Study Guide

to Accompany

Economics Today
1999-2000 Edition

by

Roger LeRoy Miller

Prepared by:

Roger LeRoy Miller
Institute for University Studies
and
Robert W. Pulsinelli
Western Kentucky University

 ADDISON-WESLEY

An imprint of Addison Wesley Longman, Inc.

Reading, Massachusetts • Menlo Park, California • New York • Harlow, England
Don Mills, Ontario • Sydney • Mexico City • Madrid • Amsterdam

Study Guide to accompany Miller, *Economics Today, 1999-2000 Edition*

Copyright © 1999 Addison Wesley Longman, Inc.

ISBN:0-321-03350-7

2 3 4 5 6 7 8 9 10-VG-02010099

TABLE OF CONTENTS

TO THE STUDENT

This *Study Guide* is designed to help you read and understand *Economics Today*, 1999-2000 Edition. Lesson one in economics is that nothing is free; a price must be paid for every activity that is performed and for every good or service that is obtained. The price that you must pay to learn economics certainly includes the course tuition and the costs of your textbook and this *Study Guide*. The price for learning economics also includes the time and effort that it will take you to read and think about this discipline. But the benefits are, potentially, enormous.

If you really learn economics you will achieve your immediate objective, which is (presumably) to make a good grade. More importantly—for the long run—if you learn to think like an economist, you will gain some very crucial insights into human behavior. You should never forget that economics is, first and foremost, a study of human behavior. An understanding of human behavior is a necessary prerequisite to attaining your personal goals and to fulfilling any goals that you might have of helping other people. Good intentions are not enough; if you really want to help people you must understand how they are likely to respond to specific policies. And economics has proven to be an invaluable aid in understanding human motivation.

HOW THIS *STUDY GUIDE* CAN HELP YOU

This student guide can help you to maximize your learning, subject to constraints on the amount of time that you can allot to this course. There are at least five specific ways in which you can benefit from this guide.

(1) The *Study Guide* can help you decide what topics are the most important. Because there are so many topics analyzed in each chapter (in *all* principles of economics textbooks) many students become confused about what is essential and what is not. You can't learn everything; the *Study Guide* can help you concentrate on the crucial topics in each chapter.

(2) If you are forced to miss a class or two (we strongly recommend that you attend class regularly, but we realize that emergencies do arise), you can use this *Study Guide* to help you learn the material discussed in your absence.

(3) There is a good chance that the questions you are required to answer in this *Study Guide* are representative of the types of questions that you will be asked during examinations.

(4) You can use this *Study Guide* to help you review for exams.

(5) Finally, this *Study Guide* can help you decide whether you really do understand the material. Don't wait until exam time to find out!

Ultimately, the way to learn economics is by reading your textbook and *thinking about the theories*. You should try to express the analysis in your own words and to apply the theory to real world circumstances. This *Study Guide* can't teach you to think like an economist—you'll have to learn to do that on your own. It can, however, provide feedback on your progress; if you can answer the questions and solve the problems, then you will know that you are on the right path.

THE CONTENTS OF THE *STUDY GUIDE*

Economics is considered to be a rather difficult subject because (a) it is theoretical in nature, (b) it uses a specialized jargon, or vocabulary, and (c) it takes (most people) much time and effort to learn. We who are economists, however, believe that our discipline is exciting and provides tremendous insights into human behavior. Your text and this *Study Guide* have been written for the precise purpose of helping you to learn economics. We always try to keep you, the student, in mind.

Before we indicate to you how we think you can best utilize this *Study Guide* to achieve your goals we want to indicate to you what it contains. Most chapters include the following sections.

1.   Putting this Chapter into Perspective

In this section we attempt to show you where the particular chapter fits into the big picture and, on occasion, offer you advice about how to study the chapter and on which ideas to concentrate.

2.   Learning Objectives

Here we list approximately ten things that you should be able to do after you have completed the chapter.

3.   Chapter Outline

This section presents a sentence outline for the chapter; it provides you with a quick overview of the contents of the chapter and it includes only the most important topics.

4.   Key Terms

This section provides a list of the most important terms used in the text chapter; these terms are crucial to your understanding and each is defined in the glossary at the end of its *Study Guide* chapter.

5.   Key Concepts

This is a list of the most important theoretical concepts used in the chapter; these too are explained in the end-of-chapter glossary.

6. Completion Questions

This set of short answer "fill-in-the-blank" questions is intended to test your knowledge of key terms, key concepts, and facts. Some will require an application of the theoretical concepts contained in the text.

7. True-False Questions

This is another objective test to help you see if you understand the main issues in the chapter. We also explain what is wrong with each false statement. We believe that this will be very helpful to you.

8. Multiple-Choice Questions

The numerous multiple-choice questions in each chapter are another objective test to help you decide whether or not you need to spend more time and effort on the chapter at hand.

9. Working with Graphs

Because graphs are so central to the study of economics, we decided to allocate an entire section (in those chapters where applicable) devoted to helping you interpret graphs. We believe that if you can master graphical analysis, the rest of economics will follow easily. The questions appearing in this section are the actual questions that we pose to our students in the classroom; teachers know that if students cannot answer such questions there is no point in moving on.

10. Problems

This section requires you to take a pencil in hand and solve specific problems that depend on your knowledge of the chapter's contents. Often students believe that they understand certain concepts, but then they cannot solve related problems. By working on these questions you will see the concepts in another light, and a deeper understanding will emerge.

11. Case Study

Here we apply chapter concepts to real life situations, in an attempt to show you how useful and interesting economics can be.

12. Answers

We have placed the answers to the *Study Guide* at the end of each chapter, and not at the end of the book. We believe that you will find this convenient.

13. Chapter Glossary

Because economics vocabulary is so important, we decided to add it to the student guide. And we have placed it where it is the most useful: at the end of the relevant chapter, not at the end of the book.

HOW TO USE THIS STUDY GUIDE

What follows is a recommended strategy for improving your grade. It may seem like an awful lot of work, but the payoffs will be high. Try the whole program for the first three or four chapters. If you feel you can skip some steps safely, then try doing so and see what happens. After all, only you can know your capabilities and individual circumstances. We do urge you, however, to give this approach a chance.

For each chapter we recommend that you follow the sequence of steps below.

1. Read the introduction, the learning objectives, the sentence outline, and the lists of key terms and concepts in this *Study Guide*; follow any study suggestions offered in the introduction.

2. Read the Chapter Summary in your text at the end of the chapter.

3. Read about half the textbook chapter (unless it is very long), being sure to underline only the most important points which you should be able to recognize after having read two chapter outlines. Put a check mark by that material that you don't understand.

4. If you find the textbook chapter easy to understand, you might want to finish reading it. Otherwise, rest for a sufficient period (you can be the judge of how long it takes you to be refreshed) before you read the second half of the chapter. Again be sure to underline only the most important points and to put a checkmark by the material you find difficult to understand.

5. After you have completed the entire textbook chapter, take a break. Then read only what *you* have underlined, throughout the entire chapter.

6. Now concentrate on the difficult material, by which you have left checkmarks. Reread this material and *think about it*; you will find that it is very exciting to figure out difficult material on your own.

7. Read each of the chapter preview questions in the textbook and write out your answer. After you have finished, compare your answers to the answers to those questions provided by your author at the end of the chapter.

8. Find the comparable chapter in this *Study Guide* and answer the completion questions, the true-false questions, the multiple-choice questions, the problems, and the working with graphs questions. Compare your answers with the answers provided at the back of the *Study Guide* chapter. Make a note of the questions you have missed and find the page(s) in your textbook upon which these *Study Guide* questions are based. If you still don't understand— ask your teacher or your student teaching assistant. (If you decided that our answers are wrong, then by all means write and tell us.)

9. Re-read the learning objectives in this *Study Guide* and decide if you are able to achieve each of these objectives.

10. Before your examination, study your class notes. Reread the *Study Guide* outline, then re-do the completion questions, the true-false questions, the multiple-choice questions, and the problems. Compare your answer with the answer at the back of the appropriate chapter in this guide. Identify your problem areas and re-read the relevant pages in the book. Think through the answers on your own. If you still can't understand the analysis, ask your teacher or your student teaching assistant for help. (Be sure to let your teacher know that you have tried to answer the questions on your own.)

If you have followed the strategy outlined above, you should feel sufficiently confident and be relaxed to do well on your exam.

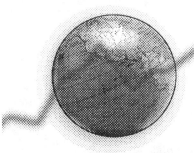

THE NATURE OF ECONOMICS

PUTTING THIS CHAPTER INTO PERSPECTIVE

The aim of Chapter 1 is to help you begin to get a feel for what economics is all about. Chapter 1 defines economics and introduces you to the theory of economic behavior. Economists are concerned with how people do in fact behave in the economic arena *and not* with how people themselves describe their actions, motivations, and beliefs. We contend that people act in ways that promote their own (sometimes broadly-defined) self-interest, and that they respond predictably to economic incentives.

By combining this theory of human behavior with the concept of marginal analysis (analyzed in later chapters) and the "other things constant" assumption, economists are able to (1) generate numerous insights and testable theories about behavior, (2) explain widely disparate social phenomena, and (3) predict how people are likely to behave under numerous circumstances.

Although an understanding of Chapter 1 cannot possibly turn you into an economist, it can certainly begin to give you a feel for "the economic way of thinking." It is a good idea to re-read this chapter every three or four weeks, just to reinforce the important perspective that it provides.

LEARNING OBJECTIVES

After you have read this chapter you should be able to

1. define economics.

2. distinguish between microeconomics and macroeconomics.

3. recognize the rationality assumption.

4. recognize elements of an economic model, or theory.

5. recognize that economics is ultimately concerned with human behavior.

6. define resource.

7. recognize why young people are more receptive to new ideas and technology than are older people.

8. distinguish between positive economics and normative economics, and be able to classify specific statements under each category.

CHAPTER OUTLINE

1. Economics, a social science, is defined as the study of how people make choices to satisfy their wants.
    a. Wants are all the things that people would consume if they had unlimited income.
    b. Because wants are unlimited and people cannot satisfy all their wants, individuals are forced to make choices about how to spend their income and how to allocate their time.

2. Economics is broadly divided into microeconomics and macroeconomics.
    a. Microeconomics studies decision making undertaken by individuals (or households) and by firms.
    b. Macroeconomics studies the behavior of the economy taken as a whole; it deals with such economy-wide phenomena as unemployment, the price level, and national income.

3. Economists assume that individuals are motivated by self-interest and respond predictably to opportunities for gain.
    a. The rationality assumption is that individuals act *as if* they were rational.
    b. Self-interest often means a desire for material well-being, but it can also be defined broadly enough to incorporate goals relating to love, friendship, prestige, power, and other human characteristics.
    c. By assuming that people act in a rational, self-interested way, economists can generate testable theories concerning human behavior.

4. Economics is a Social Science.
    a. Economists develop models, or theories, which are simplified representations of the real world.
    b. Such models help economists to understand, explain, and predict economic phenomena in the real world.
    c. Like other social scientists, economists usually do not perform laboratory experiments; they typically examine what already has occurred in order to test their theories.
    d. Economic theories, like all scientific theories, are simplifications—and in that sense they are "unrealistic."
    e. Economists, as do all scientists, employ assumptions; one important economic assumption is "all other things being equal."
    f. Models or theories are evaluated on their ability to predict, and not on the realism of the assumptions employed.
    g. Economic models relate to behavior, not thought processes.

5. Economists maintain that the unit of analysis is the individual; members of a group are assumed to pursue their own goals rather than the group's objectives.

6. Positive economics is objective and scientific in nature, and deals with testable *if this, then that* hypotheses.

7. Normative economics is subjective and deals with value judgments, or with what *ought* to be.

KEY TERMS

Aggregates
Ceteris paribus
  (other things being equal)
Economics

Incentives
Macroeconomics
Microeconomics
Models (or theory)

Resource
Wants

KEY CONCEPTS

Normative economics
Positive economics

Rationality assumption

COMPLETION QUESTIONS
Fill in the blank or circle the correct term.

1. Because it is impossible to have all that we want, people are forced to make _____.

2. Economics is a (natural, social) science.

3. Economics is the study of how people make _____ to satisfy their _____.

4. Microeconomics deals with (individual units, the whole economy).

5. A nation's unemployment level is analyzed in (microeconomics, macroeconomics).

6. (Macroeconomics, Microeconomics) studies the causes and effects of inflation.

7. Economists maintain that a member of a group usually attempts to make decisions that are in (her own, the group's) interest.

8. The rationality assumption is that individuals (believe, act as if) they are rational.

9. Economic models are (simplified, realistic) representations of the real world.

10. The *ceteris paribus* assumption enables economists to consider (one thing at a time, everything at once).

11. Younger people are (less, more) likely to try new technology and learn new ideas.

12. Economists maintain that incentives (are, are not) important to decision making.

13. Economists define self-interest (narrowly, broadly).

14. Economists take the (individual, group) as the unit of analysis.

15. Economic statements that are testable and are of an "if/then" nature are (positive, normative).

TRUE-FALSE QUESTIONS
Circle the **T** if the statement is true, the **F** if it is false. Explain to yourself why a statement is false.

T F   1.   Economics is the study of how people think about economic phenomena.

T F   2.   The economists' definition of self-interest includes only the pursuit of material goods.

T F   3.   Macroeconomics deals with aggregates, or totals, of economic variables.

T F   4.   When economists attempt to predict the number of workers a firm will employ, they are studying macroeconomics.

T F   5.   Economists maintain that people respond in a predictable way to economic incentives.

T F   6.   The rationality assumption is that individuals attempt, quite consciously, to make rational economic decisions, and will admit to it.

T F   7.   It is justifiable to criticize theories on the realism of the assumptions employed.

T F   8.   Households cannot be thought of as producers.

T F   9.   Because economics is a science, economists do not make normative statements.

T F 10.   Love and marriage and decisions regarding the number of children to have are outside the scope of economics.

MULTIPLE CHOICE QUESTIONS
Circle the letter that corresponds to the best answer.

1.   Economics is
     a.   a natural science.
     b.   nonscientific.
     c.   a social science.
     d.   usually studied through lab experiments.

2.   Wants include desires for
     a. material possessions.
     b. love.
     c. power.
     d. All of the above

3.   Which of the following areas of study is concerned, primarily, with microeconomics?
     a.   the steel industry
     b.   inflation
     c.   the national unemployment rate
     d.   national income determination

4.   Macroeconomic analysis deals with
     a.   the steel industry.
     b.   how individuals respond to an increase in the price of gasoline.
     c.   inflation.
     d.   how a change in the price of energy affects a family.

5. Economists maintain that Mr. Smith will usually make decisions that promote the interests of
    a. his colleagues at work.
    b. himself.
    c. his class.
    d. his race.

6. Economic models
    a. use unrealistic assumptions.
    b. are seldom tested in laboratories.
    c. are concerned with how people behave, not with how they think.
    d. All of the above

7. An economic model is justifiably criticized if
    a. its assumptions are not realistic.
    b. it cannot be tested in a controlled, laboratory experiment.
    c. it fails to predict.
    d. All of the above

8. New ideas and new technology
    a. will not be adopted by older people.
    b. are adopted less readily by older people, for rational reasons.
    c. are equally likely to be embraced by people of all ages.
    d. are ignored only by irrational people.

9. Economics
    a. is a natural science.
    b. is concerned with how people respond to incentives.
    c. is unconcerned with value judgments.
    d. deals with assumptions, therefore is unrealistic.

10. Concerning Native Americans, in recent years
    a. economic incentives have increased their (self-reported) numbers.
    b. their population has fallen dramatically due to high infant mortality rates.
    c. economic incentives have decreased their numbers.
    d. their living standards have fallen.

11. Which of the following is a normative economics statement?
    a. If price rises, people will buy less.
    b. If price rises, people will buy more.
    c. If price rises the poor will be injured; therefore price should not be permitted to rise.
    d. If price rises people will buy less; therefore we ought to observe that quantity demanded falls.

12. Which of the following is a positive economics statement?
    a. Full employment policies should be pursued.
    b. If minimum wage rates rise, then unemployment will rise.
    c. We should take from the rich and give to the poor.
    d. The government should help the homeless.

13. Normative economics statements
    a. are testable hypotheses.
    b. are value-free.
    c. are subjective, value judgments.
    d. can be scientifically established.

MATCHING

Choose the item in Column (2) that best matches an item in Column (1).

(1)	(2)

a. normative economics   f. nonscientific value judgments
b. macroeconomics   g. objective, scientific hypotheses
c. self-interest   h. study of individual behavior
d. positive economics   i. study of economic aggregates
e. microeconomics   j. rational behavior

CASE STUDY

Economists were surprised to discover that most people, when interviewed immediately after purchasing gasoline, did not have any idea what they had just paid per gallon. Non-economists use this as evidence against the notion that people are rational.

Economists maintain that price is an important determinant of consumer behavior, yet, apparently people don't even consider price! How can economists predict consumer behavior if consumers don't even know what price is?

Interestingly, it was discovered that at the *end of the month*, those gasoline stations that charged the highest prices sold the least amount of gasoline, and those that charged the lowest prices sold the most amount of gasoline.

Apparently, although most people didn't know the price per gallon, nevertheless *as a group*, consumers bought more of that gasoline (given quality) that was sold at a cheaper price. Consider this apparent contradiction then answer the following questions.

1. Which consumers are more likely to know the price of gasoline: owners of cab companies and fleets of automobiles, or casual drivers?

2. Is it rational for the typical buyer of gasoline to drive around to every gas station to check price each time she buys—or should she form a buying habit and do business with the same station (and check prices only occasionally)?

3. Why might it be rational for some buyers *knowingly* to pay a higher price and be a regular customer at a higher-priced station? (Hint: consider emergencies).

ANSWERS TO CHAPTER 1

COMPLETION QUESTIONS

1. choices
2. social
3. choices; wants
4. individual units
5. macroeconomics
6. macroeconomics
7. her own
8. act as if

9. simplified
10. one thing at a time
11. more
12. are
13. broadly
14. individual
15. positive

TRUE AND FALSE QUESTIONS

1. F   Economics is the study of how people make choices to satisfy their wants.
2. F   Economists have a broader definition of self-interest; wants include power, friendship, love, and so on.
3. T
4. F   The example is about microeconomics.
5. T
6. F   That assumption is merely that people act *as if* they are rational.
7. F   All theories employ unrealistic assumptions; what matters is how well they predict.
8. F   Households can be thought of as combining goods and time to produce outputs such as meals.
9. F   Economists, like other scientists, can and do make normative statements.
10. F   All of these can be subjected to economic analysis.

MULTIPLE CHOICE QUESTIONS

1.c;   2.d;   3.a;   4.c;   5.b;   6.d;   7.c;   8.b;   9.b;   10.a;
11.c;   12.b;   13.c.

MATCHING

a and f;   b and i;   c and j;   d and g;   e and h

CASE STUDY

1. People who spend *a lot* of funds on gasoline are more likely to know its price, not casual drivers.
2. It is rational to form habits and to check price only occasionally, because people value their time too.
3. You might knowingly trade with a higher-priced gasoline station because you can get to know and trust the owner who can then be relied upon to fix or tow your car in an emergency—at a reasonable price.

GLOSSARY TO CHAPTER 1

Aggregates   Total amounts or quantities; aggregate demand, for example, relates to the total demand within a nation.

***Ceteris paribus* assumption**   The assumption that all things are held equal, or constant, except those under study.

Economics   The study of how people allocate their limited resources to satisfy their unlimited wants.

Incentives   Rewards for engaging in a particular activity.

Macroeconomics   The study of the behavior of the economy as a whole, including such economy-wide phenomena as unemployment, the price level, and national income.

Microeconomics   The study of decision making undertaken by individuals (or households) and by firms.

Models, or theories   Simplified representations of the real world used to make predictions or to better understand the real world.

Normative economics   Analysis involving value judgments about economic policies; relates to whether things are good or bad. It involves statements of what *ought to* be.

Positive economics   Analysis that is strictly limited to making either purely descriptive statements or scientific predictions; for example, *If A, then B*. A statement of *what if*.

Rationality assumption   An assumption in economics in which people are assumed to behave in a reasonable way and thus will not intentionally make decisions that will leave them worse off.

Resource   Anything that can be used to produce goods and services that people value. (Also called factors of production.)

Wants   Wants are the things that people would consume if they had unlimited income.

CHAPTER 2

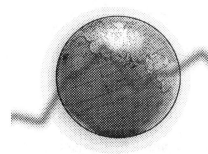

SCARCITY AND THE WORLD OF TRADE-OFFS

PUTTING THIS CHAPTER INTO PERSPECTIVE

Chapter 1 defined wants and stressed that no one can satisfy all his or her wants. Chapter 2 starts with this notion and builds upon it. People want more things—both material and nonmaterial (such as love, friendship, and affection)—than their individual and collective resources permit. Because we cannot have everything that we want, scarcity forces us to make choices. We are all faced with trade-offs; if we want more of good A, we must give up other goods. Hence the important concept of opportunity cost emerges. This concept is one of the most useful and universally applied concepts in economics, and you will do well to learn it now. As this chapter shows, the opportunity cost concept helps to decide which resource combinations are efficient, and which are not.

Resources used to produce goods and services are scarce, hence choices, trade-offs, and opportunity costs emerge when we consider resource allocation. Chapter 2 lists and defines resources.

LEARNING OBJECTIVES

After you have studied this chapter you should be able to

1. define production, scarcity, resources, land, labor, human and physical capital, entrepreneurship, goods, services, opportunity costs, production possibilities curve, technology, efficiency, inefficient point, law of increasing relative costs, specialization, absolute advantage, comparative advantage, and division of labor.

2. distinguish between a free good and an economic good.

3. determine the opportunity cost of an activity, when given sufficient information.

4. draw production possibilities curves under varying assumptions, and recognize efficient and inefficient points relating to such curves.

5. understand the difference between a person's or nation's absolute advantage and comparative advantage.

6. recognize the main issues in the debate regarding the costs and benefits of saving lives by reducing risk.

CHAPTER OUTLINE

1. Because individuals or communities do not have the resources to satisfy all their wants, scarcity exists.
    a. If society can get all that it wants of good A when the price of good A is zero, good A is not scarce.
    b. If the price of good B is zero, and society cannot get all that it wants of good B, then B is scarce.
    c. Because resources, or factors of production, are scarce, the outputs they produce are scarce.
        i.   Land, the natural resource, includes all the gifts of nature.
        ii.   Labor, the human resource, includes all productive contributions made by individuals who work.
        iii. Physical capital, the man-made resource, includes the machines, buildings, and tools used to produce other goods and services.
        iv.   Human capital, the education and training of workers.
        v.   Entrepreneurship includes the functions of organizing, managing, assembling, and risk-taking necessary for business ventures.
    d. Goods include anything from which people derive satisfaction, or happiness.
        i.   Economic goods are scarce.
        ii.   Non-economic goods are not scarce.
        iii. Services are intangible goods.
    e. Economists distinguish between wants and needs; the latter are objectively undefinable.

2. Because of scarcity, choice and opportunity costs arise.
    a. Due to scarcity, people trade off options.
    b. The production possibilities curve (PPC) is a graph of the trade-offs inherent in a decision.
        i.   When the marginal cost of additional units of a resource or good remains constant, the PPC curve is a straight line.
        ii.   When the marginal cost of additional units of a resource or good rises, the PPC curve is bowed outward.
        iii. A point on a PPC is an efficient point; points inside a PPC are inefficient; points outside the PPC are unattainable (impossible), by definition.
    c. People have an economic incentive to specialize in that endeavor for which they have a comparative advantage.
    d. The process of division of labor increases output and permits specialization.

3. Economic growth can be depicted through PPCs.
    a. There is a trade off between present consumption and future consumption.
    b. If a nation produces fewer consumer goods and more capital goods now, then it can consume more goods in the future than would otherwise be the case.

4. Drivers who face the option of using a faster carpool lane face a trade-off, for they have to take the time to arrange for there to be another passenger in the car. That "cost" must be weighed against the time saving in arriving to their destination sooner.
    a. When carpool lanes are offered for a fee to anyone, those who place a high value on their time can reduce less desirable time spent driving.
    b. Some argue that such a system is not fair, but the same argument is true for every scarce resource allocated by the price system.

KEY TERMS

Resources
Land
Labor
Physical capital
Human capital
Consumption goods

Goods
Services
Entrepreneurship
Technology
Specialization
Economic goods

Division of labor
Inefficient point
Scarcity
Production
  possibilities curve

KEY CONCEPTS

Efficiency
Absolute advantage
Comparative advantage

Opportunity cost
Least-cost combination
Production

Law of increasing
  relative costs

COMPLETION QUESTIONS
Fill in the blank or circle the correct term.

1. The factors of production include _____, _____, _____, _____, and _____.

2. People tend to specialize in those activities for which they have a(n) (comparative, absolute) advantage.

3. When people choose jobs that maximize their income, they are specializing according to their _____ advantage.

4. If at a zero price quantity demanded exceeds quantity supplied for a good, that good is a(n) _____; if at a zero price quantity supplied exceeds quantity demanded for a good, that good is a(n) _____.

5. The _____ of good A is the highest-valued alternative that must be sacrificed to attain it.

6. If the cost of additional units of a good remains constant, the production possibilities curve will be (linear, bowed outward); if the cost of additional units of a good rises, the production possibilities curve will be (linear, bowed outward).

7. Because specialized resources are more suited to specific tasks, the cost of producing additional units of a specific good will (rise, fall).

8. If an economy is inefficient, its actual output combination will lie (inside, outside) the production possibilities curve.

TRUE-FALSE QUESTIONS
Circle the **T** if the statement is true, the **F** if it is false. Explain to yourself why a statement is false.

T F 1. Most individual's needs exceed their wants.

T F 2. Because resources are scarce, the goods that they produce are also scarce.

T F   3.   For most activities no opportunity cost exists.

T F   4.   If a production possibilities curve is linear, the cost of producing additional units of a good rises.

T F   5.   At any given moment in time it is impossible for an economy to be inside its production possibilities curve.

T F   6.   The cost to society of lowering the speed limit is zero.

T F   7.   People have little incentive to specialize in jobs for which they have a comparative advantage.

T F   8.   Economic growth shifts the production possibilities curve outward.

T F   9.   If the price to a specific user is zero, the good must be a noneconomic good.

T F 10.   Only rich drivers will use for-fee fast lanes.

MULTIPLE CHOICE QUESTIONS

Circle the letter that corresponds to the best answer.

1. Because of scarcity
    a. people are forced to make choices.
    b. opportunity costs exist.
    c. people face trade-offs.
    d. All of the above.

2. Which of the following is not considered to be "land"?
    a. bodies of water
    b. fertility of soil
    c. capital
    d. climate

3. Which of the following words does not belong with the others?
    a. opportunity cost
    b. noneconomic good
    c. scarcity
    d. economic good

4. Which statement concerning a production possibilities curve is not true?
    a. A trade-off exists along such a curve.
    b. It is usually linear.
    c. Points inside it indicate inefficiency.
    d. A point outside it is currently impossible to attain.

5. The production possibilities curve is bowed outward because
    a. the relative cost of producing a good rises.
    b. of the law of decreasing relative costs.
    c. all resources are equally suited to the production of any good.
    d. All of the above.

6. When nations and individuals specialize
   a. overall living standards rise.
   b. trade and exchange increase.
   c. people become more vulnerable to changes in tastes and technology.
   d. All of the above

7. When a nation expands its capital stock, it is usually true that
   a. it must forego output of some consumer goods in the present.
   b. the human capital stock must decline.
   c. fewer consumer goods will be available in the future.
   d. no opportunity cost exists for doing so.

8. Ms. Boulware is the best lawyer and the best secretary in town.
   a. She has a comparative advantage in both jobs.
   b. She has an absolute advantage in both jobs.
   c. She has a comparative advantage in being a secretary.
   d. All of the above

9. If Ms. Chen pays for the right to use a fast carpool lane,
   a. she is definitely richer than anyone else who has not decided to do the same.
   b. she has a low opportunity cost of time.
   c. the value placed on the time saved in driving is at least equal to the fees she paid.
   d. her opportunity cost is twice the fees she paid to drive faster during rush hour.

MATCHING
Choose the item in Column (2) that best matches an item in Column (1).

(1)	(2)
a. absolute advantage	i. production possibilities curve
b. efficiency	j. specialization
c. trade-offs	k. capital
d. comparative advantage	l. ability to produce at a lower unit cost
e. resource	m. specializing in one's comparative advantage
f. economic good	n. society cannot get all it wants at at a zero price
g. inefficiency	o. highest-valued foregone alternative
h. opportunity cost	p. inside PPC

WORKING WITH GRAPHS

1. Given the following information, graph the production possibilities curve in the space provided and then use the graph to answer the questions that follow.

Combination (points)	Autos (100,000 per year)	Wheat (100,000 tons per year)
A	16	0
B	14	4
C	12	7
D	9	10
E	5	12
F	0	13

Autos per Year (in units of 100,000)

Wheat per Year (in units of 100,000 tons)

a. If the economy is currently operating at point C, what is the opportunity cost of moving to point D? to point B?

b. Suppose that the economy is currently producing 1,200,000 autos and 200,000 tons of wheat per year. Label this point in your graph with the letter G. At point G the economy would be suffering from what? At point G we can see that it is possible to produce more wheat without giving up any auto production, or produce more autos without giving up any wheat production, or produce more of both. Label this region in your graph. This region appears to contradict the definition of a production possibilities curve. What is the explanation for this result?

c. Suppose a new fertilizer compound is developed that will allow the economy to produce an additional 150,000 tons of wheat per year if no autos are produced. Sketch in a likely representation of the effect of this discovery, assuming all else remains constant.

    d.   What sort of impact (overall) will this discovery have on the opportunity cost of more wheat production at an arbitrary point on the new production possibilities curve as compared to a point representing the same level of output of wheat on the original curve?

2.   Consider the graphs below, then answer the questions that follow.

                 (a)   (b)

    a.   Which graph, a or b, shows constant relative costs of producing additional units of butter? Why?
    b.   Which graph, a or b, shows increasing relative costs of producing additional units of butter? Why?
    c.   Which graph seems more realistic, a or b? Why?

3.   Graph the probable relationship between
    a.   Income and the amount of money spent on housing.
    b.   Annual rainfall in New York City and the annual value of ice cream sales in New Orleans.
    c.   Number of vegetarians per 10,000 people and meat sales per 10,000 people.

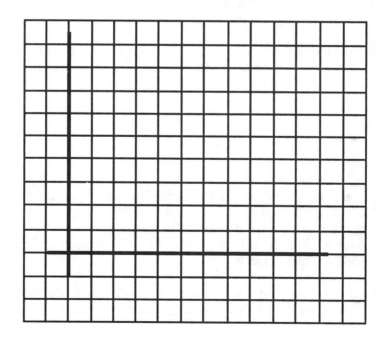

PROBLEMS

1. If a *nation* wants to increase its future consumption it must forego some present consumption because it must allocate some resources to the production of capital goods. Suppose *you* want to increase your future consumption, given a fixed lifetime income, what can you do?

2. Assume that Ms. Gentile values her time at $50 per hour because she has the opportunity to do consulting, and that Joe College values his time at $2 per hour. Assume that it costs $400 to fly from their hometown to San Francisco, and that the flight takes 6 hours. Assume that it costs $200 to take a bus, and that the bus trip takes 24 hours.
    a. What is the cheaper way to get to San Francisco for Ms. Gentile? Why?
    b. Which transportation is cheaper for Joe College? Why?

3. Suppose you have a friend currently working as a salesperson in a local computer store that sells personal computers. This friend is thinking about going back to school full-time to finish up work on her computer science degree. She explains to you that she earns $15,000 (after taxes) per year in her current job and that she estimates tuition will cost $1,600 per year. In addition she estimates fees, supplies, books, and miscellaneous expenses associated with attending school will run $800 per year. She wants to attend a university that is located directly across the street from the store where she currently works. She claims that she pays $350 per month for rent and utilities and that she spends about $200 per month on food.

    Using what you have learned, calculate and explain to your friend the opportunity cost to her of another year back at school.

4. The Hughes family consists of Mr. Hughes, Mrs. Hughes, and their son, Scotty. Assume that Mr. Hughes can earn $30 per hour (after taxes) any time he chooses, Mrs. Hughes can earn $5 per hour, and the family values homemaker activities at $6 per hour.
    a. Because the family requires income to purchase goods and services, who will probably work in the marketplace?
    b. Who will probably do the housework?
    c. If the family must pay $3 per hour to have its lawn mowed, who will be assigned that work?
    d. If Scotty can now earn $4 per hour on a job, who now might mow the grass?
    e. If wage rates in the marketplace for Mrs. Hughes rise to $7 per hour, what is the family likely to do?

CASE STUDY

Over the past twenty years the percentage of women in the labor force has increased dramatically. In recent years divorce rates, and the number of women and children officially classified as living in poverty have increased also. Some people maintain that higher percentages of women in the labor force reflect the fact that "times are tougher and it now takes two people to support a family." Others maintain that the feminist movement is the main reason for some of these changes. Almost everyone sees higher divorce rates and higher poverty rates for women and children as a serious social problem and increased human misery.

Consider, however, that over the past twenty years real (inflation-adjusted) wage rates have increased in the United States, and that therefore the opportunity cost for women staying out of the labor force has risen.

1. How might increasing female percentages in the labor force be accounted for by rational family decision-making processes?

2. Is it more rational for women to opt for divorce now than it was twenty years ago?

3. If women *choose* divorce, work, and income that is *officially* considered to be at poverty levels, are their lives necessarily worse?

ANSWERS TO CHAPTER 2

COMPLETION QUESTIONS

1. land, labor, physical capital, human capital, entrepreneurship
2. comparative
3. comparative
4. economic good; noneconomic good
5. opportunity cost
6. linear; bowed outward
7. rise
8. inside

TRUE-FALSE QUESTIONS

1. F   Wants vastly exceed needs (which can't be defined anyway) for everyone.
2. T
3. F   An opportunity cost exists for all activities.
4. F   A linear PPC implies a constant cost of production.
5. F   All an economy need be is inefficient to be inside the PPC.
6. F   If people drive more slowly they suffer opportunity costs for their time.
7. F   People can earn more income in jobs for which they have a comparative advantage.
8. T
9. F   An individual user *may* pay a zero price for a good, but that doesn't necessarily mean its a noneconomic good.
10. F   Some poor drivers will be willing to pay to save time; after all, not everyone who buys expensive caviar is extremely rich.

MULTIPLE CHOICE QUESTIONS

1.d;   2.c;   3.b;   4.b;   5.a;   6.d;   7.a;   8.b;   9.c.

MATCHING

a and l;   b and m;   c and i;   d and j;   e and k;   f and n;   g and p;   h and o

WORKING WITH GRAPHS

1.   See the following graph.

a.   The move from C to D "costs" 300,000 autos—that is, the economy must give up 300,000 autos (1,200,000 - 900,000) to make such a move. The move from C to B "costs" 300,000 tons of wheat. Notice that in both cases there are gains (C to D involves 300,000 more tons of wheat and C to B means 200,000 more autos are produced), but we measure opportunity costs in terms of movements along a production possibilities curve and what has to be given up to make the choice reflected in the move.

b.   See the preceding graph. Remember, the production possibilities curve shows all possible combinations of two goods that an economy can produce by the efficient use of all available resources in a specified period of time. Since point G is not on the production possibilities curve, the statement contained in this portion of the question does not contradict the definition of the curve. Point G is inside the curve, which implies available resources are not being used efficiently.

c.   See the preceding graph.

d.   It will lower the opportunity cost of additional wheat production.

2.   a.   Panel a shows constant relative costs because the PPC is linear.

b.   Panel b shows increasing costs because the PPC is bowed out.

c.   Panel b is more realistic because it is likely that the production of guns and butter requires specialized resources.

3.   a.   The graph should be upward sloping from left to right.

b.   There should be no systematic relationship between these two variables.

c.   The graph should be downward sloping from left to right.

PROBLEMS

1.   If you want to increase your future consumption—for retirement, say—then you will have to save more out of your current income. The principal and interest that accrue will permit you to purchase more goods in the future than you otherwise would have been able to. Note that by doing so you—as an individual—must forego some present consumption in order to increase

your future consumption. In that sense what is true for the nation is also true for an individual.

2. a. plane; flying costs her $400 plus 6 hours times $50 per hour, or $700, while taking a bus would cost her $200 plus 24 hours times $50 per hour, or $1400.
    b. bus; taking the bus costs him a total of $248 while the total cost of flying is $412 to him.

3. The opportunity cost of another year back at school for your friend is as follows:

Foregone after-tax salary	$15,000
Tuition costs	1,600
Expenses associated with school	800
Total opportunity costs	$17,400

4. a. Mr. Hughes
    b. Mrs. Hughes or Scotty
    c. Scotty
    d. The family (or perhaps Scotty) will hire someone to mow the lawn.
    e. Mrs. Hughes may enter the labor force and the family may hire someone to do housework.

CASE STUDY

1. As the opportunity cost for staying at home rises, more women will enter the labor force and substitute their work at home with (a) appliances and/or (b) hired domestic workers.
2. If they now can earn more income in the labor force, the opportunity cost to them of staying in an unhappy marriage rises.
3. Assuming that they are adults, who know the consequences of divorce, if women voluntarily choose to divorce and work at a wage rate that is near or below the "official" poverty level, all things considered, they are probably better off. Otherwise they would have stayed home and traded off material goods for unhappiness.

GLOSSARY TO CHAPTER 2

Absolute advantage   The ability to produce a good or service at an "absolutely" lower cost, usually measured in units of labor or resource input required to produce one unit of the good.

Comparative advantage   The ability to produce a good or service at a lower opportunity cost.

Consumption goods   Goods that are bought by households to be used up, such as food, clothing, and movies.

Division of labor   The segregation of a resource into different specific tasks; for example, one automobile worker puts on bumpers, another doors, and so on.

Economic goods   Any goods or services that are scarce.

Efficiency   The situation where a given output is produced at minimum cost. Or alternatively the case where a given level of inputs is used to produce the maximum output possible.

Entrepreneurship   The fifth factor of production, involving human resources that perform the functions of raising capital, organizing, managing, assembling other factors of production, and making basic business policy decisions. The entrepreneur is a risk taker.

Goods   Anything from which individuals derive satisfaction or happiness and thus is valued.

Human capital   Education and training of workers

Inefficient point   Any point inside the production possibilities frontier, where resources are being used inefficiently.

Labor   Productive contributions of humans who work, which involve both thinking and doing.

Land   The natural resources that are available without alteration or effort on the part of humans. Land as a resource includes location, original fertility and mineral deposits, topography, climate, water, and vegetation.

Law of increasing relative costs   The opportunity cost of additional units of a good generally increases as society attempts to produce more of that good. It is what causes the bowed-out shape of the production possibilities curve.

Least-cost combination   The level of input use that produces a given level of output at minimum cost.

Opportunity cost   The highest valued alternative that must be sacrificed to attain something or satisfy a want.

Physical capital   All manufactured resources, including buildings, equipment, machines, and improvements to land.

Production   Any activity that results in the conversion of natural resources, human resources, and other resources into goods and services that can be used in consumption.

Production possibilities curve (PPC)   A curve representing all possible combinations of total output that could be produced assuming (a) a fixed amount of productive resources of a given quality and (b) the efficient use of those resources.

Resources   Inputs used to produce goods and services. (Also called factors of production).

Scarcity   A situation in which the necessary ingredients for producing those things that people desire are insufficient to satisfy all wants.

Services   Things purchased by consumers that do not have physical characteristics. Examples of services are those purchased from doctors, lawyers, dentists, repair personnel, and so on.

Specialization   The division of productive activities among persons and regions so that no one individual or one area is totally self-sufficient. An individual may specialize, for example, in law or medicine. A nation may specialize in the production of coffee, computers, or cameras.

Technology   Society's pool of applied knowledge concerning how goods and services can be produced.

CHAPTER 3

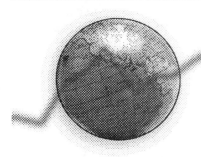

DEMAND AND SUPPLY

PUTTING THIS CHAPTER INTO PERSPECTIVE

This chapter is one of the most important chapters in the text. To students who take the time to study it, the returns are exceptionally high. Chapter 3 analyzes the economist's most indispensable tools: demand and supply. Specifically, in this chapter you will study (a) demand and supply, (b) how demand and supply determine equilibrium (or market-clearing) price, and (c) how periods of surpluses or shortages result if price is not at the equilibrium level.

It is important that you master the material in this chapter, because you will be applying and reapplying these same tools and principles to many different situations. When presented with a problem, the economist will first try to express the problem in terms of the concepts of demand and supply and then proceed to economic analysis proper. It is with this thought in mind that an anonymous writer once noted: "You can make even a parrot into a learned economist—all it must learn are the two words *supply* and *demand*."

Mastering Chapter 3, however, will require some time. Many pitfalls to understanding economics can be avoided if you learn and understand the key definitions in this chapter. You must understand *exactly* what demand and supply mean; *exactly* what quantity demanded and quantity supplied mean; *exactly* what a change in demand and a change in supply mean; *exactly* what a surplus and a shortage mean. A universal confusion exists for students and others about the distinction between a change in demand (or supply) and a change in quantity demanded (or quantity supplied). Similarly, unless you know exactly what a shortage or a surplus is, you will be continually misinterpreting economic events.

LEARNING OBJECTIVES

After you have studied this chapter you should be able to

1. define demand schedule, quantity demanded, supply schedule, quantity supplied, equilibrium, shortage, and surplus.

2. graph demand and supply curves from demand and supply schedules.

3. state the law of demand and state two reasons why we observe the law of demand.

4. enumerate five non-own-price determinants of demand and five other determinants of supply.

5. predict the effects of a change in the price of one good on the demand for (a) a substitute good, and (b) a complementary good.

6. recognize, from graphs, the difference between a change in demand and a change in quantity demanded and the difference between a change in supply and a change in quantity supplied.

7. determine from a supply curve and a demand curve what the equilibrium price and the equilibrium quantity will be.

8. explain how markets eliminate surpluses and shortages.

CHAPTER OUTLINE

1. The *law of demand* states that at higher prices a lower quantity will be demanded than at lower prices, *other things being equal*.
   a. For simplicity, things other than the price of the good itself are held constant.
   b. Buyers respond to changes in *relative*, not *absolute*, *prices*.

2. The *demand schedule* for a good is a set of pairs of numbers showing various possible prices and the quantity demanded at each price, for some time period.
   a. Demand must be conceived of as being measured in constant-quality units.
   b. A *demand curve* is a graphic representation of the demand schedule and it is negatively sloped, reflecting the law of demand.
   c. A market demand curve for a particular good or service is derived by summing all the individual demand curves for that product.

3. The determinants of demand include all factors (other than the good's own price) that influence the quantity purchased.
   a. When deriving a demand curve, other determinants of demand are held constant. When such non-own-price determinants do change, the original demand curve shifts to the left or to the right.
   b. The major *determinants of demand* are consumers' income, tastes and preferences, changes in their expectations about future relative prices, the price of substitutes and complements for the good in question, population, and age composition of the population.
   c. A change in demand is a shift in the demand curve, whereas a change in *quantity demanded* is a movement along a given demand curve.

4. Supply is the relationship between price and the quantity supplied, other things being equal.
   a. The law of supply posits generally a direct, or positive, relationship between price and quantity supplied.
      i. As the relative price of a good rises, producers have an incentive to produce more of it.
      ii. As a firm produces greater quantities in the short run, a firm often requires a higher relative price before it will increase output.
   b. A *supply schedule* is a set of numbers showing prices and the quantity supplied at those various prices.
   c. A *supply curve* is the graphic representation of the supply schedule; it is positively sloped.
   d. By summing individual supply curves for a particular good or service we derive that good or service's market supply curve.

e. The major *determinants of supply* are the prices of resources (inputs) used to produce the product, technology, taxes and subsidies, price expectations of producers, and the number of firms in an industry.

f. Any change in the determinants of supply (listed in part e) causes a change in supply and therefore leads to a shift in the supply curve.

g. A change in price, holding the determinants of supply constant, causes a movement along—but not a shift in—the supply curve.

5. By graphing demand and supply on the same coordinate system, equilibrium can be found at the intersection of the two curves.

a. *Equilibrium* is a situation in which the plans of buyers and of sellers exactly coincide, so that there is neither excess quantity supplied nor excess quantity demanded; at the equilibrium price, quantity supplied equals quantity demanded.

b. At a price below the equilibrium price, quantity demanded exceeds quantity supplied, and *excess demand*, or a *shortage*, exists.

c. At a price above the equilibrium price, quantity supplied exceeds quantity demanded, and an *excess supply*, or a *surplus*, exists.

d. Seller competition forces price down, and eliminates a surplus.

e. Buyer competition forces price up, and eliminates a shortage.

KEY TERMS

Demand schedule	Supply curve	Equilibrium price
Demand curve	Market demand	Money price
Supply schedule		

KEY CONCEPTS

Relative price	Complements
Law of supply	Equilibrium
Normal goods	Shortage, or excess quantity demanded
Inferior goods	Surplus, or excess quantity supplied
Substitutes	Subsidy

COMPLETION QUESTIONS
Fill in the blank or circle the correct term.

1. A _____ relates various possible prices to the quantities demanded at each price, and a _____ relates various prices to the quantities supplied at each price.

2. A change in quantity demanded is a (movement along, shift in) the demand curve; and a change in demand is a _____ the demand curve.

3. At the intersection of the supply and demand curves, the quantity supplied equals the quantity demanded, and at that price a(n) _____ exists; at a price above that intersection, quantity supplied exceeds quantity demanded and a(n) _____ exists; at a price below that intersection, quantity demanded exceeds quantity supplied, and a(n) _____ exists.

4. The law of demand is that, other things being equal, more is bought at a (lower, higher) price and less is bought at a _____ price.

5. There is a(n) (direct, inverse) relationship between price and quantity demanded, and demand curves will be (positively, negatively) sloped.

6. When the other determinants of demand change, the entire demand curve shifts; the five major non-own-price determinants of demand are_____, _____, _____, _____, and _____.

7. If the demand for pizza rises, given the supply, then the equilibrium price of pizza will (rise, fall) and the equilibrium quantity will _____.

8. The law of supply relates prices to quantities supplied; in general, as price rises, quantity supplied _____. Therefore a(n) (direct, inverse) relationship exists, and the supply curve is (positively, negatively) sloped.

9. The supply curve is positively sloped because as price rises, producers have an incentive to produce (less, more).

10. When the determinants of supply change, the entire supply curve will shift; five major determinants of supply are _____, _____, _____, _____, and _____.

11. Videocassettes and videocassette players are (substitutes, complements); if the price of videocassette players rises, then the demand for video cassettes will _____.

12. When the price of peaches rises, the demand for pears rises; peaches and pears are (substitutes, complements).

13. *Analogy*: An excess quantity supplied is to a surplus as a(n) _____ is to a shortage.

14. A rise in demand causes the demand curve to shift to the (left, right); an increase in quantity demanded occurs when there is a movement (up, down) the demand curve.

15. By convention, economists plot (price, quantity) on the vertical axis and (price, quantity) on the horizontal axis.

16. Without a used CD market the quantity demanded for new CDs at a given price would be (smaller, larger).

TRUE-FALSE QUESTIONS
Circle the **T** if the statement is true, the **F** if it is false. Explain to yourself why a statement is false.

T F   1. A demand schedule relates quantity demanded to quantity supplied, other things being constant.

T F   2. A change in the quantity demanded of cigarettes results from a change in the price of cigarettes.

T F   3. A graphical representation of a demand curve is called a demand schedule.

T F   4. An increase in price leads to a leftward shift in demand and a rightward shift in supply.

T F   5. The existence of a used CD market decreases the demand for new CDs.

T F   6. Buyers are concerned with absolute, not relative prices.

T F   7. As producers increase output in the short run, the cost of additional units of output tends to rise.

T F   8. If the price of tennis racquets rises, the demand for tennis balls will tend to rise also.

T F   9. If the price of butter rises, the demand for margarine will rise.

T F   10. If price is below the equilibrium price, a shortage exists.

MULTIPLE CHOICE QUESTIONS
Circle the letter that corresponds to the best answer.

1. A demand schedule
    a. relates price to quantity supplied.
    b. when graphed, is a demand curve.
    c. cannot change.
    d. shows a direct relationship between price and quantity demanded.

2. If the price of milk rises, other things being constant,
    a. buyers will drink less milk.
    b. buyers will substitute milk for other beverages.
    c. the demand for milk will fall.
    d. the demand for cola drinks will fall.

3. Which of the following will **NOT** occur if the price of hamburger meat falls, other things being constant?
    a. The demand for hamburger buns will increase.
    b. People will substitute hamburgers for hot dogs.
    c. The demand for hot dogs will rise.
    d. The quantity of hamburgers demanded will increase.

4. If the price of good A rises and the demand for good B rises, then A and B are
    a. substitutes.
    b. complements.
    c. not related goods.
    d. not scarce goods.

5. Several years ago some cities in North Carolina passed a law that limited showers to 4 minutes, with a possible 30-day jail sentence for violators. Which of the following statements is probably true for those cities?
    a. A surplus of water existed.
    b. The price of water was too high.
    c. A shortage of water would exist regardless of how high its price got.
    d. The price of water was below the equilibrium price.

6. If the supply of gasoline rises, with a given demand, then
    a. the relative price of gasoline will rise.
    b. the equilibrium price of gasoline will rise.
    c. the equilibrium quantity of gasoline will increase.
    d. the equilibrium price and equilibrium quantity of gasoline will increase.

7. If income falls and the demand for steak falls, then steak is a(n)
    a. substitute good.
    b. complement good.
    c. normal good.
    d. inferior good.

Consider the graphs below when answering questions 8 and 9.

8. Given the figure above,
    a. the equilibrium price is P_1, the equilibrium quantity is P_2.
    b. the equilibrium quantity is P_1.
    c. the equilibrium price is P_3, the equilibrium quantity is Q_1.
    d. the equilibrium quantity is Q_1, the equilibrium price is P_1.

9. Which of the following is *not* true?
    a. A shortage exists at P_2.
    b. The equilibrium price is P_1.
    c. An excess quantity demanded exists at P_3.
    d. The market-clearing price is P_1.

10. If the demand for hamburgers rises, with a given supply, then
    a. the supply of hamburgers will rise because price rises.
    b. the equilibrium price of hamburgers will fall and the equilibrium quantity will rise.
    c. the equilibrium quantity and the equilibrium price of hamburgers will rise.
    d. the quantity supplied of hamburgers will decrease.

11. If a shortage exists at some price, then
    a.   sellers can sell all they desire to sell at that price.
    b.   sellers have an incentive to raise the price.
    c.   buyers cannot get all they want at that price.
    d.   All of the above

12. Which of the following will lead to a rise in supply?
    a.   an increase in the price of the good in question
    b.   a technological improvement in the production of the good in question
    c.   an increase in the price of labor used to produce the good in question
    d.   All of the above

13. Which of the following probably will **NOT** lead to a fall in the demand for hamburgers?
    a.   a decrease in income
    b.   an expectation that the price of hamburgers will rise in the future
    c.   a decrease in the price of hot dogs
    d.   a change in tastes away from hamburgers

14. When a demand curve is derived,
    a.   quantity is in constant-quality units.
    b.   the price of the good is held constant.
    c.   money income changes.
    d.   consumer tastes change.

15. If a surplus exists at some price, then
    a.   sellers have an incentive to raise the price.
    b.   buyers have an incentive to offer a higher price.
    c.   sellers cannot sell all they wish to at that price.
    d.   seller inventories are falling.

MATCHING
Choose the item in Column (2) that best matches an item in Column (1).

(1)	(2)
a. excess quantity demanded	k. relation between price and quantity demanded
b. supply curve	l. law of supply
c. demand curve	m. population increases
d. bread and butter	n. raw material prices rise
e. eyeglasses and contact lenses	o. community money income falls
f. demand shifts to the left	p. market clearing price
g. supply shifts to the left	q. surplus
h. equilibrium price	r. complements
i. equilibrium quantity rises	s. substitutes
j. excess quantity supplied	t. shortage

WORKING WITH GRAPHS

1. Use the demand schedule below to plot the demand curve on the following coordinate system. Be sure to label each axis correctly.

Price per bottle of shampoo	Quantity demanded of bottles of shampoo per week (in thousands)
$6	8
$5	10
$4	12
$3	14
$2	16
$1	18

2.   Use the supply schedule below to plot the supply curve on the coordinate system in problem 1.

Price per bottle of shampoo	Quantity supplied of bottles of shampoo per week (in thousands)
$6	18
$5	15
$4	12
$3	9
$2	6
$1	3

3.   Using the graphs from problems 1 and 2, indicate on the graph the equilibrium price and the equilibrium quantity for bottles of shampoo. What is the equilibrium price? the equilibrium quantity?

4.   Continuing with the same example, assume that the government puts a price ceiling at $3 per bottle of shampoo. What is the quantity demanded at that price? the quantity supplied? Does a surplus or a shortage exist at that price?

5.   Consider the two graphs below, in panels a and b.

(a)   (b)

Which panel shows an increase in quantity demanded? Which shows a rise in demand?

6.   Distinguish between a fall in supply and a decrease in quantity supplied, graphically, using the space below. Use two panels.

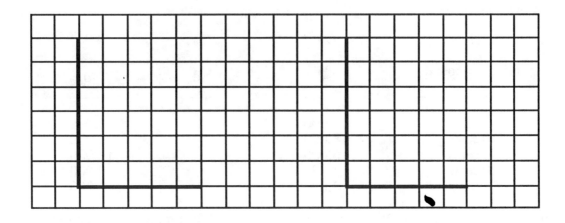

7.   Consider the graphs below in panel (a). Then show, in panel (b), the new equilibrium price (label it P_1) and the new equilibrium quantity (label it Q_1) that results due to a change in tastes in favor of the good in question.

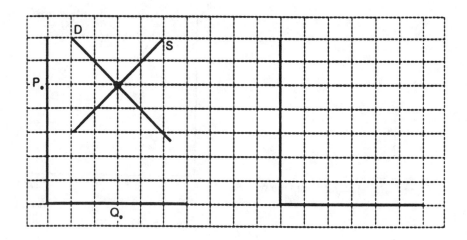

PROBLEMS

1.   In the table below, monthly demand schedules for turkey are indicated. Assume that column 2 represents quantities demanded in October, column 3 represents November, and column 4 represents December.

(1)	(2)	(3)	(4)
Price per pound	Q_d	Q_d	Q_d
5 cents	10,000		16,000
10 cents	8,000		14,000
15 cents	6,000		12,000
20 cents	4,000		10,000
25 cents	2,000		8,000

Fill in column 3 yourself. What happens to the demand for turkey in November relative to October and December? Why?

2.   List the non-own-price determinants of demand that will lead to a decrease in demand. Be specific.

3.   List the nonprice (other) determinants of supply that will lead to a rise in supply. Be specific.

4. Concerning oranges, indicate whether each event leads to (i) a rightward shift in demand, (ii) a leftward shift in demand, (iii) an increase in quantity demanded, (iv) a decrease in quantity demanded, (v) a rightward shift in supply, (vi) a leftward shift in supply, (vii) an increase in quantity supplied, (viii) a decrease in quantity supplied.

    (Note: some events may lead to more than one of the above.)

    _____ a) An early frost in Florida destroys some orange groves.
    _____ b) Migrant workers organize a union and raise wage rates.
    _____ c) The price of oranges rises.
    _____ d) The price of oranges falls.
    _____ e) The Federal government lowers the price of oranges below equilibrium and freezes the price at the lower level.
    _____ f) Orange growers leave the industry.
    _____ g) Lemons (but not oranges) are demonstrated to cause cancer in lab rats.
    _____ h) The government subsidizes orange growers at 3 cents per orange.
    _____ i) News is released that the government forecast is for a poor orange crop this year.
    _____ j) The price of lemons rises (assume now that orange growers can also grow lemons).

5. For each of the statements (a) through (j) in the previous question, decide whether the market clearing *(equilibrium)* price will rise, fall, or be unaffected.

    a) _____   f) _____
    b) _____   g) _____
    c) _____   h) _____
    d) _____   i) _____
    e) _____   j) _____

CASE STUDY

College professors are excited by ideas and love to debate profound philosophical issues. For many, the topic that seems to really get their blood boiling is the campus parking problem. It seems that a parking shortage exists at many colleges, and faculty senates all over the country provide a forum for endless debate of various solutions. Faculty members think that their employers have a "duty" to provide parking for them; students think that parking should be provided for them, because they are crucial to the university. Administrators, in their heart of hearts, believe that they are what make universities important; hence they lay claim to special parking privileges.

1. Draw a probable demand curve for campus parking, with the number of parking spaces on the horizontal axis and the price of parking permits on the vertical axis. Why is such a curve likely to be negatively sloped? (Clue: Are there substitutes for parking one's car on campus?)

2. Draw a probable supply curve on the same coordinate system as in problem (1). Why is such a curve likely to be (at least slightly) upward sloping?

3. Label the equilibrium price P_e and label a price P_1 at which a shortage exists. The price P_1 is the one suggested to exist on many college campuses.

4. How can the parking shortage be eliminated? Why? How will a higher price allocate parking spaces? Is such a solution fair?

ANSWERS TO CHAPTER 3

COMPLETION QUESTIONS

1. demand curve or schedule; supply curve or schedule
2. movement along; shift in
3. equilibrium; surplus; shortage
4. lower; higher
5. inverse; negatively
6. income, tastes and preferences, prices of related goods, expectations about future relative prices, population
7. rise; rise
8. increases; direct; positively
9. more
10. prices of inputs, technology, taxes and subsidies, price expectations, number of firms in industry
11. complements; fall
12. substitutes
13. excess quantity demanded
14. right; down
15. price; quantity
16. smaller

TRUE AND FALSE

1. F   A demand schedule relates quantity demanded to price.
2. T
3. F   A graphical representation of a demand schedule is a demand curve.
4. F   An increase in price leads to a decrease in quantity demanded and an increase in quantity supplied.
5. F   It increases the demand for new CDs.
6. F   Buyers respond to changes in relative prices.
7. T
8. F   The demand for tennis balls will tend to *fall*, because they are complements.
9. T
10. T

MULTIPLE CHOICE QUESTIONS

1.b;   2.a;   3.c;   4.a;   5.d;   6.c;   7.c;   8.d;   9.a;   10.c;
11.d;   12.b;   13.b;   14.a;   15.c.

MATCHING

a and t;   b and l;   c and k;   d and r;   e and s;   f and o;   g and n;   h and p;
i and m;   j and q

WORKING WITH GRAPHS

1. See graphs.
2. See graphs.

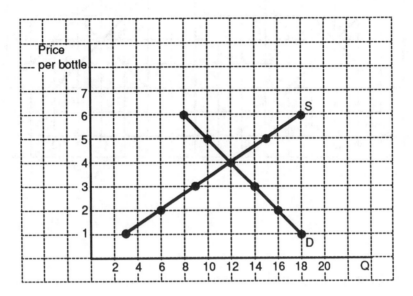

3. $4; 12 bottles
4. 14 bottles; 9 bottles; shortage
5. Panel (a); Panel (b)
6.

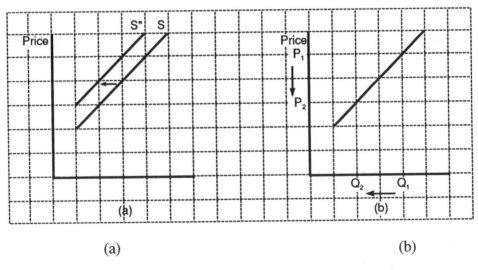

(a)	(b)
A decrease in supply	A decrease in quantity supplied

7.

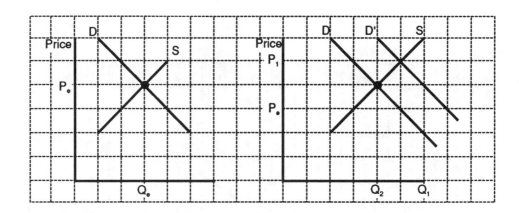

PROBLEMS

1.   Rises, due to Thanksgiving, much relative to October, and (perhaps) slightly relative to December.
2.   Income falls for a normal good; change in tastes occurs away from the good; price of a substitute falls or price of a complement rises; expectations exist that the good's future relative price will fall; decrease in population occurs.
3.   Reduction in the price of inputs; decrease in a sales tax on the good or increase in the (per unit) subsidy of the good; expectation that the future relative price will fall; increase in the number of firms in the industry.

4.   a.   vi and iv   f.   vi and iv
      b.   vi and iv   g.   i and vii
      c.   iv and vii   h.   v and iii
      d.   iii and viii   i.   i
      e.   iii and viii   j.   i and vi

5.   a.   rise   f.   rise
      b.   rise   g.   rise
      c.   be unaffected   h.   fall
      d.   be unaffected   i.   rise
      e.   be unaffected   j.   rise

CASE STUDY

1.   See graphs, question 3. As the price of parking permits rises, faculty and students will find substitutes. They will join car pools, walk, ride bicycles, park off-campus, come to campus less often, and so on.
2.   If price rises to sufficiently high levels, the administration will find it profitable to increase the quantity supplied of parking places. In the short run this may be accomplished by laying out parking lots more efficiently, re-painting lines, allocating some spaces specifically to economy cars, and so on. In the long run, more lots can be paved or parking structures can be constructed.

3.   See graphs.

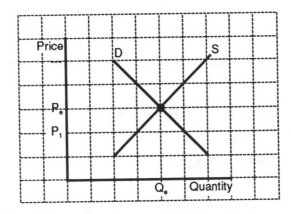

4.   The shortage can be eliminated by allowing the price of parking permits to rise from P_1 to P_e. This price rise will lead to a decrease in the quantity demanded and to an increase in the quantity supplied of parking places. Parking spaces will be allocated to the highest bidders. Whether or not this is a "fair" way to allocate parking spaces is a normative issue and therefore depends on one's value judgments.

GLOSSARY TO CHAPTER 3

Complements   Two goods are complements if both are used together for consumption or enjoyment. The more you buy of one, the more you buy of the other. For complements, a change in the price of one causes an opposite shift in the demand for the other.

Demand curve   A graphic representation of the demand schedule. A negatively sloped line showing the inverse relationship between the price and the quantity demand.

Demand schedule   A schedule of how much of a good or service people will purchase at each different possible price during a specified time period.

Equilibrium   A situation where quantity supplied equals quantity demanded at a particular price.

Inferior good   Those goods for which demand falls as income rises.

Law of supply   A principal stating that generally the higher the price of a good, the larger the quantity sellers will make available over a specified time period, other things being equal.

Market clearing, or equilibrium, price   The price that clears the market, where quantity demanded equals quantity supplied; the price at which the demand curve intersects the supply curve.

Market demand   The demand of all consumers in the marketplace for a particular good or service. The summing at each price of the quantity demanded by each individual.

Money price   That price that we observe today in terms of today's dollars. Also called the *absolute, nominal,* or *current* price.

Normal good   A good for which demand rises as income rises. Most goods are normal goods.

Relative price   The price of a commodity expressed in terms of the price of another commodity or the (weighted) average price of all other commodities.

Shortage   A situation in which quantity demanded is greater than quantity supplied at a price below the market–clearing price.

Subsidy   A negative tax; a payment to a producer (or consumer) from the government, usually in the form of a cash grant.

Substitutes   Two goods are substitutes when either one can be used for consumption. The more you buy of one, the less you buy of the other. For substitutes, the change in the price of one causes a shift in demand for the other in the same direction as the price change.

Supply curve   The graphic representation of the supply schedule; a line (curve) showing the supply schedule, which slopes upward (has a positive slope).

Supply schedule   A schedule showing the relationship between price and quantity supplied, other things being equal, for a specified period of time.

Surplus   A situation in which quantity supplied is greater than quantity demanded at a price above the market-clearing price.

CHAPTER 4

EXTENSIONS OF DEMAND AND SUPPLY ANALYSIS

PUTTING THIS CHAPTER INTO PERSPECTIVE

In Chapter 3 you learned how the forces of supply and demand, with buyers and sellers transacting voluntarily, determine market-clearing or equilibrium price. Sellers compete with sellers for sales, and buyers compete with buyers for goods and services. If price is above equilibrium, a surplus exists and seller competition forces price down toward equilibrium; if price is below equilibrium, a shortage exists and buyer competition forces price up toward equilibrium. Prices adjust until surpluses and shortages are eliminated.

Because resources are scarce, outputs are scarce and somehow scarce outputs must be allocated (or rationed) to people. Under voluntary exchange, when supply and demand forces are unrestricted, goods and services are allocated to the highest bidders. In effect, goods and services go to those customers who are willing to give up more of *other* goods and services.

In this chapter you learn that (a) it takes time for price adjustments to eliminate surpluses and shortages; (b) when governments prevent prices from falling or rising, then prolonged surpluses and prolonged shortages arise, respectively; (c) if price is not allowed to allocate goods to the highest bidder then some other rationing system must—and will—emerge to determine how a specific good will be allocated. Nonprice rationing systems include waiting, discrimination, power, force, coupons, and lotteries, to name a few.

LEARNING OBJECTIVES

After you have studied this chapter you should be able to

1. define price system, voluntary exchange, terms of exchange, transactions costs, price controls, price ceiling, price floor, nonprice rationing devices, black market, rent control, minimum wage, and import quota.

2. predict what happens to equilibrium price and equilibrium quantity when supply increases or decreases relative to demand, and when demand increases relative to supply.

3. predict what happens to the relative price of a good or resource if it becomes more or less scarce.

4. differentiate between the causes of short-run and long-run (prolonged) shortages.

5. explain how labor shortages eventually disappear, given wage rate flexibility.

39

6. recognize various methods of rationing goods and services.

7. recognize, from graphs, how a black market emerges.

8. enumerate several consequences of rent control.

9. recognize several consequences of government quantity restrictions.

10. recognize the consequences of price floors and the causes of prolonged surpluses.

CHAPTER OUTLINE

1. In a price system (free enterprise) voluntary exchange typically determines price; buyers and sellers transact with a minimum amount of governmental interference.
    a. Under a system of voluntary exchange, the terms of exchange (the terms, usually price, under which trade takes place) are set by the forces of supply and demand.
    b. Markets reduce transactions costs (all the costs associated with exchanging, including such costs associated with gathering information and enforcing contracts).
    c. Under voluntary exchange *both* buyers and sellers are presumed to benefit—otherwise the transactions would not continue.

2. Changes in demand and/or supply lead to changes in the equilibrium price and the equilibrium quantity.
    a. If demand shifts to the right (left), given supply, then the equilibrium price rises (falls) and the equilibrium quantity rises (falls).
    b. If supply shifts to the right (left), given demand, then the equilibrium price falls (rises) and the equilibrium quantity rises (falls).
    c. When both supply and demand change, it is not always possible to predict the effects on the equilibrium price and the equilibrium quantity.

3. Prices and wage rates aren't always perfectly flexible.
    a. If prices are inflexible, published prices will not change very much, but such hidden price rises as a quality reduction might occur.
    b. Markets do not always move to equilibrium (given a change in demand or supply) immediately; hence shortages can emerge in the short run.
    c. Short-run labor shortages could arise if employers are reluctant to bid wage rates up and it takes time for people to learn new skills.

4. Price reflects relative scarcity and performs a rationing function.
    a. If an input or output becomes less scarce (more scarce), its relative price will fall (rise).
    b. If governments prevent prices from rising to their equilibrium level, via a price control or ceiling, then goods cannot (legally) be allocated to the highest bidders and prolonged shortages result; other forms of rationing emerge.
    c. During prolonged shortages, such nonprice rationing devices as cheating, long lines, first-come first-served, political power, physical force, and other non-market forces arise.
    d. Governments also interfere in markets by putting price floors on price; for example, governments impose minimum wage rates, and they have put price floors on agricultural goods, which have caused surpluses.

5. Rent controls are governmentally imposed price ceilings on rental apartments, which lead to predictable results; non-price rationing for apartments results.

6. The government has put price floors in several markets.
    a. For many years, price supports created minimum prices for agricultural goods.
    b. When the government sets minimum wages above the equilibrium, some unemployment is created.
    c. Governments sometimes restrict quantity directly through import quotas, which prohibit the importation of more than a specified quantity of a particular good in a one-year period.

KEY TERMS

Price ceiling	Price floor	Black market
Transactions costs	Minimum wage	Import quota

KEY CONCEPTS

Price controls	Rent control	Price system
Voluntary exchange	Terms of exchange	Nonprice rationing devices

COMPLETION QUESTIONS

Fill in the blank or circle the correct term.

1. Resources are scarce; therefore we cannot have all we want at a (zero, positive) price and there will be various ways in which people will _____ for resources.

2. If demand shifts to the left, given supply, then the equilibrium price will (rise, fall) and the equilibrium quantity will _____.

3. If supply shifts to the right, given demand, then the equilibrium price will _____ and the equilibrium quantity will _____.

4. If both demand and supply shift to the right then the equilibrium price (will rise, will fall, is indeterminate) and the equilibrium quantity (will rise, will fall, is indeterminate).

5. If both demand and supply shift to the left, then the equilibrium price (will rise, will fall, is indeterminate), and the equilibrium quantity (will rise, will fall, is indeterminate).

6. If the demand for good A or resource A rises relative to its supply, it has become relatively (less scarce, more scarce) and its relative price will (rise, fall); if the demand for good or resource B falls relative to its supply, then it has become relatively _____, and its relative price will _____.

7. If the published price of good A remains constant, but its quality falls, then its relative price has actually (risen, fallen). If the published price of good A remains constant, but people have to wait in line to get it, then the price of good A has actually _____, because people have an opportunity cost for their _____.

8. If the demand for a labor skill rises relative to its supply, that skill becomes (less scarce, more scarce) and its relative price will (rise, fall); this leads to a(n) (decrease, increase) in the number of people willing to learn that skill.

9. Price performs a(n) _____ function; inputs or outputs go to the _____ bidders, if people are free to exchange voluntarily in markets; if such

economic freedoms do not exist, then other (price, nonprice) determinants will allocate goods and services.

10.   Price controls that put a price ceiling on goods and services create (surpluses, shortages); and price floors create (surpluses, shortages).

11.   If governments place price (floors, ceilings) on goods, then black markets might emerge.

12.   Rent control is a form of price (floor, ceiling); rent control (increases, reduces) the future supply of apartment construction, (increases, reduces) tenant mobility, (improves, causes a deteriation in) the quality of the existing stock of apartments, and hurts _____.

13.   By prohibiting the sale and use of tobacco products, the government would cause the supply of cigarettes to shift to the (left, right), makes cigarettes (more, less) scarce, and causes their relative price to (rise, fall).

14.   Import quotas, licensing arrangements, and outright bans on specific goods are forms of government (price, quantity) restrictions.

15.   An import quota tends to (lower, raise) price to consumers.

16.   If governments put price floors on agricultural goods, a (shortage, surplus) will result.

TRUE-FALSE QUESTIONS
Circle the **T** if the statement if true, the **F** if it is false. Explain to yourself why a statement is false.

T F   1.   If supply shifts to the left, given demand, then the equilibrium price and the equilibrium quantity will rise.

T F   2.   If demand shifts to the left, given supply, then the equilibrium price and the equilibrium quantity will fall.

T F   3.   If both supply and demand shift to the right, then equilibrium price and equilibrium quantity are indeterminate.

T F   4.   If the supply of good A increases relative to its demand, then good A is now more scarce, and its relative price will rise.

T F   5.   If published price is constant, but it takes consumers longer to wait in lines, the true (full) price has really risen.

T F   6.   If markets are flexible and no market restrictions exist, then surpluses and shortages won't occur, even in the short run.

T F   7.   Minimum wage laws are a form of price ceiling.

T F   8.   Rent controls help the poor who are looking for apartments, because rents are lower.

T F   9.   Black markets, in effect, cause price to rise for certain buyers.

T F 10.   Agricultural surpluses arise when governments put price ceilings on such goods.

MULTIPLE CHOICE QUESTIONS
Circle the letter that corresponds to the best answer.

1. Because resources are scarce,
    a. buyers compete with buyers for outputs.
    b. there must be some method for rationing goods.
    c. people cannot have all they want at a zero price.
    d. All of the above

2. If markets are free and prices are flexible,
    a. equilibrium price cannot be established.
    b. shortages and surpluses eventually disappear.
    c. shortages and surpluses can't arise.
    d. equilibrium quantity cannot be established.

3. If demand shifts to the right (given supply), then equilibrium
    a. quantity will rise.
    b. price is indeterminate.
    c. price and equilibrium quantity are indeterminate.
    d. price will fall.

4. If supply shifts to the right (given demand), then equilibrium
    a. quantity will rise.
    b. price will rise.
    c. price and equilibrium quantity will fall.
    d. price and equilibrium quantity rises.

5. If both supply and demand shift to the left, then equilibrium
    a. price is indeterminate and equilibrium quantity rises.
    b. price is indeterminate and equilibrium quantity falls.
    c. price falls and equilibrium quantity falls.
    d. price falls and equilibrium quantity is indeterminate.

6. If the demand for good A falls relative to its supply, then
    a. good A is now relatively more scarce.
    b. good A is now relatively less scarce.
    c. the relative price of good A will rise.
    d. the actual price of good A will rise, even if A is not price flexible.

7. If the demand for good B rises relative to it supply, then
    a. good B is now relatively more scarce.
    b. the relative price of good B will rise.
    c. the actual price of good B will rise, even if good B is price inflexible.
    d. All of the above

8. If the demand for good A rises relative to its supply, and markets are price-flexible, then
    a. no shortage of A can exist in the long run.
    b. no shortage of A can exist in the short run.
    c. the published price of A remains constant, but its actual price falls.
    d. the published price of A remains constant, but its actual price rises.

9. If the demand for good A rises relative to its supply, and markets are price-inflexible, then
   a. a shortage can exist in the short run.
   b. a shortage can exist in the long run.
   c. the published price of A might remain constant, but its actual price rises.
   d. All of the above

10. If the demand for economists falls relative to their supply, then
    a. more college students will major in economics.
    b. some economists will change professions.
    c. a shortage of economists will result, in the long run.
    d. All of the above

11. Which of the following can influence how a society rations a specific good?
    a. Price system that rations to the highest bidder
    b. Political power
    c. Religion
    d. All of the above

12. Prolonged shortages arise if
    a. demand increases relative to supply.
    b. price floors are set by governments.
    c. prices are not allowed to rise to equilibrium.
    d. buyers are allowed to compete for goods.

13. Black markets may arise if
    a. price ceilings exist.
    b. price floors exist.
    c. governments do not intervene in the market.
    d. equilibrium price is too low.

14. Rent controls
    a. are a form of price floor.
    b. help the homeless who need apartments.
    c. make tenants less mobile.
    d. reduce litigation in society.

15. If an effective minimum wage is imposed, then
    a. more workers will be unable to find jobs.
    b. the quantity of labor demanded will fall.
    c. some workers will move to sectors not covered by minimum wages.
    d. All of the above

16. Prolonged agricultural surpluses can arise if governments
    a. set price above equilibrium.
    b. institute price floors, or price supports.
    c. purchase the excess supply.
    d. All of the above

MATCHING
Choose the item in Column (2) that best matches an item in Column (1).

(1)   (2)

a. price floor   e. buyer competition
b. price ceiling   f. rent control
c. scarce resources   g. minimum wage law
d. nonprice rationing   h. black market, long lines

WORKING WITH GRAPHS

1. Consider the graphs below, then answer the questions that follow.

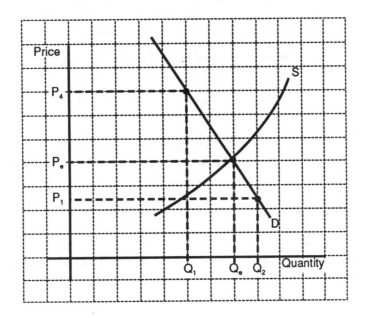

a. The market-clearing price is _____?
b. If the government imposes a price ceiling at P_1, what will be the quantity supplied? The quantity demanded? What exists at that price?
c. Given the quantity that will be forthcoming at the permitted price of P_1, what will the actual or black market price be?
d. Other than via a black market transaction, how can the actual price paid by buyers exceed the permitted price, P_1.
e. If price had been permitted to rise to equilibrium, what would be the quantity supplied by sellers? Is that amount greater or lesser than the quantity at P_1? Why?

2.   Consider the following supply and demand curves for labor, and then answer the questions.

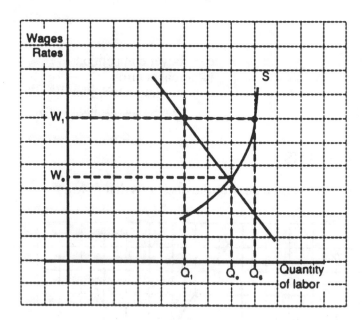

a.   What is the equilibrium wage rate? The equilibrium quantity of labor?

b.   If the government sets a minimum wage rate at W_1, what is the quantity of labor demanded by employers? The quantity of labor supplied by workers? What exists at the minimum wage rate?

c.   Is there a shortage or surplus of *jobs*? How might such jobs be allocated (that is, how will employers go about deciding who gets the jobs)?

3.   During September of 1989, the then "drug Czar" William T. Bennett, Director of the Office of National Drug Control Policy, and Nobel Prize winning economist Milton Friedman debated the case for the prohibition of drugs in various letters to the editor, in the *Wall Street Journal*. Bennett, who favors prohibition, maintained that if drugs were legalized price would fall, and therefore, the total amount of drug usage in the U.S. would rise. Friedman, who favors legalization of drugs (to adults) maintained that, once legalized, the demand for drugs would fall because (1) the appeal to people who want the excitement of doing something "taboo" would disappear, and (2) addicts who have only a $2 a day habit have less of an incentive to get other people hooked on drugs (to support their own habit) than if they had a $200 a day habit.

a.   Is Bennett correct when he says that once legalized, price will fall? Why?

b.   If the demand for drugs shifts to the left, and the supply of drugs to the right, what happens to the price of drugs?

c.   If the demand for drugs shifts to the left (Friedman) and the supply of drugs shifts to the right (Bennett), what happens to the equilibrium quantity?

d.   How does your answer to (c) help you decide whether drug usage will rise or fall if drugs are legalized? What information is necessary to resolve this issue?

PROBLEMS

1. In a 1950's movie entitled "Under the Yum-Yum Tree," Jack Lemmon played a lecherous landlord who was extremely wealthy.
   a. How do you imagine he created a shortage of his own luxury apartments, and what criteria do you imagine he used to decide who was able to rent such apartments?
   b. Does rent control force landlords to discriminate in the selection of tenants? What criteria might they use to make such selections?

2. In 1979 the rock group "The Who" gave a concert in Cincinnati, and 11 people died outside Riverfront Coliseum when the gates were opened and the crowd rushed in to get choice seats. What other method of allocating the scarce resource "choice seats" would have prevented this tragic event?

CASE STUDY

In California, 1984, an oil company was convicted of charging prices that were above the legally-set price, and forced to charge, for a short time, prices below market prices to atone. Customers were then faced with a choice between (1) waiting in line for low-priced gasoline or (2) not waiting and purchasing gasoline of a similar quality at a higher price across the street. Two economists surveyed customers who chose each of those options.

1. What kinds of people waited in line for the lower-priced gasoline?

2. What kinds of people frequented the higher-priced gasoline stations?

ANSWERS TO CHAPTER 4

COMPLETION QUESTIONS

1. zero; compete
2. fall; fall
3. fall; rise
4. is indeterminate; will rise
5. is indeterminate; will fall
6. more scarce; rise; less scarce; fall
7. risen; risen; time
8. more scarce; rise; increase
9. rationing; highest; nonprice
10. shortages; surpluses
11. ceilings
12. ceiling; reduces; reduces; causes a deteriation in; landlords and low income apartment hunters
13. left; more; rise
14. quantity
15. raise
16. surplus

TRUE-FALSE QUESTIONS

1. F   The equilibrium quantity falls.
2. T
3. F   Equilibrium quantity rises.
4. F   Good A is now less scarce, and its relative price will fall.
5. T
6. F   No, surpluses and shortages can exist—in the short run.
7. F   They are a price floor.
8. F   That group is hurt because they will be discriminated against, and because the housing stock diminishes.
9. T
10. F   Price ceilings cause shortages.

MULTIPLE CHOICE QUESTIONS

1.d;   2.b;   3.a;   4.a;   5.b;   6.b;   7.d;   8.a;   9.d;   10.b;
11.d;   12.c;   13.a;   14.c;   15.d;   16.d.

MATCHING

a and g;   b and f;   c and e;   d and h.

WORKING WITH GRAPHS

1. a. P_e
    b. Q_1; Q_2; shortage
    c. P_4
    d. quality deterioration, long lines that increase opportunity costs
    e. Q_e; greater; a higher price induces sellers to produce more.

2. a. W_e; Q_e
    b. Q_1; Q_6; surplus of labor, or unemployment
    c. shortage; family influence, political power, bribes, racial or gender preference

3. a. He is correct, because the supply curve will shift to the right as the costs and risks of drug-dealing fall.
    b. falls; Therefore Bennett is right.
    c. It is impossible to predict the net effect on the equilibrium quantity.
    d. The real issue is an empirical one; Will supply rise by more than demand falls, or vice versa?

PROBLEMS

1. a. He set rents far below the market-clearing levels, and many people wanted his apartments; he rented only to "lovely young ladies."
    b. Yes; gender, beauty, race, number of children, age, ability to pay, pets, and so on.

2. Instead of "first-come, first-served seating," ticket sellers could have raised the price of choice seats and used assigned seating. Shortly thereafter, the city of Cincinnati passed a resolution that outlawed first-come, first-served seating.

CASE STUDY

1. People who had low opportunity costs for their time: teenagers, homemakers, senior citizens, low-income people.
2. People who had high opportunity costs for their time: professionals, business executives, high income people.

GLOSSARY TO CHAPTER 4

Black market A market in which goods are traded at prices above their legal maximum prices.

Import quota A government-set physical supply restriction on goods from abroad

Minimum wage A wage floor legislated by government, below which it is illegal to pay workers.

Nonprice rationing devices All those methods used to ration scarce goods that are price controlled. Whenever the price system is not allowed to work, there will exist nonprice rationing devices to ration the affected goods and services.

Price ceiling A legal maximum price that can be charged for a particular good or service.

Price controls Government mandated controls on either minimum or maximum prices that can be charged for goods and services.

Price floor A legal minimum price below which a good or service cannot be sold. Legal minimum wages are an example.

Price system An economic system in which relative prices are constantly changing to reflect changes in supply and demand for different commodities. The prices of those commodities are signals to everyone within the system about what is relatively scarce and what is relatively abundant.

Rent control Price ceilings placed on rents in particular municipalities.

Terms of exchange   The terms under which the trading takes place. Usually the terms of exchange are given by the price at which a good is traded.

Transaction costs All of the costs associated with exchanging, including the informational costs of finding out price and quality, service record, durability, etc., of a product, plus the cost of contracting and enforcing that contract.

Voluntary exchange   The act of trading, usually done on a voluntary basis in which both parties to the trade are subjectively better off after the exchange.

CHAPTER 5

THE PUBLIC SECTOR

PUTTING THIS CHAPTER INTO PERSPECTIVE

To date you have learned that scarcity is a human condition, that economists study how resources are allocated to satisfy wants, and that there are many potential determinants of how resources are rationed in specific situations. In Chapter 5 we analyze how governments influence resource use—or more specifically, how individuals and groups use the institution of government to influence resource use.

It is important to master this chapter because our overall goal is to understand how resources are rationed in the American economy. The role of the government in our economy has grown tremendously since World War II; some maintain that it is nearly as important as the price system in determining resource use in the United States.

It is generally agreed that the price system is an efficient resource allocator. Typically the value of output will be maximized (opportunity costs will be minimized) if the price system is permitted to allocate resources to satisfy wants. Nevertheless, the resource allocation that results from a price system is not always efficient. In this chapter you learn that if externalities exist, then the price system will transmit *incorrect* signals, and resource misallocation will result as the economy overproduces or underproduces specific goods and services. Similarly, because of the "free rider" problem, the price system will underproduce public goods. For these reasons the government has an *economic* function to perform; it can help to correct resource misallocation by providing the correct signals to economic agents.

The government has important *political* functions to perform also; it affects the output of merit and demerit goods and it redistributes income if the political process decides that the income distribution that results from the price system is unfair.

It is impossible to analyze the public sector without understanding the role of taxes. In this chapter we distinguish between marginal and average tax rates and analyze the effects of raising tax revenues through various types of tax systems.

LEARNING OBJECTIVES

After you have studied this chapter you should be able to

1. define antitrust legislation, monopoly, spillover or externality, third parties, effluent fee, market failure, property rights, private goods, public goods, principle of rival consumption,

exclusion principle, free-rider problem, merit good, demerit good, transfer payment, transfers in kind, marginal and average tax rates, proportional, progressive, and regressive taxation, capital gain, capital loss, retained earnings, tax incidence.

2. enumerate the five economic functions of government.

3. predict whether a specific good will be overproduced, underproduced, or produced in just the right amount if resources are allocated by the price system.

4. identify which graphs take into account an externality and which do not.

5. list the two ways in which a government can correct for negative externalities.

6. identify the three ways in which a government can correct for positive externalities.

7. list four characteristics of public goods that distinguish them from private goods.

8. distinguish between a marginal and an average tax rate.

9. calculate the tax burden for individuals with different incomes, given different tax structures.

10. recognize the costs and benefits of a flat tax.

CHAPTER OUTLINE

1. The government provides many economic functions that affect the way in which resources are allocated.
   a. If a benefit or cost associated with an economic activity *spills over* to *third parties*, the price system will misallocate resources; a proper role for government is to correct such externalities.
      i. If a negative externality exists, the price system will over-allocate resources to that industry; the government can correct this by taxing or regulating such activities.
      ii. If a positive externality exists, the price system will under-allocate resources to that industry; the government can correct this by financing additional production, by providing special *subsidies*, or by regulation.
   b. A legal system that defines and enforces property rights is crucial to the American capitalistic economy.
   c. Because a competitive price system transmits correct signals, an important role for government is to promote competition.
   d. A price system will underallocate resources to the production of *public goods*.
      i. Characteristics of public goods include:
         (1) They are usually indivisible.
         (2) They can be used by more people at no additional cost.
         (3) Additional users of public goods do not deprive others of any of the services of the good.
         (4) It is difficult to charge individual users a fee based on how much they themselves consume of the public good.
      ii. Because public goods must be consumed collectively, individuals have an incentive to take a *free ride* and not pay for them.
      iii. Because the price system underproduces public goods, a proper role of government may be to ensure their production.
   e. In recent years the government has taken on the economic role of ensuring economywide stability: full employment, price stability, and economic growth.

2. The government provides political functions that also affect resource allocation.
    a. Governments subsidize the production of *merit goods* and tax or prohibit the production of *demerit goods*.
    b. By combining a progressive tax structure with *transfer payments*, the government attempts to redistribute income from higher to lower income groups. (Although many "loopholes" frustrate such a policy.)

3. Governments tax in order to obtain revenues to finance expenditures.
    a. The marginal tax rate is the change in the tax payment divided by the change in income.
    b. The average tax rate equals the total tax payment divided by total income.

4. There are three main types of taxation systems.
    a. Under a *proportional taxation* system, as a person's income rises, the percentage of income paid (rate of taxation) in taxes remains constant.
    b. Under a *progressive taxation* system, as a person's income rises, the percentage of income paid in taxes rises.
    c. Under a *regressive taxation* system, as a person's income rises, the percentage of income paid in taxes falls.

5. The federal government imposes income taxes on individuals and corporations, and it collects Social Security taxes and other taxes.
    a. The most important tax in the U.S. economy is the personal income tax; recently some have proposed a consumption tax, which taxes people based on what they actually spend.
    b. The difference between the buying and selling price of an asset, such as a share of stock or a plot of land, is called a capital gain if a profit results, and a capital loss if it doesn't.

6. The corporate income tax is a moderately important source of revenue for the various governments in the U.S. economy.
    a. Corporate stockholders are taxed twice: once on corporate income and again when dividends are received or when the stock is sold.
    b. The incidence of corporate taxes falls on people—consumers, workers, management, and stockholders—not on such inanimate objects as "corporations."

7. An increasing percentage of federal tax receipts is accounted for each year by taxes (other than income) levied on payrolls, such as Social Security taxes and unemployment compensation.

8. Major sources of revenue for states and local governments are sales and excise taxes.

9. The Internal Revenue Code is extremely complicated. Americans expend an opportunity cost of about $70 billion a year filling out their tax returns.

10. High marginal tax rates may lead to less work, early retirements, fewer second jobs, and people entering the labor market later. High marginal tax rates may lead to a reduced saving rate.

11. An alternative to the current income tax system is a national sales tax, which might be at a rate of 15 percent on all final purchases of goods and services at the retail level with a rebate for every household earning less than, say, $20,000.00.

KEY TERMS

Antitrust legislation

Monopoly

Subsidy

Capital gain

Merit good

Demerit good

Effluent fee

Transfer payment

Capital loss

Retained earnings

Government, or political, goods

KEY CONCEPTS

Spillover or externality

Third parties

Market failure

Principle of rival consumption

Exclusion principle

Private goods

Public goods

Tax incidence

User charge system

Marginal tax rate

Average tax rate

Transfers in kind

Proportional taxation

Progressive taxation

Regressive taxation

Free-rider problem

Tax bracket

Property rights

COMPLETION QUESTIONS

Fill in the blank or circle the correct term.

1. The five economic functions of federal government in our capitalistic system are
    _____, _____, _____,
    _____, _____.

2. If there are disputes in an economic arena, the _____ often acts as a "referee" to help settle the dispute.

3. Antitrust legislation, in theory, is supposed to (decrease, promote) competition in the private sector.

4. If externalities are an important result of an economic activity, then the price system is (inefficient, efficient).

5. If Mr. Johnson buys an automobile from General Motors, then those people not directly involved in the transaction are considered _____.

6. Pollution is an example of a (negative, positive) externality.

7. When there are spillover costs, a price system will (under, over) allocate resources to the production of the good in question.

8. If third parties benefit from a transaction, then (negative, positive) externalities exist, and the price system will allocate resources (inefficiently, efficiently).

9. Positive and negative externalities are examples of market _____.

10. A government can correct negative externalities by imposing taxes and by _____ the industry or firms in question.

11. A government can correct positive externalities by _____, _____, _____.

12. If a positive externality exists for good B, a price system will produce too _____ of good B.

13. Public goods have four distinguishing characteristics. They are usually _____; they can be used by more people at _____ additional cost; additional users (do, do not) deprive others of the services of a public good; it is very (easy, difficult) to charge individuals based on how much they used the public good.

14. A free rider has an incentive to (pay, not pay) for a public good.

15. Demerit goods are goods for which society wants to (decrease, increase) production.

16. Americans spend $70 billion of (opportunity, explicit) cost filling out their tax returns.

17. A national sales tax would be assessed on (all, only final) goods and services.

18. Many government, or political, goods are provided to consumers at a (zero, positive) price; but the opportunity cost to society of providing government goods is (zero, positive).

19. If the price of an asset rises after its purchase, the owner receives a _____ gain; if the price falls, the owner suffers a _____ loss.

20. The marginal tax rate applies only to the (first, last) tax bracket.

21. The corporate income tax is paid by one or more of the following groups: _____, _____, and _____.

TRUE-FALSE QUESTIONS
Circle the **T** if the statement is true, the **F** if it is false. Explain to yourself why a statement is false.

T F 1. In the U.S. economy the government plays only a minor role in resource allocation, because the country is capitalistic.

T F 2. Governments provide a legal system, but this important function is not considered an economic function.

T F 3. One aim of antitrust legislation is the promotion of competition.

T F 4. If externalities, or spillovers, exist, then a price system misallocates resources, so that inefficiency exists.

T F 5. If a negative externality exists, buyers and sellers are not faced with the true opportunity costs of their actions.

T F 6. If a positive externality exists when good A is produced, a price system will underallocate resources into the production of good A.

T F   7.   One way to help correct for a negative externality is to tax the good in question, because that will cause the price of the good to fall.

T F   8.   A price system will tend to overallocate resources to the production of free goods, due to the free rider problem.

T F   9.   Scarcity exists in the market sector, but not in the public sector.

T F   10.   If third parties are hurt by the production of good B and they are not compensated, then too many resources have been allocated to industry B.

T F   11.   Deciding what is a merit good and what is a demerit good is easily done and does not require value judgments.

T F   12.   The federal individual income tax is regressive.

T F   13.   The largest source of receipts for the federal government is the individual income tax.

T F   14.   In a progressive tax structure, the average tax rate is greater than the marginal tax rate.

T F   15.   Positive economics confirms that a progressive taxation system is more equitable than a regressive taxation system.

T F   16.   In the United States the tax system that yields the most revenue to all governments combined is the corporate tax.

T F   17.   When corporations are taxed, consumers and corporate employees are also affected.

MULTIPLE CHOICE QUESTIONS
Circle the letter that corresponds to the best answer.

1.   Which of the following is not an economic function of government?
   a.   income redistribution
   b.   providing a legal system
   c.   ensuring economywide stability
   d.   promoting competition

2.   A price system will misallocate resources if
   a.   much income inequality exists.
   b.   demerit goods are produced.
   c.   externalities exist.
   d.   All of the above

3.   Which of the following does not belong with others?
   a.   positive externality
   b.   negative externality
   c.   demerit good
   d.   public good

4. The exclusion principle
    a. does not work for public goods.
    b. does not work for private goods.
    c. causes positive externalities.
    d. makes it easy to assess user fees on true public goods.

5. Which of the following statements concerning externalities is true?
    a. If a positive externality exists for good A, A will be overproduced by a price system.
    b. If externalities exist, then resources will be allocated efficiently.
    c. Efficiency may be improved if the government taxes goods for which a positive externality exists.
    d. The output of goods for which a positive externality exists is too low, from society's point of view.

6. Which of the following is **NOT** a characteristic of public goods?
    a. indivisibility
    b. high extra cost to additional users
    c. exclusion principle does not work easily
    d. difficult to determine how each individual benefits from public goods

7. Market failure exists if
    a. Mr. Smith cannot purchase watermelons in his town.
    b. buyers and sellers must pay the true opportunity costs of their actions.
    c. third parties are injured and are not compensated.
    d. the government must provide merit goods.

8. Which of the following will properly correct a negative externality that results from producing good B?
    a. subsidizing the production of good B
    b. letting the price system determine the price and output of good B
    c. forcing buyers and sellers of good B to pay the true opportunity costs of their actions.
    d. banning the production of good B

9. Merit and demerit goods
    a. are examples of public goods.
    b. are examples of externalities.
    c. indicate market failure.
    d. are not easily classified.

10. Which of the following is most unlike the others?
    a. income tax
    b. sales tax
    c. consumption tax
    d. value added tax

11. A switch from the current progressive income tax to a national sales tax
    a. would not change our tax system very much.
    b. would lead to more taxes on savings.
    c. would cause the current structure of the IRS to be greatly reduced.
    d. more Internal Revenue agents would be hired.

12.   If the government taxes group A and gives to group B, then economic incentives for
   a.   group A may be reduced.
   b.   group B may be reduced.
   c.   both may change so as to reduce output.
   d.   All of the above.

13.   If Mr. Ayres loves good A, he can convey the intensity of his wants if good A is
   a.   a private good.
   b.   a public good.
   c.   not subject to the exclusion principle.
   d.   expensive.

14.   The free rider problem exists
   a.   for private goods.
   b.   for goods that must be consumed collectively.
   c.   only if people can be excluded from consumption.
   d.   All of the above

15.   In a progressive tax structure,
   a.   the marginal tax rate exceeds the average tax rate.
   b.   equity exists.
   c.   the average tax rate rises as income falls.
   d.   All of the above

16.   Which of the following statements is true?
   a.   Under a regressive tax structure the average tax rate remains constant as income rises.
   b.   If upper-income people pay more taxes than lower income people, equity must exist.
   c.   The U.S. federal personal income tax system is progressive.
   d.   At very high income levels, the Social Security tax and employee contribution become progressive.

17.   The tax incidence of the corporate income tax falls on
   a.   corporate stockholders.
   b.   corporate employees.
   c.   consumers of goods and services produced by corporations.
   d.   All of the above

18.   Which of the following statements about the Social Security tax is **NOT** true?
   a.   It is a progressive tax.
   b.   It came into existence in 1935.
   c.   It is imposed on employers and employees.
   d.   It is a payroll tax.

19.   If Mr. Romano faces a 90 percent marginal tax rate,
   a.   the next dollar he earns nets him ninety cents.
   b.   his total tax payments equal 90 percent of his total income.
   c.   he has a strong incentive to not earn extra income.
   d.   his average tax rate must be falling.

20.   A proportional tax system
   a.   is unfair.
   b.   cannot be consistent with people's ability to pay such taxes.
   c.   means that upper income people pay smaller percentages of their income in taxes than do lower income people.
   d.   requires upper income people to pay more tax dollars than lower income people pay.

MATCHING
Choose the item in Column (2) that best matches an item in Column (1).

(1)	(2)
a. antitrust legislation	g. pollution
b. spillover	h. externality
c. positive externality	i. national defense
d. negative externality	j. alcohol
e. government good	k. monopoly
f. demerit good	l. flu shots

PROBLEMS

1. Complete the following table for three taxes and then indicate what type of tax each is.

Income	Tax 1		Tax 2		Tax 3	
	Tax paid	Average tax rate	Tax paid	Average tax rate	Tax paid	Average tax rate
$ 1,000	$ 30	_____	$ 10	_____	$ 100	_____
3,000	90	_____	60	_____	270	_____
6,000	180	_____	180	_____	480	_____
10,000	300	_____	400	_____	700	_____
15,000	450	_____	750	_____	900	_____
20,000	600	_____	1200	_____	1000	_____
30,000	900	_____	2100	_____	1200	_____

2. Suppose the above table had a fourth tax as shown below. Find the average and marginal tax rates and explain what type tax it would be.

Income	Tax paid	Average tax rate	Marginal tax rate
$ 1,000	$ 30	_____	_____
3,000	120	_____	_____
6,000	300	_____	_____
10,000	500	_____	_____
15,000	600	_____	_____
20,000	700	_____	_____
30,000	900	_____	_____

3. One important purely economic function of government is to promote competition, which presumably makes the price system more efficient. During the 1970s the OPEC oil cartel was able to restrict output dramatically, which permitted the cartel to charge much higher prices and earn higher profits. How did consumers, businesses, and other governments react to the higher relative price of oil? Were such actions rational, from the point of view of the individuals involved? Did such decisions lead to a misallocation of resources from *society's* point of view? (Hint: the OPEC price was artificially high because the cartel reduced output and repressed competition.)

4. In the text five economic functions of the government and two political functions were analyzed. Place each of the following governmental activities in one (or more) of these seven categories in the space provided at the far right of each letter.

a) Providing aid to welfare recipients   _____
b) Passing antitrust laws   _____
c) Subsidizing the arts   _____
d) Prohibiting the sale and possession of drugs   _____
e) Providing national defense   _____
f) Enforcing a progressive tax structure   _____
g) Enforcing contracts   _____
h) Providing public education to children   _____
i) Prosecuting fraud   _____
j) Providing funds for AIDS research   _____
k) Creating jobs to reduce unemployment   _____

WORKING WITH GRAPHS

1. Consider the graph below, then answer the questions. Assume S represents industry supply and S' includes pollution costs to society as well as industry private costs.

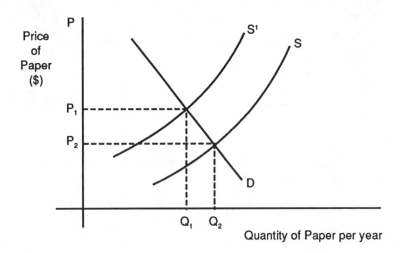

a. If no governmental intervention takes place, what will be the market equilibrium price? The market equilibrium quantity?

b. At the market equilibrium quantity (Q_2), which is higher: private costs or social costs?

c. From *society's* point of view, what is the price that reflects the true opportunity costs of paper? From that same point of view, what is the optimal quantity of paper?

d. Considering your answers in the above three questions, will a price system produce too little, or too much paper.

e. Does a negative externality or a positive externality exist?

2.   Consider the graphs below, then answer the questions that follow. Assume that D represents private market demand and that D' represents benefits that accrue to third parties as well as private benefits.

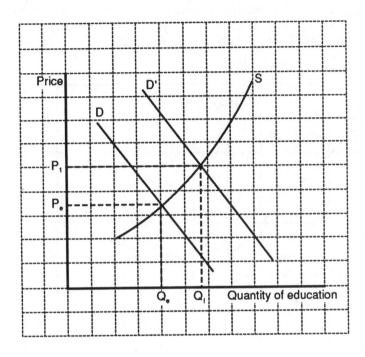

a.   If no government intervention occurs, what will be the market equilibrium price? The market equilibrium quantity?

b.   At the market equilibrium quantity, which is greater, private benefits or social benefits?

c.   From *society's* point of view, what is the optimal price and the optimal quantity of education?

d.   In this example, does the price system provide too much, or too little education?

e.   Is there a positive externality or a negative externality for this good?

3. Suppose you know the demand and supply of fertilizer locally, and you have graphed them as shown in the graphs that follows. The fertilizer plant that operates in your town is also producing pollution. This pollution is a constant amount per unit of output (proportional to output) at the plant. If the government decides to try to combat the pollution problem by imposing a $20-per-ton tax on fertilizer produced, show graphically what will happen to the fertilizer market. Will the level of pollution in your town be reduced? If so, by how much? If not, can you offer a solution to the pollution problem?

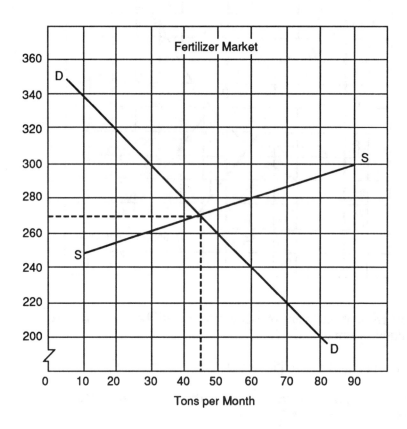

4. a. Draw supply and demand curves for good A, for which no externalities exist, and indicate the optimal quantity of output, the price that reflects the opportunity cost to buyers and sellers of that good, and whether the price system has over-, or under-, or properly allocated resources into industry A.

    b. Draw private supply and demand curves for good B, for which negative externalities exist. Draw another curve on that coordinate system which reflects negative externalities. Indicate the optimal output quantity and price from society's point of view, and compare them to the output quantity and price that would result from a price system.

    c. Draw private supply and demand curves for good C, for which positive externalities exist. Draw another curve which reflects the positive externalities associated with good C. Indicate the optimal price and output quantity of good C from society's point of view, and compare them to the output quantity and price that result from the price system.

CASE STUDY

Many people believe that smokers impose negative externalities on non-smokers in the form of "second-hand smoke." As a consequence smoking has been banned in many public buildings, on airplane flights, and so on. Some cities require non-smoking sections in restaurants; many people maintain that smoking should not be permitted in *any* restaurants. Some day it may be illegal to smoke at all.

1.   Do you think that the evidence regarding the ill effects of smoking on third parties is strong?

2.   Is such evidence crucial to intelligent policy-making?

3.   Regarding restaurants, is a ban on smoking necessary? Can a market, voluntary exchange solution emerge?

ANSWERS TO CHAPTER 5

COMPLETION QUESTIONS

1. providing a legal system, promoting competition, correcting externalities, providing public goods, ensuring economywide stability
2. government
3. promote
4. inefficient
5. third parties
6. negative
7. over
8. positive; inefficiently
9. failure
10. regulating
11. subsidizing production, financing production, regulation
12. little
13. indivisible; zero; do not; difficult
14. not pay
15. decrease
16. opportunity
17. only final
18. zero; positive
19. capital; capital
20. last
21. stockholders, consumers, employees

TRUE-FALSE QUESTIONS

1. F Even in capitalist countries the government plays a major role.
2. F It is an economic function because by enforcing contracts government can promote trade and commerce.
3. T
4. T
5. T
6. T
7. F A tax will cause the price of the good to *rise*, which is a movement in the correct direction.
8. F The free rider problem deals with goods that are *scarce*, but for which the exclusion principle does not work well.
9. F Scarcity exists in the public sector too; after all, the government uses and allocates scarce goods.
10. T
11. F Whether or not a good is a merit good requires value judgments.
12. F It is progressive.
13. T
14. F For average taxes to rise with income (a progressive tax) the marginal tax rate must exceed the average tax rate.
15. F "Equitable" requires normative statements.
16. F No, the personal income tax does so.
17. T

MULTIPLE CHOICE QUESTIONS

1.a;   2.c;   3.c;   4.a;   5.d;   6.b;   7.c;   8.c;   9.d;   10.a;
11.c; 12.d; 13.a; 14.b; 15.a; 16.c; 17.d; 18.a; 19.c; 20.d.

MATCHING

a and k;   b and h;   c and l;   d and g;   e and i;   f and j

PROBLEMS

1. Tax 1: 3 percent; 3 percent; 3 percent; 3 percent; 3 percent; 3 percent; 3 percent; proportional

    Tax 2: 1 percent; 2 percent; 3 percent; 4 percent; 5 percent; 6 percent; 7 percent; progressive

    Tax 3: 10 percent; 9 percent; 8 percent; 7 percent; 6 percent; 5 percent; 4 percent; regressive

2. ATR: 3 percent; 4 percent; 5 percent; 5 percent; 4 percent; 3.5 percent; 3 percent

    MTR: 3 percent; 4.5 percent; 6 percent; 5 percent; 2 percent; 2 percent; 2 percent

    The average tax rate for this tax initially rises and then falls, as does the marginal tax rate. As a result, this tax is progressive up to an income of $6,000, proportional from there to $10,000, and regressive for levels of income above $10,000. Thus this tax is a combination of all three types of taxes as income varies. Can you graph the ATR and MTR for this tax? Can you think of any taxes that might behave in this manner?

3. Consumers joined car pools, drove less often, bought smaller cars, and endured less comfortable temperatures at home; businesses invested in the production of such oil substitutes as solar energy, nuclear energy, shale oil, coal, etc.; governments subsidized the production of gasohol and shale oil, etc. Such actions were rational because they were responses to a perceived increase in the relative price of oil and its distillates. From society's point of view, such actions led to a misallocation because the lack of competition caused the price system to transmit an incorrect signal. The signal was that oil had become more scarce—but the signal was induced by an artificial restriction of supply.

4. a. redistribution
    b. promoting competition
    c. providing merit goods
    d. discouraging demerit goods
    e. providing public goods
    f. redistribution
    g. providing legal systems
    h. correcting positive externality
    i. providing legal system
    j. correcting negative externality
    k. stabilizing economy

WORKING WITH GRAPHS

1. a. P_2; Q_2
    b. social costs
    c. P_1; Q_1
    d. too much
    e. negative

2. a. P_e; Q_e
    b. social benefits
    c. P_1; Q_1
    d. too little
    e. positive

3. The supply curve after the tax is imposed shifts to S_1—that is, upward by $20 at each quantity. The equilibrium quantity falls from 45 tons per month to below 40 tons per month as a result. Thus the quantity of fertilizer produced has declined by more than 10 percent. This means that the output of pollution has declined by more than 10 percent, because the output of pollution is a constant per unit of output of fertilizer.

The result of the analysis should not be extended in a general fashion without regard to other possible effects that a tax of this nature might have. We might also wish to consider other factors before imposing a pollution tax. Among these factors are the effects of the increased price of the fertilizer, the likely reduction in employment as a result of the reduced quantity of fertilizer produced, and the ability of alternative methods of pollution control to achieve the same results.

4. a. The market price and the equilibrium quantity are at the socially optimal values because no externalities exist; resources are allocated properly into industry A.
   b. The *new* curve you draw, which reflects a negative externality, should be a supply curve that lies to the left of (above) the original curve, labeled S_1. The optimal price-quantity combination exists where S_1 intersects the demand curve; the socially optimal price is higher than the market price, and the socially optimal quantity is lower than the market quantity.
   c. The new curve should be a demand curve, D', that lies to the right of (above) the original demand curve. The socially optimal price-output combination is where D' intersects the supply curve; price will be higher and output will be higher than the market price-output combination.

CASE STUDY

1. So far the evidence is mixed.
2. Such evidence is crucial, otherwise smokers will be needlessly harmed.
3. Specialization would arise; some restaurants will ban smoking, others will permit it. Consumers can take their choice.

GLOSSARY FOR CHAPTER 5

Antitrust legislation   The enactment of laws that restrict the formation of monopolies and that regulate certain anticompetitive business practices.

Average tax rate   The total tax payment divided by total income. It is the proportion of total income paid in taxes.

Capital gain   The positive difference between the purchase price and the sale price of an asset. If a share of stock is bought for $5 and then sold for $15, the capital gain is $10.

Capital loss   The negative difference between the purchase price and the sale price of an asset.

Demerit good   The opposite of a merit good; one which the political process has decided is socially undesirable, e.g., heroin.

Effluent fee   A charge for the right to pollute based on the amount of discharge.

Exclusion principle   A characteristic of public goods; no one can be excluded from the benefits of a public good, even if he or she hasn't paid for it.

Free-rider problem   A problem associated with public goods in which individuals presume that others will pay for the public goods, so that, individually, they can escape paying for their portion without a reduction in production occurring.

Government, or political, goods   Goods (and services) provided by the public sector; they can be either private or public goods.

Marginal tax rate   The change in the tax payment divided by the change in income, or the percentage of additional dollars that must be paid in taxes. The marginal tax rate is applied to the last tax bracket of taxable income.

Market failure   A situation in which an unfettered market leads to either an under- or overallocation of resources to a specific economic activity. Spillovers, or externalities, are cases of market failure.

Merit good   A good that has been deemed socially desirable via the political process, e.g., museums.

Monopoly   A firm that has great control over the price of a good. In the extreme case, a monopoly is the only seller of a good or service.

Principle of rival consumption   Stated briefly, when I use a private good, my use excludes the possibility of your using it simultaneously, we are rivals in the consumption of that private good.

Private goods   Goods that can only be consumed by one individual at a time. Private goods are subject to the principle of mutual exclusivity.

Progressive taxation   A tax system in which, as one earns more income, a higher percentage of the additional dollars is taxed. The marginal tax rate exceeds the average tax rate as income rises.

Property rights   The rights of an owner to use and to exchange property.

Proportional taxation   A tax system in which, as the individual's income goes up, the tax bill goes up in exactly the same proportion. Also called a *flat rate tax*.

Public goods   Goods for which the principle of rival consumption does not apply; they can be jointly consumed by many individuals simultaneously at no additional cost and with no reduction in the quality or quantity of the public good.

Regressive taxation   A tax system in which, as more dollars are earned, the percentage of tax paid on them falls. The marginal tax rate is less than the average tax rate as income rises.

Retained earnings   Profits kept by corporations rather than distributed as dividends.

Spillover, or externality   A situation in which a benefit or a cost associated with an economic activity spills over to third parties.

Subsidy   Negative tax; payment to producers or consumers of a good or service. For example, farmers often get subsidies for producing wheat, corn, or peanuts.

Tax bracket   A specified interval of income to which a specific and unique marginal tax is applied.

Tax incidence   The distribution of tax burdens among various groups in society.

Third parties   Parties who are external to negotiations and activities between buyers and sellers. For example, if you agree to buy a car with no brakes and then run over me, I am a third party to the deal struck between you and the seller of the car, and my suffering is the negative externality.

Transfer payments   Money payments made by governments to individuals for which no services or goods are concurrently rendered. Examples are welfare, Social Security, and unemployment insurance benefits.

Transfers in kind   Payments for which no goods or services are rendered concurrently, which are in the form of actual goods and services, such as food stamps, low-cost public housing, and medical care.

User charge system   A system of distributing government, or political, goods and services whereby the consumer pays more or less directly for those goods and services by specific taxes according to use or specific fees according to use.

CHAPTER 6

ECONOMIES IN TRANSITION

PUTTING THIS CHAPTER INTO PERSPECTIVE

Our concern is with how the different economic systems answer the three fundamental questions facing all societies: *what* to produce, *how*, and *for whom*.

Under market capitalism private property rights to goods and services, including labor, are extended to individuals who make voluntary exchanges as buyers and sellers. Governments enforce such property rights.

Despite many years of central planning experience, communist, or socialist, economies did not live up to their economic promise; problems still abound in the few remaining such economies. One major problem is the enormous administrative task involved in planning a modern economy; even sophisticated computers haven't been able to make a dent in the problem. Planners haven't been able to get around the problem of issuing specific orders or rules for production plans; enterprise directors and workers often find it advantageous to follow the letter, rather than the spirit, of the rules. Finally, such economies have an enormous incentive problem; it is not easy to get people to be productive and innovative if they are not rewarded sufficiently. It is not surprising, therefore, that communist economies have collapsed in the Soviet Union and in Eastern Europe. While you are reading this chapter note how important property rights are; a successful economic system requires well-defined property rights.

In Chapter 6 we describe the economic systems of Russia and the People's Republic of China, as well as how economic power may shift in the world.

LEARNING OBJECTIVES

After you have studied this chapter you should be able to

1. define economic system resource allocation, communism, market capitalism, laissez-faire, property rights, least-cost combination, mixed economy, privatization, and incentive structure.

2. describe the four faces of capitalism.

3. recognize the characteristics of the four stages of frontier capitalism.

4. describe how market capitalism answers the three fundamental economic questions.

5. recognize the least-cost combination of inputs.

6. recognize the main elements of recent economic reforms in the Russian and Chinese economic systems.

CHAPTER OUTLINE

1. In its theoretical form market capitalism has the following attributes:
    a. Private property rights are enforced by a judicial system.
    b. Prices are set by the forces of supply and demand.
    c. Resources flow to their most profitable use.
    d. Risk-taking in the business sphere, and the costs and benefits to doing so, are undertaken by individuals and not by the state.
    e. "What", "how", and "for whom" are determined by market forces.

2. Under capitalistic nations the price, or market, system answers the three economic questions.
    a. The forces of supply and demand determine "What, and how much to produce"; market price must be sufficiently high to make a good profitable for producers to produce.
    b. Profit maximization via the price system assures that the "How" question is answered so that the least-cost combination of resources will be used to produce outputs.
    c. Under such a system "For Whom" is answered by the distribution of money income; those with high money incomes get more goods than those with low money incomes.
        i.   The quantity, quality, and type of the various human and nonhuman resources that a person owns determines his or her money income.
        ii. A specific good or service is allocated to the highest bidders; hence the market rations each output to specific individuals.
    d. Under capitalism voluntary exchanges in markets take place; as such, resources (inputs) are allocated to businesses, and goods and services (outputs) are allocated to households.

3. An alternative form of economic system is communism; in its purest form it had the following attributes:
    a. Restricted private property rights existed, with respect to the major factors of production.
    b. Prices were (mostly) set by the state, not by the forces of supply and demand.
    c. The mobility of labor and other resources was severely restricted; a centralized planning authority allocates resources.
    d. "What", "how", and "for whom" were determined by the government.
    e. Economic risk-taking was done by the state, not by individuals.
    f. Taxation was used to redistribute income.

4. Real-world economies are comprised of elements from both pure market capitalism and pure command socialism; they are mixed economies. In the past many predicted that the two economic systems would converge, becoming more like the command socialist economy; the collapse of the Soviet Union and Eastern-bloc economic systems changed this notion. Today it appears that convergence will be toward the mixed economy model that exists in the United States.

5. Because people respond to economic incentives, a successful economic system requires well-defined property rights that are enforced by the state; such a system encourages wealth creation.

6. These are four types of capitalism in existence: consumer, producer, family, and frontier.

7. When a centralized economy collapses, black markets arise, then small businesses emerge, followed by the development of financial markets; in the final stages of frontier capitalism foreign investments are attracted and privatization occurs.

8. Russia, the most important part of the former Soviet Union, evolved into a system in which only a small elitist group lived well.
    a. In its transition phase, it is privatizing rapidly.
    b. The lack of a strong legal system has led to business wars.

9. China has also been in transition, since 1979.
    a. Privatization is proceeding more slowly than in Russia.
    b. In special economic zones capitalism is flourishing.
    c. The rule of law is still precarious in China.

KEY TERMS

Socialism   Command socialism   Mixed economy
Communism   Property rights

KEY CONCEPTS

Incentive structure   Resource allocation   Laissez faire
Least-cost combination   Privatization   Economic system

COMPLETION QUESTIONS
Fill in the blank or circle the correct term.

1. Under communism, economic decisions were made by (a central authority, many individuals); the closer we go to a pure capitalist system, the (less, more) political centralization there is.

2. One of the important features of a socialist economy is that the nonlabor means of production are owned by the _____.

3. The forces that determine relative rewards from production in a socialist state are set by the (market, government).

4. People respond to incentives, therefore property rights (are, are not) important.

5. In its purest form, market capitalism has the following attributes: _____, _____, _____, _____, and _____.

6. Resource allocation involves answering the three basic questions of _____, _____, and _____ goods and services will be produced.

7. Real world economies are _____ economies, because they have elements of both _____ and _____ economies.

8. Under _____ individuals have vast, government-protected private property rights.

9. Central planning is important under _____.

10. Under (planning, a price system) resources will be more likely allocated such that the least-cost combination will be chosen by producers.

11. Under capitalism specific goods and services are allocated to the (highest bidders, rich).

12. Markets (reduce, increase) transaction costs.

13. The four types of capitalism are _____, _____, _____, and _____.

14. In recent years China has become (less, more) decentralized; individuals have gained (less, more) control over economic decisions.

15. In 1989-90 command socialism (communism) was demonstrated to be an obvious economic (failure, success).

TRUE-FALSE QUESTIONS
Circle the **T** if the statement is true, the **F** if it is false. Explain to yourself why a statement is false.

T F 1. Under communism, producers followed the commands of many individuals, through the market.

T F 2. Under communism, all factors of production were owned by the state.

T F 3. In real world communist economies, no wage rate differentials existed.

T F 4. In communist economies, economic risk-taking was undertaken mostly by individual enterprises.

T F 5. In the real world, economies are a mixture of capitalistic and socialistic economies.

T F 6. In China, recent price reforms have not been successful in special enterprise zones.

T F 7. Privatization is relatively painless for formerly command economies.

MULTIPLE CHOICE QUESTIONS
Circle the letter that corresponds to the best answer.

1. In command socialist economies,
    a. all factors of production were owned by the state.
    b. no wage differentials existed.
    c. an economic plan was developed by government decision makers.
    d. households did not own durable goods.

2. In recent years the Russian economy is moving toward
    a. less income inequality.
    b. more privatization.
    c. more government control of industry.
    d. dramatic increases in private property rights.

3. Which of the following is **NOT** a key attribute of any actual socialist system?
   a. The government owns the major productive resources.
   b. No form of property rights exist.
   c. Relative rewards for production are set by the state.
   d. Wage differentials induce production.

4. In the Russian economy recently there has (have) been a(n)
   a. restructuring of the economy.
   b. reforming of the price system.
   c. increasing incentives by allowing more income inequality.
   d. All of the above.

5. Under market capitalism
   a. income inequality is too extreme.
   b. a price system allocates resources.
   c. central planning plays a huge role.
   d. what to produce is determined, in theory, by the government.

6. Since the early 1990s, Russian has engaged in
   a. almost nonexistent privatization.
   b. extremely rapid privatization.
   c. an increase in price controls.
   d. the nationalization of the housing market

7. For an economic system to be successful
   a. a legal system must be developed.
   b. property rights must be defined and enforced.
   c. incentives must be provided to people.
   d. All of the above

MATCHING
Choose the item in column (2) that best matches an item in column (1).

(1)	(2)
a. market capitalism	f. transfer property rights from government to private sector
b. communism	g. fundamental economic questions
c. privatization	h. governmental resource allocation
d. what, how, for whom	i. voluntary exchange
e. least-cost combination	j. efficient resource allocation

PROBLEMS

1. Under a pure capitalistic system, consumer sovereignty helps to answer *what, how* and *for whom*.
   a. Explain how *for whom* is affected if *what* changes, for example if tastes change in favor of tiddlywinks playoffs and away from professional football.
   b. Explain how *for whom* is affected if *how* changes because unions increase wage rates relative to other factors of production.
   c. Explain how a change in *for whom* (taxing some and giving to others) might change *what* to produce.

2. Assume that, given its resource base, an economy is able to produce output combinations A, B, C, and D. Society values combination A at $10,000, combination B at $20,000, combination C at $30,000, and combination D at $15,000.
    a. What is the opportunity cost of producing combination A?
    b. What is the opportunity cost of producing combination B?
    c. What is the opportunity cost of producing combination C?
    d. What is the opportunity cost of producing combination D.
    e. If the community wanted to maximize the value of its output, given its resource base, which combination should it produce?
    f. If the community wanted to minimize the opportunity cost of its output, which combination would it choose?

CASE STUDY

How should developed countries help the former communist bloc countries that have renounced the command economy system in favor of a more capitalistic, market-oriented, approach? Answers from different ends of the political spectrum will, of course, differ. Free market economists are in agreement that aid in the form of financial gifts and bailouts should be minimal and short-lived. Instead, they believe that those countries can achieve increased living standards in the long run only if they protect private property rights and permit foreign investments. Consumers in advanced nations can also receive benefits if they open their markets (i.e., reduce trade barriers) to the changing nations. "Trade, not aid" would seem to them to be a better permanent solution.

1. How can those newly emerging market economies produce goods and services that advanced countries will buy if their economies are devastated?

2. How will consumers in advanced economies benefit by opening their markets to ex-communist countries? Will everyone in advanced economies benefit?

ANSWERS TO CHAPTER 6

COMPLETION QUESTIONS

1. a central authority; less
2. state
3. government
4. are
5. private property rights, prices set by supply and demand, resources flow to most profitable use, risk-taking assumed by individuals, what, how, and for whom determined by market forces

6. what, how, for whom
7. mixed, market, planned
8. market capitalism
9. command socialism
10. a price system
11. highest bidders
12. reduce
13. consumer, producer, family, and frontier.
14. more, more
15. failure

TRUE-FALSE QUESTIONS

1. F Commands were set by a centralized government.
2. F Labor was not completely owned by the state.
3. F They existed, and in some cases were quite large.
4. F It was assumed by the state.
5. T
6. F Just the opposite is the case.
7. F Prices and unemployment typically rise in the short run.

MULTIPLE CHOICE QUESTIONS

1.c;   2.b;   3.b;   4.d;   5.b;   6.b;   7.d.

MATCHING

a and i;   b and h;   c and f;   d and g;   e and j

PROBLEMS

1. a. The incomes of football players will fall; incomes of those people who are dexterous and have the skills required of tiddlywinks competition will rise. Thus a change in tastes (*what*) redistributes income from one group to another, and so *for whom* changes.
   b. If wage rates rise relative to the price of capital and land, then producers will increase their demand for nonlabor resources; nonlabor resources will be substituted for labor. Income will be redistributed from some newly laid-off laborers to people who own property or are skillful at designing and producing capital. Thus a change in *how* leads to changes in *for whom*.
   c. To the extent that people with low incomes have tastes different than people with high incomes, then *what* is produced will be affected.

2. a. $30,000   c. $20,000   e. C
   b. $30,000   d. $30,000   f. C

CASE STUDY

1. All economies (and all individuals) have a comparative advantage in producing something; also, if they permit multi-national companies to invest in their countries they will be able to export salable goods.
2. Consumers will pay lower prices for imported goods and services; hence their living standards will rise. However, those businesses and laborers that are replaced by imported goods will be harmed—at least in the short run.

GLOSSARY TO CHAPTER 6

Command socialism   An economy in which there is virtually no private property, such that the state owns virtually all the factors of production. Decisions about what and how much, by whom, and for whom are decided by command from a central authority.

Communism   A theoretical economic political system as outlined by Karl Marx in which the state withers away and we observe "from each according to his ability, to each according to his need."

Economic system   The institutional means through which resources are used to satisfy human wants.

Incentive structure   The motivational rewards and costs that individuals face in any given situation. Each economic system has its own incentive structure.

Laissez faire   An economic system in which the government minimizes its activity within the economy.

Least-cost combination   The combination of input use that produces a given level of output at minimum cost.

Mixed economy   An economic system in which the decision about how resources should be used is made partly by the private sector and partly by the government or public sector.

Privatization   The sale or transfer of state-owned property and businesses to the private sector, in part or in whole.

Property rights   The right of an owner to use and to exchange property.

Resource allocation   The assignment of resources to specific uses. More specifically, it means determining what will be produced, how it will be produced, and for whom it will be produced.

Socialism   An economic system in which the state owns the major share of productive resources except labor. Also, socialism usually involves the redistribution of income.

CHAPTER 7

THE MACROECONOMY: UNEMPLOYMENT AND INFLATION

PUTTING THIS CHAPTER INTO PERSPECTIVE

In your lifetime you will hear the words *recession, depression, inflation*, and *unemployment* thousands of times. Chapter 7 is important because it introduces and defines these terms which are crucial to macroeconomics. In fact, a proper understanding of these terms is important to anyone who wants to be sufficiently literate in economics and wants to be able to understand or influence economic policy.

First, let's place these terms in perspective. Over long periods, output in the U.S. economy has grown at an average annual rate of just over 3%. As annual output rises, so do employment and living standards. Unfortunately national output does not grow smoothly; although the long-run trend is approximately 3% per year, in any given period *actual* growth is likely to be above or below that rate. When actual economic growth is less than 3%—indeed it can even be a negative number when the level of national output is falling—a recession is sometimes said to exist. Unemployment usually accompanies recession and slow (or negative) growth rates. When the actual national output growth rate exceeds the 3% trend rate, then the economy is in an expansion (or boom) phase. Unfortunately, during expansion phases inflation often is a side effect. To complicate things even further, deviations from the trend line growth are irregular in timing, magnitude, and duration.

While you are studying this chapter (and after you finish your study of economics) keep in mind that in practice these oft-spoken words—recession, depression, unemployment, and inflation—are difficult to conceptualize, to define, and to measure. Because a certain amount of arbitrariness is involved in defining these terms, the interpretation of what changes in these variables mean with regard to the economic well-being of the community is a tricky business. Further, because interpretation of changes in the statistics that purport to represent these concepts is difficult, it is also difficult to conduct economic policy. Stated differently, if our economic data do not transmit reliable and accurate information, then we should exercise great prudence when we develop economic policy to stabilize the economy. We return to this last, exceedingly important point in later chapters. For now, as you study Chapter 7, just try to see how slight changes in definitions—changes which might be quite reasonable—can actually change the magnitude of such variables as unemployment and inflation.

LEARNING OBJECTIVES

After you have studied this chapter you should be able to

1. define the following terms: stock, flow, labor force, unemployment rate, discouraged worker, labor force participation rate, frictional unemployment, cyclical unemployment, seasonal unemployment, structural unemployment, job loser, reentrant, job leaver, new entrant, wait unemployment, full employment, purchasing power, inflation, underground economy, base year, price index, consumer price index, producer price index, GDP deflator, deflation, hyperinflation, unanticipated inflation, anticipated inflation, nominal or market rate of interest, real rate of interest, creditor, debtor, cost-of-living adjustments, repricing (menu) cost of inflation, business fluctuations, recession, expansion, and purchasing power.

2. calculate the unemployment rate, given specific information.

3. recognize the four categories under which an individual is officially counted as being among the unemployed.

4. list the major types of unemployment.

5. distinguish between the effects of anticipated and unanticipated inflation.

6. predict whether a specific group benefits or is economically injured by unanticipated inflation.

7. calculate a price index for a given market basket that includes a small quantity of goods.

8. distinguish between stocks and flows.

9. recognize the types of business fluctuations and list shocks that can cause such fluctuations.

CHAPTER OUTLINE

1. When unemployment exists, the economy is inefficient and households forego goods and services.
    a. The unemployment rate is the percentage of the measured labor force that is unemployed.
    b. The calculation of the official unemployment rate is complicated and somewhat arbitrary.
    c. Four official categories of reasons for unemployment are: job losers, job leavers, re-entrants, new entrants.
    d. The unemployment rate varies directly with the average duration of unemployment, other things being constant.
    e. Because of the *discouraged worker* phenomenon, the official unemployment rate understates true unemployment.

2. Unemployment has been categorized into four types: frictional, cyclical, seasonal, and structural.
    a. *Frictional unemployment* exists when people are between steady jobs.
    b. *Cyclical unemployment* is due to recessions and depressions.
    c. *Seasonal unemployment* results from differences in the demand for labor over the seasons of the year.
    d. *Structural unemployment* results when resources are reallocated so that individuals with specific skills cannot find jobs for long periods.

3. Full employment is impossible to attain because of frictional unemployment.
    a. "Full employment" is said to prevail when only frictional unemployment exists.
    b. Wait unemployment is caused by such wage rigidities as minimum wages set by governments and unions.

4. Inflation is a sustained rise in a weighted average of all prices.

5. Measures of inflation include the *consumer price index*, the *producer price index*, and the GDP deflator.
    a. The consumer price index measures the cost of an unchanging representative basket of consumer goods through time.
    b. The producer price index measures the cost of an unchanging basket of goods sold in primary markets by producers of commodities in all stages of processing.
    c. The GDP deflator measures the value of *all* goods and services produced by an economy; the "basket" changes over time.

6. The ill effects of inflation are accounted for mostly by unanticipated inflation; if inflation is fully anticipated, ill effects are slight.

7. The *nominal interest rate* is (approximately) equal to the sum of the *real interest rate* and the anticipated inflation rate.
    a. If inflation is unanticipated, *creditors* are worse off because the real value of their monetary assets falls.
    b. If inflation is unanticipated, *debtors* are better off because the real value of their monetary debts falls.

8. Besides the transfer of wealth from creditors to debtors during periods of unanticipated inflation, there are other effects.
    a. Inflation reduces the value of cash holdings.
    b. Resources must be allocated to predict inflation and to avoid its ill effects.

9. The ups and downs in economic activity are called business fluctuations.
    a. Inflation tends to be higher during an expansion phase, and unemployment rates are lower.
    b. During a contraction phase unemployment rates are higher and the inflation rate is lower.

10. Such external shocks as bad weather and rapid and unanticipated price rises in strategic resources such as oil also cause business fluctuations.

KEY TERMS

Labor force	New entrant	Producer price index
Contraction	Base year	GDP deflator
Job loser	Price index	Stock
Reentrant	Consumer price index	Flow
Job leaver	Recession	Expansion

KEY CONCEPTS

Frictional unemployment
Discouraged workers
Participation rate
Cyclical unemployment
Seasonal unemployment
Structural unemployment
Real rate of interest
    unemployment

Nominal, or market,
    rate of interest
Unanticipated inflation
Cost-of-living adjustments
Business fluctuations
Anticipated inflation
Repricing, or menu cost of
    inflation

Deflation
Creditor
Debtor
Purchasing power
Inflation
Hyperinflation
Wait unemployment

COMPLETION QUESTIONS
Fill in the blank or circle the correct term.

1.   This chapter deals with unemployment and _____.

2.   A _____ is measured per unit of time, while _____ is measured at a given moment in time.

3.   The unemployment rate is calculated by dividing the number of unemployed by the sum of the (a) employed plus the (b) _____.

4.   If a person is able to work and last looked for a job five weeks ago, she (is, is not) in the labor force.

5.   Homemakers are officially considered as (unemployed, employed, not in the labor force).

6.   Discouraged workers currently are not looking, but have looked, for a job, and they are counted officially as (employed, unemployed, not in the labor force); because of this official classification, some people believe that the measured unemployment rate (overstates, understates) true unemployment.

7.   The percentage of working-age individuals who are in the labor force is called the labor force _____.

8.   Unemployment has been categorized into four basic types: frictional, _____, _____, and _____.

9.   If imperfect information exists within job markets, then some frictional unemployment is (desirable, undesirable), both from the individual's and society's point of view.

10.   _____ unemployment varies with the business cycle.

11.   There is consensus among economists that the current "full" employment rate for the U.S. economy is consistent with about _____ percent actual unemployment.

12.   Many of the problems associated with inflation have occurred because the inflation rate was _____.

13.   The nominal interest rate equals the real interest rate (plus, minus) the anticipated inflation rate.

14.   When inflation is unexpected, (debtors, creditors) benefit at the expense of (debtors, creditors).

15.   In unanticipated deflation occurs, debtors are economically (worse, better) off.

16.   When the inflation rate is extremely high it is referred to as _____; when the price level falls this phenomenon is referred to as _____.

17.   The CPI and the PPI measure the cost of a(n) (unchanging, changing) basket of goods through time.

18.   To the extent that price indexes do not adjust for quality improvements, they (overstate, understate) the true rate of inflation.

19.   Wait unemployment is due to _____.

20.   Business fluctuations can be caused by _____ shocks such as poor weather or large, unanticipated price rises in key resources such as oil.

TRUE-FALSE QUESTIONS

Circle the **T** if the statement is true, the **F** if it is false. Explain to yourself why a statement is false.

T F   1.   Business fluctuations tend to be relatively constant in timing, magnitude, and duration, at least in the United States.

T F   2.   The dating of recession and expansion phases is somewhat arbitrary.

T F   3.   As inflation occurs, the purchasing power of a unit of money falls.

T F   4.   The opportunity costs due to unemployment, in terms of foregone national output, are usually trivial.

T F   5.   Homemakers and students are officially counted as part of the labor force.

T F   6.   People who are not working and who last looked for a job within the past four weeks are officially unemployed.

T F   7.   If the average duration of unemployment rises, other things being constant, the unemployment rate will fall.

T F   8.   People not working who have looked for a job six months ago but are not looking now are counted as discouraged workers, and therefore are officially unemployed.

T F   9.   Re-entrants are considered to be unemployed.

T F   10.   Because of imperfect information in the labor market, there will always be some frictional unemployment.

T F   11.   Anticipated inflation causes fewer economic problems than unanticipated inflation.

T F   12.   During periods of correctly anticipated inflation, debtors gain at the expense of creditors.

T F 13.   The unemployment rate is higher in the contraction phase of a business cycle.

T F 14.   Income is a flow, inflation is a flow, and the number unemployed is a stock.

T F 15.   The CPI measures the cost of an unchanging basket of goods and services.

MULTIPLE CHOICE QUESTIONS
Circle the letter that corresponds to the best answer.

1. Business fluctuations are
    a. nonperiodic recurrent fluctuations in overall economic activities.
    b. of similar duration.
    c. of similar magnitude.
    d. All of the above

2. The U.S. labor force includes
    a. the unemployed.
    b. people in mental institutions.
    c. children.
    d. None of the above

3. Which of the following statements is **NOT** a stock concept?
    a. The number of unemployed.
    b. National income.
    c. The number of job losers.
    d. The number of job finders.

4. Which of the following is a flow concept
    a. National income
    b. Inflation rate
    c. Consumption
    d. All of the above

5. Which of the following persons is **NOT** like the others?
    a. job finder
    b. job leaver
    c. new entrant
    d. re-entrant

6. Which of the following persons is officially unemployed?
    a. a housewife
    b. a student
    c. a resident in an institution
    d. a nonworking individual who has looked for a job within the past week

7. If the average duration of unemployment rises, other things being constant,
    a. the participation rate will rise.
    b. the unemployment rate will rise.
    c. total employment must fall.
    d. total unemployment must fall.

8. Which of the following statements is false?
   a. It is possible for the total number of employed and the total number of unemployed to rise in the same period.
   b. It is possible for the total number of employed to rise and the unemployment rate to rise in the same period.
   c. If the average duration of unemployment falls, other things being constant, the unemployment rate will fall.
   d. The definitions of employment, unemployment, and labor force are not subject to disagreement among economists.

9. Discouraged workers are officially
   a. unemployed.
   b. employed.
   c. not in the labor force.
   d. in the labor force.

10. If homemakers were counted in the labor force and considered employed, then
   a. the female participation rate would rise.
   b. the overall official unemployment rate would fall.
   c. overall official employment would rise.
   d. All of the above

11. If inflation is anticipated
   a. it is costless to society.
   b. debtors gain.
   c. it costs less to society than if unanticipated.
   d. creditors gain.

12. Which of the following is least like the others
   a. frictional unemployment
   b. seasonal unemployment
   c. discouraged worker unemployment
   d. cyclical unemployment

13. The teenage unemployment rate is usually high because
   a. many are new entrants in the labor force.
   b. teenagers have a shorter duration of unemployment than adults.
   c. teenagers stay on a given job longer than adults.
   d. All of the above

14. Because there is always frictional unemployment, "full" employment is considered to exist if
   a. every man, woman, and child is working.
   b. everyone age 16 and over is working.
   c. the unemployment rate is relatively small.
   d. the unemployment rate is 12%.

15. If the inflation rate is anticipated,
   a. net creditors will be hurt.
   b. inflation may not be a major problem.
   c. net debtors will be hurt.
   d. people will hold more cash than they want to hold.

16. Unanticipated deflation
    a.   hurts net debtors.
    b.   causes no economic problems.
    c.   hurts people who hold cash.
    d.   hurts fixed income groups.

17. Which of the following statements is true?
    a.   If there is zero anticipated inflation, the nominal interest rate equals the real interest rate.
    b.   The real interest rate equals the nominal interest rate plus the anticipated inflation rate.
    c.   The real interest rate equals the nominal interest rate divided by the anticipated inflation rate.
    d.   Borrowers will not permit lenders to raise the nominal interest rate if all expect that the inflation rate will rise.

18. Which of the following groups is *most* hurt by unanticipated inflation?
    a.   workers with cost of living adjustment clauses in their labor contracts
    b.   Social Security recipients
    c.   workers who sign new work agreements every day
    d.   wealthy people who hold much cash in their wall safes

19. The consumer price index
    a.   measures the cost of an unchanging basket of goods and services.
    b.   does not take into account relative price changes, and therefore is biased.
    c.   does not completely account for quality changes, and therefore is biased.
    d.   All of the above

MATCHING
Choose the item in Column (2) that best matches an item in Column (1).

(1)	(2)
a. labor force	i. re-entrant
b. wait unemployment	j. GDP deflator
c. unemployed	k. job gainer
d. price index	l. employed and unemployed
e. employed	m. minimum wage law
f. inflation	n. falling purchasing power of money
g. business fluctuation	o. cyclical unemployment
h. recession	p. expansion

PROBLEMS

1.   Assume that the employment data are (in millions)

Noninstitutional population (≥16)	193.190
Resident armed forces	1.568
Civilian labor force	129.600
Total labor force	131.168
Employed	119.754

    a.   Calculate the number of people (16 years old and over) not in the labor force.
    b.   Calculate the number of unemployed civilian workers.
    c.   What is the civilian unemployment rate?
    d.   What would be the unemployment rate if resident armed forces were counted in the labor force?

2. The CPI measures the cost of an unchanging representative basket of goods and services through time. Suppose the following occur: (a) inflation, (b) an increase in the relative price of energy, and (c) a decrease in the relative price of food. What does the law of demand predict concerning household purchases of food and energy? If households respond predictably, will the CPI overstate or understate the hardships associated with increases in the overall price level?

3. Suppose that an economic slump occurs and that (a) many minorities stop looking for jobs because they know that the probability of finding a job is low, and (b) many people who are laid off start doing such work at home as growing food, painting, repairing their houses and autos, and so on. Which of these events implies that the official unemployment rate overstates unemployment, and which implies the opposite?

4. Consider the following table for an economy that produces only four goods:

Goods & Services	1982 Price	1982 Quantity	2000 Price	2000 Quantity
Pizza	$ 4	10	$ 8	12
Cola	12	20	36	15
T-shirts	6	5	10	15
Business equipment	25	10	30	12

Assuming a 1982 base year:

a. What is nominal GDP for 1982 and for 2000?
b. What is real GDP for 1982? For 2000?
c. What is the implicit GDP price deflator for 1982? For 2000?
d. What is the CPI for 1982? For 2000?

5. From the list below, classify each of the unemployed individuals as represented either (F) frictional, (S) structural, or (C) cyclical unemployment.

_____ a) James Engine is an auto worker from Detroit who has been laid off because of the recent sharp decline in GDP, which has resulted in a severe decrease in auto sales.

_____ b) Digs McDuff, from western Kentucky, finds he can no longer get work in the coal mines because of new automated mining techniques.

_____ c) Priscilla Primm is unable to locate work after finishing her high school education and entering the labor force.

_____ d) Leroy Cosighn, an aerospace engineer, finds himself unemployed because of large cutbacks in defense spending. Since our space program is also on a tight budget, Leroy hasn't been able to locate alternative work for the past two months.

_____ e) Oscar Hammerhead, a skilled carpenter, has found himself out of work because of the housing slump brought on by high interest rates and the recession.

_____ f) Alice Weatherby quits her job as a salesperson out of frustration stemming from her lack of promotion. She begins to look for a management position in a similar work setting.

_____ g) Patricia Matren reenters the labor force after having a child and is unable to locate suitable work.

_____ h) Flaps Peterson, an airline pilot, suddenly finds himself laid off because of the dramatic decline in the demand for air transportation caused by the recent recession.

6. Suppose we define our relevant "market basket" of goods as containing the following:

   10 apples   4 pounds of bananas
    7 oranges   2 pineapples

   Suppose we also have the following price information for the years 1995 and 2000:

Fruit	1995	2000
Apples	$ .10 each	$ .18 each
Oranges	.15 each	.23 each
Bananas	.25 per pound	.20 per pound
Pineapples	.50 each	.65 each

   What is the 2000 FPI (fruit price index) using 1995 as the base year? What does this index tell us?

CASE STUDY

Suppose you went to your local grocery store and counted 200 cans of Campbell Soup on the shelves. Then you came back two weeks later and counted again, discovering that there were still 200 cans on the shelves.

1. Can you conclude that the grocery has not sold any of this soup during the two-week period?

2. Is this an optimal stock of soup for the store to hold on hand? What determines this number?

3. Draw an analogy and a lesson regarding the number of people who are unemployed every month?

ANSWERS TO CHAPTER 7

COMPLETION QUESTIONS

1. inflation
2. flow; stock
3. unemployed
4. is not
5. not in the labor force
6. not in the labor force; understates
7. participation rate
8. cyclical; seasonal; structural
9. desirable
10. Cyclical

11. 5.5%
12. unanticipated
13. plus
14. debtors; creditors
15. worse
16. hyperinflation; deflation
17. unchanging
18. overstate
19. wage rate rigidities
20. external

TRUE-FALSE QUESTIONS

1. F All are highly variable.
2. T
3. T
4. F Costs could be in the hundreds of billions of dollars.
5. F They are not in the offically measured labor force.
6. T
7. F The unemployment rate will rise.
8. F They are, officially, not in the labor force.
9. T
10. T
11. T
12. F Neither group gains or benefits at the expense of the other because the nominal interest rate will reflect the anticipated inflation rate.
13. T
14. T
15. T

MULTIPLE CHOICE QUESTIONS

1.a; 2.a; 3.b; 4.d; 5.a; 6.d; 7.b; 8.d; 9.c; 10.d;
11.c; 12.c; 13.a; 14.c; 15.b; 16.a; 17.a; 18.d; 19.d.

MATCHING

a and l; b and m; c and i; d and j; e and k; f and n; g and p; h and o

PROBLEMS

1. a. 62.022 million   b. 9.846 million   c. 0.076   d. 0.075

2. The law of demand predicts that households will purchase less energy and more food. Because the CPI measures the cost of purchasing an unchanging basket, it will overstate the hardships of inflation.

3. If minorities become discouraged from looking for jobs, they will not be counted as officially unemployed, and therefore the actual employment rate will understate "true" unemployment. If people perform do-it-yourself activities, they are "really" working, but they won't be counted in the labor force if they quit looking for a job; or they will be counted as unemployed if they continue their job search. Either way, such do-it-yourself activities cause the official unemployment rate to overstate the "true" unemployment rate.

4. a. Nominal GDP for 1982 = ($4) (10) + ($12) (20) + ($6) (5) + ($25) (10) = $560. Nominal GDP for 2000 = ($8) (12) + ($36) (15) + ($10) (15) + ($30) (12) = $1,146.
   b. Real GDP for 1982 = $560. Real GDP for 2000 = ($4) (12) + ($12) (15) + ($6) (15) + ($25) (12) = $618.
   c. Implicit GDP deflator for 1982 = (nominal GDP1982/real GDP1982) x 100 = ($560/$560) x 100 = 100.0. Implicit GDP deflator for 2000 = (nominal GDP2000/real GDP2000) x 100 = ($1146/$618) x 100 = 185.4.
   d. CPI for 1982 = 100, because it is the base year. CPI for 2000 = (P2000Q1982/P1982Q1982) x 100 = ($850/$310) x 100 = 2.74.
   P2000Q1982 = ($8) (10) + ($36) (20) + ($10) (5) = $850.
   P1982Q1982 = ($4) (10) + ($12) (20) + ($6) (5) = $310.

5. a. C; b. S; c. F; d. S; e. C; f. F; g. F; h. C

6.

Fruit	Q-00	P-00	Total	Q-00	P-95	Total
Apples	10	$.18	$1.80	10	$.10	$1.00
Oranges	7	.23	1.61	7	.15	1.05
Bananas	4	.20	.80	4	.25	1.00
Pineapples	2	.65	1.30	2	.50	1.00
			$5.51			$4.05

Therefore, the FPI = $5.51 / $4.05 = 1.36. This means that on average, fruit is 1.36 times more expensive in 2000 than in 1995. In other words, fruit prices (to the extent that they are measured by our market basket) have risen 36 percent from 1995 to 2000.

Notice that fruit prices have risen at a different rate across different types of fruit. Bananas have actually become cheaper in the above problem. Remember, a price index measures *average* overall tendencies by calculating the ratio of costs of the same "market basket" of goods at *two or more* points in time.

CASE STUDY

1. No, they may not be the *same cans* of soup.
2. Weekly sales, opportunity costs of shelf space.
3. If the number of unemployed remains at about the same number every month, this is not a severe problem if the people that are unemployed are different people each month.

GLOSSARY TO CHAPTER 7

Anticipated inflation The inflation rate that we believe will occur; when it does, we are in a situation of fully anticipated inflation.

Base year The year that is chosen as the point of reference for comparison of prices in other years.

Business fluctuations   The ups and downs in overall business activity, as evidenced by changes in national income, employment, and the price level.

Consumer Price Index (CPI)   A statistical measure of a weighted average of prices of a specified set of goods and services purchased by wage earners in urban areas.

Contraction   The phase of the business cycle in which there is a slowdown in the pace of national economic activity.

Cost-of-living adjustments (COLAs)   Clauses tacked onto contracts that allow for increases in specified nominal values in order to take account of changes in the cost of living or Consumer Price Index.

Creditor   Individuals or businesses that have more savings than debt. In other words, a net creditor receives interest on savings that exceed any interest payments made on what is owed.

Cyclical unemployment   Unemployment resulting from business recessions that occur when aggregate (total) demand is insufficient to create full employment.

Debtor   Individuals or businesses whose debt exceeds accumulated savings. In other words, a net debtor pays more in interest on debt than is received in the form of interest and dividends on savings.

Deflation   The situation in which the average of all prices of goods and services in an economy is falling.

Discouraged workers   Individuals who have stopped looking for a job because they are convinced that they will not find a suitable one. Typically, they became convinced after unsuccessfully searching for a job.

Expansion   A business fluctuation in which overall business is rising more rapidly than usual.

Flow   A quantity measured per unit of time, such as income or the number of people who are fired every month.

Frictional unemployment   Unemployment associated with frictions in the system that may occur because of costly job market information. Because workers do not know about all job vacancies that may be suitable, they must search for appropriate job offers. This takes time, so they remain frictionally unemployed.

GDP deflator   A price index measuring the changes in prices of all goods and services produced by the economy.

Hyperinflation   Extremely rapid rise of the average of all prices in an economy.

Inflation   The situation in which the average of all prices of goods and services in an economy is rising.

Job leaver   An individual in the labor force who voluntarily quits.

Job loser   An individual in the labor force who was employed and whose employment was involuntarily terminated or who was laid off.

Labor force   Individuals aged 16 years or older who either have jobs or are looking and available for jobs; the number of employed plus the number of unemployed.

New entrant   An individual who has never held a full-time job lasting two weeks or longer, but is now in the labor force.

Nominal, or market, rate of interest   That rate of interest expressed in contracts today, in terms of today's dollars; whatever rate of interest you have to pay for credit or obtain from your savings.

Participation rate   The ratio of the number in a group that is in the labor force to the total number in the group.

Producer Price Index (PPI)   A statistical measure of a weighted average of prices of those commodities that firms purchase from other firms.

Price index   The cost of today's market basket of goods expressed as a percentage of the cost of the same market basket during a base year.

Purchasing power   The value of your money income in buying goods and services. If your money income stays the same but the price of one good that you are buying goes up, your effective purchasing power falls.

Real rate of interest   The nominal rate of interest minus the anticipated rate of inflation.

Recession   A period of time during which the rate of growth of business activity is slower than usual.

Reentrant   An individual who used to work full time but left the labor force and has now reentered it looking for a job.

Repricing, or menu, cost of inflation   The cost associated with recalculating and printing new prices when there is inflation.

Seasonal unemployment   Unemployment resulting from the seasonal pattern of work in specific industries, usually due to seasonality in demand or to changing weather conditions, rendering certain work difficult, if not impossible; for example, agriculture, construction, and tourist industries generate seasonal unemployment.

Stock   The quantity of something, measured at a given point in time. Stocks are defined independently of time, although they are assessed at a point in time.

Structural unemployment   Unemployment resulting from fundamental changes in the structure of the economy. Structural unemployment occurs, for example, when the demand for a product falls drastically so that workers specializing in the production of that product find themselves out of work.

Unanticipated inflation   Inflation at a rate which comes as a surprise to an individual; unanticipated inflation can be either at a higher or lower rate than anticipated.

Wait Unemployment   Unemployment that is caused by wage rigidities that are a function of minimum wages, unions, and other factors.

CHAPTER 8

MEASURING THE ECONOMY'S PERFORMANCE

PUTTING THIS CHAPTER INTO PERSPECTIVE

Chapter 8 presents an introduction to national income accounting, the main procedure used to measure the economy's performance between two points in time. More specifically, this chapter shows exactly how gross domestic product, net national product, national income, personal income, and disposable personal income are calculated.

There are three main goals in Chapter 8. First, the chapter introduces you to the concepts and definitions of national income accounting. In order to understand the macroeconomic theories analyzed in the next four chapters, you must be familiar with the meaning of the key terms in this chapter. Furthermore, before policymakers can perform the governmental economic function of stabilizing the economy, they must be able to (a) understand how the macroeconomy works, and (b) measure the key economic variables with accuracy. After all, economic policy is not likely to be successful unless we know how the economy is actually performing and how to change it in desired directions. Such knowledge requires more than a nodding acquaintance with the material in this chapter.

The second objective of this chapter is to indicate that the value of national output is identical to the value of national income. It is important for you to understand that total expenditures for output determine the value of national output and, in turn, that total expenditures become income to those people who have produced national output.

Third, Chapter 8 stresses that national income accounting is a very imprecise measure of national output and that it is an even less precise measure of comparing economic welfare (well-being) for the residents of other nations. In later chapters we analyze the problems involved in conducting policy to affect variables that can be only crudely measured.

It may be necessary for you to memorize some of the material in this chapter—in particular, how each of those income/output measures mentioned in the first paragraph of this preview are defined. Perhaps the task can be made easier if you try to understand what each term actually tries to measure; each one really does attempt to measure something different.

LEARNING OBJECTIVES

After you have studied this chapter you should be able to

1. define total income, final goods and services, gross domestic product, intermediate goods, value added, expenditure approach, income approach, durable consumer goods, nondurable

consumer goods, gross private domestic investment, producer durables or capital goods, fixed investment, inventory investment, depreciation or capital consumption allowance, net domestic product, net investment, indirect business taxes, nonincome expense items, national income, personal income, disposable personal income, nominal values, real values, constant dollars, purchasing power parity, and foreign exchange rate.

2. distinguish between flows and stocks, intermediate and final goods, durable and nondurable goods, nominal and real values, goods and services, and gross and net private domestic investment.

3. recognize whether a transaction is or is not included in gross domestic product.

4. recognize whether the inability to include an activity in gross domestic product causes our measure to overstate or understate output and/or economic welfare.

5. list the three general categories of purely financial transactions.

6. distinguish between the expenditure approach and the income approach to deriving gross domestic product.

7. recognize the major components of GDP, using the expenditure approach and using the income approach.

8. derive GDP, NDP, NI, PI, and DPI when given sufficient information.

9. convert nominal GDP into real GDP, given the GDP price deflator.

10. point out problems with measuring GDP and with making international comparisons of GDP.

11. recognize some determinants of the size of a nation's underground economy.

CHAPTER OUTLINE

1. *National income* accounting is a measurement system used to estimate national income and its components.

2. In order to eliminate the effects of inflation and deflation, statisticians convert nominal GDP into real GDP by dividing the former by a price index.

3. Gross domestic product (GDP), is the market value of all the final goods and services produced by factors of production located within a nation's borders.
   a. In order to avoid double counting, only final goods and services are counted in GDP determination.
   b. Because nonproductive transactions do not contribute to output or to economic welfare, they are excluded from GDP determination.
      i. Such financial transactions as (a) purchases and sales of securities and (b) private and public transfers are non-productive activities; they are therefore excluded from GDP determination.
      ii. The transfer of used goods is considered a nonproductive activity because by definition used goods are produced (and counted) in a previous period.
      iii. Other transactions excluded from GDP determination are homemaker activities, underground activities, most illegal activities, and do-it-yourself activities; in principle most of these activities *should* be counted in GDP determination, but they are difficult to measure.

4.   There are two basic approaches to measuring GDP: the *expenditure approach* and the *income approach*.

5.   The expenditure approach measures GDP by summing the value of household consumption expenditures, government expenditures, *gross private domestic investment*, and *net exports*.
     a.   Household consumption expenditures fall into three categories: *durable, nondurable,* and services.
     b.   Government expenditures equal the cost of goods and services purchased by governments, because such goods are usually provided at a zero price to users.
     c.   Gross private domestic investment equals the sum of fixed investment, inventory investment, and consumer expenditures on new residential structures.
     d.   Net exports equal the value of exports minus the value of imports.
     e.   *Net domestic product* (NDP) equals gross domestic product minus *depreciation.*
     f.   Indirect business taxes include the value of excise, sales, and property taxes.
     g.   Depreciation is also referred to as capital consumption allowances; indirect business taxes plus depreciation equal nonincome expense items.

6.   Other components of national income accounting are *national income* (NI), *personal income* (PI), and *disposable personal income* (DPI).
     a.   National income equals NDP minus indirect business taxes; using the income approach, NI equals the sum of all factor payments to resource owners.
     b.   Personal income equals NI *minus* corporate taxes, Social Security contributions, and undistributed corporate profits, *plus* public transfer payments; using the income approach, PI equals the amount of income that households actually receive before they pay their personal income taxes.
     c.   Disposable personal income equals PI minus personal income taxes and nontax payments; DPI equals the income that households have to spend for consumption and saving.

7.   Because we are really interested in variations in the real output of the economy, nominal GDP is divided by a GDP price deflator in order to obtain real GDP.

8.   Real GDP divided by population yields per capita real GDP; this latter statistic provides a better measure of a nation's living standard.

9.   The official GDP measure *underestimates* national output and economic welfare because it does not take into account do-it-yourself activities, homemaker's services, some illegal activities, and underground economy activities. In general, an underground economy will be more important the higher are marginal tax rates on income and the higher are legally mandated benefits that employers must pay to workers.

10. Because GDP is difficult to measure, international GDP comparisons are very difficult; a recent improvement is the purchasing power parity concept, which takes into account the costs of goods and services that are not traded internationally—and therefore are not reflected in foreign exchange rates.

KEY TERMS

Total income
Durable consumer good
Nondurable consumer good
Net Investment
Gross domestic product

Gross private domestic
    investment
Fixed investment
Inventory investment

Indirect business taxes
Personal income
Disposable personal income
Net domestic product

KEY CONCEPTS

Intermediate goods

Expenditure approach

Income approach

Producer durables

Nominal values

Depreciation

Nonincome expense items

Constant dollars

Value added

Real values

Purchasing power parity

Foreign exchange rate

Capital consumption allowance

Final goods and services

COMPLETION QUESTIONS

Fill in the blank or circle the correct term.

1. Inflation causes us to (understate, overstate) the value of output and economic welfare, while deflation causes us to (understate, overstate) such values. For that reason, economists attempt to correct for price level changes; they attempt to convert the less accurate (nominal, real) values into the more accurate (nominal, real) values.

2. GDP represents the total market value of all (final, final and intermediate) goods and services produced during a year.

3. Values that are calculated at a moment in time are referred to as _____; values that are calculated over a time interval are _____ values. Examples of flows include income, consumption, and saving; examples of stocks include _____ and _____.

4. In order to avoid double counting, _____ goods are not counted; only final goods are included in national income accounting.

5. Nonproductive activities, such as financial transactions, (are, are not) counted in GDP determination; if you sell your 4-year-old car to your friend, this activity (is, is not) counted in GDP determination.

6. When a person receives a Social Security payment, the value (is, is not) counted as a productive activity; counting transfers as a productive activity would be an example of _____ counting.

7. Do-it-yourself activities, homemakers' activities, and (legal) underground economy activities (are, are not) productive activities; such activities (are, are not) counted in the official GDP figures; for that reason the GDP figures (overestimate, underestimate) national output and economic welfare.

8. The two basic methods of GDP determination are the _____ approach and the _____ approach. The expenditure approach to national income includes the sum of the values of _____, _____, _____, and _____. The income approach estimates national income by summing _____, _____, _____, and _____.

9. Because many government goods and services are provided to users free of charge, such items are valued at their _____ of production.

10. Consumer durable goods are arbitrarily defined as items that last more than _____ year(s).

11. Net investment equals gross private domestic investment minus _____.

12.   Net exports are identical to total exports (plus, minus) total imports.

13.   Gross domestic product minus depreciation equals _____;   nonincome expense items include indirect business taxes and _____; national income equals NDP minus _____; personal income minus personal income taxes and nontax payments equals _____.

14.   When nominal GDP is divided by the _____, real GDP is determined; when real GDP is divided by population, _____ is determined.

15.   GDP accounting has been criticized. GDP understates productive activities and economic welfare because it (includes, excludes) household production, do-it-yourself activities, and otherwise legal activities in the _____ economy. Because various things such as pollution (are, are not) subtracted from GDP, GDP overstates economic welfare.

16.   The purchasing power parity approach to making international comparisons of living standards (does, does not) consider relative costs of goods that are not traded internationally.

TRUE-FALSE QUESTIONS
Circle the **T** if the statement is true, the **F** if it is false. Explain to your self why a statement is false.

T   F   1.   Inflation causes us to overstate national income and output.

T   F   2.   Gross domestic product is a stock concept.

T   F   3.   Both final and intermediate goods are counted when measuring GDP.

T   F   4.   Homemakers' activities are nonproductive transactions.

T   F   5.   When Mr. Smith purchases a share of stock, investment rises; therefore GDP rises.

T   F   6.   Public transfers are counted in GDP, but private transfers are not.

T   F   7.   A nation's underground economy becomes larger as marginal tax rates rise on income.

T   F   8.   Whether or not a good is durable is an arbitrary decision.

T   F   9.   In the expenditure approach, the value G equals the sum of all the receipts governments realize from the sale of their services, plus taxes.

T   F   10.   When a person purchases a new pair of socks, consumption takes place in the official GDP accounts.

T   F   11.   If net exports rise, other things being constant, then GDP rises.

T   F   12.   Corporate income taxes are a form of indirect business tax.

T   F   13.   The sum of household consumption plus household saving equals disposable personal income.

T   F   14.   GDP minus depreciation equals net private domestic investment.

T   F   15.   The expenditure approach is identical to the income approach because of the way in which profit is defined.

MULTIPLE CHOICE QUESTIONS

Circle the letter that corresponds to the best answer.

1. Concerning real vs. nominal values,
   a. people respond to changes in real values.
   b. economists attempt to convert real into nominal values.
   c. current values are real values.
   d. nominal values have been adjusted for changes in the price level.

2. Gross domestic product includes
   a. only intermediate goods and services.
   b. only final goods and services.
   c. both intermediate and final goods.
   d. neither intermediate nor final goods.

3. In order to avoid overstating national output and income,
   a. intermediate goods are ignored.
   b. used good transactions between non-businesses are ignored.
   c. public and private transfers are ignored.
   d. All of the above

4. Which of the following is a nonproductive transaction?
   a. Mr. Gentile gives his niece $50 for her birthday.
   b. Mrs. Patullo cooks for her family.
   c. Mrs. Arianas is a waitress in the "underground" economy.
   d. All of the above

5. Which of the following activities is ignored in the official national income accounts?
   a. Mr. Pulsinelli gives his son $500 for Christmas.
   b. Mrs. Pulsinelli sells her used car to the Harrymans.
   c. Beth Pulsinelli paints her own house.
   d. All of the above

6. *Analogy*: Consumption is to stock as _____ is to flow.
   a. inventory value
   b. GDP
   c. NDP
   d. saving

7. When Capra purchases a bottle of French wine,
   a. consumption falls.
   b. investment rises by the purchase price.
   c. consumption rises by the purchase price.
   d. net exports fall.

8. Net investment equals
   a. GDP minus capital consumption allowances.
   b. gross private domestic investment plus depreciation.
   c. gross private domestic investment minus depreciation.
   d. planned saving minus net saving.

9. If total exports exceed total imports, other things being constant, then
    a. total expenditures fall.
    b. net exports are positive.
    c. GDP falls.
    d. investment rises.

10. GDP minus depreciation equals
    a. net investment.
    b. capital consumption allowances.
    c. NDP.
    d. NI.

11. Which is **NOT** a component of indirect business taxes?
    a. sales taxes
    b. excise taxes
    c. corporate income taxes
    d. property taxes incurred by business persons

12. Which of the following is a nonincome expense item?
    a. depreciation
    b. excise and sales taxes
    c. property taxes incurred by businesspersons
    d. All are nonincome expense items.

13. National income
    a. minus depreciation equals NDP.
    b. plus depreciation plus indirect business taxes equals GDP.
    c. minus inflation equals real GDP.
    d. plus transfer payments equals PI.

14. Which of the following is **NOT** included in national income?
    a. corporate taxes
    b. Social Security taxes
    c. transfer payments
    d. undistributed corporate profits

15. Which of the following is a transfer payment?
    a. Mr. Farano pays his son for painting the house.
    b. Mr. Scheifele gets paid for tending bar but does not declare his income.
    c. Mrs. Niemeck gets paid by a state government for teaching.
    d. Mrs. Carson receives Social Security benefits.

16. Which of the following best represents a nation's standard of living?
    a. nominal GDP
    b. real GDP
    c. per capita real GDP
    d. per capita nominal GDP

17. Which of the following activities is **NOT** considered in GDP determination and therefore causes economic welfare to be overestimated?
    a. do-it-yourself activities
    b. pollution damage
    c. homemaker activities
    d. private and public transfers

18. Forecasters have difficulty in predicting economic recessions because
    a. Data from government agencies are often revised
    b. Government price indices are unreliable
    c. It is difficult to measure recent technological improvements
    d. All of the above

MATCHING
Choose the item in Column (2) that best matches an item in Column (1).

(1)	(2)
a. expenditure approach	j. depreciation
b. income approach	k. NDP
c. intermediate good	l. C+I+G+net exports
d. capital consumption allowance	m. wages+rents+profits+interest payments
e. GDP minus depreciation	n. flour used by a baker
f. nonincome expense item	o. bread used by a family
g. final good	p. price-level adjusted GDP
h. constant dollars	q. capital good
i. producer durable	r. indirect business taxes

PROBLEMS

1. What happens to the official measure of GDP if
    a. a woman marries her butler?
    b. an addict marries his cocaine supplier?
    c. homemakers perform the same jobs but switch houses and charge each other for their services?

2. What happens to economic welfare in the three examples in problem 1 above?

3. Consider the following table and then
    a. Calculate real GDP for each of the years indicated.

Year	Nominal GDP	GDP Deflator	Real GDP (1972 dollars)
1980	2631.7	178.42	_____
1981	2957.8	195.60	_____
1982	3069.3	207.38	_____
1983	3304.8	215.34	_____
1984	3661.3	223.38	_____

    b. Interpret what a GDP deflator of 223.38 for the year 1984 means.
    c. Determine whether or not inflation occurred over the 1980-1984 period.

4. Suppose you are given the following information about some hypothetical economy and its national income accounts. Use this information to answer the questions that follow. (Amounts are in billions of dollars)

Indirect business taxes	$148
Corporate profits	101
Corporate income taxes	56
Retained earnings	24
Proprietors' income	73
Rents and interest earned (R + I)	98
Exports	18
Imports	10
Net domestic product	1436
Government expenditures on goods & services	323
Transfer payments	230
Social Security contributions	120
Consumption expenditures	1055
Gross investment	220
Disposable personal income	1123

a. Find GDP.
b. Find depreciation (capital consumption allowances).
c. Find domestic factor income receipts.
d. Find wages and salaries.
e. Find personal income.
f. Find personal income taxes.
g. Find net exports.

5. Suppose you own a small skateboard factory that has sales, expenses, and profits as shown below.

Total sales		$25,000
Expenses		
Wages and salaries	9,000	
Interest on loans	800	
Rent	3,200	
Raw materials	7,000	
Tools and equipment	1,000	
Profits		$ 4,000

What is the value added to GDP of the productive activities of your firm?

CASE STUDY

In this chapter you learned that homemaker activities are not counted in GDP calculations, and that therefore our nation's GDP is underestimated. Assume for the following questions that, other things constant, estimates are now made regarding the value of homemaker services.

1. What happens to measured national income, measured consumption, and measured saving?

2. What happens to the measured saving/national income ratio?

3. If larger percentages of women leave homemaker chores and find jobs in the labor force, will GDP be measured more, or less, accurately?

ANSWERS TO CHAPTER 8

COMPLETION QUESTIONS

1. overstate; understate; nominal; real
2. final
3. stocks; flow; inventory value, bank accounts
4. intermediate
5. are not; is not
6. is not; double
7. are; are not; underestimate
8. expenditure; income; consumption, government expenditures, investment, net exports; wages, interest, rents, profits

9. cost
10. three
11. depreciation; or capital consumption allowance
12. minus
13. NDP; depreciation; indirect business taxes; disposable personal income
14. GDP deflator; per capita real GDP
15. excludes; underground; are not
16. does

TRUE-FALSE QUESTIONS

1. T
2. F   GDP is measured per unit of time; hence it is a flow concept.
3. F   Only final goods are counted, to avoid double counting.
4. F   They are productive; if someone outside the family did them, you would probably have to pay for such services.
5. F   Common stock purchases are simply financial transactions.
6. F   Neither is counted, as should be the case.
7. T
8. T
9. F   G equals the value (at cost) of government purchases of goods and services.
10. T
11. T
12. F   They are direct taxes.
13. T
14. F   It equals NDP.
15. T

MULTIPLE CHOICE QUESTIONS

1.a; 2.b; 3.d; 4.a; 5.d; 6.a; 7.d; 8.c; 9.b; 10.c;
11.c; 12.d; 13.b; 14.c; 15.d; 16.c; 17.b; 18.d.

MATCHING

a and l; b and m; c and n; d and j; e and k; f and r; g and o; h and p; i and q

PROBLEMS

1. a. falls; b. unaffected, because illegal activities not counted anyway; c. rises

2. a. remains constant; b. difficult to tell; it depends on one's value judgment;
    c. remains constant

3. a.

Year	Real GDP (1972 dollars)
1980	1475.0
1981	1512.2
1982	1480.0
1983	1534.7
1984	1639.0

    b. The overall price level in 1984 was about 2.23 times higher than it was in 1972 (the base year).
    c. Inflation occurred in every year over that period because the GDP deflator went up every year.

4. a. To get GDP: $C + I + G + X = 1055 + 220 + 323 + 8 = 1606$
    b. To get depreciation: $GDP - NDP = 1606 - 1436 = 170$
    c. To get domestic factor income: $NDP - \text{sales taxes} = 1436 - 148 = 1288$
    d. To get wages and salaries: domestic factor income - corp. profits - prop. income - R & I $= 1288 - 101 - 73 - 98 = 1016$
    e. To get PI: domestic factor income - corp. tax - soc. sec. - ret. earn. + trans. pay. = $1288 - 56 - 120 - 24 + 230 = 1318$
    f. To get personal income taxes: $PI - DPI = 1318 - 1123 = 195$
    g. To get net exports: $X = \text{exports} - \text{imports} = 18 - 10 = 8$

5. Value added is measured by the difference in the cost of the raw materials used to produce a product and the final value of that product. Thus

    value added = total sales - cost of raw materials or
    value added = $25,000 - $7,000 = $18,000

CASE STUDY

1. Rises; rises; stays the same.
2. Falls.
3. More accurately.

GLOSSARY TO CHAPTER 8

Capital consumption allowance   Another name for depreciation; the amount that businesses would have to save in order to take care of the deterioration of machines and other equipment.

Constant dollars   Dollars expressed in terms of real purchasing power using a particular year as the base or standard of comparison.

Depreciation   Reduction in the value of capital goods over a one-year period due to physical wear and tear and also to obsolescence; also called capital consumption allowance.

Disposable personal income (DPI)   Personal income after personal income taxes have been paid.

Durable consumer goods   Goods used by consumers that have a life span of more than one year; that is, goods that endure and can give utility over a longer period of time.

Expenditure approach   A way of computing national income by adding up the dollar value of current market prices of all final goods and services.

Final goods and services   Those goods and services that are at their final stage of production and will not be transformed into yet another good or service. For example, wheat is not a final good or service because it is used to make bread. But bread is.

Fixed investment   Purchases by businesses of newly produced producer durables, or capital goods, such as production machinery and office equipment.

Foreign exchange rate   The price of one currency in terms of another.

Gross domestic product (GDP)   The total market value of all final goods and services produced by factors of production located within the borders of a nation in a one-year period.

Gross private domestic investment   The creation of capital goods, such as factories and machines, that can yield production and hence consumption in the future. Also included in this definition are changes in business inventories and repairs made to machines or buildings.

Income approach   A way of measuring national income by adding up all components of national income, including wages, interest, rent and profits.

Indirect business taxes   All business taxes except the tax on corporate profits. Indirect business taxes include sales and business property taxes.

Intermediate goods   Goods used up entirely in the production of final goods.

Inventory investment   Changes in the stocks of finished goods and goods in process, as well as changes in the raw materials that businesses keep on hand. Whenever inventories are decreasing, inventory investment is negative; whenever they are increasing, inventory investment is positive.

Net investment   Gross private domestic investment minus an estimate of the wear and tear on the existing capital stock. Net investment therefore measures the change in our capital stock over a one-year period.

Net domestic product (NDP)   GDP minus depreciation.

Nominal values   The values of variables such as GDP and investment expressed in current dollars, also called money values. Otherwise stated, measurement in terms of actual market prices at which goods are sold.

Nondurable consumer goods   Goods used by consumers that are used up within a year.

Nonincome expense items   The total of indirect business taxes and depreciation.

Personal income (PI)   The amount of income that households actually receive before they pay personal income taxes.

Producer durables, or capital goods   Durable goods having an expected service life of more than one year that are used by businesses to produce other goods and services.

Purchasing power parity   Adjustments in exchange rate conversions that take into account the differences in the true cost of living across countries.

Real values   Measurement of economic values after adjustments have been made for changes in prices between years.

Total income   The yearly amount earned by the nation's resources (factors of production). Total income therefore includes wages, rent, interest payments, and profits that are received, respectively, by workers, landowners, capital owners, and entrepreneurs.

Value added   The dollar value of an industry's sales minus the value of intermediate goods (for example, raw materials and parts) used in production.

CHAPTER 9

ECONOMIC GROWTH— TECHNOLOGY, RESEARCH & DEVELOPMENT, AND KNOWLEDGE

PUTTING THIS CHAPTER INTO PERSPECTIVE

This chapter is concerned with economic growth: its definition, impact on living standards, and its determinants. In order to have growth, saving must occur. New growth theorists emphasize other determinates of growth, such as technology. Here technology improvements are a function of the size of the reward. Having an open economy also appears to be important for growth, as is investment in human capital.

LEARNING OBJECTIVES

After you have studied this chapter you should be able to

1. define economic growth, labor productivity, new growth theory, patent and innovation.

2. identify the main determinants of economic growth.

3. indicate how economic growth affects production possibilities curves.

4. determine whether or not specific policies can contribute to economic growth.

CHAPTER OUTLINE

1. Economic growth is defined as the rate of increase in per-capita real GDP.
   a. Graphically, economic growth can be viewed as a rightward shift in a countries production possibilities curve.
   b. Numerically, economic growth is the sum of the rate of growth of capital, plus the rate of growth of labor, plus the rate of growth of the product of those growth rates.

2. Saving, or non-consumption of income, is an important determinant of economic growth.
   a. When people save they free up resources from the production of consumer goods.
   b. If such freed resources are then allocated to the production of capital or investment goods, economic growth will occur.
   c. Thus, if people consume less today, they can consume more in the future.

3. New growth theorists maintain that if technological advances are rewarded, they will be forthcoming.
   a. Patents provide property rights to intellectual achievements and inventions; thus patents encourage economic growth.
   b. As long as it is profitable for people to find new ideas, they will be forthcoming, and economic growth will continue.

    c.   If people have incentives to increase their human capital through education and training, economic growth will be enhanced.

4.   Although many people disagree, it can be shown empirically that population growth is associated with economic growth; hence immigration may be viewed as a contributing factor to economic growth.

5.   When property rights are well defined, capital accumulation will ensue, and economic growth will be enhanced.

KEY TERMS

Economic growth	New growth theory	Innovation
Labor productivity	Patent	

COMPLETION QUESTIONS
Fill in the blank or circle the correct term.

1.   Economic growth is the _____ in per-capita real GDP.

2.   Graphically, economic growth shows a _____ shift in a nation's production possibilities curve.

3.   Numerically, economic growth is equal to the _____ of the growth rate of capital and the growth rate of labor, plus _____.

4.   Other things constant, if people wish to consume more in the future they must _____ more now.

5.   New growth theorists predict that technology, research, and innovation (need not, must be) rewarded.

6.   Inventors usually require _____ to be useful.

7.   When people invest in education and training, economists refer to this as increases in human _____.

8.   Economic growth is enhanced by _____, _____, _____, _____, and _____.

TRUE-FALSE QUESTIONS
Circle the **T** if the statement is true, the **F** if it is false. Explain to yourself why a statement is false.

T F   1.   Economic growth benefits low-income people.

T F   2.   Large changes in a nation's growth rate are required before significant changes in living standards can occur.

T F   3.   If people save more a nation's growth rate probably will rise.

T F   4.   If an underdeveloped nation better protects property rights, its economic growth rate will rise, other things constant.

T F   5. Inventions, research, and technology occur automatically, according to the new growth theorists.

T F   6. Economic growth must eventually approach zero, because resources are finite.

T F   7. Inventions contribute to economic growth.

T F   8. When a nation invests in education, human capital increases and economic growth is enhanced.

T F   9. Underdeveloped countries can increase their economic growth by opening their economies to foreign investment.

T F   10. Empirically, immigration can be shown to reduce a nation's living standards.

MULTIPLE CHOICE QUESTIONS
Circle the letter that corresponds to the best answer.

1. Economic growth initially leads to
    a. higher living standards.
    b. increased leisure.
    c. increased pollution.
    d. All of the above.

2. When economic growth occurs, the production possibilities curve
    a. shifts leftward.
    b. shifts rightward.
    c. is unaffected.
    d. rotates about the vertical axis.

3. Economic growth
    a. shifts the production possibilities curve leftward.
    b. assures full employment.
    c. may be uneven over time.
    d. creates unemployment.

4. Which of the following contributes to economic growth?
    a. Technological progress.
    b. Well-defined property rights.
    c. Human capital investment.
    d. All of the above

5. Before capital accumulation can take place,
    a. saving must decline.
    b. household saving must be converted into business investments.
    c. a large resource base is necessary.
    d. households must forego future consumption for more present consumption.

6. Which of the following does **NOT** contribute to economic growth?
    a. Protected property rights
    b. Investments in education
    c. Nationalization of foreign investments
    d. Increasing the ratio of investment to real GDP

7. Which of the following is **NOT** true?
   a. Saving, if converted into investment, will contribute to economic growth.
   b. Economic growth can help people of all income levels.
   c. Economic growth assures full employment.
   d. Immigration increases a nation's growth rate, other things constant.

8. Which of the following is most **UNLIKE** the others?
   a. Patents
   b. Nationalization of businesses
   c. Capital accumulation
   d. Well-defined property rights

9. Which of the following will likely increase productivity?
   a. Increase in population.
   b. Investment in research and development.
   c. Higher corporate taxes.
   d. Elimination of patent protection.

MATCHING
Choose the item in Column (2) that best matches an item in Column (1).

(1)	(2)
a. contracts enforced by government	f. innovations
b. economic growth	g. rate of change of per-capita real GDP
c. inventions	h. education
d. human capital	i. non-consumption of income
e. saving	j. well-defined property rights

PROBLEMS

1. Consider the hypothetical economy depicted in the following table, then answer the following questions. (Hint: each of the following questions is based on a change from one year to the next. For example, the situation in question "a" exists when going from year 1 to year 2.) Note that quantity of labor represents number of workers per year, and productivity of labor represents the real value of the output of each worker over the year.

Year	Quantity of Labor (millions)	Productivity of Labor (thousands of $)	Real GDP (billions of $)	Population (millions)	Per Capita Real GDP (thousands of $)
1	1	$10.0	$10.0	2	$ 5.0
2	1	10.3	10.3	2	5.15
3	2	10.3	20.6	4	5.15
4	2.5	12.875	32.1875	4	8.046875
5	3.125	16.09375	50.292969	4	10.058594

   a. If the quantity of labor remains constant and the productivity of labor rises by 3 percent, what happens to real GDP? Given those changes and a constant population, what happens to per capita real GDP?

b. If the quantity of labor doubles and the productivity of labor remains constant, what happens to real GDP? Given those changes and a doubling of population, what happens to per capita real GDP?

c. If the quantity of labor rises by 25 percent and labor productivity rises by 25 percent, what happens to real GDP? Given those changes and a constant population, what happens to per capita real GDP?

d. If the quantity of labor rises by 25 percent and labor productivity rises by 25 percent and population rises by 25 percent, what happens to per capita real GDP?

CASE STUDY

The years since 1989 have been remarkable years for economists who are interested in the determinants of economic growth—and remarkable years for people who follow the news. In one country after another, the people, and even the leaders, admitted that their economic systems were a failure. Central planning proved unable to compete with capitalism as an economic system.

Many economists are now concerned with how to generate economic growth in those countries. Should the economies combine planning with increasingly larger private sectors? Should they adopt capitalism and forget about planning altogether? Or should they attempt to develop a new, untried, path to economic growth?

1. Many people in those countries still believe that foreigners should not be allowed to "dominate" their economies. In essence, then, they want to restrict the amount of foreign investment and immigration into their countries. What advice would you give the leaders in those countries with respect to these issues?

2. How can economically advanced nations help those countries?

ANSWERS TO CHAPTER 9

COMPLETION QUESTIONS

1. rate of increase
2. rightward
3. sum; their productivity rate of growth
4. save
5. must be
6. innovations
7. capital
8. well defined property rights, saving, investments in human capital, open economies, population growth

TRUE-FALSE QUESTIONS

1. T
2. F   A small change in the growth rate leads to enormous changes in living standards over time.
3. T
4. T
5. F   New growth theorists maintain that incentives are required to bring forth such things.
6. F   As long as incentives to develop new ideas exist, economic growth will occur.
7. T
8. T
9. T
10. F   Immigration and growth rates are positively correlated.

MULTIPLE CHOICE QUESTIONS

1.d;   2.b;   3.c;   4.d;   5.b;   6.c;   7.c;   8.b;   9.b.

MATCHING

a and j;   b and g;   c and f;   d and h;   e and i.

PROBLEMS

1. a. rises by 3 percent; rises by 3 percent
   b. doubles; remains constant
   c. rises by 56.25 percent (note: this equals the sum of their changes plus their product); rises by 56.25 percent
   d. rises by 25 percent

CASE STUDY

1. Evidence shows that the more open an economy, the faster its rate of growth. Moreover, immigration seems to help growth.

2. They might be able to help them with short-term loans, but sustained help would require opening domestic markets to exports from those countries and encouraging multinationals to invest there.

GLOSSARY TO CHAPTER 9

Economic growth   Increases in per capita real GDP measured by its rate of change per year.

Innovation   Transforming an invention into something that is useful to humans.

Labor productivity   Total domestic output (GDP) divided by the number of workers (output per worker).

New growth theory   A relatively modern theory of economic growth that examines the factors that determine why technology, research, innovation, and the like are undertaken, and how they interact.

Patent   A government grant that gives an inventor the exclusive right or privilege to make, use, or sell his or her invention for a limited time.

CHAPTER 10

MICRO FOUNDATIONS: AGGREGATE DEMAND AND AGGREGATE SUPPLY

PUTTING THIS CHAPTER INTO PERSPECTIVE

In Chapter 10 the aggregate demand curve and the short-run and long-run aggregate supply curves are derived. You must master these curves if you are to understand the modern theory of the price level and modern theories of inflation (the rate at which the price level is rising). Such curves also play a prominent role in the explanation of stagflation—the simultaneous existence of high unemployment rates and high inflation rates. Stagflation erupted several times in the 1970s and that phenomenon led economists to rethink old macroeconomic models and to develop new models. The aggregate demand/aggregate supply model can also be used to explain the Great Depression.

Modern theories of how to combat inflation or unemployment also depend on a thorough understanding of the aggregate demand curve and the aggregate supply curve. This is an important chapter—one that will reward your efforts handsomely. You should read your text carefully and master this chapter in your student learning guide. Much of what is in this chapter appears in today's headlines; Chapter 10 will help you to make sense of these headlines and to analyze the story behind them.

LEARNING OBJECTIVES

After you have studied this chapter you should be able to

1. define aggregate demand, aggregate supply, aggregate demand curve, short-run aggregate supply curve, interest rate effect, open economy effect, real-balance effect, aggregate demand shock, long-run aggregate supply curve, endowments, contractionary gap, expansionary gap, demand-pull inflation, and cost-push inflation.

2. distinguish between aggregate demand and an aggregate demand curve and between short-run aggregate supply and short-run aggregate supply curve.

3. predict whether an aggregate demand curve (or short-run aggregate supply curve) will shift to the right or to the left when specific changes in nonprice-level determinants occur.

4. determine the price level and the equilibrium real national income level when given an aggregate demand curve and a short-run aggregate supply curve.

5. list three reasons why the aggregate demand curve is negatively sloped.

6. recognize changes that will shift the aggregate demand curve.

7. recognize reasons why the short-run aggregate supply curve is positively sloped.

8. distinguish between the short-run and the long-run aggregate supply curve.

9. distinguish between a contractionary gap and an expansionary gap.

10. distinguish between cost-push and demand-pull inflation.

CHAPTER OUTLINE

1. The *aggregate demand* curve indicates the various quantities of all goods and services demanded at various price levels.
   a. The aggregate demand curve is downward sloping for at least three reasons.
      i. When the price level rises (falls), those people who own cash balances will experience a reduction (increase) in the purchasing power of their wealth; they consequently will plan to spend less (more) on goods and services.
      ii. When the price level rises (falls), people want to hold more (less) money in order to make the same transactions; given the supply of money, this increase (decrease) in the relative demand for money will cause interest rates to rise (fall); planned purchases on consumer durables and capital goods will therefore fall (rise).
      iii. When the price level rises (falls), domestic residents will export less (more) and import more (less); these two effects (which result from international relative price changes) cause a decrease (increase) in planned purchases of domestically produced goods and services.
   b. When the nonprice-level determinants of *aggregate demand* change, the aggregate demand curve shifts.
      i. If the money supply rises (falls), then the AD curve will shift to the right (left); if taxes rise (fall), the AD curve will shift to the left (right).
      ii. If expectations about the future economic outlook become more (less) favorable, the AD curve will shift to the right (left).
      iii. If a nation's exchange rate decreases (increases), the AD curve will shift to the right (left).

2. The *aggregate supply* curve shows the relationship between planned rates of total production for the entire economy and various price levels.
   a. The long-run aggregate supply (LRAS) curve relates the nation's level of real national output of goods and services to the price level, when full information and full adjustments have occurred.
      i. The LRAS curve is vertical at that level of real national output determined by tastes, technology, and the endowments of resources that exist in the nation.
      ii. The LRAS curve is vertical in the long run because a higher price level for output will be accompanied by higher costs for producers; hence after all these adjustments are made producers have no incentive to increase output merely because the price level is higher.
      iii. The LRAS curve shifts rightward over time, as technological improvements occur and as the nation's endowments increase.
   b. The short-run aggregate supply (SRAS) curve shows how real national output changes with the price level in the short run, before full adjustment is made and before full information is available.
      i. If the price level rises, while input costs remain the same, producers have an incentive to increase output; if prices rise and some costs remain constant, it is profitable to increase output.
      ii. Producers are able to expand output in the short run in response to price level increases because
         1. firms can use existing workers more intensively.
         2. existing capital equipment can be used more intensively.

          3.   if wage rates don't rise, it is profitable for firms to hire the unemployed or new entrants to the labor force.

        iii. At some point the SRAS curve becomes very steep; it becomes harder and harder to find more workers at existing wage rates.

        iv. The SRAS curve, therefore, is positively sloped and becomes steeper and steeper as the price level gets higher.

    c. Changes in the nonprice-level determinants of *short-run aggregate supply* lead to shifts in the short-run aggregate supply curve.

        i.   If input costs rise (fall), the SRAS curve shifts to the left (right).

        ii. An increase (decrease) in labor or in its productivity will shift the SRAS curve to the right (left).

        iii. Temporary changes in the above shift SRAS, but not LRAS.

3.   The price level and the equilibrium output (real national income) level are determined at the intersection of the AD curve with SRAS and LRAS.

4.   Unanticipated shifts in the AD and the AS curves are called aggregate demand shocks and aggregate supply shocks, respectively.

    a. A short war, such as the Persian Gulf War, shifts the AD curve rightward; the equilibrium price level rises and the equilibrium output level rises.

    b. If the war is prolonged, the SRAS curve shifts upward, and the new equilibrium position is at a higher price level, but at the old, initial, national output level.

5.   Changes in a nation's endowments of land, labor, and capital, or changes in technology, shift the LRAS curve.

6.   If full-employment equilibrium does not exist, then either an expansionary gap or a contractionary gap exists.

    a. An expansionary gap exists when the equilibrium level of real national income is greater than the full-employment level.

    b. A contractionary gap exists when the equilibrium level of real national income is less than the full-employment level.

7.   There are two types of inflation—demand pull and cost-push.

    a. Demand-pull inflation is caused by increases in aggregate demand that are not matched by increases in aggregate supply.

    b. Cost-push inflation is caused by continual left-ward shifts in the short-run aggregate-supply curve.

KEY TERMS

Aggregate demand	Expansionary gap	Aggregate supply
Endowments	Cost-push inflation	Contractionary gap
Demand-pull inflation		

KEY CONCEPTS

Aggregate demand curve	Aggregate supply shock
Short-run aggregate supply curve	Interest rate effect
Real balance effect	Open economy effect
Aggregate demand shock	Long-run aggregate supply curve

COMPLETION QUESTIONS
Fill in the blank or circle the correct term.

1. The sum of all planned expenditures in an economy is called (aggregate demand, aggregate demand curve); the sum of planned production in the economy is called (aggregate supply, aggregate supply curve).

2. The aggregate demand curve relates planned purchase rates of all goods and services to various _____; the aggregate supply curve relates planned rates of total production for the entire economy to various _____.

3. The aggregate demand curve is _____ sloped due to three effects: _____, _____, and _____.

4. When the price level rises (other things being constant), the real wealth of people who hold cash balances (falls, rises); therefore planned purchases of goods and services will (fall, rise).

5. When a nation's price level falls (other things being constant) its exports (rise, fall) and its imports (rise, fall); therefore the planned purchases of its output will (rise, fall).

6. When the price level rises, people will want to hold (more, less) money; this increase in the demand for money causes interest rates to (rise, fall); such a change in the interest rate causes households to plan to purchase (more, fewer) consumer durables, and businesses to plan to purchase (more, fewer) capital goods.

7. Nonprice determinants of aggregate demand include _____, _____, _____, and _____.

8. If government spending rises and taxes fall, the AD curve will shift to the (left, right); if the economic forecast is rosy, the AD curve will shift to the (left, right); if the money supply falls, the AD curve shifts to the _____.

9. The short-run aggregate supply curve is _____ sloped; as the price level rises in the short run, planned production by businesses (rises, falls).

10. If changes in production costs lag behind changes in the price level, producers will have an incentive to produce (more, less) as the price level rises.

11. The short-run AS curve will shift if there is a change in any of the following non-price-level determinants of aggregate supply: _____, _____, and _____.

12. If wage rates fall, the short-run AS curve will shift to the _____; if technological improvements occur and if the prices of raw materials fall permanently, the long-run AS curve will shift to the _____.

13. The price level and the equilibrium national output level are determined where the SRAS curve and the AD curve _____.

14. At very high price levels, the SRAS curve becomes very (flat, steep) because it becomes (more difficult, easier) to get more labor at relatively fixed wage rates.

15. A temporary increase in an input price shifts only the (LRAS, SRAS).

16. An unanticipated shift in the AD curve is called a _____.

17. If equilibrium does not exist, then either a _____ or a _____ exists.

18. Continual leftward shifts in the SRAS cause _____.

TRUE-FALSE QUESTIONS
Circle the **T** if the statement is true, the **F** if it is false. Explain to yourself why a statement is false.

T F 1. Aggregate demand relates planned purchases to price levels.

T F 2. The aggregate supply curve relates planned rates of total production to various price levels.

T F 3. As the price level falls, other things being constant, the purchasing power of cash balances rises.

T F 4. As the price level of a nation rises, other things being constant, the value of its imports and exports falls.

T F 5. As the price level falls, other things being constant, the demand for money falls and the interest rate rises.

T F 6. If the price level falls, the AD curve shifts to the right.

T F 7. If the price level rises and the costs of inputs don't rise immediately, producers have an incentive to increase output.

T F 8. The short-run aggregate supply curve is positively sloped.

T F 9. If productivity rises and raw material prices fall, then the SRAS curve will shift to the right.

T F 10. If the price level falls and wage rates don't, producers have an incentive to produce less.

T F 11. Producers can expand output in the short run by adding to their capital stock.

T F 12. The SRAS curve becomes very flat at higher and higher price levels.

T F 13. The LRAS curve is vertical because firms can make adjustments and information is complete.

T F 14. A demand shock that shifts the AD curve rightward will probably cause national output to rise and the price level to fall.

T F 15. The LRAS curve is vertical and doesn't shift in a growing economy.

T F 16. If neither a contractionary nor an expansionary gap exists, then full employment equilibrium exists.

T F 17. Cost-push inflation involves continual shifts inward in the short-run aggregate supply curve.

MULTIPLE CHOICE QUESTIONS
Circle the letter that corresponds to the best answer.

1. *Analogy*: price is to demand as the price level is to
   a. aggregate demand.
   b. aggregate supply.
   c. aggregate demand curve.
   d. aggregate supply curve.

2. Aggregate demand includes
   a. planned production rates by businesses.
   b. planned saving.
   c. planned purchases by households and businesses.
   d. various price levels.

3. The aggregate demand curve
   a. relates planned purchases to various price levels.
   b. is negatively sloped.
   c. includes planned expenditures on consumption, investment, and governmentally provided goods.
   d. All of the above

4. The aggregate demand curve is negatively sloped because, other things being constant,
   a. as the price level rises, the demand for money falls.
   b. as the price level falls, the purchasing power of cash balances rises.
   c. as the price level falls, the AD curve shifts to the right.
   d. as the price level rises, exports rise.

5. When the price level falls, other things being constant,
   a. the demand for money falls.
   b. the interest rate falls.
   c. household and business planned expenditures rise.
   d. All of the above

6. Which of the following does **NOT** occur when the price level rises, other things being constant?
   a. Exports rise, imports fall.
   b. The demand for money rises.
   c. The purchasing power of cash balances falls.
   d. Aggregate demand falls.

7. Which of the following does **NOT** cause the AD curve to shift?
   a. an increase in taxes
   b. a decrease in the real interest rate
   c. a decrease in the price level
   d. a change in the money supply

8. Concerning the SRAS curve, an increase in the price level
   a. has no effect on planned production.
   b. leads to an increase in output if input prices rise proportionally.
   c. causes a decrease in planned production in the long run.
   d. causes an increase in planned production.

9. If the price level rises faster than costs of production rise, then
    a.   profits per unit fall.
    b.   producer have an incentive to increase output.
    c.   the aggregate supply curve shifts to the right.
    d.   the aggregate supply curve shifts to the left.

10. Which of the following causes the SRAS curve to shift to the left?
    a.   a fall in wage rates
    b.   rises in productivity
    c.   technological improvements
    d.   increase in raw material costs

11. Which of the following will **NOT** shift the LRAS curve?
    a.   a change in the price level
    b.   a new oil discovery
    c.   freer trade among nations
    d.   economic growth

12. The LRAS curve
    a.   is a short-run phenomenon.
    b.   shows national output rising with the price level.
    c.   does not shift over time, due to economic growth.
    d.   reflects the price level/national output situation when costs freely adjust to price-level changes.

13. If unused capacity and significant unemployment exist, then the SRAS curve is
    a.   vertical over a broad range.
    b.   downward sloping.
    c.   horizontal or slightly upward sloping.
    d.   the same as the LRAS curve.

14. At the intersection of the SRAS curve, LRAS curve, and the AD curve,
    a.   the equilibrium price level is determined.
    b.   the equilibrium national output level is determined.
    c.   economy wide equilibrium exists.
    d.   All of the above

15. An unanticipated rightward shift in the AD curve
    a.   is a supply shock.
    b.   is a demand shock.
    c.   will cause the output level to fall.
    d.   will cause the price level to fall.

16. Massive technological changes in the computer industry probably will cause the
    a.   SRAS curve to shift upward.
    b.   LRAS curve to shift rightward.
    c.   AD curve to shift leftward.
    d.   AD curve to shift rightward because the price level will rise.

17. Both unemployment and the price level rise if the
    a.   AD curve shifts to the right.
    b.   AD curve shifts to the left.
    c.   SRAS curve shifts to the left.
    d.   SRAS curve shifts to the right.

18. A temporary rise in production costs
   a.   shifts the LRAS curve rightward.
   b.   shifts the SRAS curve upward.
   c.   shifts the AD curve leftward.
   d.   shifts the AD curve rightward.

19. Which of the following is most **UNLIKE** the others?
   a.   Rosy economic outlook.
   b.   Rise in a nation's exchange rate.
   c.   Tax decreases.
   d.   Increase in money supply.

MATCHING
Choose the item in Column (2) that best matches an item in Column (1).

(1)	(2)
a. aggregate demand	h. change in government spending or taxing
b. aggregate supply	i. changes in imports and exports due to price changes
c. aggregate demand shift	j. planned production
d. aggregate demand shock	k. changes in the demand for money due to changes in the price level
e. real balances effect	l. planned expenditures
f. open economy effects	m. unanticipated change in investment expenditures
g. interest rate effects	n. change in the value of cash balances

WORKING WITH GRAPHS

1. Consider the short-run graphs below, then answer the questions that follow.

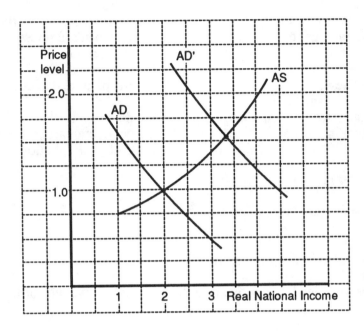

a. What is the equilibrium price level, given the AS and AD curves? What is the equilibrium level of real national income?
b. What could cause the AD curve to shift to AD'? Answer the remaining questions assuming that AD has shifted to AD'.
c. Given AS and the previous AD curve, what now happens to the price level? Why?
d. Given AS and the previous AD curve, what now happens to the equilibrium level of real national income? Why?
e. If full employment exists at real national income level $2, what exists at the new equilibrium level?

PROBLEMS

1.   Assuming the economy is operating at equilibrium, predict what happens to the equilibrium price level and the equilibrium real national income level as a result of
a.   productivity increases.
b.   an increase in the labor participation rates.
c.   a significantly lower marginal tax rate.
d.   economic growth.
e.   a temporary rise in raw material prices.
f.   an increase in population.
g.   a decrease in raw material prices.
h.   a decrease in government spending.
i.   an improvement in expectations about the future economic outlook.
j.   an increase in the price of oil.
k.   technological improvements.
l.   a temporary increase in investment spending.
m.   a permanent increase in investment spending.

ANSWERS TO CHAPTER 10

COMPLETION QUESTIONS

1. aggregate demand; aggregate supply
2. price levels; price levels
3. negatively; real-balance, interest, substitution of foreign goods
4. falls; fall
5. rise, fall; rise
6. more; rise; fewer, fewer
7. government spending and taxing policies, exchange rates, expectations, money supply, real interest rates
8. right; right; left
9. positively; rises
10. more
11. wage rates, productivity, technology, raw material prices
12. right; right
13. intersect
14. steep, more difficult
15. SRAS
16. demand shock
17. contractionary gap; expansionary gap
18. cost-push inflation

TRUE-FALSE QUESTIONS

1. F The AD *curve* relates planned purchases to price levels.
2. T
3. T
4. F The value of exports falls, imports rise.
5. F Interest rates fall.
6. F A lower price level leads to a movement down the AD curve; no shift.
7. T
8. T
9. T
10. T
11. F By assumption, this option is not available in the short run.
12. F It becomes very steep as labor becomes more difficult to obtain at constant wage rates.
13. T
14. F The price level will rise too.
15. F It shifts rightward in a growing economy.
16. T
17. T

MULTIPLE CHOICE QUESTIONS

1.a; 2.c; 3.d; 4.b; 5.d; 6.a; 7.c; 8.d; 9.b; 10.d; 11.a;
12.d; 13.c; 14.d; 15.b; 16.b; 17.c; 18.b; 19.b.

MATCHING

a and l; b and j; c and h; d and m; e and n; f and i; g and k

WORKING WITH GRAPHS

1. a. 1.0, 2
   b. Increase in government expenditures, decrease in taxes, increase in money supply, increase in population, rosier expectations
   c. Rises, because a general shortage of goods and services now exists at the previous price level.
   d. Rises, because producers have an incentive to produce more as the price level rises.
   e. Expansionary gap.

PROBLEMS

1. a. The SRAS and LRAS curves shift to the right; therefore national output rises, and the price level falls.
    b. The SRAS curve shifts to the right; therefore national output rises, and the price level falls.
    c. The SRAS curve shifts to the right; therefore national output rises, and the price level falls.
    d. The LRAS curve shifts to the right as potential output increases; national output rises, and the price level falls.
    e. Temporary rise in price level, temporary reduction in national output.
    f. The AD curve shifts to the right; therefore national output and the price level rise.
    g. The SRAS curve shifts to the right; therefore the price level falls and national output rises.
    h. The AD curve shifts to the left; national output falls and the price level falls.
    i. The AD curve shifts to the right; therefore national output rises, and the price level rises.
    j. The SRAS curve shifts to the left; therefore national output falls, and the price level rises.
    k. The SRAS and LRAS curves shift to the right; therefore national output rises; and the price level falls.
    l. The AD curve shifts to the right; therefore national output and the price level rise in the short run.
    m. LRAS shifts as well as AD; national output rises, the effect on the price level is uncertain.

GLOSSARY TO CHAPTER 10

Aggregate demand   All planned expenditures for the entire economy summed together.

Aggregate demand curve   Planned purchase rates for all goods and services in the economy at various price levels.

Aggregate demand shock   Any unexpected shock that causes the aggregate demand curve to shift inward or outward.

Aggregate supply   All planned production for the entire economy summed together.

Aggregate supply shock   Any unexpected shock that causes the aggregate supply curve to shift inward or outward.

Contractionary gap   When the equilibrium level of national income is below the full-employment level.

Cost-push inflation   Inflation caused by continual decreases in the short-run aggregate supply curve.

Demand-pull inflation   Inflation caused by increases in aggregate demand not matched by increases in aggregate supply.

Endowments   The various resources in an economy, including both physical resources and such human resources as ingenuity and management skills.

Expansionary gap   When the equilibrium level of real national income is greater than the full-employment level.

Interest rate effect   Changes in the price level change the amount of money people want to hold which, other things constant, changes the interest rate, which changes the aggregate demand for goods and services.

Long-run aggregate supply curve   The vertical curve representing real output of goods and services that is possible given endowments and under full employment.

Open economy effect   Changes in the domestic price level change the value of exports and imports for a nation.

Real balance effect   A change in the price level causes a change in the purchasing power of currency which then changes the desired rate of consumption at all income levels.

Short-run aggregate supply curve   The relationship between planned rates of total production for the entire economy and the price level, in the short run.

CHAPTER 11

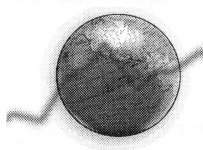

CLASSICAL AND KEYNESIAN MACRO ANALYSIS

PUTTING THIS CHAPTER INTO PERSPECTIVE

Chapter 11 continues the development of our macroeconomic models. The main objective of macroeconomics is to explain how the equilibrium levels of GDP and employment are determined. Chapter 10 provided an overview of how the equilibrium price level and the equilibrium GDP level are determined simultaneously through the AS/AD approach.

In this chapter short run GDP is determined in the Classical and the Keynesian models. The essential difference is that in the classical model the price level is assumed flexible, and in the Keynesian model it is assumed to be constant—at least in the short run. In the Keynesian model a depression situation is assumed, hence it is reasonable to assume a fixed price level and a horizontal range for the AS curve. In that range GDP is said to be demand-determined.

In this chapter we apply the AS/AD framework to analyze the results of a change in a nation's exchange rate, and to indicate how it is possible to have economic growth without inflation.

LEARNING OBJECTIVES

After you have studied this chapter you should be able to

1. define Say's law, money illusion, and Keynesian short-run aggregate supply curve.

2. recognize the main assumptions and conclusions of the classical model.

3. recognize the shape of the classical long-run aggregate supply curve, and predict the effects of a change in aggregate demand in this model.

4. recognize the shape of the Keynesian short-run aggregate supply curve and predict the effects of a change in aggregate demand in this model.

5. predict the effects on the AS curve and the AD curve of a change in a nation's exchange rate.

6. use the AS/AD approach to recognize how it is possible to have economic growth without inflation.

CHAPTER OUTLINE

1. The classical model was developed in the 18th and 19th centuries; it attempted to explain the determinants of the price level and GDP.
   a. Say's law is that supply creates its own demand.
   b. The classical model assumes (1) pure competition, (2) wage and price flexibility, (3) self-interest, and (4) no money illusion.
   c. In this model the interest rate changes until household saving is equated to business planned investment, thereby assuring that every dollar that leaves the economic system as saving comes back in as a dollar invested.
   d. Because the LRAS curve is vertical in the classical model, changes in AD merely change the price level; GDP is supply determined.

2. John Maynard Keynes developed what is now the Keynesian model during the 1930s, a depression period.
   a. This model assumes that prices and wages are constant in the short run, hence the SRAS curve has a horizontal range.
   b. Changes in AD, consequently, lead to changes in GDP, but not the price level; in this model GDP is demand determined in the short run.

3. If we relax the assumption of a fixed price level we operate on the upward portion of the SRAS curve.
   a. An increase in AD leads to an increase in GDP, but some of the increase will be checked off by a rising price level that leads to wealth, interest rate, and foreign goods substitution effects.
   b. A decrease in AD will lead to a decrease in GDP, but some of the decrease will be abated by a falling price level, which leads to wealth, interest rate, and foreign goods substitution effects.

4. If a nation's exchange rate rises in value, its SRAS curve will shift rightward, as imported raw material prices fall, and its AD curve will shift leftward as its imports rise and its exports fall; the net effect is a lower price level, while the net effect on GDP is indeterminate.

5. It is possible to have economic growth without inflation.
   a. Economic growth shifts the short-run and long-run AS curves rightward.
   b. Rightward shifts in the AD curve, therefore, can be offset by leftward shifts in AS.

KEY TERMS

Say's law

KEY CONCEPTS

Money illusion   Keynesian short-run aggregate supply curve

COMPLETION QUESTIONS
Fill in the blank or circle the correct term.

1. Say's Law maintains that _____ creates its own _____.

2. The major assumptions of the classical model are _____,
   _____, _____, and _____.

3. If people respond to changes in absolute prices, when relative prices are unaltered, then they suffer from a _____ illusion.

4. In the classical model desired household saving and desired business investment are equated by the _____ rate; and at the equilibrium wage rate full employment (does, does not) exist.

5. In the classical model the LRAS curve is (horizontal, vertical) therefore changes in the AD curve lead to changes in _____, but not to changes in _____.

6. In the Keynesian range, prices and wage rates are (fixed, flexible), hence the SRAS curve is (horizontal, vertical); changes in AD lead to changes in _____, but not in _____.

7. Saving is a(n) (leakage from, injection into) the circular flow and is a potential problem; if saving is offset by _____, which is a(n) (leakage from, injection into) the circular flow, then full employment will prevail.

8. Saving represents a _____ curve; investment represents a _____ curve. Saving and investment are brought into equality by the _____ rate, in the classical model.

9. If much unused capacity and massive unemployment exist, the economy will be operating in the _____ range of the SRAS curve; in that range, increases in the AD curve will lead to increases in _____ but no changes in the _____; in that range, national income is said to be _____ determined.

We relax the assumption of a fixed price level in questions 10, 11, 12, and 13.

10. An increase in AD causes the price level to_____, but some of that effect is reduced because of the following effects: _____, _____, and _____.

11. A decrease in AD causes the price level to_____, but some of the effect is reduced.

12. Nation A's exchange rate has increased. As a result its SRAS curve will shift to the _____, and its AD curve will shift to the _____; the net effect is that nation A's price level will _____ and its GDP change will _____.

13. Country Z's exchange rate has weakened. As a result its AD curve will _____ and its SRAS curve will ____; the net effect on country Z is that its GDP change will _____ and its price level will _____.

14. As economic growth occurs, a nation's short-run AS curve will shift _____ and its long-run AS curve will shift _____. Consequently, if the AD curve shifts rightward during periods of economic growth inflation (will, will not, may not) result.

TRUE-FALSE QUESTIONS
Circle the **T** if the statement is true, the **F** if it is false. Explain to yourself why a statement is false.

T F   1. The classical model preceded the Keynesian model.

T F   2. Say's Law says that demand creates its own supply.

T F   3.   In the classical model, prices and wages are fixed.

T F   4.   A money illusion exists if people respond to relative, not absolute, price or wage rate changes.

T F   5.   In the classical model, household desired saving equals business desired investment because the interest rate adjusts until they are equated.

T F   6.   The classical model is consistent with the horizontal range of the SRAS curve.

T F   7.   In the horizontal range of the SRAS curve, real GDP is demand determined.

T F   8.   If the AD curve shifts in the classical model, then the price level will change, but the level of real national output remains constant.

T F   9.   If the AD curve shifts in the Keynesian range, the price level changes, as does real GDP.

T F   10.   If the interest rate falls, investment spending will rise.

T F   11.   If the price level can change, a rightward shift in AD will cause real GDP to rise and the price level to fall.

T F   12.   If a nation's exchange rate weakens, its SRAS curve will shift leftward, its AD curve will shift rightward, and its price level will rise.

T F   13.   Economic growth causes a nation's long-run AS curve to shift to the right, but its short-run AS curve to shift to the left.

MULTIPLE CHOICE QUESTIONS
Circle the letter that corresponds to the best answer.

1.   The classical model assumes
    a. prices and wages are constant.
    b. pure competition.
    c. people suffer from money illusion.
    d. altruism is the main motivating force.

2.   Say's Law
    a. was developed by J. M. Keynes.
    b. maintains that demand creates its own supply.
    c. maintains that supply creates its own demand.
    d. implies that general overproduction is likely under capitalism.

3.   In the classical model, saving
    a. is an injection into the income stream.
    b. and investment are determined by national disposable income.
    c. causes unemployment.
    d. is a leakage from the circular flow.

4. In the classical model, when households save,
    a. that money becomes a part of supply of saving curve.
    b. business investment offsets such saving.
    c. full employment will still prevail.
    d. All of the above

5. In the Keynesian model, in a depression
    a. the economy operates in the horizontal range of the SRAS curve.
    b. prices and wages are flexible.
    c. the interest rate adjusts until desired saving equals desired investment.
    d. All of the above

6. When economic growth occurs, a nation's
    a. short-run AS curve shifts leftward
    b. short-run and long-run AS curves shift rightward
    c. long-run AS curve becomes horizontal
    d. price level must rise

7. In the horizontal range of the SRAS curve,
    a. the price level is constant.
    b. the classical model assumptions apply.
    c. national income is supply determined.
    d. full employment exists.

8. If a nation's exchange rate rises, its
    a. SRAS curve shifts leftward, due to input cost reductions.
    b. AD curve shifts rightward, due to falling imports.
    c. price level will fall.
    d. GDP will rise, unambiguously.

9. If a nation's exchange rate falls, its
    a. SRAS curve shifts leftward, due to input cost increases.
    b. AD curve shifts rightward, due to increased exports and decreased imports.
    c. price level rises.
    d. All of the above.

10. Which of the following will **NOT** shift the classical investment curve?
    a. a change in the interest rate
    b. a change in profit expectations
    c. a change in business taxes
    d. a change in technology and innovation

11. In the classical model, if AD shifts to the right, then
    a. real national income rises.
    b. the price level rises.
    c. real national income falls.
    d. the price level is unaffected.

12. In the Keynesian range of SRAS, if AD shifts to the left, then
    a. the price level falls.
    b. real national income is unchanged.
    c. real national income falls.
    d. the price level rises.

MATCHING
Choose the item in Column (2) that best matches an item in Column (1).

(1)	(2)
a. Say's law	h. confusion between absolute and relative prices
b. fixed price level	i. leftward shift in AD
c. money illusion	j. Keynesian range
d. stronger exchange rate	k. classical model
e. weaker exchange rate	l. leftward shift in SRAS
f. economic growth	m. expenditure on capital goods
g. investment	n. rightward shifts in AS

WORKING WITH GRAPHS

1. Using the coordinate system below, answer the questions that follow.

   a. Assuming a flexible price level and an open economy draw an equilibrium situation using the AS/AD model.
   b. Assume that this nation's exchange rate has weakened, draw in the new AD and the new SRAS curves.
   c. What happens to GDP and the price level?

CASE STUDY

During the late 1970s in the United States, the inflation rate was high, and so was the unemployment rate. Some economists suggested that this problem could be solved by reducing tax rates dramatically.

1. What effect would a dramatic tax rate decrease have on
   a. labor supply?
   b. investment?
   c. saving?
   d. economic growth?

2.   What would happen to the short-run aggregate supply curve?

3.   How might a dramatic decrease in taxes solve the problem of high inflation and high unemployment?

ANSWERS TO CHAPTER 11

COMPLETION QUESTIONS

1. supply; demand
2. pure competition; price-wage flexibility; self-interest; no money illusion
3. money
4. interest; does
5. vertical; price level; real GDP
6. fixed; horizontal; real GDP; the price level
7. leakage; investment; injection into
8. supply; demand; interest
9. horizontal; real GDP; price level; demand
10. rise; wealth; interest rate; foreign goods substitution effects
11. fall
12. right; left; fall; be indeterminate
13. shift rightward; shift leftward; be indeterminate; rise
14. rightward; rightward; may not

TRUE-FALSE QUESTIONS

1. T
2. F   Say's law is that supply creates its own demand.
3. F   They are flexible in the classical model.
4. F   Money illusion results when people respond to absolute, but not relative price changes.
5. T
6. F   The SRAS curve is vertical in the classical model.
7. T
8. T
9. F   Price level is constant, real GDP changes.
10. T
11. F   Real GDP rises, but the price level rises too.
12. T
13. F   Both curves shift rightward.

MULTIPLE CHOICE QUESTIONS

1.b;   2.c;   3.d;   4.d;   5.a;   6.b;   7.a;   8.c;   9.d;   10.a;
11.b;   12.c.

MATCHING

a and k;   b and j;   c and h;   d and i;   e and l;   f and n;   g and m.

WORKING WITH GRAPHS

a. N.A.
b. The AD curve should shift rightward; the AS curve should shift leftward.
c. Effect on GDP is indeterminate; price level should rise.

CASE STUDY

1. a. increase; b. increase; c. increase; d. increase.
2. It shifts to the right.
3. Rightward shifts in the SRAS curve cause the price level to fall and GDP to rise (which causes unemployment to fall).

GLOSSARY TO CHAPTER 11

Keynesian short-run aggregate supply curve   The horizontal portion of the aggregate supply curve in which there is unemployment and unused capacity in the economy.

Money illusion   The ability to be fooled by changes in money prices rather than relative prices.

Say's law   A dictum of J.B. Say that supply creates its own demand; by producing goods and services, an equal means and a willingness to purchase other goods and services are created.

CHAPTER 12

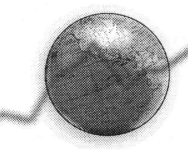

CONSUMPTION, INCOME, AND THE MULTIPLIER

PUTTING THIS CHAPTER INTO PERSPECTIVE

In this chapter we analyze in detail the model developed by John Maynard Keynes, introduced in Chapter 11. Recall that Keynes' model assumed high levels of excess capacity and unemployment; hence the price level is assumed constant.

Chapter 12 analyzes the consumption, saving, and investment functions, how equilibrium is determined, and how shifts in the planned expenditures curve lead to multiplier effects.

LEARNING OBJECTIVES

After you have studied this chapter you should be able to

1. define saving, savings, consumption, dissaving, autonomous consumption, average propensity to consume, average propensity to save, marginal propensity to consume, marginal propensity to save, 45-degree reference line, wealth, lump-sum tax, and multiplier.

2. distinguish between flow variables and stock variables.

3. relate consumption and saving to income.

4. distinguish between the marginal propensity to consume (save) and the average propensity to consume (save).

5. calculate marginal and average propensities to consume (save), given the relevant information.

6. distinguish between the causes of a movement along and a shift in the consumption (saving) curve.

7. list the main determinants of planned business investment spending and recognize how each affects such spending.

8. predict what will happen to national income and employment if total planned expenditures do not equal real national income.

9. calculate the autonomous consumption or autonomous investment multiplier, given the relevant information.

10. calculate the change in the equilibrium level of national income due to a change in autonomous expenditures, given the marginal propensity to consume.

CHAPTER OUTLINE

1. The sum of *consumption* expenditures and *saving* equals income, by definition.
    a. Saving, consumption, and income are flows which, therefore, are measured per unit of time; *savings* and wealth are stocks whose values are measured at a given moment in time.
    b. Investment, which is a flow, includes expenditures by firms for capital goods.

2. John Maynard Keynes maintained that planned real saving and planned real consumption were determined by real disposable income.
    a. For the household, planned real consumption is typically plotted on the vertical axis and real disposable income on the horizontal axis; the planned saving curve can be derived by subtracting the planned consumption curve from the 45 degree line.
    b. *Autonomous consumption* is that consumption that is independent of income, and it is the value of the vertical intercept on the consumption function; if consumption is positive at zero national income, then *dissaving* must exist over the lower range of the consumption function.
    c. The *average propensity to consume* (APC) equals total real consumption divided by total real disposable income; the *average propensity to save* (APS) equals total real saving divided by total real disposable income.
    d. The *marginal propensity to consume* (MPC) equals the change in real consumption divided by the change in real disposable income; the *marginal propensity to save* (MPS) equals the change in real saving divided by the change in real disposable income.
    e. The APC + APS = 1; and the MPC + MPS = 1.
    f. When real disposable income changes, a movement along the consumption curve results; when there is a change in the nonincome determinants of consumption, the consumption curve shifts.

3. The nonincome determinants of consumption include wealth, future income or inflationary expectations, and population.
    a. If wealth increases, the consumption function shifts upward; if wealth decreases, it shifts downward.
    b. If households expect better times ahead, the consumption function shifts upward; expected worse times will shift it downward.
    c. An expectation that the inflation rate will fall may shift the consumption function downward.
    d. An increase in population shifts the consumption function upward; a decrease in population shifts it downward.

4. Investment includes business expenditures on plants and equipment and on inventories; such expenditures are more variable than household consumption expenditures because expectations play a more important role in investment expenditures.
    a. An inverse relationship exists between investment expenditures and the interest rate.
    b. Non-interest rate determinants of investment spending include expectations, innovation and technology, and business taxes.
        i. If the future looks rosier, then more investment expenditures will be made at any interest rate; the investment curve will shift to the right.
        ii. Improvements in technology and innovation shift the planned investment curve to the right.
        iii. If business taxes rise, the planned investment curve shifts to the left; a reduction in such taxes shifts it to the right.

5. The simplified Keynesian model, which considers only household consumption expenditures and business investment expenditures, is useful because it provides insights and serves as a foundation for more complicated models.

6. Real consumption depends on real disposable income and it is also related to real national income; the latter relationship is more convenient for our analysis.
    a. A portion of the consumption function is autonomous, or independent of real national income.
    b. Net investment is dependent on the interest rate; for simplicity we assume that it is autonomous, or independent of national income.
    c. The 45-degree reference line indicates where planned expenditures equal real national income per year.

7. The equilibrium level of real national income occurs at that income level where the planned expenditures curve intersects the 45-degree reference line.
    a. Once the equilibrium real national income level is determined, the employment level is also determined because a functional relationship exists between those two variables in the short run.
    b. At all other income levels disequilibrium exists.
        i.   If total planned expenditures exceed real national income, then business inventories will fall involuntarily and businesses will find it profitable to increase output and employment.
        ii. If total planned expenditures are less than real national income, then business inventories will rise involuntarily and businesses will find it profitable to decrease output and employment.

8. When *autonomous expenditures* change, the planned expenditures curve shifts and there will be a *multiplier effect.*
    a. If autonomous consumption, autonomous investment, autonomous government expenditures, or net exports change, the planned expenditures curve shifts by an identical amount.
    b. Equilibrium real national income per year will change by a multiple of the change in autonomous expenditure, in the same direction.

9. A multiplier effect exists because one person's expenditure is another person's income, and changes in autonomous spending lead to successive rounds of spending and income creation.
    a. The steeper the slope of the planned expenditure curves (the MPC), the greater is the multiplier.
    b. The simple multiplier equals the reciprocal of the MPS.
    c. Because of the multiplier effect, fluctuations in economic activity will be magnified.

KEY TERMS

45-degree reference line	Average propensity to consume
Saving	Marginal propensity to consume
Wealth	Average propensity to save
Dissaving	Marginal propensity to save
Consumption	

KEY CONCEPTS

Autonomous consumption	Lump-sum tax
Multiplier	Consumption function

COMPLETION QUESTIONS
Fill in the blank or circle the correct term.

1. Saving is a(n) (leakage from, injection into) the circular flow and is a potential problem; if saving is offset by _____, which is a(n) (leakage from, injection into) the circular flow, then full employment will prevail.

2. Saving represents a _____ curve; investment represents a _____ curve. Saving and investment are brought into equality by the _____ rate, in the classical model.

3. If much unused capacity and massive unemployment exist, the economy will be operating in the _____ range of the SRAS curve; in that range, increases in the AD curve will lead to increases in _____ but no changes in the _____; in that range, national income is said to be _____ determined.

4. Saving is a (stock, flow) concept, while savings is a _____ concept.

5. The sum of planned consumption and planned saving equals _____, by definition; when real disposable income rises, planned real consumption _____ and planned real saving _____.

6. The average propensity to save (APS) equals saving divided by _____; the APC plus the APS equal _____.

7. The marginal propensity to consume (MPC) equals the change in consumption (divided by, plus, minus) the change in real disposable income; one minus the MPC equals the _____.

8. The amount of consumption that is (dependent on, independent of) income is called autonomous consumption; when autonomous consumption exists, the vertical intercept of the consumption function is (negative, zero, positive), and the APC (falls, remains constant, rises) as real disposable income rises.

9. Dissaving exists when consumption expenditures (equal, are less than, exceed) income.

10. The consumption function will shift if autonomous consumption changes due to changes in such nonincome determinants of consumption as _____, _____, _____, and _____.

11. Investment varies (directly, inversely) with changes in the interest rate; the planned investment curve shifts if there are changes in _____, _____, or _____.

12. Along the 45-degree reference line, planned total expenditures equal real _____; where the planned expenditures line intersects the 45-degree reference line (equilibrium, disequilibrium) exists; where those curves do not intersect, _____ exists.

13. In the model in which government and foreign transactions are ignored, household planned consumption expenditures plus business investment expenditures equal aggregate _____.

14. If total planned expenditures exceed real national income, business inventories will _____ involuntarily and businesses will find it profitable to (increase, decrease) output and employment; if total planned expenditures are less than real national income, business inventories will _____ involuntarily and businesses will find it profitable to _____ output and employment.

15. If autonomous government purchases of goods and services (G) are added to the aggregate expenditures curve, the aggregate expenditures curve will shift (upward, downward) and equilibrium real national income per year will (rise, fall).

16. If exports and imports are added to the aggregate expenditure curve and imports exceed exports, then net exports are a (positive, negative) number and equilibrium real national income will (rise, fall) by an amount (greater than, equal to, less than) net exports.

TRUE-FALSE QUESTIONS
Circle the **T** if the statement is true, the **F** if it is false. Explain to yourself why a statement is false.

T F 1. The APC plus the MPC equals 10, by definition.

T F 2. In the Keynesian model, if wealth rises, the consumption function shifts upward.

T F 3. In the Keynesian model, the APC falls and the APS rises as national income rises.

T F 4. If autonomous consumption is positive, then the vertical intercept of the consumption curve is positive.

T F 5. If real disposable income rises, the consumption function will shift upward.

T F 6. On average, disposable income is about 85 percent of national income.

T F 7. The 45-degree reference line indicates planned expenditures at each level of real national income.

T F 8. Autonomous consumption and autonomous investment vary directly with real national income.

T F 9. The equilibrium level of real national income is found at the point at which the planned expenditures curve intersects the 45-degree reference line.

T F 10. If total planned expenditures exceed real national income, then business inventories will fall and businesses will increase output.

T F 11. In the short run, employment and real national income (output) are directly related.

T F 12. Ignoring the government and foreign sectors, if planned saving is less than planned investment, then planned expenditures are less than real national income.

T F 13. If autonomous expenditures rise, then the planned expenditures curve will shift upward.

T F 14. If autonomous expenditures rise by $1 billion, national income will probably rise by more than $1 billion.

T F 15.   If the price level falls, the planned expenditures curve will shift upward.

T F 16.   If the MPC is 0.75, a $1 billion increase in autonomous expenditures will cause national income to rise by $4 billion, if the SRAS curve is horizontal.

MULTIPLE CHOICE QUESTIONS
Circle the letter that corresponds to the best answer.

1.   Autonomous real consumption
    a.   varies directly with real disposable income.
    b.   varies inversely with real disposable income.
    c.   changes with changes in wealth.
    d.   equals planned saving.

2.   The 45-degree reference line
    a.   indicates planned expenditures.
    b.   is a line along which planned expenditures equal real national income.
    c.   is the consumption function.
    d.   is the autonomous investment function.

3.   If planned investment is autonomous, then
    a.   it is independent of real national income.
    b.   it is independent of the interest rate.
    c.   it varies directly with real national income.
    d.   it varies inversely with real national income.

4.   At that level of income where the planned expenditures curve intersects the 45-degree reference line (ignoring G and X)
    a.   equilibrium exists.
    b.   unplanned inventory changes equal zero.
    c.   planned saving equals planned investment.
    d.   All of the above

5.   Changes in autonomous expenditures
    a.   affect the 45-degree reference line.
    b.   shift the planned expenditures curve.
    c.   are movements along the planned expenditures curve.
    d.   lead to equal increases in real national income.

6.   The consumption function analyzed in the text
    a.   has an autonomous component that varies with income.
    b.   indicates that real consumption falls as real income rises.
    c.   shifts if autonomous consumption changes.
    d.   is the same as the autonomous investment function.

7.   If total planned expenditures exceed real national income, then
    a.   business inventories will rise involuntarily.
    b.   business inventories will fall involuntarily.
    c.   equilibrium exists.
    d.   real national income will fall.

8. If total planned expenditures are less than real national income, then
   a. business inventories will rise involuntarily.
   b. business inventories will fall involuntarily.
   c. equilibrium exists.
   d. real national income will rise.

9. Which of the following is most unlike the others?
   a. consumption function
   b. investment function
   c. 45-degree reference line
   d. planned expenditures curve

10. If business inventories rise involuntarily, then
    a. equilibrium exists.
    b. total planned expenditures are less than real national income.
    c. real national income will rise.
    d. businesses will hire more labor.

11. If the short run, total employment and real national income/output
    a. are inversely related.
    b. are directly related.
    c. are independent of each other.
    d. reflect the law of demand.

12. If planned saving exceeds planned investment, then (ignoring government and foreign transactions)
    a. total planned expenditures are less than real national income.
    b. national income exceeds planned expenditures.
    c. business inventories will rise involuntarily, and national income will fall.
    d. All of the above

13. In macroeconomic equilibrium (ignoring government and foreign transactions)
    a. planned saving equals planned investment.
    b. actual inventories equal actual investment.
    c. actual saving does not equal actual investment.
    d. saving plus investment equals consumption.

14. As the MPC rises, the multiplier
    a. falls.
    b. rises.
    c. is unaffected.
    d. changes in an unpredictable way.

15. If the MPC is 1/2, then (ignoring price level effects)
    a. the multiplier is 12.
    b. changes in autonomous income lead to equal changes in national income.
    c. shifts in the planned expenditures curve lead to a change in equilibrium real national income that equals twice the value of the shift.
    d. the APC must fall as real income falls.

16. The multiplier
    a. relates changes in autonomous expenditures to changes in equilibrium real national income.
    b. deals with shifts in the planned expenditures curve.
    c. implies that economic fluctuations are magnified.
    d. All of the above

17. When the price level rises,
    a. the planned expenditures curve shifts downward.
    b. the 45-degree reference line shifts upward.
    c. autonomous expenditures rise.
    d. the multiplier effect is increased.

18. If the planned expenditures curve shifts downward when the price level rises, and upward when the price level falls, then
    a. the multiplier effect is lessened.
    b. the economy can pull out of a recession faster.
    c. economic fluctuations due to shocks will be lessened.
    d. All of the above

19. *Analogy*: Saving is to income as _____ is to wealth.
    a. income
    b. savings
    c. investment
    d. consumption

20. Saving plus consumption equal
    a. investment.
    b. aggregate demand.
    c. disposable income.
    d. 1.

21. Which of the following causes the consumption function to shift?
    a. an increase in real disposable income
    b. a decrease in real disposable income
    c. an increase in wealth
    d. an increase in investment

22. If autonomous consumption is positive, then
    a. the vertical intercept of the consumption function is positive.
    b. the APC falls as real disposable income rises.
    c. dissaving occurs at very low real disposable income levels.
    d. All of the above

23. Autonomous consumption
    a. varies with disposable national income.
    b. varies with wealth.
    c. changes lead to movements along a given consumption curve.
    d. if positive, means that the vertical intercept of the consumption function is zero.

24. If the MPC = 0.8 then the
    a. APC = 0.2.
    b. MPS = 0.2.
    c. APS = 0.2.
    d. vertical intercept of the consumption function is positive.

25. If real disposable income rises by $100 and consumption rises by $75, then
    a. the APC = 0.75.
    b. the MPC = 0.25.
    c. the MPS = 0.25.
    d. the MPC = $75.

26. If the APC falls as real disposable income rises, then
    a. the APS must rise as real disposable income rises.
    b. the APS is constant.
    c. the MPC must be falling.
    d. the vertical intercept of the saving function must be positive.

27. If the APC falls as real disposable income rises, the
    a. vertical intercept of the consumption function is positive.
    b. vertical intercept of the saving function is negative.
    c. APS rises from a negative number to zero to a positive number.
    d. All of the above.

MATCHING
Choose the item in Column (2) that best matches an item in Column (1).

(1)	(2)
a. planned investment is less than planned saving	h. planned expenditures equal national income
b. equilibrium	i. falling national income
c. recession	j. multiplier
d. reciprocal of MPS	k. planned expenditures are less than national income
e. APC	l. non income determinants of consumption
f. MPC	m. total consumption divided by total income
g. autonomous consumption	n. change in consumption divided by change in income

WORKING WITH GRAPHS

1. Using the graphs provided, answer the questions that follow.

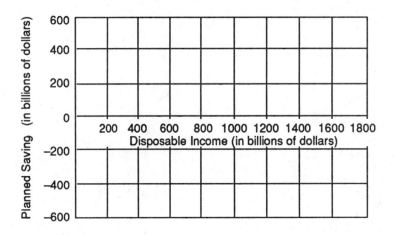

a. Graph the saving function in the space provided in panel (b).
b. What is the break-even level of disposable income?
c. What is the MPC? What is the MPS?
d. What is the APC at $800 billion of disposable income?
e. What is the APC at $1600 billion of disposable income?
f. What is the APC at $1200 billion of disposable income?

2. Draw an AS and an AD curve, using the classical model assumptions. Then show what happens if the money supply is increased, other things constant.

3. Draw an AS and an AD curve, using the Keynesian Range model assumptions. Then show what happens if government expenditures are increased, other things constant.

4. Given the following information about a hypothetical economy, complete the table below and then represent this economy in a planned expenditures diagram and a saving/investment diagram in the space provided. Include a 45-degree reference line and indicate the level of equilibrium national income. (The figures are given in billions of dollars per year.)

$C = \$200 + .80Y$ $I = \$160$

Y	I	C	Total Planned S	Inventory Expenditures	Changes
800	_____	_____	_____	_____	_____
900	_____	_____	_____	_____	_____
1500	_____	_____	_____	_____	_____
1800	_____	_____	_____	_____	_____
2000	_____	_____	_____	_____	_____
2400	_____	_____	_____	_____	_____

where   C = planned consumption   S = planned saving
        Y = real national income   I = planned investment

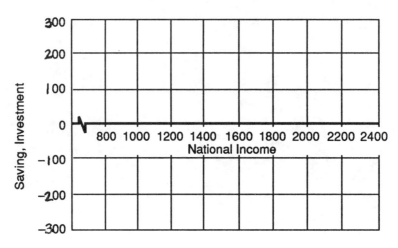

5. Consider the graphs below, then answer the questions that follows. (Note that G = government spending and X = net imports.)

a. What is the value of net exports?
b. What is the MPC for this economy?
c. What is the value of the equilibrium level of real national income?
d. What is the multiplier for this economy?

PROBLEMS

1. Suppose that for a particular economy, MPS = 1/4. Complete the following table under the assumption that autonomous investment has just increased by $2000 (using the simple Keynesian model).

	Change in Income	Change in Consumption	Change in Saving
Round 1	2000	_____	_____
Round 2	1500	_____	_____
Round 3	_____	_____	_____
All other rounds	_____	_____	_____
Total	_____	_____	_____

2. Answer the following assuming a simple Keynesian economy:
    a. If the MPC = 3/4, and the current equilibrium level of real national income is $1240 billion, what will be the new equilibrium level of income if autonomous investment falls by $10 billion?
    b. Given the same initial equilibrium level of real national income and the same decrease in investment, what would be the new equilibrium if MPC is 4/5 rather than 3/4?

3.   Consider the graphs below, then answer the questions that follow. [Ignore G and X]

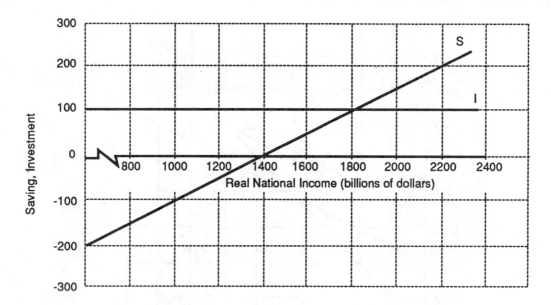

a.   What is the value of autonomous saving?
b.   What is the value of autonomous consumption?
c.   What is the value of autonomous investment?
d.   At real national income $2,000 billion do planned expenditures equal, exceed, or are they less than, real national income? Why?
e.   At real national income $1600 billion are unplanned inventories rising, falling, or remaining constant? Why?
f.   What is the equilibrium level of real national income? Why?

4. Assume that you know that the MPC for a particular economy is three-fourths.
a.   If the break-even income is $10,000, what will be the level of consumption if income is $14,000?
b.   If income drops to $8,000, what will be the level of consumption? Of saving?

CASE STUDY

Over the past ten years or so, the average propensity to save (APS) in the U.S. has been relatively low. Researchers have found that our national Social Security system, Medicare, and various other programs that aid the elderly may have an important effect on our national APS.

1.   How do government-provided income maintenance services to the elderly affect the saving-consumption decision of people during their working years?
2.   If the government forced people to save amounts that they would have saved anyway, what would happen to the saving rate?

ANSWERS TO CHAPTER 12

COMPLETION QUESTIONS

1. leakage from; investment; injection into
2. supply; demand; interest
3. horizontal; real national income (output), price level; demand
4. flow; stock
5. disposable income; rises, rises
6. income; 1
7. divided by; MPS
8. independent of; positive, falls
9. exceed
10. expectations, wealth, population
11. inversely; profit expectations, innovation and technology, business taxes
12. national income; equilibrium; disequilibrium
13. planned expenditures
14. fall; increase; rise; decrease
15. upward; rise
16. negative; fall; greater than

TRUE-FALSE QUESTIONS

1. F   The APC plus the APS equals 1.0.
2. T
3. T
4. T
5. F   No shift, just a movement along (up) the C-function.
6. T
7. F   At every point along the 45-degree line; planned expenditures equal national income.
8. F   Autonomous here means independent of income.
9. T
10. T
11. T
12. F   Planned expenditures would exceed national income.
13. T
14. T
15. T
16. T

MULTIPLE CHOICE QUESTIONS

1.c;	2.b;	3.a;	4.d;	5.b;	6.c;	7.b;	8.a;	9.c;	10.b;
11.b;	12.d;	13.a;	14.b;	15.c;	16.d;	17.a;	18.d;	19.b;	20.c;
21.c;	22.d;	23.b;	24.b;	25.c;	26.a;	27.d.			

MATCHING

a and k;   b and h;   c and i;   d and j;   e and m;   f and n;   g and l

WORKING WITH GRAPHS

1. a.

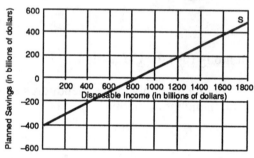

b. $800 billion

c. 1/2; 1/2

d. 1

e. 3/4

f. 5/6

2.

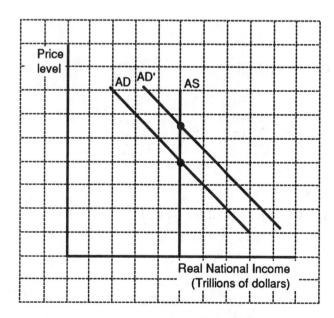

A money supply increase shifts the AD curve to AD', which causes the price level to rise; real national output remains at the full employment/full capacity level.

3.

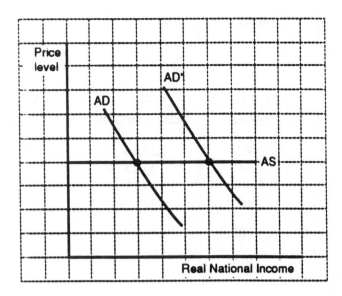

An increase in G shifts the AD curve to AD'; real national income rises, but the price level remains constant in the Keynesian Range.

4.

Y	I	C	S	Total Planned Expenditures	Inventory Changes
800	160	840	-40	1000	-200
900	160	920	-20	1080	-180
1500	160	1400	100	1560	-60
1800	160	1640	160	1800	0
2000	160	1800	200	1960	40
2400	160	2120	280	2280	120

5. a. $200 billion; b. 0.5;   c. $1800 billion; d. 2.0

PROBLEMS

1.

	Change in Income	Change in Consumption	Change in Saving
Round 1	2000	$1500.00	$ 500.00
Round 2	1500	1125.00	375.00
Round 3	1125	843.75	281.25
All other rounds	3375	2531.25	843.75
Total	$8000	$6000.00	$2000.00

2. a. $1200 billion
    b $1190 billion

3. a.   - $200 billion
    b. $200 billion
    c. $100 billion
    d.   Less than, because planned saving > planned investment
    e.   Falling, because at that income level planned investment > planned saving
    f. $1800 billion, because only here does planned saving equal planned investment.

4. a. $13,000
    b. $8,500; -$500 (dissaving)

CASE STUDY

1. If government programs reduce the need for people to finance their future consumption, working people will substitute present consumption for future consumption; that is, they will save less now.
2. If government forces people to save what they would have saved anyway, the APS will be unaffected—assuming the interest rate is the same.

GLOSSARY TO CHAPTER 12

Average propensity to consume (APC)   Consumption divided by disposable income; for any given level of income, the proportion of total disposable income that is consumed.

Average propensity to save (APS)   Saving divided by disposable income; the proportion of total disposable income that is saved.

Autonomous consumption   That part of consumption that is independent of, or does not depend on, the level of disposable income. Changes in autonomous consumption shift the consumption function.

Consumption   That which is spent on new goods and services out of a household's current income. Whatever is not consumed is saved. Consumption includes such things as buying food and going to a concert.

Consumption function   The relationship between the amount consumed and disposable income. A consumption function tells us how much people plan to consume out of various disposable income levels.

Dissaving   Negative saving. A situation where spending exceeds income. Dissaving can occur when a household is able to borrow or use up existing owned assets.

45-degree reference line   The line along which planned expenditures equal real national income per year; a line that bisects the total planned expenditures/real national income quadrant.

Lump-sum tax   A tax that does not depend on the level of income, or on the circumstances of the taxpayer.

Marginal propensity to consume (MPC)   The ratio of the change in consumption to the change in disposable income. A .8 marginal propensity to consume tells us that an additional $100 in take-home pay will lead to an additional $80 consumed.

Marginal propensity to save (MPS)   The ratio of the change in saving to the change in disposable income. A .2 marginal propensity to save indicates that out of an additional $100 in take-home pay, $20 will be saved. Whatever is not saved is consumed. The marginal propensity to save plus the marginal propensity to consume must always equal 1, by definition.

Multiplier   The ratio of the change in the equilibrium level of real national income to the change in autonomous expenditures; that number by which a change in autonomous investment or autonomous consumption, for example, is multiplied to get the change in the equilibrium level of real national income.

Saving   The act of not consuming all of one's current income. Whatever is not consumed out of spendable income is, by definition, saved. Saving is an action measured over time (flow), whereas **savings** are an existing accumulation of wealth resulting from the act of saving in the past (stock).

Wealth   The stock of assets owned by a person, household, firm, or nation. For a household, wealth can consist of a house, cars, computers, bank accounts, and cash.

CHAPTER 13

FISCAL POLICY

PUTTING THIS CHAPTER INTO PERSPECTIVE

You have already learned how macroeconomic equilibrium is determined. In Chapter 12 it was pointed out that, unlike the classical economists, Keynes maintained that there is nothing in a capitalistic (free enterprise) economy that assures full employment or price stability. The existence of contractionary gaps and expansionary gaps implies that equilibrium and unemployment (or inflation) can exist simultaneously.

Chapter 13 is a continuation of Chapter 12. Here you learn that if we wish to pursue the normative economics goals of full employment and price stability, then fiscal policy can be employed. Fiscal policy is the deliberate changing of government expenditures and/or taxes in order to attain such national economic goals as full employment, price stability, economic growth, and an international payments equilibrium. (In later chapters we develop the analysis of the other major stabilization tool, monetary policy, which can be employed to attain those same national goals.)

This chapter indicates how fiscal policy may be employed to counteract expansionary gaps and contractionary gaps. It also indicates that fiscal policy measures can be offset by indirect effects (changes in interest rates and the Ricardian equivalence theorem), direct effects (government expenditures that compete with the private sector cause an offsetting reduction in business investment), open economy effects (deficit spending leads to an offsetting reduction in net exports as higher domestic interest rates cause the country's exchange rate to rise).

You also learn in this chapter that changes in marginal tax rates affect the labor-leisure tradeoff, the household saving-investment tradeoff, and business investment decisions.

Fiscal policy analysis is a rather complex business. We must be careful to distinguish between *discretionary* fiscal policy (in which conscious stabilization policies are pursued by policymakers) and automatic fiscal policy. The latter occurs automatically, without any conscious policy-making decisions, as a result of a progressive tax structure, unemployment compensation, the corporate income tax, and other taxes.

An important, if sad, lesson to be learned in this chapter is that fiscal policy is very difficult to implement. First there are the technical problems. Are the data accurate? How much crowding out will occur? How long or how variable are the various fiscal policy time lags? Then there are the political questions. If you leave this chapter with the feeling that fiscal policy is more an art than a science, then you are on the right track.

LEARNING OBJECTIVES

After you have studied this chapter you should be able to

1. define fiscal policy, direct expenditure offsets, automatic, or built-in, stabilizers, crowding out, recognition time lag, action time lag, effect time lag, Ricardian equivalence theorem, and supply-side economics.

2. recognize the proper fiscal policy required to eliminate output gaps and expansionary gaps.

3. distinguish between the effects of fiscal policy when the economy is operating on the LRAS curve and when it is not.

4. recognize four effects that limit the effectiveness of fiscal policy.

5. indicate how an expansionary fiscal policy can cause net exports to fall.

6. distinguish between discretionary fiscal policy and automatic fiscal policy.

7. enumerate the major problems associated with conducting fiscal policy.

8. recognize how changes in marginal tax rates can affect the labor-leisure tradeoff, the saving-consumption decision, and the business investment decision.

9. distinguish among the three fiscal policy time lags.

CHAPTER OUTLINE

1. Fiscal policy is the discretionary changing of government expenditures and/or taxes in order to achieve such national economic goals as high employment and price stability.
   a. If a contractionary gap exists, then expansionary fiscal policy is in order; if government expenditures increase (lump-sum taxes fall) the aggregate demand curve shifts rightward and the contractionary gap can be eliminated, at a higher price level.
   b. If an expansionary gap exists, then contractionary fiscal policy is called for; if government expenditures decrease (lump-sum taxes increase) the aggregate demand curve shifts leftward and the expansionary gap can be eliminated, at a lower price level.
   c. If the economy is already operating on LRAS, shifts in the AD curve lead to *temporary* increases (decreases) in real GDP which are untenable because they are off LRAS; in the long run input owners revise their expectations upward (downward) and the SRAS curve shifts upward (downward); in the long run GDP will be at the LRAS level and the price level change will be greater than the change in the short run.

2. There are various effects that offset fiscal policy.
   a. Two indirect effects can possibly offset fiscal policy.
      i. If government expenditures are financed by borrowing (deficit spending) then the interest rate may rise, which will cause a reduction in (a) business investment and (b) household expenditures on such durable goods as housing and automobiles.
      ii. If households perceive deficit spending as an increase in their future tax liabilities, the Ricardian equivalence theorem predicts that they will save more, hence the AD curve may not shift at all: household current consumption falls by the amount that G rises.

b. A direct effect may also offset fiscal policy; to the extent that government expenditures compete with the private sector, then increases in G are offset by decreases in private investment.

c. The open economy effect may also offset fiscal policy; deficit spending may cause the interest rate to rise, which induces foreigners to purchase domestic U.S. assets, which causes the relative price of the domestic currency to rise; in turn net exports fall, which partially offsets an expansionary fiscal policy.

d. Supply side effects can result from fiscal policy effects of changing tax rates; changes in marginal tax rates may affect the labor-leisure tradeoff, the household saving-consumption decision, and business investment.

3. The recognition, action, and the effect time lags reduce the effectiveness of fiscal policy.

4. A progressive income tax and unemployment compensation are two examples of automatic, or built-in stabilizers; they are not discretionary, and they move the economy automatically toward high employment levels.

5. During normal times when there is not excessive unemployment or inflation, fiscal policy actions by the Congress have proven to be relatively ineffective—usually too little too late to help in minor recessions.

KEY TERMS

Recognition time lag
Action time lag

Effect time lag
Supply side economics

KEY CONCEPTS

Fiscal policy
Ricardian equivalence theorem
Automatic, or built-in, stabilizers

Crowding out effect
Direct expenditure effect

COMPLETION QUESTIONS
Fill in the blank or circle the correct term.

1. Discretionary fiscal policy is defined as a _____ change in taxes and/or government spending in order to change equilibrium national income and employment.

2. If a contractionary gap exists, it can be offset by (contractionary, expansionary) fiscal policy; such a policy entails (decreasing, increasing) government expenditures or (decreasing, increasing) taxes, which will cause the aggregate demand curve to shift (leftward, rightward); national output should (fall, rise) and the price level should (fall, rise).

3. If an expansionary gap exists, it can be eliminated if government expenditures (decrease, increase) or if taxes are (decreased, increased); this will cause the AD curve to shift (leftward, rightward) and national income will (fall, rise).

4. If the economy is *already* operating on its long run aggregate supply curve, then fiscal policy actions which shift the AD curve will cause real national income to change (temporarily, permanently) and the price level will change (more, less) in the long run, relative to the short run.

5. If government expenditures are financed by borrowing, a federal budget (deficit, surplus) will result, which may cause the interest rate to (fall, rise), which in turn will cause business investment and household consumption on (durable, nondurable) goods to (fall, rise); hence fiscal policy effects will be (reduced, increased).

6. If households perceive government deficit spending as an increase in their future tax liabilities, they may save (less, more) according to the _____ theorem; hence fiscal policy effects will be (reduced, increased).

7. To the extent that government expenditures compete with the private sector, then such expenditures will (induce more, discourage) business investment expenditures; hence fiscal policy effects of an increase in G will be (reduced, enlarged).

8. If U.S. deficit spending causes the U.S. interest rate to rise, foreigners will want to purchase U.S. _____, which will lead to a(n) (decrease, increase) in the international demand for the dollar; hence U.S. exports will (fall, rise) and U.S. imports will (fall, rise); hence the expansionary effects of an increase in G will be (reduced, enlarged) by this open economy effect.

9. Supply side effects can result from fiscal policy tax changes; if marginal tax rates rise this can induce laborers to substitute _____ for _____, and households might be induced to save (less, more) because the after tax return to saving will fall; because the after-tax return on investment will fall, we expect business to invest (less, more).

10. The super rich (do, do not) change their behavior when marginal tax rates change.

11. If government expenditures or taxes change over the business cycle without deliberate action taken by Congress, then this is referred to as automatic fiscal policy, or built-in _____; examples of automatic fiscal policy include _____ and _____; automatic fiscal policy (increases, decreases) the magnitude of business cycle fluctuations.

12. Discretionary fiscal policy is (easy, difficult) to conduct because it usually takes (little, much) time for Congress to enact such policy.

13. If the public perceives that deficit spending creates future tax liabilities, and if people wish to leave money to their heirs, then current saving may well (decrease, increase); hence the net effect of deficit spending on interest rates is (to lower them, to raise them, uncertain).

14. There are three time lags that hamper fiscal policy: _____, _____, and _____. The existence of time lags makes conducting fiscal policy (easier, harder) for policymakers.

15. Because of automatic stabilizers, when the economy is in an expansion phase government transfers (rise, fall) and tax revenues (rise, fall); hence expansions (other things constant) generate government budget (surpluses, deficits).

16. The existence of automatic stabilizers makes our economy (less, more) stable; they also make it (difficult, easy) to distinguish discretionary from automatic fiscal policy.

TRUE-FALSE QUESTIONS
Circle the **T** if the statement is true, the **F** if it is false. Explain to yourself why a statement is false.

T   F   1.   Fiscal policy may involve changes in taxes and/or government spending.

T   F   2.   If an expansionary gap exists, fiscal policy calls for increased G and/or reduced taxes.

T   F   3.   If a contractionary gap exists, proper fiscal policy requires a federal government budget surplus—or a larger surplus if one already exists.

T   F   4.   If an economy is already operating on its LRAS curve, an expansionary fiscal policy will, eventually, cause the price level to rise by less than it would if the economy had been operating at a SRAS curve.

T   F   5.   If government expenditures are financed by borrowing, a federal deficit is created which could cause interest rates to rise.

T   F   6.   If interest rates rise as a result of deficit spending, expansionary fiscal policy effects will be magnified.

T   F   7.   If interest rates rise as a result of deficit spending, then foreigners may want to purchase more assets in the U.S., which would cause the value of the U.S. dollar to rise on international exchange rate markets.

T   F   8.   If households perceive an increase in federal deficit spending as an increase in their future tax liabilities they may save more now, which would reduce the effects of expansionary fiscal policy.

T   F   9.   If government expenditures directly compete with the output of the private sector, then business investment will fall and tend to offset the effects of such a fiscal policy.

T   F   10.   Crowding out implies that if federal deficits cause interest rates to rise, businesses will reduce investments and this will tend to offset fiscal policy effects.

T   F   11.   Because of the time lags involved in fiscal policy, policymakers can more easily achieve national economic goals, because they have more time to solve the problem.

T   F   12.   If federal deficit spending causes interest rates to rise, households will purchase more consumer durables and businesses will invest more.

T   F   13.   If fiscal policy is pursued by raising marginal tax rates, laborers may choose to work less and businesses might choose to make fewer investments.

MULTIPLE CHOICE QUESTIONS
Circle the letter that corresponds to the best answer.

1.   Fiscal policy
     a.   deals with automatic stabilizers.
     b.   is relatively easy to conduct.
     c.   deals with discretionary actions by policymakers.
     d.   calls for stabilizing changes in the money supply.

2. If a contractionary gap exists, proper fiscal policy could entail
   a. increased government spending.
   b. decreased taxes.
   c. deficit spending.
   d. All of the above.

3. If government expenditures rise to counteract a contractionary gap
   a. the AD curve shifts rightward.
   b. the AD curve shifts leftward.
   c. taxes must rise to finance such expenditures.
   d. the price level will fall.

4. If an expansionary gap exists
   a. contractionary fiscal policy is called for.
   b. G should rise to cause the price level to fall.
   c. expansionary fiscal policy is called for.
   d. taxes should fall, to stimulate the economy.

5. If a contractionary gap exists, then
   a. the equilibrium income exceeds the full-employment income level.
   b. it can be filled by increases in G or decreases in taxes, or some combination of both.
   c. it can be filled by decreases in G or increases in taxes, or some combination of both.
   d. the economy is in an expansion phase.

6. If the economy is operating on its short-run aggregate supply curve and an expansionary gap exists
   a. a contractionary fiscal policy is called for.
   b. leftward shifts in AD that cause some unemployment will be helpful.
   c. contractionary fiscal policy will eventually change only the price level.
   d. All of the above

7. If an expansionary gap exists, it can most efficiently be eliminated by some combination of
   a. increases in G, decreases in taxes.
   b. decreases in G, decreases in taxes.
   c. decreases in G, increases in taxes.
   d. increases in G, increases in taxes.

8. Which of the following will **NOT** offset fiscal policy?
   a. the multiplier effect
   b. G financed by increased taxes
   c. G financed by borrowing (deficit spending)
   d. automatic stabilizers

9. Which of the following can offset an expansionary fiscal policy?
   a. higher interest rates resulting from deficit spending
   b. private investment falling in areas competing with government expenditures
   c. perceptions by households that larger deficits imply increased future tax liabilities
   d. All of the above

10. Which of the following may well result from higher interest rates brought on by deficit spending?
    a. increased purchases of consumer durable goods
    b. increased business investment
    c. a rising exchange rate for the domestic economy
    d. All of the above

11. If taxes fall, then
    a. the planned expenditures curve shifts downward.
    b. the aggregate demand curve shifts to the right.
    c. the aggregate supply curve shifts to the left.
    d. national income will fall.

12. If government expenditures exceed tax receipts then, other things being constant,
    a. a surplus exists.
    b. a balanced budget exists.
    c. a deficit exists.
    d. the economy must contract.

13. If marginal tax rates rise
    a. laborers may choose less income (work), which is taxed, and more leisure, which is not taxed.
    b. the tax base could shrink.
    c. productivity could fall eventually, as business investment falls.
    d. All of the above

14. Fiscal policy
    a. if discretionary, only involves changing taxes.
    b. is difficult to implement because of time lag problems
    c. if automatic, is destabilizing.
    d. All of the above

15. Choose the statement that is **NOT** true.
    a. Time lags make fiscal policy difficult.
    b. Fiscal policy is conducted solely by the executive branch of the U.S. government.
    c. Crowding out reduces the impact of an expansionary fiscal policy.
    d. The Ricardian equivalence theorem implies that fiscal policy may be quite ineffective.

MATCHING
Choose an item in Column (2) that best matches an item in Column (1).

(1)

a. stabilization policy
b. discretionary fiscal policy
c. automatic stabilizer
d. contractionary gap
e. expansionary gap
f. time lags
g. deficit spending

(2)

h. recognition, action, effect
i. change in tax law
j. tax receipts less than government spending
k. unemployment compensation
l. recession period
m. inflationary period
n. conscious attempt to achieve high employment and price stability

WORKING WITH GRAPHS

1.   Consider the graphs below, then answer the questions that follow.

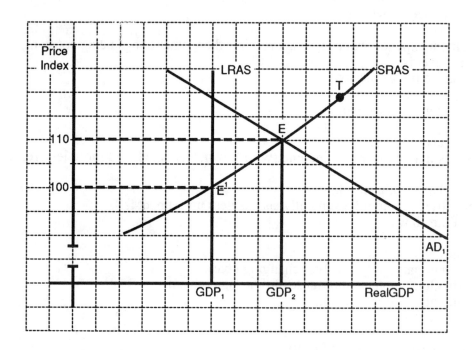

a.   What is the short-run equilibrium level of real GDP? What type of gap exists? Is this real income level sustainable?
b.   What type of fiscal policy would you recommend? Be specific.
c.   Continuing (b) above, you want the new AD curve to shift through what point?
d.   The long-run result of your fiscal policy is to cause what to happen to real GDP? To the price index?

2. Consider the graphs below, then answer the questions that follow.

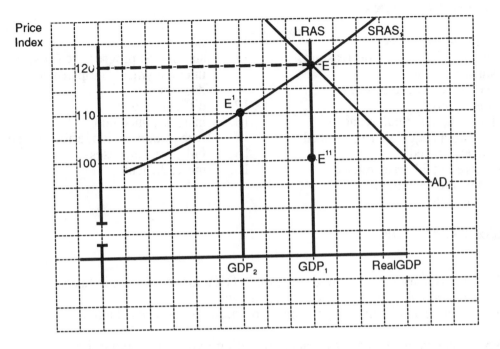

a. What is the short-run equilibrium level of real GDP? The long-run equilibrium level of real GDP? The short-run equilibrium price level?

b. Assume that it is desirable to get the short-run equilibrium price level to 110. What type of fiscal policy would you suggest? (Be specific) You want the new AD curve to come through what point? What will be the new short-run level of real GDP? Is this level sustainable? Why not?

c. Continuing (b) above, what will happen to the short-run aggregate supply curve? Why?

d. What will be the long-run level of real GDP?

CASE STUDY

In 1993, Bill Clinton was sworn in as president of the United States. In *his* perception at least, the economy was in a deep recession and something had to be done. He proposed a combination of tax increases and reductions in government spending. Is this what you would consider a proper fiscal policy in such circumstances? Why, or why not?

To be fair, it should be noted that President Clinton felt that the U.S. economy's woes were due to its high federal deficits and the accumulating public debt. To the extent that a reduction in such deficits will cause a reduction in interest rates and a perceived reduction in future tax liabilities by households—and given the fact that the economy was actually *growing* in 1993, is President Clinton's plan more plausible?

ANSWERS TO CHAPTER 13

COMPLETION QUESTIONS

1. deliberate, or conscious
2. expansionary; increasing; decreasing; rightward; rise, rise
3. decrease, increased; leftward, fall
4. temporarily; more
5. deficit; rise; durable; fall; reduced
6. more, Ricardian equivalence; reduced
7. discourage; reduced
8. assets; increase; fall; rise; reduced
9. leisure; income resulting from working; less; less
10. do
11. stabilizers; progressive tax structure, unemployment compensation; decreases
12. difficult; much
13. increase; uncertain
14. recognition, action, effect; harder
15. fall, rise; surpluses
16. more; difficult

TRUE-FALSE QUESTIONS

1. T
2. F   An expansionary gap calls for a decrease in G and/or an increase in taxes.
3. F   A contractionary gap calls for deficit spending.
4. F   No, the price level will change by more because output won't change.
5. T
6. F   No, higher interest rates will cause offsetting expenditure reductions in the private sector.
7. T
8. T
9. T
10. T
11. F   Time lags make fiscal policy more difficult because of the uncertainty they generate.
12. F   No, less of such expenditures will occur in response to a higher interest rate.
13. T

MULTIPLE CHOICE QUESTIONS

1.c;   2.d;   3.a;   4.a;   5.b;   6.d;   7.c;   8.a;   9.d;   10.c;
11.b;   12.c;   13.d;   14.b;   15.b.

MATCHING

a and n;   b and i;   c and k;   d and l;   e and m;   f and h;   g and j

WORKING WITH GRAPHS

1. a. GDP_2; expansionary gap; no, because it is above the full-employment level of real GDP
   b. Contractionary; Reduce G and or increases taxes.
   c. E'
   d. Fall to GDP_1; fall to 100

2. a. GDP$_1$; GDP$_1$; 120.
   b. Contractionary; reduce G, increase taxes; E'; GDP$_2$; No, because it is below the real GDP consistent with LRAS.
   c. It will shift downward (rightward) as factors of production become accustomed to the lower price level.
   d. GDP$_1$

CASE STUDY

The combination of increased taxes and decreased government expenditures makes no sense if the economy is in a recession. Because the economy *actually* was growing, such a policy would be less damaging. Moreover, to the extent that federal deficits actually do cause higher interest rates and household perception of future tax liabilities, such a policy makes some sense.

GLOSSARY TO CHAPTER 13

Action time lag The time required between recognizing an economic problem and putting policy into effect. While the action time lag is short for monetary policy, it is quite long for fiscal policy, which requires congressional approval.

Automatic, or built-in, stabilizers Tax systems, such as the progressive income tax, that cause changes in the economy with government action.

Crowding-out effect The tendency of expansionary fiscal policy to cause a decrease in planned investment or planned consumption in the private sector; this decrease results from the rise in interest rates.

Direct expenditure effects Actions taken by the private sector that offset fiscal policy actions.

Effect time lag The time that elapses between the onset of policy and the results of that policy.

Fiscal policy The discretionary changing of government expenditures and/or taxes in order to achieve national economic goals, such as high employment with price stability.

Recognition time lag The time required to gather information about the current state of the economy.

Ricardian equivalence theorem The proposition that an increase in the government budget deficit has no effect on aggregate demand.

Supply-side economics Generally applies to attempts at creating incentives for individuals and firms to increase productivity; explores the factors that cause the aggregate supply curve to shift.

CHAPTER 14

DEFICIT SPENDING AND THE PUBLIC DEBT

PUTTING THIS CHAPTER IN PERSPECTIVE

The federal government can finance its expenditures in *only* three ways: by taxing, by borrowing from the private sector, and by creating money. This chapter concentrates on the first two, and later chapters analyze the implications of the third.

Today, concern about the federal deficit has waned, because unexpectedly high tax receipts have reduced it or eliminated it. Be assured, though, that because of Medicare and Social Security spending, it will become an important issue again.

Whenever the deficit becomes an issue again, economists will debate whether it is correctly measured and whether it really creates a burden on future generations. The key point is to understand that some government expenditures are actually *investments* rather than provisions for current consumption. As a consequence, treating all G as if it is a consumption overstates government expenditures in the years in which such governmental investments are made.

Equally important, to the extent that the government generates a relatively high rate of return on such investments, future generations will not be burdened by inheriting a smaller capital stock. Furthermore, even if the public debt is owed to foreigners, future generations will benefit from such investments and be better able to pay the debt to foreigners.

We conclude, therefore, that we should really try to ascertain whether or not government investments are generating a high rate of return. Clearly, wasteful government expenditures could well leave future generations with an economic burden.

LEARNING OBJECTIVES

After you have studied this chapter you should be able to

1. define entitlement, operating budget, capital budget, public debt, gross public debt, and net public debt.

2. distinguish between the gross public debt and the net public debt.

3. distinguish between the federal budget deficit and the public debt.

4. list the three ways our federal government can finance its expenditures.

5.   distinguish between an operating budget and a capital budget, and recognize the importance of this distinction for the debate regarding the annual federal budget deficit.

6.   recognize how federal government deficits can contribute to trade deficits.

7.   list reasons for believing that our federal deficit is mismeasured.

8.   recognize the main issues in the debate as to whether current federal deficits burden future generations.

CHAPTER OUTLINE

1.   The federal government finances government expenditures in three ways: taxing, borrowing from the private sector, and creating money.

2.   Federal deficit spending results when government expenditures exceed tax revenues and the government borrows to finance the difference.

3.   The public debt is the total value of all outstanding federal government securities.
   a.   The net public debt equals the gross public debt minus all government interagency borrowing.
   b.   The ratio of annual interest payments on the public debt to national income has increased steadily since 1970; it has more than doubled since 1975.
   c.   Part of our net public debt is owned by foreigners. Foreign ownership of the public debt increased after 1970, fell in the 1980's, but is now over 38 percent.

4.   Deficit spending can impose a burden on future generations in two ways.
   a.   Unless national income grows dramatically too, future generations will have to be taxed at a higher rate to retire the debt.
   b.   To the extent that current government expenditures on consumption goods crowds out private investment, future generations will inherit a smaller capital stock (reduced wealth).

5.   To the extent that we owe our public debt to ourselves, *all* members of future generations need not be burdened; some will be better off and others will be worse off, but as a *group* they can't be worse off.

6.   To the extent that government expenditures are made on investment goods, then if the rate of return on such investments is sufficiently high, future generations need not be burdened with a reduced capital stock or a lesser ability to pay foreigners who own our debt.

7.   If the economy is operating at a level substantially below full employment, crowding out need not occur and deficit spending need not place a burden on future generations.

8.   There have been various proposals to decrease the U.S. federal deficit.
   a.   Increasing taxes could, in principle, eliminate the deficit but this method would raise taxes substantially at current spending levels; hence it is not politically wise to do so; taxing the "rich" simply would not generate anywhere near the amount of tax revenues to do the job.
   b.   Reducing expenditures, especially on entitlements (which currently represent 50 percent of the federal budget outlay) would help; this method is not politically feasible either.

    c.   A balanced budget amendment has been proposed to decrease our deficit; past proposals have not been effective and such an act would merely increase the amount of "off budget" expenditures.

9.   Empirical evidence implies that a linkage may exist between our nation's federal deficits and its international trade deficit.

10.   Theoretically, higher budget deficits cause higher domestic interest rates, which in turn induces foreigners to purchase our federal (and private) debt; hence foreigners may substitute purchases of our debt for purchases of our export goods, thereby contributing to a trade deficit.

11.   Some economists maintain that we are incorrectly measuring the deficit and, consequently, overstating its importance.
    a.   Businesses typically develop an operating budget and a capital budget.
    b.   Because our federal deficit figures do not separate expenditures for current operations from investment-type outlays (i.e. we don't have a capital budget) we overstate current spending on capital goods in the year in which they are purchased—and overstate the deficit.
    c.   There are many budget deficit estimates; each is calculated differently and none gives a complete picture of the "true" deficit.
    d.   Some deficits do not fully indicate our federal government's future liabilities in such areas as military (and civilian!) pension plans, and the savings and loan bailout.

KEY TERMS

Entitlement
Public debt

Gross public debt
Net public debt

COMPLETION QUESTIONS
Circle the correct term or fill in the blank.

1.   The federal government can finance its expenditures in three ways: _____, _____, and _____.

2.   If government expenditures exceed its tax revenues a federal _____ exists; if such an excess is financed by borrowing from the private sector, then we say that _____ spending has occurred, and the _____ debt will (fall, rise).

3.   The net public debt subtracts out all government _____ borrowing, hence it is more relevant than the gross public debt.

4.   The ratio of annual interest payments on the public debt to national income has (doubled, tripled, quadrupled) since 1975; since 1978 the percent of our public debt owned by foreigners has (decreased, increased) somewhat.

5.   Current deficit spending can burden future generations if they must be taxed at (lower, higher) rates to retire the debt; they can also be burdened if crowding out leaves them with a smaller _____ stock, which will reduce their wealth.

6.   To the extent that we owe our public debt to ourselves, future generations, as a *group*, (will, will not) be burdened, because some members of future generations will inherit the securities sold by the government to finance the debt.

7. To the extent that current government expenditures are made on (investment, consumption) goods that yield a relatively high return, future generations will inherit a (smaller, larger) capital stock and a higher income from which they can pay the public debt.

8. Crowding out is less likely to occur if deficit spending is made when the economy is operating at (low, high) levels of unemployment.

9. Various proposals to decrease our federal deficit include increased _____, decreased _____, especially on _____, and a _____ amendment. The latter could lead to an increase in _____-budget spending.

10. A linkage may exist between our nation's federal deficits and its _____ deficit; federal deficits may cause domestic interest rates to rise, which induces foreigners to substitute purchases of our federal _____ for purchases of our exports. Other things constant a trade _____ will emerge.

11. Some economists maintain that we incorrectly measure our federal deficits. We overestimate true current government expenditures because we do not use a _____ budget; we underestimate the magnitude of our deficits because we do not account for such future federal government liabilities as _____.

TRUE-FALSE QUESTIONS
Circle the **T** if the statement is true, the **F** if it is false. Explain to yourself why a statement is false.

T F 1. Our federal government can finance its expenditures by taxing, borrowing, or by creating money.

T F 2. Federal deficits emerge if the government borrows from other domestic federal agencies to finance its expenditures.

T F 3. When the federal deficit is increased, the public debt rises.

T F 4. The deficit is a stock concept, while the public debt is a flow concept.

T F 5. It is not politically feasible to finance all of our government expenditures through taxation.

T F 6. A balanced budget amendment will probably reduce the number of off-budget government expenditures.

T F 7. If federal deficits are owed to foreigners, future domestic residents must be burdened economically.

T F 8. If federal budget deficits cause interest rates to rise, crowding out results.

T F 9. Federal budget deficits can cause trade deficits.

T F 10. To the extent that our measure of the current deficit ignores future government liabilities, it overstates our true deficit.

T F 11. If we do not devise a capital budget, then government expenditures on investment goods overstate the true current deficit.

T F 12.   Future generations need not be burdened if deficit spending is used to finance investment projects that have relatively high rates of return.

T F 13.   If we owe the public debt to ourselves, then future generations will be burdened.

MULTIPLE CHOICE QUESTIONS
Circle the letter that corresponds to the best answer.

1.   Our federal government can finance its expenditures by
    a.   borrowing from our other government agencies.
    b.   running trade deficits.
    c.   taxing.
    d.   All of the above

2.   When the federal government finances its deficit by borrowing
    a.   the public debt rises.
    b.   the money supply rises.
    c.   taxes must rise.
    d.   the public debt falls.

3.   The following has been proposed to eliminate the deficit:
    a.   raise taxes.
    b.   reduce government expenditures on entitlements.
    c.   pass a balanced budget amendment.
    d.   All of the above

4.   Which of the following will probably **NOT** occur if the federal deficit rises?
    a.   Interest rates will fall.
    b.   Foreigners will wish to purchase our debt.
    c.   Foreigners will tend to import less of our goods.
    d.   U.S. exports will fall.

5.   Which of the following is factually correct?
    a.   Empirical evidence shows that federal budget deficits have been associated with growing trade deficits.
    b.   Since 1970, the percent of our public debt owed to foreigners has decreased.
    c.   The ratio of tax revenues to GDP has increased dramatically since 1975.
    d.   The U.S. federal deficit is very high as compared to that of other developed nations.

6.   The public debt
    a.   is the value of all borrowing in the U.S.
    b.   is a flow concept.
    c.   is the total value of all outstanding federal governmental securities.
    d.   falls as deficit spending increases.

7.   Deficit spending could impose a burden on future generations if
    a.   people realize that the public debt is a future tax liability.
    b.   government expenditures are made on investment goods instead of consumption goods.
    c.   crowding out reduces our capital stock.
    d.   All of the above

8. If government deficits are financed by borrowing from the private sector or borrowing from foreigners
    a. the public debt rises.
    b. U.S. trade deficits could arise.
    c. future tax liabilities may increase for existing households.
    d. All of the above

9. If federal deficits increase during periods of high unemployment
    a. the unemployment rate will probably rise.
    b. crowding out need not occur.
    c. interest rates will probably fall.
    d. the public debt will fall.

10. If people realize that the public debt is a future tax liability, then deficit spending will
    a. induce more households to save more.
    b. burden future generations.
    c. cause crowding out to occur.
    d. lead to higher interest rates.

11. If our federal government deficits are large, then
    a. trade surpluses arise.
    b. interest rates will fall, as inflation results.
    c. foreigners may purchase our deficit debt and fewer of our goods and services.
    d. our public debt must burden future generations.

MATCHING
Choose an item in Column (2) that best matches an item in Column (1).

(1)	(2)
a. crowding out	g. result of higher interest rates
b. flow	h. guaranteed governmental benefits
c. trade deficits	i. subtraction of interagency debt
d. entitlement	j. substitution of assets for imports
e. net public debt	k. value of outstanding government securities
f. public debt	l. federal deficit

CASE STUDY

Suppose you learn that Mrs. Stone owed $5,000 two years ago, and now owes $10,000. Can you conclude that she is worse off today than she was two years ago? No, because her *income* might have more than doubled, and/or her *assets* might have increased by more than $5,000, so that her net worth actually increased.

This example is constructive because it points out that you must have a complete financial picture of an individual, or you can reach fallacious conclusions. Can we make an analogy to conclusions regarding U.S. budget deficits? Do so. What information would we need to determine if increased U.S. budget deficits imply that the U.S. is becoming financially insolvent?

ANSWERS TO CHAPTER 14

COMPLETION QUESTIONS

1. taxing, borrowing from the private sector, creating money
2. budget deficit; deficit; public; rise
3. intragency
4. doubled; decreased
5. higher; capital
6. will not
7. investment; larger
8. high
9. taxation; expenditures; entitlements; balanced budget; off
10. trade; debt securities; deficit
11. capital; private and public pensions;

TRUE-FALSE QUESTIONS

1. T
2. F   No, borrowing from the private sector (or foreign governments) is required.
3. T
4. F   The deficit is a flow concept, it is calculated between two points in time; the public debt is a stock concept, it is calculated at a specific point in time.
5. T
6. F   A balanced budget amendment would *increase* the amount of off-budget expenditures.
7. F   Not if government expenditures are made on investment goods that yield a relatively high rate of return.
8. T
9. T
10. F   It *under*states the true deficit.
11. T
12. T
13. F   Some members of future generations will be burdened, others will not, therefore one cannot say the whole generation is burdened.

MULTIPLE CHOICE QUESTIONS

1.c;   2.a;   3.d;   4.a;   5.a;   6.c;   7.c;   8.d;   9.b;   10.a;
11.c.

MATCHING

a and g;   b and l;   c and j;   d and h;   e and i;   f and k

CASE STUDY

The analogy is worth considering. Hence it is the *ratio* of government deficits to *national income* that matters—not just the size of the deficits. And, really, what we would like to know is what is happening to the United States' net worth—which is the difference between the value of all of its assets (land holdings, capital stock, gold, etc.) and the value of its liabilities (including the future liabilities mentioned in the text). What is happening to the *ratio* of our public debt to our net worth is what is really crucial. Alas, such information is not easily obtained.

GLOSSARY TO CHAPTER 14

Entitlements   The rights to guaranteed benefits under a governmental program such as Social Security or unemployment compensation.

Gross public debt   All federal government debt irrespective of who owns it.

Net public debt   Gross public debt minus all government interagency borrowings.

Public debt   The total value of all outstanding federal government securities.

CHAPTER 15

MONEY AND THE BANKING SYSTEM

PUTTING THIS CHAPTER INTO PERSPECTIVE

Chapter 15 is the first chapter in Part Five: Money, Monetary Policy, and Stabilization. Until now, we have analyzed how the equilibrium level of real national income and employment are determined in the short run and how fiscal policy can be used to eliminate contractionary gaps and expansionary gaps.

The aim of Chapter 15 is to introduce you to the concepts essential to an explanation of where money fits into macroeconomics—the main goal of Part Five. Chapter 15 explains that money is that good or "thing" that performs the essential functions of money, namely, a medium of exchange, a unit of accounting, a store of value, and a standard of deferred payment. And Chapter 15 distinguishes between the two basic approaches to measuring money: the transactions approach (M1) and the liquidity approach (M2). Each approach stresses a different function of money and a different point of view as to the role that money plays in the economy.

In order for policymakers to achieve such national economic goals as full employment, price stability, economic growth, and an equilibrium in the international balance of payments, it is necessary that they fully understand how the banking system operates and how it is influenced by the central bank—the Federal Reserve System. This is what Chapter 15 attempts to do.

This chapter introduces a lot of new terms, and you should resist the temptation to memorize. Unless you are advised differently by your teacher, you should try merely to understand the main distinctions between M1 and M2. Each component in M1 is a medium of exchange; each can be used *directly* to purchase goods and services. Each item in M2 (which includes all the items in M1) has liquidity as a distinguishing feature; each item in M2 can be converted easily into other assets without loss of nominal value and with small transaction costs. In other words, the *nominal* value of M2 items is not subject to capital losses (or gains); as changes occur in the economy, M2 items maintain their nominal (but not necessarily real) values.

Keep in mind that the two methods reflect differing approaches as to the essential feature of money. The M1 approach views money as a medium of exchange; if money is essentially a medium of exchange, then as the money supply rises or falls we should expect total expenditures to rise and fall respectively.

On the other hand, the M2 approach maintains that the essential feature of money is that it is the most liquid asset. People hold a variety of assets in their asset portfolios and reach an equilibrium when they have an optimal amount of money and other (less liquid) assets. When this equilibrium is disturbed as a result of changes in the money supply, their asset portfolios become "too liquid" or "too illiquid" and their behavior changes in a predictable way.

Thus M1 and M2 reflect different theories of the essential nature of money and therefore two different theories about how changes in the supply of money affect the macroeconomy. In general, however, they predict similar results, as other chapters demonstrate.

LEARNING OBJECTIVES

After you have studied this chapter you should be able to

1. define currency, liquidity, fiduciary monetary system, M1, M2, barter, near monies, depository institutions, central bank, Fed, financial intermediation, financial intermediary, assets, liabilities, commercial bank, and thrift institutions.

2. list the four functions of money.

3. list three advantages of a money system over a barter system.

4. rank assets according to their liquidity.

5. distinguish between the transactions approach and the liquidity approach to measuring money.

6. list the components of M1.

7. recognize the two main reasons that people accept the dollar as money in the United States.

8. enumerate and recognize the six functions of the Federal Reserve System.

9. match specific financial intermediaries with their probable asset/liability characteristics.

CHAPTER OUTLINE

1. There are four traditional functions of money; money is that "thing" that serves these four functions.
    a. Money is a *medium of exchange*; money is that for which people exchange their productive services or that which they give for goods and services.
    b. Money is a unit of accounting; the monetary unit is used to value goods and services relative to each other.
    c. Money acts as a *store of value*; money is an asset that is a convenient store of generalized purchasing power.
    d. Money is a standard of deferred payment; money is used to pay future obligations or debts.

2. *Liquidity* is the degree to which an asset can be acquired or disposed of without loss in terms of nominal value and with small transactions costs.
    a. Money is the most liquid of all assets.
    b. Different goods have served as money throughout history.

3. Today the United States is on a *fiduciary monetary system*.
    a. The dollar is money in the United States because it is acceptable by virtually everyone in exchange for goods and services.

b. Another reason the dollar is money in the United States is because it has predictability of value in the future.

4. There are two basic approaches to measuring the money supply.
   a. The *transactions approach* to measuring money—M1—stresses that the essence of money is that it is a medium of exchange.
      i. M1 includes *currency*—monetary coins and paper money.
      ii. M1 also includes checkable deposits (accounts on which people can write checks).
      iii. M1 also includes the value of traveler's checks issued by non-bank institutions.
   b. Although credit cards seem to act as a medium of exchange, they are not really money.
   c. The *liquidity approach* to measuring money—M2—stresses that money is a highly liquid asset; such assets have an unchanging *nominal* value.
      i. M2 includes all the items in M1.
      ii. M2 also includes savings deposits in all depository institutions.
      iii. M2 also includes statement savings deposits, passbook savings accounts, time deposits (small-denomination and savings certificates), money market deposit accounts, overnight repurchase agreements at commercial banks, overnight Eurodollars, and retail money market mutual fund balances.

5. The current U.S. banking structure has evolved into a complex phenomenon that includes a central bank (the Fed), *commercial banks*, *thrift institutions*, and other *depository institutions* of recent vintage.

6. Financial institutions act as financial intermediaries; that is, they perform the function of transferring funds from savers to investors.

7. The Federal Reserve System, the *central bank* of the United States, was established in 1913 to counter the periodic financial panics that had occurred.
   a. The Fed organizational chart shows a Board of Governors, 12 Federal Reserve district banks having 25 branches, and a Federal Open Market Committee that determines Fed policy actions.
   b. Commercial banks and other depository institutions are required by the Fed to keep a certain percentage of their deposits on reserve with Fed district banks.

8. There are seven major functions performed by the Fed.
   a. It supplies the country with fiduciary currency.
   b. It provides a system of check collection and clearing.
   c. It holds depository institutions' reserves.
   d. It acts as the government's fiscal agent.
   e. It supervises member banks.
   f. It acts as a lender of last resort.
   g. It regulates the money supply, which is its most important function.

KEY TERMS

Money market deposit accounts	Repurchase agreement	Eurodollar deposits
Commercial bank	Central bank	Thrift institution
M1	The Fed	Assets
M2	Financial intermediaries	Liabilities
Depository institutions	Transactions accounts	Money supply
Checkable deposits	Certificate of deposit	Traveler's checks
Savings deposits	Money market mutual funds	Time deposit

KEY CONCEPTS

Liquidity	Liquidity approach	Unit of accounting
Fiduciary monetary system	Barter	Store of value
Money	Transactions approach	Standard of deferred
Near monies	Medium of exchange	payment
Financial intermediation		

COMPLETION QUESTIONS
Fill in the blank or circle the correct term.

1.   Because money is accepted for goods and services, it is used as a _____; it also performs the functions of _____, _____, and a _____.

2.   _____ is the most liquid of all assets, because it maintains its (nominal, real) value.

3.   For an exchange to take place in a barter economy, a _____ coincidence of wants must exist; when a money system replaces a barter economy, specialization (decreases, increases) transaction costs.

4.   The opportunity cost of holding money is foregone _____ earnings; the benefit to holding money is increased _____.

5.   The United States is on a _____ monetary system, which means the dollar is backed by (gold, faith that it can be exchanged for goods); items are used as money because of their _____ and _____ of value.

6.   M1 is the _____ approach to measuring money; M1 includes _____, _____, and _____; each can be used to make _____.

7.   M2 is the _____ approach to measuring money; M2 components are characterized by high _____ because they maintain their nominal value.

8.   The U.S. central bank is the _____; it was established in 1913 to counter the financial _____ that occurred periodically.

9.   Depository institutions include commercial banks, _____, _____, and _____; depository institutions are required to keep a certain percentage of their _____ on reserve with Federal Reserve district banks.

10. The Fed has seven major functions: it _____, _____, _____, _____, _____, _____ and _____; the Fed's most important function is _____.

11. When inflation occurs, the price level (rises, falls), and the value of a unit of money (rises, falls).

12. Financial intermediaries perform the function of transferring household _____ to business _____.

TRUE-FALSE QUESTIONS
Circle the **T** if the statement is true, the **F** if it is false. Explain to yourself why a statement is false.

T F 1. Exchange in a money economy requires a double coincidence of wants.

T F 2. In a money economy, specialization is encouraged and transaction costs fall, relative to a barter economy.

T F 3. An asset is liquid if it can be disposed of at a low transaction cost without loss of nominal value.

T F 4. There is no opportunity cost to holding money, because it is the most liquid of all assets.

T F 5. M1 and M2 are the same thing.

T F 6. Barter economies are more efficient than money economies.

T F 7. In the United States the dollar is backed by gold and silver.

T F 8. Currency and transactions accounts are money because of their acceptability and their predictability of value.

T F 9. E-cash eliminates currency and coins and works through the Internet.

T F 10. The components of M1 are less liquid than the components of M2.

T F 11. The components of M2 all are used as a medium of exchange.

T F 12. Credit cards are officially counted in M2.

T F 13. The value of M2 always exceeds the value of M1.

T F 14. The Fed requires depository institutions to hold a certain percentage of their deposits on reserve.

T F 15. Currency is the highest percentage of M1.

T F 16. The Fed's most important function is to supply the economy with fiduciary currency.

T F 17. The Fed is prohibited from being a lender of last resort.

T F 18. When the price level falls, the value of money rises.

T F 19. Financial intermediation is the process of transforming business investments into household saving.

MULTIPLE CHOICE QUESTIONS
Circle the letter that corresponds to the best answer.

1. Which of the following is a function of money?
   a. medium of exchange
   b. unit of accounting
   c. store of value
   d. All of the above

2. Which is **NOT** considered money?
   a. checkable deposits
   b. traveler's checks issued by nonbanks
   c. credit cards
   d. currency

3. Which of the following is a characteristic of M2?
   a. high liquidity
   b. medium of exchange
   c. significant changes in nominal value
   d. real value does not vary during inflationary periods

4. Which of the following is an advantage of money over barter?
   a. permits more specialization of labor
   b. does not require a double coincidence of wants
   c. reduces transaction and storage costs
   d. All of the above

5. Which of the following assets are probably the least liquid?
   a. savings account balances
   b. shares of stock in a major corporation
   c. office buildings
   d. automobiles

6. Which of the following is most **UNLIKE** the others?
   a. currency
   b. passbook savings account
   c. checking accounts
   d. traveler's checks issued by nonbanks

7. Which of the following is **NOT** a component of M1?
   a. savings deposits
   b. nonbank traveler's checks
   c. currency
   d. All of the above

8. Regarding U.S. financial institutions,
   a. they are becoming less similar.
   b. the distinctions among them are becoming blurred.
   c. very few changes have occurred since the 1970s.
   d. they all have pretty much the same composition of assets and liabilities.

9. Which of the following is not a part of M1?
   a. nonbank traveler's checks
   b. credit card limits
   c. currency
   d. checkable deposits

10. Which of the following is a depository institution?
    a. commercial bank
    b. savings and loan association
    c. credit union
    d. All of the above

11. *Analogy*: M1 is to the transactions approach as M2 is to the _____.
    a. unit of accounting approach
    b. liquidity approach
    c. barter approach
    d. medium of exchange approach

12. Which of the following is the most important function of the Fed?
    a. It regulates the money supply.
    b. It supervises member banks.
    c. It supplies the economy with fiduciary currency.
    d. It holds depository institutions' reserves.

13. Barter
    a. increases specialization of labor.
    b. makes money less useful.
    c. increases transaction costs.
    d. eliminates the need for a double coincidence of wants.

14. Near monies
    a. are used as a medium of exchange.
    b. are highly liquid.
    c. include currency and demand deposits.
    d. All of the above

15. Under a fiduciary monetary standard, money is backed by
    a. gold.
    b. public faith that money can be exchanged for goods and services.
    c. precious metals that can be exchanged for goods and services.
    d. the Treasury's assets.

16. Currency
    a. is not a component of M2.
    b. earns no interest.
    c. is illiquid.
    d. cannot be used in transactions.

MATCHING
Choose the item in Column (2) that best matches an item in Column (1).

(1)	(2)
a. M1	f. ease of conversion into money
b. M2	g. checkable deposit
c. currency	h. coins and paper money
d. bank liability	i. transactions approach
e. liquidity	j. liquidity approach

PROBLEMS

1. Below you are given hypothetical figures in billions of dollars for various items relating to the supply of money.

Currency	226.6
Checkable deposits	567.0
Money market mutual fund shares	329.1
Small-denomination time deposits	1,141.2
Overnight repurchase agreements & Eurodollars	81.6
Traveler's checks	7.6
Savings deposits	413.7
Money market deposit accounts	489.3

    a.   Find the value of M1.
    b.   Find the value of M2.

CASE STUDY

In the late 1970s and in the 1980s a number of financial innovations seem to have blurred the distinction between M1—the transactions concept of money—and other assets. At least a portion of the funds in the interest-bearing transactions accounts under M1 represent *savings*. Consequently it may no longer be possible to view M1 as a measure of pure *transactions* balances.

Moreover, some portions of M2, such as money market funds, allow (limited) check-writing privileges. This means that some portions of M2, which are not included in M1, are in fact transactions accounts. In short, some of M1 is non-transaction-related and some transaction-related accounts are not included in M1.

1. If financial innovations induce people to move money from one account into another (seeking higher after-tax, risk-adjusted rates of return), can the meaning of M1 and M2 change?

2. If your answer to (a) above is yes, is it possible to get changes in the money measures, even though nothing essential is happening?

3. What are the consequences of yes answers to (a) and (b) above, with respect to measurement and money-supply control?

ANSWERS TO CHAPTER 15

COMPLETION QUESTIONS

1. medium of exchange; unit of accounting, store of value, standard of deferred payment
2. money, nominal
3. double; decreases
4. interest; liquidity
5. fiduciary; faith that it can be exchanged for goods; acceptability, predictability
6. transactions; currency, checkable deposits, traveler's checks; transactions
7. liquidity; liquidity
8. Fed; panics
9. savings and loans associations, credit unions, mutual savings banks; total deposits
10. supplies fiduciary currency, performs check clearing and collection, holds reserves of depository institutions, acts as the government's fiscal agent, supervises member banks, lender of last resort; the regulation of the money supply
11. rises, falls
12. saving, investors

TRUE-FALSE QUESTIONS

1. F That statement is true for a barter economy.
2. T
3. T
4. F The opportunity cost of holding money is foregone interest.
5. F M2 includes non-checkable deposits (near monies).
6. F Barter economies require a double coincidence of wants and they limit opportunities for specialization.
7. F The U.S. is on a fiduciary monetary standard.
8. T
9. T
10. F They are more liquid.
11. F They are all highly liquid, but some are not a medium of exchange.
12. F Credit cards, by definition, are not a part of M2.
13. T
14. T
15. F Checkable deposits are.
16. F Its most important function is to regulate the money supply.
17. F That is a *function* of the Fed's.
18. T
19. F It is the process of transferring household saving to business investment.

MULTIPLE CHOICE QUESTIONS

1.d;   2.c;   3.a;   4.d;   5.c;   6.b;   7.a;   8.b;   9.b;   10.d;
11.b;   12.a;   13.c;   14.b;   15.b;   16.b

MATCHING

a and i; b and j; c and h; d and g; e and f

PROBLEMS

1. a. M1 = $801.2 billion
   b. M2 = $3,256.1 billion

CASE STUDY

1. yes
2. yes
3. Measurement becomes more difficult, and so does control.

GLOSSARY TO CHAPTER 15

Assets That which is owned; those things to which a business or household holds legal claim.

Barter The direct exchange of goods and services for other goods and services without the use of money.

Central bank   A banker's bank, usually an official institution that also serves as a country's treasuries bank. Central banks normally regulate commercial banks.

Certificate of deposit   A time deposit with a fixed maturity date offered by banks and other financial institutions.

Checkable deposits   Any deposits in a thrift institution or a commercial bank on which a check may be written.

Commercial bank Business firms that are chartered by a government agency to engage in the banking business and to accept demand deposits and make commercial loans.

Depository institutions Financial institutions that accept deposits from savers and lend those deposits out at interest.

Eurodollar deposits   Deposits denominated in U.S. dollars but held in banks outside the United States, often in overseas branches of U.S. banks.

Fiduciary monetary system   A system in which currency is issued by the government, and its value is based uniquely on the public's faith that the currency represents command over goods and services.

Financial intermediaries Those institutions that play the role of intermediaries between ultimate lenders (savers) and ultimate borrowers.

Financial intermediation The process by which financial institutions accept savings from households and lend the savings to businesses and other households.

Liabilities That which is owed; the legal claims against a business or household by non-owners.

Liquidity The degree to which an asset can be converted into another asset without loss of nominal value.

Liquidity approach   A method of measuring the money supply by looking at money as a temporary store of value.

M1 The total value of currency plus checkable deposits in commercial banks and other checking accounts in thrift institutions, as well as traveler's checks not issued by banks.

M2 M1 plus (a) savings and small-denomination time deposits at all depository institutions; (b) overnight repurchase agreements at commercial banks; (c) overnight Eurodollars issued to U.S. residents by foreign branches of U.S. banks worldwide; (d) balances in money market mutual funds; and (e) retail money market deposit accounts (MMDAs).

Medium of exchange   Any asset that sellers will accept as payment.

Money   Anything that is universally accepted as a medium of exchange.

Money market deposit accounts   Accounts issued by banks yielding a market rate of interest with a minimum balance requirement and a limit on transactions. They have no minimum maturity.

Money market mutual funds   Funds of investment companies that obtain funds from the public that are held in common and used to acquire short maturity credit instruments, such as certificates of deposit and securities sold by the U.S. government.

Money supply   The amount of money in circulation. There are numerous ways of defining the money supply.

Near monies   Assets that are almost money. They have a high degree of liquidity, they can be easily converted into money without loss in value. Time deposits and short-term U.S. government securities are examples.

Repurchase agreement (REPO)   An agreement made by a bank to sell treasury or federal agency securities to its customers, coupled with an agreement to repurchase them at a price that includes the accumulated interest.

Savings deposits   Funds that can be withdrawn at any time without payment of a penalty, but still earn interest.

Standard of deferred payment   An essential property of money which makes it desirable to use as a means of settling debts that mature in the future.

Store of value   The ability of an item to hold value over time; a necessary property of money.

The Fed   The Federal Reserve System; the central bank of the United States.

Thrift institutions   Financial institutions that receive most of their funds from the savings of the public; they include credit unions, mutual savings banks, and savings and loan associations.

Time deposit   A deposit in a financial institution that, in principle, requires a notice of intent to withdraw or must be left for an agreed- upon period. Withdrawal of funds prior to the end of the agreed-upon period can result in a penalty payment.

Transactions accounts   Checking account balances in commercial banks and other types of financial institutions, such as credit unions and savings banks; any accounts in financial institutions on which you can easily write checks without many restrictions.

Transactions approach   A method of measuring the money supply by looking at money as a medium of exchange.

Traveler's checks   Financial instruments purchased from a bank or a non-banking organization that can be used as cash upon a second signature by the purchaser.

Unit of accounting A measure by which prices are expressed; the common denomination of the price system; a central property of money.

CHAPTER 16

MONEY CREATION AND DEPOSIT INSURANCE

PUTTING THIS CHAPTER INTO PERSPECTIVE

Stabilization policy is one of the important roles of the government. In Chapter 13 fiscal policy was analyzed, and Chapter 15 explored the structure of the banking system, the essence and the functions of money, and how money is measured. Before we can analyze the other major stabilization tool, monetary policy, we must study how banks create money (to be more specific, checkable deposits). That is precisely the main objective of Chapter 16: to explain how the Fed and the depository institutions together determine and change the money supply.

To explain how depository institutions operate and how the money expansion process works, we employ a convenient tool—the balance sheet. (If you have taken a course in accounting, you will recognize our balance sheet as a simplified balance sheet; it is a stock concept.) Be sure to note the distinction between balance sheets that show the overall position of a bank and those that deal with *changes* in individual items in the balance sheet; also be sure to concentrate on the checkable deposit entry and reserves (especially excess reserves).

The essence of deposit creation is that when total bank (read: depository institution) reserves rise, individual banks will acquire excess reserves and will have an incentive to make loans—because reserves earn no interest for banks. Banks lend by creating checking accounts for borrowers, and checking accounts, as was pointed out in Chapter 15, are a part of the money supply.

A second major objective in Chapter 16 is to analyze the determinants of the money multiplier. When the Fed buys or sells T-bills (short-term Treasury securities) on the open market, via open-market operations, the money supply will change by a multiple of the value of the T-bill. The reciprocal of the required reserve ratio defines the *maximum* money multiplier. The *actual* money multiplier depends on the extent to which banks are prepared to hold excess reserves and the extent to which the public wishes to hold currency instead of transactions accounts. In the unlikely case that banks hold zero excess reserves and there are no currency drains during the money creation process, the actual money multiplier will be equal to the maximum money multiplier.

A third objective is to show that the Federal deposit insurance system that insures depository institutions is flawed and how that system has contributed to the crisis in the depository institutions industry. The concepts of asymmetric information, adverse selection, and moral hazard are employed to do exactly that.

LEARNING OBJECTIVES

After you have studied this chapter you should be able to

1. define money multiplier, fractional reserve system, total reserves, legal reserves, required reserve ratio, legal reserves, required reserves, excess reserves, balance sheet, open market operations, discount rate, federal funds market, federal funds rate, asymmetric information, adverse selection, and moral hazard.

2. distinguish among legal, required, and excess reserves.

3. calculate required reserves given total reserves and the required reserve ratio.

4. recognize from a balance sheet whether a bank is in a position to make new loans.

5. distinguish between the situations in which a bank receives a deposit written on another bank and one written on the Fed.

6. show, using balance-sheet accounts, what happens when the Fed engages in open-market operations.

7. calculate the maximum money multiplier, given the required reserve ratio.

8. recognize forces that reduce the money multiplier.

9. distinguish among the three ways in which the Fed changes the money supply.

10. recognize flaws in the deposit insurance system, and understand how such flaws contribute to depository institution risk-taking; and relate the behavior of the main characters in the S&L crisis to the concepts of adverse selection and moral hazard.

CHAPTER OUTLINE

1. Changes in money supply growth are linked to changes in economic growth, to the inflation rate, and to the business cycle.

2. The Federal Reserve and depository institutions together determine the total money supply in the United States, which has a fractional reserve banking system.

3. Depository institutions are required to maintain a specified percentage of their customer deposits as reserves.
   a. *Legal reserves* constitute what depository institutions are allowed by law to claim as reserves; today that consists of deposits held at Fed district banks and vault cash.
   b. *Required reserves* are the minimum amount of legal reserves that a depository institution must hold in reserve; they are expressed as a ratio of required reserves to total deposits.
   c. *Excess reserves* are the difference between actual (total) legal reserves and required reserves.

4. A balance sheet indicates the relationship between reserves and total deposits in a depository institution.
   a. When a bank receives a deposit drawn on another bank, its total reserves rise by the amount of the deposit; and its excess reserves rise also; the bank lends an amount equal to its excess reserves by creating a checkable account.

b. The total money supply is unaffected, however, because the bank on which the deposit was drawn will lose an equal number of deposits—and excess reserves—so no net change in total reserves results, and therefore the total money supply is not altered.

5. The Fed can affect the level of reserves in the banking system; therefore, it can change the money supply by a multiple of its transactions.
   a. *Open-market operations* are the buying and selling of U.S. government securities, on the open market, by the Fed.
   b. If the Fed purchases a $100,000 U.S. government security from a bond dealer, it pays for the security by writing a check on itself; when the bond dealer deposits the check, this becomes a bank liability *and* a bank asset/reserve; the bank's excess reserves rise and no other bank's reserves fall; banking system total reserves rise.

6. If the Fed sells a $100,000 U.S. government security to a bond dealer on the open market, the bond dealer pays for it by check, and the Fed reduces the reserves of that bank, while no other bank's reserves have increased; the net effect is a reduction in the banking system's total reserves.

7. When total banking system reserves change, the money supply will change by a multiple of the reserve change.
   a. If the Fed purchases a $100,000 government security, total banking system reserves rise and the money supply will rise by a multiple of $100,000.
   b. Continuing this example, if the required reserve ratio is 20 percent, then total new deposits will equal $500,000.
   c. A financial transaction must increase (decrease) total banking system reserves in order for a multiple expansion (contraction) to occur.

8. The maximum money multiplier equals the reciprocal of the required reserve ratio; the actual change in the money supply equals the *actual* money multiplier times the change in total reserves.
   a. There are two major forces that reduce the *money multiplier*.
      i. Currency drains reduce the money multiplier.
      ii. If depository institutions hold excess reserves, the actual money multiplier will be less than the maximum.
   b. The M1 multiplier has varied from about 2.5 to about 3.5 since 1960; the M2 multiplier has increased steadily over that period, from about 6.5 to over 12.

9. There are three ways in which the Fed can change the money supply: through open market operations, by changing the discount rate, and by changing reserve requirements.

10. Federal deposit insurance was created during the Great Depression in order to prevent bank runs.
    a. There have been three major flaws in the deposit insurance system: the insurance price has been too low, and the rate charged has been the same for all institutions, regardless of the riskiness of an institution's portfolio, and the system insures deposits, not depositors.
    b. Those flaws have encouraged managers of depository institutions to assume greater risk than they would otherwise; a moral hazard exists for such managers.
    c. The adverse selection problem also exists; knowing that depositors have little or no incentive to monitor bank manager decisions, people willing to engage in fraudulent and risky behavior are attracted to this industry.
    d. Both the moral hazard problem and the adverse selection problem result from asymmetric information.
    e. Increased risk-taking, in conjunction with adverse economic circumstances, led to large numbers of depository institution failures and governmentally forced mergers.

KEY TERMS

Reserves	Required reserve ratio	Open market operations
Legal reserves	Excess reserves	Discount rate
Required reserves	Balance sheet	Federal funds market
Asset	Liability	Net worth

KEY CONCEPTS

Money expansion multiplier	Federal funds rate	Moral hazard
Fractional reserve banking system	Asymmetric information	Adverse selection
Money multiplier process	Federal deposit insurance (FDIC)	Bank run

COMPLETION QUESTIONS
Fill in the blank or circle the correct term.

1. There is a strong link between growth in the _____ and economic growth, the inflation rate, and the business cycle.

2. Total transactions deposits are determined by the Federal Reserve and _____ institutions.

3. Predecessors to modern-day banks were _____ and money-lenders who had secure vaults and who eventually realized that at any given time only a small _____ of total deposits left with them were withdrawn; this was the beginning of _____ banking.

4. Legal reserves constitute anything that depository institutions are permitted by law to claim as such; today legal reserves include _____ and _____.

5. Required reserves are the (minimum, maximum) amount of legal reserves that a depository institution must hold; the required reserve ratio is the ratio of required reserves to _____; excess reserves equal _____ minus _____.

6. When an individual bank has zero excess reserves it (can, cannot) extend more loans; when an individual bank receives a new deposit, its total reserves (fall, rise) by the amount of the deposit and its excess reserves (fall, rise). That bank can now increase its lending by the size of _____.

7. If Bank A receives a deposit that is a check written on Bank B, then Bank A's excess reserves will (rise, fall) and Bank B's will _____; overall banking system excess reserves will (rise, fall, remain unaltered); the total money supply will _____.

8. Assume the Fed purchases a $1 million security on the open market from a bond dealer who deposits it in Bank A. Bank A's total reserves rise by $_____ and its excess reserves rise by a fraction of that amount; as a result of this transaction other banks find that their reserves are (decreased, unaltered, increased); the money supply has (decreased, remained constant, increased).

9. If the Fed sells a $1 million security on the open market, total banking system reserves will (fall, rise), and the _____ will contract by a multiple of $1 million.

10. If the required reserve ratio is 10 percent, then the maximum money multiplier equals _____; the actual money multiplier will be less than the maximum due to _____ and _____.

11. If Mr. Calvo deposits a $200 check in Bank A, the $200 increase in Mr. Calvo's checking account is a(n) (asset, liability) of Bank A; Bank A's (assets, liabilities) will also rise by $200 because Bank A's reserves rise by that amount.

12. The Federal deposit insurance system was created during the _____; it was instituted to prevent bank _____.

13. The Federal deposit insurance system has three flaws: the rate charged to depository institutions has been too (low, high), each depository institution has been charged (the same, a different) rate, and the system insures (deposits, depositors).

14. Because individual depository institutions don't pay rates that reflect the riskiness of their portfolios, Federal deposit insurance (encourages, discourages) risk-taking by depository institutions.

15. Both the moral hazard problem and the adverse selection problem stem from a(n) _____ of information. The moral hazard problem results because one party to the transaction has superior information (before, after) the transaction, while the adverse selection problem results because one party has superior information (before, after) the transaction.

16. Our deposit insurance system encourages depositors to (ignore, monitor closely) the loan portfolio of depository institutions, hence bank managers have an incentive to take on (less, more) risk and the _____ problem results.

17. Our deposit insurance system encourages depositors to (ignore, monitor closely) the behavior of bank owners and bank managers. Hence people who are willing to take excessive risk or people who are willing to engage in fraudulent behavior are (discouraged from, encouraged to) enter(ing) the banking industry, and the _____ problem results.

TRUE-FALSE QUESTIONS
Circle the **T** if the statement is true, the **F** if it is false. Explain to yourself why a statement is false.

T F   1. Together, the Fed and depository institutions determine the total money supply.

T F   2. Early goldsmiths discovered that at any given time only a small percentage of people who left gold with them for safekeeping asked for their gold.

T F   3. Legal reserves equal required reserves plus excess reserves.

T F   4. Today legal reserves include only vault cash for banks.

T F   5. Total deposits multiplied by the required reserve ratio equals excess reserves.

T F   6. If an individual bank has excess reserves, it can make loans.

T F   7. When a depository institution makes a loan, it creates checkable deposits.

T F 8.   When Mr. Plick deposits a $1000 check in his checkable account in Bank A, Bank A's assets and liabilities each rise by $1000.

T F 9.   The Fed pays interest to depository institutions that hold reserves with Federal Reserve district banks.

T F 10. Depository institutions have an incentive to minimize their excess reserves.

T F 11. If a financial transaction increases total reserves in the banking system, the money supply will rise.

T F 12. The actual money multiplier will equal the maximum money multiplier, if banks hold excess reserves.

T F 13. When people receive checks they deposit the whole check; they never withdraw part in currency.

T F 14. The Fed can cause an increase in the money supply by lowering the required reserve ratio.

T F 15. A money multiplier exists due to a fractional reserve system.

T F 16. The maximum money multiplier equals the reciprocal of the marginal propensity to save.

T F 17. Federal deposit insurance rates have not varied with the riskiness of a depository institution's portfolio.

T F 18. If the government subsidizes failing banks, bank managers have less incentive to avoid risk or to be efficient.

T F 19. There is a link between the inflation rate and the rate of growth of the money supply.

T F 20. The adverse selection problem implies that if depositors have little or no incentive to monitor bank behavior, so some unscrupulous people will attempt to perform banking services.

T F 21. The adverse selection problem, but not the moral hazard problem, stems from an asymmetric information situation.

T F 22. The moral hazard problem results from asymmetric information that exists before a transaction.

MULTIPLE CHOICE QUESTIONS
Circle the letter that corresponds to the best answer.

1.   Under a fractional reserve system, depository institutions
    a.   cannot keep 100 percent of their deposits on reserve.
    b.   must keep 100 percent of their deposits on reserve.
    c.   are required to keep a certain percentage of their total deposits on reserve.
    d.   cannot hold excess reserves.

2. Early goldsmiths and moneylenders
    a. charged a fee for providing safekeeping for valuables deposited with them.
    b. were the original bankers.
    c. discovered that they could lend out depositors' gold at interest, because only a fraction of gold deposits were requested at any given time.
    d. All of the above

3. If depository institutions were not required to hold reserves,
    a. they would not hold any reserves.
    b. the Fed would have less control over the money supply.
    c. monetary control would be easier for the Fed.
    d. they would hold 100 percent of their deposits on reserve.

4. Today in the United States depository institution legal reserves include
    a. vault cash and deposits at Federal Reserve district banks.
    b. U.S. government securities.
    c. gold.
    d. All of the above

5. Which of the following is most **UNLIKE** the others?
    a. flow
    b. stock
    c. wealth
    d. balance sheet

6. *Analogy*: the required reserve ratio is to the money multiplier as the _____ is to the national income multiplier.
    a. balance sheet
    b. excess reserve
    c. bond dealer
    d. marginal propensity to save

7. If the Fed purchases $1 million worth of T-bills on the open market, and the required reserve ratio is 10 percent, then
    a. the money supply will increase by $10 million, at a minimum.
    b. the money supply will decrease by $10 million.
    c. the money supply will increase by $10 million, at a maximum.
    d. the money supply will increase by $5 million, at a maximum.

8. If the Fed raises the required reserve ratio from 10 percent to 20 percent, then the maximum money multiplier
    a. will rise from 5 to 10.
    b. will fall from 10 to 5.
    c. is unaffected.
    d. cannot be calculated, due to leakages.

9. In the United States excess reserves
    a. earn interest.
    b. always equal zero.
    c. must be positive before lending can occur.
    d. All of the above

10. Legal reserves minus required reserves equal
    a. the required reserve ratio.
    b. actual reserves.
    c. vault cash plus deposits at Fed District Banks.
    d. excess reserves.

11. Which of the following will increase total reserves in the banking system?
    a. Mr. Patullo deposits a check in Bank A, drawn on Bank B.
    b. The Fed sells a security to Mrs. Damson.
    c. Mr. Farano sells a security to the Fed and deposits the check he receives in Bank C.
    d. Mr. Capano withdraws $100 from his checking account.

12. When Mr. McKay deposits a $1000 check in Bank A,
    a. Bank A's reserves (assets) rise by $1000.
    b. Mr. McKay's deposit is an additional liability for Bank A.
    c. Bank A's excess reserves rise and it can increase its lending.
    d. All of the above

13. If Bank B has negative excess reserves, then it
    a. is meeting its reserve requirements.
    b. will call in loans and not relend as old loans are paid off.
    c. must increase its lending.
    d. must shut down.

14. If the required reserve ratio is 10 percent and the Fed sells a $10,000 security on the open market, the money supply will
    a. rise by $10,000 at a minimum.
    b. rise by $100,000 at a maximum.
    c. fall by $100,000 at a maximum.
    d. fall by $10,000.

15. If the required reserve ratio is 10 percent, then
    a. the actual money multiplier is 10.
    b. the maximum money multiplier is 10.
    c. the national income multiplier is 10.
    d. excess reserves equal 0.

16. The actual change in the money supply equals the actual money multiplier
    a. times the change in reserves.
    b. plus the change in reserves.
    c. times the change in excess reserves.
    d. plus the change in excess reserves.

17. Deposit insurance
    a. is unnecessary in a fractional reserve system.
    b. helps to prevent bank runs.
    c. implies that the government should subsidize failing banks.
    d. decreases depository institution risk-taking under the current system.

18. As it now operates, the Federal deposit insurance system
    a. subsidizes depository institutions.
    b. charges the same insurance rate to all banks (currently zero for most).
    c. encourages depository institutions to assume more risk.
    d. All of the above

19. Asymmetry of information that occurs
    a. before a transaction could lead to a moral hazard problem.
    b. after a transaction could lead to an adverse selection problem.
    c. before a transaction could lead to an adverse selection problem.
    d. presents no economic problem.

20. The moral hazard problem implies that
    a. asymmetry of information exists.
    b. unscrupulous people have an incentive to own and operate banks.
    c. asymmetry of information existed before a transaction.
    d. All of the above

21. Which of the following is an example of adverse selection?
    a. Unhealthy people wish to obtain group health insurance.
    b. Unscrupulous people wish to occupy jobs that are difficult to monitor.
    c. People with cancer wish to buy insurance from companies that don't require a health examination.
    d. All of the above

MATCHING
Choose an item in Column (2) that best matches an item in Column (1).

(1)	(2)
a. money multiplier	e. moral hazard
b. asymmetry of information	f. 10 maximum money multiplier
c. required reserve ratio	g. reciprocal of required reserve ratio
d. 10 percent required reserve ratio	h. ratio of required reserves to total deposits

PROBLEMS

1. The following table contains several different required reserve ratios that might be imposed on depository institutions. In column 2, calculate the maximum money multiplier for each of the figures given in column 1. In column 3, calculate the maximum amount by which a single depository institution can increase its loans for each dollar's worth of excess reserves on deposit. In column 4, calculate the amount by which the entire banking system can increase deposits for each dollar of excess reserves in the system.

1	2	3	4
12 1/2%	_____	_____	_____
16 2/3%	_____	_____	_____
20%	_____	_____	_____
30%	_____	_____	_____
33 1/3%	_____	_____	_____

2. Below you are given a series of bank balance sheets. Assume that each case presented is independent. Use the information given to post the changes that would result from the specified action in each case. Show reductions using a minus sign and additions with a plus sign.

	Assets	Liabilities
A. A small business writes a check to pay back a $2000 loan from the same bank.	Reserves: Loans & Securities:	Demand Deposits:
B. The bank makes a $500 loan to you and credits your checking account.	Reserves Loans & Securities:	Demand Deposits:
C. The bank sells $500 in Treasury Bills to the Fed to make up a reserve deficiency.	Reserves: Loans & Securities:	Demand Deposits:
D. You cash a $25 check (at your bank) for date money.	Reserves: Loans & Securities:	Demand Deposits:

3. Suppose you have the balance sheets for three banks, as given in the table below. Assume that the reserve requirement is 20 percent. Then:
   a. Compute the required reserves and place these in row A.
   b. Compute the excess reserves and place these in row B.
   c. Compute the amount of new loans each bank can extend in a multibank system and place these in row C.
   d. Compute the amount of new loans each bank could extend if each were a monopoly bank and place these in row D (Note: This is equivalent to viewing each of the balance sheets below as the balance sheet for the entire banking system.)

Assets	1	2	3
Reserves	$ 5,000	$ 6,000	$ 6,000
Loans	10,000	10,000	10,000
Securities	5,000	6,000	7,000
Liabilities			
Demand deposits	17,500	20,000	18,000
Net worth	2,500	2,000	5,000

	1	2	3
A. Required Reserves	_____	_____	_____
B. Excess Reserves	_____	_____	_____
C. New Loans (single bank)	_____	_____	_____
D. New Loans (monopoly bank, i.e, all banks in the system)	_____	_____	_____

4. Assume a 5 percent required reserve ratio, zero excess reserves, no cash drain, and a ready loan demand. The Fed buys a $1 million T-bill from a depository institution.
   a. What is the maximum money multiplier?
   b. By how much will total deposits rise?

5. The Fed purchases a $1 million T-bill from Mr. Mondrone, who deposits it in Bank 1. Using T-accounts, show the immediate effects of this transaction of the Fed and Bank 1.

6. Continuing the example from problem 5:
   a. Indicate Bank 1's position more precisely using a balance sheet account, if required reserves equal 5 percent of demand deposits.
   b. By how much can Bank 1 increase its lending?

7. Suppose you are the president of a small commercial bank. You have recently hired a new loan officer with little experience. Your bank is "loaned up" —in other words, you have no excess reserves. Your new loan officer comes to you very excited and explains that one of your customers has just deposited $5000 in the bank, so he just approved an auto loan for another customer who was at his desk when the new deposit was made. The loan was for $5000. Can you explain to your new employee why this loan might get the bank into difficulty?

8. In contrast with question 7, suppose your bank holds a monopoly of all commercial banking services in the United States and simply has branches that serve various parts of the country. If the reserve requirement is 20 percent, how much of the $5000 deposit can you safely lend? Explain your answer.

CASE STUDY

The fundamental problem facing depository institutions is that they accept deposit liabilities that are convertible into currency at a one-to-one exchange rate on demand. You and I, as depositors, extend credit to depository institutions (in the form of our deposits) and we expect to get every penny back when we want it. Because such deposits are the major components of the money supply, the United States is on, essentially, a credit-based money system. Because banks are subject to runs, the system may be unstable; hence (some say) the need for federal deposit insurance and the resulting problems analyzed in the text.

Recently some economists have advocated replacing the credit-based money system with money market mutual fund (MMMF) accounts; owners of such accounts are *part owners* of the funds' assets. Thus, MMMF money is *equity* based—not credit based. If the MMMF overall portfolio decreases in value, each shareholder *immediately* absorbs his share of the loss: there is, therefore, no incentive to cash in shares, and no runs or panics will result. Even if shareholders do withdraw, they merely withdraw their own—now reduced in value—share of the fund's portfolio.

1. Are MMMF's run-proof? Why, or why not?

2. In light of the fact that depository institutions offer subsidized deposit insurance, are MMMF's at a competitive disadvantage?

3. Because the MMMF's can only offer, by law, limited checking privileges to shareholders, are MMMF's at a competitive disadvantage?

4. If the disadvantages in (b) and (c) are eliminated, will MMMF's become the dominant component of the money supply?

ANSWERS TO CHAPTER 16

COMPLETION QUESTIONS

1. money supply
2. depository
3. goldsmiths; fraction; fractional reserve
4. vault cash; reserves at Federal Reserve district banks
5. minimum; total deposits; actual (total) legal reserves; required reserves
6. cannot; rise; rise; its excess reserves
7. rise, fall; remain unaltered; remain constant
8. $1 million; unaltered; increased
9. fall, money supply
10. 10; cash drains; excess reserves
11. liability; assets
12. 1930s Great Depression; runs
13. low, the same, deposits
14. encourages
15. asymmetry; after; before
16. ignore, more; moral hazard
17. ignore; encouraged to; adverse selection

TRUE-FALSE QUESTIONS

1. T
2. T
3. T
4. F Deposits held at Federal Reserve district banks also count as legal reserves.
5. F That product equals required reserves.
6. T
7. T
8. T
9. F Reserves do not earn interest.
10. T
11. T
12. F Excess reserves lower the actual money multiplier.
13. F They often withdraw cash.
14. T
15. T
16. F It equals the reciprocal of the required reserve ratio.
17. T
18. T
19. T
20. T
21. F Both result from asymmetric information.
22. F For the moral hazard problem, the asymmetric information exists *after* the transaction.

MULTIPLE CHOICE QUESTIONS

1.c; 2.d; 3.b; 4.a; 5.a; 6.d; 7.c; 8.b; 9.c; 10.d;
11.c; 12.d; 13.b; 14.c; 15.b; 16.a; 17.b; 18.d; 19.c; 20.a;
21.d

MATCHING

a and g; b and e; c and h; d and f

PROBLEMS

1. column 2: $8, 6, 5, 3 1/3, 3;   column 3: $1, 1, 1, 1, 1
   column 4: $8, 6, 5, 3 1/3, 3

2.

Assets	Liabilities
Reserves: 0	Demand Deposits: -$2000
Loans & Securities: -$2000	

Assets	Liabilities
Reserves: 0	Demand Deposits: +$500
Loans & Securities: +$500	

Assets	Liabilities
Reserves: +$500	Demand Deposits: 0
Loans & Securities: -$500	

Assets	Liabilities
Reserves: -$25	Demand Deposits: -$25
Loans & Securities: 0	

3. a. Required reserves: $3500, $4000, $3600
   b. Excess reserves: $1500, $2000, $2400
   c. New Loans: $1500, $2000, $2400
   d. New Loans: $7500, $10,000, $12,000

4. a. 20   b. $20 million

5.

The Fed		Bank 1	
Assets	Liabilities	Assets	Liabilities
+$1,000,000 U.S. gov. securities	+$1,000,000 depository institution reserves	+$1,000,000 reserves	+$1,000,000 demand deposits owned by Mr. Mondrone

6. a.

Bank 1

Assets		Liabilities	
Total reserves	+$1,000,000	Demand deposits	+$1,000,000
Required reserves + (50,000)			
Excess reserves + ($950,000)			
Total	+$1,000,000	Total	+$1,000,000

   b. $950,000

7. In order to illustrate the effects of our eager loan officer's actions, we may look at our bank's balance sheet. Initially, we can see no problems, as shown by the balance sheet below, after the new deposit and the loan.

Hometown Bank

Assets		Liabilities	
		Demand Deposits	
Reserves	+ $5,000	Depositors	+ $5,000
Loans	+ 5,000	Borrower	+ 5,000
Total	+ 10,000		+ 10,000

The demand deposits have been broken down by source so we can see more clearly what happens. As the balance sheet now stands, both reserves and demand deposits have increased by $5000 as a result of the deposit, and no problems occur.

Presumably, the borrower wishes to purchase a car with the $5000 loan. As a result, the borrower will probably write a check to the auto dealer. If the auto dealer uses another bank to hold its deposits, then after the auto purchase and the check clearing, our bank's balance sheet would appear as below.

Hometown Bank

Assets		Liabilities	
		Demand Deposits	
Reserves	$ 0	Depositor	+ $5,000
Loans	+ 5,000	Borrower	0
Total	+ 5,000		+ 5,000

Since we were told in the question that the bank was "loaned up," we can see from the balance sheet that our bank now has no reserves with which to cover the latest demand deposits. Indeed, our eager loan officer has put our bank in a position of a reserve deficiency. Our bank must obtain reserves to meet the legal reserve requirement. This may be done by borrowing reserves, liquidating loans, or by not relending as old loans mature.

8. If our bank were the only commercial bank in the United States, it would then be possible for our loan officer to make the $5000 loan without putting our bank into a deficient reserve position. This is true because if our bank were the only bank, any loans made and spent would wind up back in our bank as deposits of those who had received payments for which the loans were made. This action would not draw down our reserves to a deficient level. Therefore this monopoly bank can safely lend $20,000.

CASE STUDY

1   Yes. Because shareholders bear no default risk; they are owners of the funds and their shares rise and fall in value immediately, as the market value of the fund's portfolio changes.

2. Yes. If depository institutions had to pay the full cost of their deposit insurance, their costs would rise relative to the MMMF's which (typically) do not buy deposit insurance (because it is unnecessary).

3. Yes. By law MMMF's can offer only limited checking, which limits their usefulness to depositors.
4. The answer is probably yes, but this is an empirical—not a theoretical—question.

GLOSSARY TO CHAPTER 16

Adverse selection   A problem resulting from asymmetric information that exists before a transaction.

Asset Anything of value that is owned.

Asymmetric information   An imbalance of information that exists between two parties in a transaction.

Balance sheet   A statement of the assets and liabilities of a business entity.

Bank runs   Attempts by many of a bank's depositors to exchange deposits for cash.

Discount rate   The interest rate that the Federal Reserve charges for reserves that it lends to depository institutions.   It is sometimes referred to as the rediscount rate or, in Canada and England, as the bank rate.

Excess reserves   The difference between legal reserves and required reserves.

Federal Deposit Insurance Corporation (FDIC)   A government agency that insures the deposits held in member banks; all members of the Fed and other banks that qualify can join.

Federal funds market   A private market (made up mostly of banks) in which banks can borrow reserves from other banks that want to lend them.   Federal funds are usually lent for overnight use.

Federal funds rate   The interest rate that depository institutions pay to borrow reserves in the interbank federal funds market.

Fractional reserve banking system   A system of banking whereby member banks keep only a fraction of their deposits on reserve.

Legal reserves   Those reserves that depository institutions are allowed by law to claim as reserves—for example, deposits held at district Federal Reserve banks and vault cash.

Liability Anything that is owed.

Money multiplier   The reciprocal of the required reserve ratio, assuming no leakages into currency and no excess reserves.   It is equal to 1/required reserve ratio.

Money multiplier process   The process by which an injection of "new" money into the banking system leads to a multiple expansion in the total money stock.

Moral hazard   A problem resulting from asymmetric information that exists after a transaction.

Net worth The difference between assets and liabilities.

Open market operations The buying and selling of existing U.S. government securities (such as bonds) in the open private market by the Federal Reserve System.

Required reserve ratio The percentage of total reserves that the Fed requires depository institutions to hold in the form of vault cash or in a reserve account with the Fed.

Required reserves The value of reserves that a depository institution must hold in the form of vault cash or in a reserve account with the Fed.

Reserves In the U.S. Federal Reserve System, deposits held by district Federal Reserve banks for depository institutions, plus depository institutions' vault cash.

CHAPTER 17

MONETARY POLICY

PUTTING THIS CHAPTER INTO PERSPECTIVE

Chapter 17 explores the ins and outs of monetary policy which, you will recall, is the changing of the money supply by the Fed in order to attain such national economic goals as high employment, price level stability, economic growth, and an equilibrium in the international balance of payments. To add to this perspective, you may further recall that an important function of government is to stabilize the economy, and monetary policy and fiscal policy are the two major stabilization tools.

This chapter explains how the three main tools of monetary policy—open market operations (OMO's), changes in the discount rate, and changes in reserve requirements—can change the money supply.

In order to conduct monetary policy, the first step is to have a model, or theory, of how changes in the money supply actually affect such macro-economic variables as the interest rate, national income, and national output. Chapter 17 first shows how money "fits in" the macroeconomy by analyzing three models: the crude quantity theory of money and price, the Keynesian model, and the monetarist model. You should try to explain to yourself how, starting from equilibrium, a change in the money supply affects changes in the economy in each model.

In the crude quantity theory of money and price, an increase in the money supply leads to increased spending (velocity is constant); because full employment is assumed (predicted), this increased spending leads to an increase in the price level; in turn this induces people to hold more money to fulfill the transactions and the precautionary motives. The price level continues to rise until the community wants to hold the, now larger, money supply. Given the economy's tendency toward full employment anyway, monetary policy is rather unnecessary.

According to Keynesians, money fits in as follows: (a) the supply of money and the demand for money determine the interest rate; (b) given profit expectations, the interest rate determines the rate of net investment spending (and helps to determine spending on consumer durables); and (c) given the consumption function and G and X, we add investment spending to determine the total planned expenditures curve, or the location of the AD curve.

Now, how does *monetary policy* work? According to Keynesians, the transmission mechanism, or chain of causality, is as follows: (a) a change in the money supply, given the demand for money, changes the interest rate; (b) given profit expectations, a change in the interest rate changes autonomous investment spending; (c) a change in autonomous investment spending, other things being constant, shifts the aggregate demand curve and leads to a change in the equilibrium level of real national income; (d) a change in real national income leads to a change in employment, in the short run.

According to the monetarists, households arrange their wealth portfolio, of which money is one component, according to desired liquidity, desired risk, comparable rates of return, and so on. When the money supply is increased via monetary policy, people are induced to exchange bonds for money because the Fed offers higher prices for bonds; this in turn reduces interest rates *and* increases the degree of liquidity in the community's portfolio. In turn, people may respond to each of these changes by purchasing durable consumer goods.

After you have the big picture of how money fits in and how monetary policy works, then you can concentrate on some of the ins and outs of monetary policy. Should the Fed target interest rates or the monetary stock (M1 or M2)? Should the Fed follow a monetary rule or use its discretion? These are interesting and important questions.

This is a very important chapter, one that is full of information and theory. If you allocate more time to mastering it, you will be in a good position to master macroeconomics. After all, much of what you have learned to this point is also in this chapter--or lurking in the background.

LEARNING OBJECTIVES

After you have studied this chapter you should be able to

1. define transactions demand, precautionary demand, asset demand, monetarism, monetary rule, monetary policy targets, and income velocity of money.

2. list the three reasons for holding money and recognize the main determinant of each.

3. enumerate the three main tools of monetary policy and show an understanding of how they work.

4. determine what happens to the price of a bond when the market interest rate changes.

5. recognize how changes in the money supply affect interest rates, investment spending, equilibrium real national income, and employment in the Keynesian model, and recognize how monetary policy works in the aggregate supply/aggregate demand model and in the equation of exchange approach.

6. use the equation of exchange to determine what happens to the price level when the money supply changes.

7. recognize the main tenets of the monetarist school and evaluate reasons why they favor a monetary rule.

8. list problems involved in the conduct of monetary policy.

9. recognize the main issues involved in setting interest rate versus money supply targets.

10. recognize specific disagreements between the monetarists and the Keynesians.

11. predict the effect on the price level when the supply of money changes relative to the demand for money.

CHAPTER OUTLINE

1. Monetary policy is the Fed's changing of the money supply (or the rate at which it grows) in order to achieve national economic goals.

2. People want to hold money (hence we analyze the demand for money) in order to make foreseen transactions (the transactions demand for money), to make unforeseen expenditures and meet emergencies (precautionary demand for money), and to have a store of value (asset demand for money).
    a. The opportunity cost of holding money is foregone interest earnings.
    b. The demand curve for money is negatively sloped because there is a tradeoff between the benefits to holding money and the costs of holding money; in short, as the (opportunity) cost of holding money rises at higher interest rates, people want to hold less money.

3. When the money supply is increased there is a direct and an indirect effect on the economy.
    a. Money supply increases (decreases) directly lead people to spend more (less) because they now have an excess (a shortage) of money balances.
    b. Not all of the excess balances will be spent on goods and services; some excess balances will be used to purchase interest-earning assets, which will cause the interest rate to fall; thus, indirectly, spending will increase on business investment and on consumer durables.
    c. In the real world the money supply usually rises regularly; hence, policy deals with changes in the rate of growth of the money supply.

4. In the long run the higher price level that results from a rightward shift in the AD curve (due to an increase in the money supply) will generate an upward shift in the SRAS curve; ultimately the economy will operate on the LRAS curve, at a higher price level.

5. The Fed has three tools at its disposal when it conducts monetary policy.
    a. Open market operations (OMO) occur when the Fed buys (sells) bonds in order to increase (decrease) the money supply.
        i.   In order to induce people to buy (sell) bonds the Fed must offer them at a higher (lower) price; changes in bond prices lead to opposite direction changes in interest rates.
        ii. When the Fed purchases (sells) bonds on the open market depository institution reserves rise (fall) and such institutions increase (decrease) their lending by creating (destroying) deposits—money.
    b. The Fed can change the discount rate on loans to depository institutions; a lower (higher) discount rate induces depository institutions to borrow more (less) from the Fed which increases (decreases) the institutions reserves and leads to more (less) lending and an increase (decrease) in the money supply.
    c. Although it does so infrequently, when the Fed changes the reserve requirement of depository institutions it creates or reduces excess reserves, which ultimately changes the money supply, or the rate at which it grows.

6. An expansionary monetary policy, if it reduces interest rates, will cause net exports to rise—an effect which is the opposite to an expansionary fiscal policy (which may cause interest rates to rise).

7. An abundance of empirical evidence, and economic theory, suggests that if the supply of money is consistently increased relative to the demand for money, the relative price of money will fall continuously—inflation will ensue.

8. The demand for money consists of several components.
   a. People desire to hold money for the transactions motive
   b. People desire to hold money for the precautionary motive.
   c. People desire to hold money for the asset motive.
      i. The total demand for money curve is negatively sloped.
      ii. The equilibrium interest rate is where the total demand for money curve intersects the money supply curve; at any other interest rate a surplus or a shortage of money exists.
      iii. In this model, a change in the money supply (given the demand for money) changes the interest rate, which changes autonomous investment spending, which shifts the planned expenditures curve, which changes national income by the multiplier effect.
   d. Monetarism is the modern quantity theory of money.
      i. The tenets of monetarism are: significant money supply changes lead to significant price level changes in the same direction; money supply changes affect national output and employment only in the short-run, but affect only the price level in the long run; fiscal policy is ineffective; the monetary time lags are long and variable, which makes monetary policy difficult to conduct; policymakers should follow a monetary rule instead of using their own discretion.
      ii. In this model, money supply changes upset the community's equilibrium regarding its wealth portfolio; people substitute among bonds, money, equities, and durable goods as the Fed changes the money supply.

9. Some policymakers wish to conduct monetary policy by selecting and meeting interest rate targets, while others wish to attain money stock growth targets.
   a. The Fed cannot, in a meaningful way, target interest rates and the money supply at the same time.
   b. In general, if the demand for money is relatively stable, the Fed should target the money supply; if the demand for money is less stable than private and public expenditures, then the Fed should target interest rates.

KEY TERMS

Asset demand   Precautionary demand
Transactions motive   Demand for money

KEY CONCEPTS

Monetary rule   Equation of exchange
Crude quantity theory of money and price   Income velocity of money
Monetarists

COMPLETION QUESTIONS
Fill in the blank or circle the correct term.

1. The Fed (can, cannot) control the supply of money, but it (can, cannot) control the demand for money.

2. The _____ theory of money and price predicts that changes in the price level are determined by changes in the quantity of money in circulation.

3. If the supply of money rises relative to its demand, the price level will (rise, fall) and the value of a unit of money will (rise, fall).

4. The number of times, on average, that each monetary unit is spent on final goods and services is called the _____.

5. In crude quantity theory of money model, in the long run national output (will, will not) be at full employment, and velocity (is, is not) constant; hence if the money supply doubles, the price level will _____.

6. People hold money for three motives: _____-_____, _____, and _____.

7. The transactions demand for money varies (directly, inversely) with nominal national income; the asset demand for money varies (directly, inversely) with the interest rate.

8. When the interest rate rises, bond prices (rise, fall); when bond prices rise, the interest rate _____; the opportunity cost of holding money is foregone _____.

9. In the Keynesian model, a fall in the interest rate causes autonomous net investment to (rise, fall), which in turn causes the aggregate demand curve to shift (rightward, leftward); then _____ and employment will rise.

10 If the current interest rate is below the equilibrium rate, an excess _____ exists and the community will attempt to (buy, sell) bonds, thereby forcing the price of bonds _____ and the interest rate _____.

11. Monetarists maintain that full employment is normal in the long run. They believe the following: that the income velocity of money (is, is not) stable; that changes in the money supply lead to changes in the price level in the (same, opposite) direction; that money supply changes affect _____ and _____ in the short run; but that in the long run only the _____ is affected by money supply changes.

12. Monetarist critics of the Fed (do, do not) want the Fed to pursue discretionary monetary policy; they want the Fed to follow a _____.

13. The three main tools the Fed employs to conduct monetary policy are _____, _____, and _____.

14. When the Fed buys bonds on the open market the price of bonds tends to (fall, rise) and the interest rate (falls, rises); also bank reserves (fall, rise) which leads to a(n) (decrease, increase) in bank lending; ultimately the money supply (falls, rises).

15. If the Fed raises the discount rate this will (discourage, encourage) bank borrowing from it and maybe (decrease, increase) bank reserves which leads to a(n) (decrease, increase) in bank deposit creation; the money supply will (fall, rise) and interest rates will probably (fall, rise) in the short run.

16. If the Fed raises reserve requirements banks will find it (harder, easier) to meet reserve requirements; banks will (call in loans, lend more) and the money supply will (fall, rise).

17. An expansionary monetary policy will tend to cause the interest rate to fall, which may lead to a(n) (decrease, increase) in net exports; an expansionary fiscal policy financed by deficits may cause the interest rate to (fall, rise), which may lead to a (decrease, increase) in net exports.

TRUE-FALSE QUESTIONS
Circle the **T** if the statement is true, the **F** if it is false. Explain to yourself why a statement is false.

T F   1.   An important objective of monetary policy is to assist the economy in maintaining high employment without undue inflation.

T F   2.   The Fed can control the supply of money but not the demand for money.

T F   3.   The crude quantity theory of money maintains that if the money supply is doubled, the price level is halved.

T F   4.   The asset demand for money motive stresses money's role as a medium of exchange.

T F   5.   The asset demand for money motive stresses money's role as a liquid store of value.

T F   6.   The opportunity cost of holding money is loss of liquidity.

T F   7.   When interest rates rise, the price of existing bonds falls.

T F   8.   In the Keynesian model, the supply of and the demand for money directly determine net investment spending.

T F   9.   If an excess quantity demanded for money exists, people will attempt to sell bonds, which drives interest rates up.

T F   10.   If the Fed buys bonds on the open market, bank reserves will rise, and so will bank lending.

T F   11.   The Fed cannot target both the interest rate and the money supply.

T F   12.   If the demand for money is more stable than private expenditures, the Fed should target the money supply.

T F   13.   If the Fed wants to increase the money supply, it will raise the discount rate or raise reserve requirements.

T F   14.   Monetarists believe that discretionary monetary policy is effective, but that fiscal policy is not.

T F   15.   An expansionary monetary policy tends to increase a nation's net exports, while an expansionary fiscal policy tends to decrease its net exports.

T F   16.   Keynesians prefer a monetary rule to discretionary fiscal policy because they believe that the demand for money is unstable.

MULTIPLE CHOICE QUESTIONS
Circle the letter that corresponds to the best answer.

1.   The demand for money curve
    a.   is upward sloping.
    b.   is flat.
    c.   is downward sloping.
    d.   denies a link between the money supply and the price level.

2. In the equation $M_S V = PQ$, according to the crude quantity theory,
    a. M_S is independent of the price level.
    b. V is the number of times each dollar is spent, on average, per year.
    c. Q is the real price level.
    d. P rises as V falls, other things constant.

3. In the crude quantity theory, as the money supply rises (other things constant),
    a. the quantity demanded for money rises.
    b. velocity rises.
    c. velocity falls.
    d. the price level rises proportionately.

4. Which of the following stresses money's role as a medium of exchange?
    a. transactions demand
    b. precautionary demand
    c. asset demand
    d. miserly demand

5. Which of the following stresses money's role as a liquid store of value?
    a. transactions demand
    b. precautionary demand
    c. asset demand
    d. miserly demand

6. The opportunity cost of holding money is
    a. foregone liquidity.
    b. foregone interest income.
    c. convenience.
    d. security.

7. The demand for money curve
    a. reflects a preference for money over bonds.
    b. shows a negative relationship between the quantity demanded for money and the interest rate.
    c. shows that people want to substitute money for bonds at low interest rates.
    d. All of the above.

8. When interest rates rise,
    a. bond prices rise.
    b. bond holders experience capital losses.
    c. bond prices are unaffected.
    d. bond holders experience capital gains.

9. An excess quantity supplied of money
    a. exists at all interest rates above equilibrium.
    b. causes interest rates to rise.
    c. induces people to want to sell bonds.
    d. All of the above

10. The intersection of the supply of and the demand for money determines the
    a. aggregate demand curve.
    b. planned expenditures curve.
    c. price level.
    d. interest rate.

11. An expansionary monetary policy is beneficial if
    a. the unemployment rate is relatively high.
    b. a recession exists.
    c. the price level is falling.
    d. All of the above

12. According to Keynesians, an increase in the money supply will
    a. reduce the interest rate.
    b. reduce net investment spending.
    c. reduce total planned expenditures.
    d. All of the above

13. Which of the following clearly is **NOT** a result of an expansionary monetary policy?
    a. higher price level
    b. lower inflation rate
    c. increase in nominal national income
    d. increased total expenditures

14. A contractionary monetary policy
    a. shifts the AD curve rightward.
    b. shifts the AD curve leftward.
    c. shifts the LRAS curve, but not the AD curve.
    d. None of the above

15. If the velocity of money is less stable than private expenditures, then the Fed
    a. should target the interest rate.
    b. should pursue fiscal policy.
    c. should target a monetary aggregate.
    d. cannot target the interest rate.

16. The equation of exchange states that
    a. expenditures equal receipts.
    b. spending equals saving.
    c. saving equals investment.
    d. aggregate demand exceeds aggregate supply.

17. According to the crude quantity theory (assuming V and Q are constant), if the money supply is tripled, the price level will
    a. rise.
    b. fall.
    c. triple.
    d. more than triple,

18. Traditional Keynesians maintain that
    a. investment is a function of the interest rate.
    b. monetary policy works through changes in the interest rate.
    c. the Fed should target interest rates, not the money supply.
    d. All of the above

19. Which of the following is **NOT** a tenet of monetarism?
    a. Monetary policy is destabilizing.
    b. The Fed should follow a monetary rule, and not use its discretion.
    c. Changes in the money supply affect only the price level, in the long run.
    d. Keynesian multipliers are sufficiently reliable to conduct stabilization policies.

20. Globalized money capital markets
    a.   affect fiscal policy results but not monetary policy results.
    b.   make monetary policy more difficult.
    c.   facilitate monetary policy.
    d.   do not affect the conduct of monetary policy.

MATCHING
Choose the item in Column (2) that best matches an item in Column (1).

(1)	(2)
a. equation of exchange	h. nondiscretionary monetary policy
b. monetarism	i. preference for liquidity
c. velocity	j. monetary aggregate
d. transactions motive	k. crude quantity theory of money
e. monetary target	l. reciprocal of k
f. monetary rule	m. inflation a monetary phenomenon
g. asset motive	n. money as a medium of exchange

WORKING WITH GRAPHS

1.   On the next page in panel (a) is the investment demand function for the economy. Panel (b) represents the supply and demand functions for money. The interest rate in the economy is currently 12 percent. The money supply is $200 billion. Panel (c) is the Keynesian model of the economy, which is currently at an equilibrium level of output and income of $800 billion. Full employment output and income is $1000 billion. Further assume that the reserve requirement is 20 percent and there are no excess reserves in the banking system. Also assume that the economy's MPC is 0.6. Autonomous investment is currently $180 billion. Fill in the paragraph that follows the graphs.

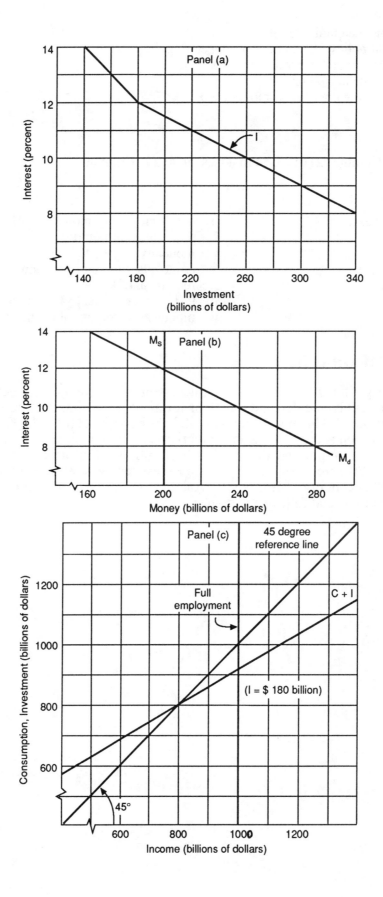

If the goal of the monetary authorities is to reach full employment, the Fed would want to (increase, decrease) the money supply by $_____, which would (raise, lower) interest rates to _____ percent. This would (increase, decrease) the level of autonomous investment by $ _____ to $_____. This (increase, decrease) in investment would be subject to a multiplier effect of _____ and therefore increase equilibrium level of income and output by $_____ to $_____. Assuming the Fed chose buying securities on the open market to (increase, decrease) the money supply, how many dollars of securities must the Fed purchase from the nonbank public to (increase, decrease) the money supply that would be consistent with full-employment equilibrium? $_____.

2. Analyze the graphs below, then answer the questions that follow.

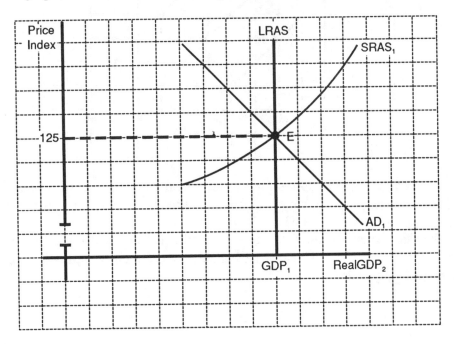

Assume that the economy is operating at point E, and that the Fed wants to reduce the price level.

a. Should it reduce or increase the money supply?
b. Should it buy or sell bonds on the open market?
c. Should it raise or lower the discount rate?
d. If the Fed follows your advice what will happen to the AD curve? (Draw it on your book or on a piece of paper).
e. What will happen to real GDP and the price level? Label the new short run equilibrium point as A.
f. After resource supplies adjust to the new price level, what happens to the SRAS curve? (Draw it.)
g. Indicate the new position in which both long run and short run equilibrium exist by labeling it B.
h. Compare the price level and real GDP level at points E and B.

3.   Analyze the graphs below and answer the questions that follow.

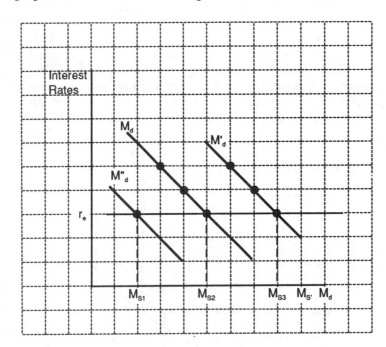

a. If the Fed targets the interest rate at r_e, and if the demand for money shifts leftward (falls) from M_d to M''_d, what happens to the money supply? Is this a stabilizing change in the money supply? Why?

b. If the Fed targets the interest rate at r_e, and if the demand for money shifts rightward (increases) from M_d to M'_d, what happens to the money supply? Is this a stabilizing money supply change? Why?

PROBLEMS

1. Suppose the economic advisors to the president feel it is necessary to raise our national income. These advisors and the president are traditional Keynesians. The chairman of the Fed is called to the Oval Office and told to stimulate the economy. Although the chairman does not have to obey, he decides to accept the directive.

Below you will find a series of interrelated questions concerning the execution of this directive. Be careful! An early mistake can affect your remaining answers. Circle the correct answer for each question.

1. The Fed will do which of the following?
    a. sell securities
    b. raise the discount rate
    c. buy securities
    d. raise reserve requirements

2. This action will
    a. lower the reserve requirement.
    b. raise the excess reserves of member banks.
    c. cause banks to increase their participation in the IMF.
    d. lower the amount of reserves required that are on deposit with the Fed.

3. We know banks are profit maximizers. They will therefore
   a. lend out excess reserves, which create more demand deposits.
   b. lend out excess reserves, which decrease demand deposits.
   c. call in outstanding loans.
   d. a and b

4. After the results of question 3,
   a. the money supply will decrease.
   b. the money supply will increase.
   c. the money supply will increase initially but then will return to its previous level.
   d. there will be no effect on the money supply.

5. If you have answered question 4 correctly, what will happen next?
   a. The interest rate will decrease, and investment will decrease.
   b. The interest rate will go up, with no effect on investment.
   c. The interest rate will remain unaffected.
   d. The interest rate will decrease, and investment will increase.

6. With the correct answer to question 5, we know that
   a. national income will increase by the amount of investment.
   b. national income will decrease by the amount of investment.
   c. national income will change by more than the amount by which investment will change.
   d. national income will change by less than the amount by which investment will change.

7. The change in national income will be
   a. change in I times 1 / (1 - MPS).
   b. change in I times 1 / (1 - MPC).
   c. change in I times 1 / (1 - MPC - MPS).
   d. change in I times change in the interest rate.

2. Given the equation of exchange MV = PQ and M = $50, V = 4, and Q = $100 then
   a. What does P equal?
   b. If M doubles, to $100, what happens to P?
   c. If M is reduced to $25, what happens to P?

3. Given the equation of exchange MV = PQ and M = $100, V = 5, and PQ = nominal national income then
   a. What is the value of nominal national income?
   b. If price level equals 1, what is the value of real national income?
   c. If the money supply triples, other things constant, what is the value of nominal national income? of real national income?

ANSWERS TO CHAPTER 17

COMPLETION QUESTIONS

1. can; cannot
2. crude quantity
3. rise; fall
4. income velocity of money
5. will; is; double
6. transactions; precautionary; asset
7. directly; inversely
8. fall; falls; interest earnings
9. rise; rightward; real national income
10. quantity demanded for money; sell; downward; upward
11. is; same; national output; employment; price level
12. do not; monetary rule
13. open market operations; changing the discount rate; changing reserve requirements
14. rise; falls; rise; increase; rises
15. discourage; decrease; decrease; fall; rise
16. harder; call in loans; fall
17. increase; rise; decrease

TRUE-FALSE QUESTIONS

1. T
2. T
3. F   The price level will also double.
4. F   It stresses money's role as a store of value.
5. T
6. F   The opportunity cost is foregone interest earnings.
7. T
8. F   They determine the interest rate; hence investment is indirectly determined.
9. T
10. T
11. T
12. T
13. F   No, the Fed would lower them.
14. F   They believe that neither is effective.
15. T
16. F   Monetarists prefer a monetary rule; Keynesians prefer an activist monetary policy.

MULTIPLE CHOICE QUESTIONS

1.c;	2.b;	3.d;	4.a;	5.c;	6.b;	7.d;	8.b;	9.a;	10.d;
11.d;	12.a;	13.b;	14.b;	15.a;	16.a;	17.c;	18.d;	19.d;	20.b

MATCHING
a and k;   b and m;   c and l;   d and n;   e and j;   f and h;   g and i

WORKING WITH GRAPHS

1. increase, $40 billion, lower, 10; increase, $80 billion; $260 billion; increase; 2 1/2; $200 billion, $1000 billion; increase, increase; $8 billion in securities from the nonbank public. **Note**: This problem actually requires you to work backward in order to obtain the

necessary increase in the money supply. That is, you must first find how much of an increase in autonomous investment is required to increase the equilibrium level of income by $200 billion (change in I x multiplier = change in income). Substitute 2 1/2 for the multiplier and $200 billion for the change in investment (I). Now go to panel (a) and find how much the interest rate must fall to increase investment by $80 billion. Then find how much the money supply must increase to lower the interest rate to 10 percent. The answer is obviously $40 billion. If the Fed purchased $8 billion of securities from, for example, businesses and security dealers, they would deposit this in their checking accounts, which would increase demand deposits in the banking system by $8 billion. Finally, the money multiplier of 5 would increase the money supply by the necessary $40 billion.

2.   a. reduce; b. sell;   c. raise;   d. It will shift leftward, to AD_2 on the graph below; e. both fall;   f. It shifts downward, to $SRAS_2$.   g. See the graph below.   h. Real GDP is the same; the price level is lower.

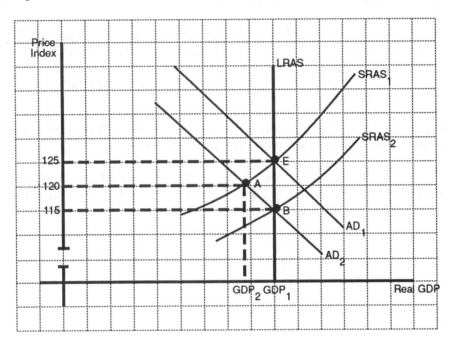

3.   a. Decreases to M_{S1}. Yes, because if the demand for money falls and the supply of money falls, then the interest rate will be unaffected and private spending won't change due to a change in the money supply.
      b. Increases to M_S3. Yes, because if the demand for money rises and the supply of money rises, then the interest rate will be unaffected; hence private spending won't change due to an unstable demand for money.

PROBLEMS

1.c   2.b   3.a   4.b   5.d   6.c   7.b
2. a.$P = 2$ b.it doubles; $P = 4$ c.it is halved, $P = 1$
3. a.$500   b.$500   c.$1500; $500

GLOSSARY TO CHAPTER 17

Asset demand   The demand for money as a store of value.

Crude quantity theory of money and price   Changes in the money supply lead to proportional changes in the price level.

Demand for money   An inverse relationship between the opportunity cost of holding money (interest receipts foregone) and the quantity of money demanded.

Equation of exchange   The number of monetary units times the number of times each unit is spent on final goods and services is identical to the price level times output (or national income).

Income velocity of money   The number of times per year a dollar is spent on final goods and services. It is equal to NNP divided by the money supply.

Monetarists   Those who believe that inflation is a monetary phenomenon and that changes in money supply growth rates can directly and indirectly affect aggregate demand.

Monetary rule   A type of monetary policy in which there is a rule specifying the annual rate of growth of some monetary aggregate.

Precautionary demand   A motive for holding money in order to meet unplanned expenditures and emergencies; it generates the precautionary demand for money.

Transactions demand   The motive that causes individuals and businesses to want to hold money as a medium of exchange to make payments. The result is that the transactions demand for money varies directly with nominal national income.

ISSUES IN STABILIZATION POLICY

PUTTING THIS CHAPTER INTO PERSPECTIVE

Economists are no strangers to controversy. In every generation one economic theory has claimed the minds and souls of a majority, but significant minority points of view have also existed. And at times these minority views have become the majority conventional wisdom. Interestingly enough, economists (and their intellectual heirs) have carried on some debates for centuries. In Chapter 18 we introduce other theories—rational expectations, or new classical, real business cycles, and new Keynesian. You should not be concerned with deciding which theory is "correct," nor should you worry about memorizing every little detail of each theory. Instead try to concentrate on only the main issues, which are summarized for you in Table 18-1.

The single most important issue in macroeconomics—and one that has been debated hotly by economists since the eighteenth century—is whether or not capitalism is stable. Such an economy is often shocked by random forces (gold and silver discoveries in the past, changes in taste, technology, and profit expectations always). If a shocked economy eventually returns to the original, near full employment equilibrium position, then it is stable; if not, it is unstable.

If capitalism is stable, then stabilization policy is not necessary unless it takes *too long* to return to equilibrium and can use some help. If capitalism is unstable, it *should* be stabilized by the government (through monetary policy and fiscal policy), *if it is possible to stabilize it.*

In recent years several exciting advances in macroeconomic theory have emerged, and such advances have caused the age-old "is capitalism stable" debate to evolve. Monetarists maintain that monetary policy only works in the short run by fooling laborers and employers into underestimating the actual rate of inflation. If economic agents expect the inflation rate to be less than it actually is, then more inflation can "buy" less unemployment and the Phillips curve is negatively sloped. But because in the long run, the true rate of inflation will be known by economic agents, the trade-off between inflation and unemployment will disappear. Eventually the actual unemployment rate will equal the natural unemployment rate; short-run Phillips curves are negatively sloped, but long-run Phillips curves are vertical at the natural unemployment rate (reflecting the vertical long-run aggregate supply curve, which is *now* conceived of as the real GDP level consistent with the natural rate of unemployment.

The rational expectations hypothesis (REH) model, however, rejects even this conception of how monetary policy works. The REH maintains that because economic agents are rational, they will use all the information available to them when they make decisions—including the probability that specific monetary and fiscal policies will be enacted. The REH proponents contend that policy-makers cannot cause economic agents to make *systematic* expectational (forecasting) errors.

They conclude that economic agents are just as likely to *over*estimate the true inflation rate as they are likely to *under*estimate it. Unannounced monetary policy can affect real national income (output) and employment, but it is just as likely to reduce them as to increase them! Furthermore, *announced* stabilization policies will have little or no effect on real national income and employment.

While the REH model is not widely accepted, it nevertheless presents a challenge to modern macroeconomists, and it certainly will cause the economics discipline to evolve toward more rigorous and more robust models. In addition, it provides more controversy for a contentious group of social scientists.

In this chapter also note that economists have also long debated the issue of the extent of competition and price wage flexibility/rigidity, an issue closely related to the "is capitalism stable" controversy. New Keynesian theories—small-menu cost theory and efficiency wage theory are modern, more subtle, versions of the Keynesian wage rate rigidity theory. Not to be outdone, the new classical economists have developed new theories that incorporate price wage flexibility: rational expectations and real business cycle theories.

New growth theorists maintain that stabilization policies to eliminate business cycles are largely irrelevant. Instead, they claim, we should be concerned with encouraging innovation, which contributes to growth—and business cycles.

LEARNING OBJECTIVES

After you have studied this chapter you should be able to

1. define active policymaking, passive policymaking, Phillips curve, natural rate of unemployment, new Keynesian economics, rational expectations hypothesis, policy irrelevance proposition, real business cycle theory, small-menu cost theory, and efficiency wage theory.

2. interpret a Phillips curve.

3. answer questions that indicate an understanding of why the Phillips curve might be negatively sloped in the short run, and vertical in the long run.

4. distinguish between the effects of an announced (anticipated) and an unannounced (unanticipated) monetary policy, according to the rational expectations hypothesis.

5. recognize the implications of price wage inflexibility for small-menu cost theory and efficiency wage theory.

6. recognize the essential features of the real business cycle theory.

7. recognize similarities and distinctions among the traditional classical, traditional Keynesian, modern monetarist, new classical and new Keynesian models.

8. recognize why new growth theorists think stabilization policies to eliminate business cycles is largely an unimportant undertaking.

CHAPTER OUTLINE

1. Some economists have argued that a trade-off exists between the rate of unemployment and the rate of inflation.

a. If such a relationship (called a *Phillips curve*) existed, policy-makers could simply try to balance the problems associated with inflation with those associated with unemployment; they could then select the "optimal" mix of unemployment and inflation consistent with societal values.

b. In reality no such policy option exists; the Phillips curve relationship has proved to be unstable.

2. A consistent short-run trade-off between inflation and unemployment seems to have existed in the past, when the actual inflation rate was relatively low for long periods.

a. In recent years the inflation rate has been much more variable.

b. If workers underestimate the true inflation rate, they will be fooled into accepting a lower wage rate than they bargained for, and the actual unemployment rate will fall.

3. The natural rate of unemployment is determined by (a) frictional unemployment and (b) unemployment due to price and wage rigidities in the economic system.

4. NAIRU is that rate of unemployment below which the rate of inflation tends to rise and below which it tends to fall.

5. The Friedman-Phelps model indicates how monetary policy can account for the Phillips curve trade-off between inflation and unemployment in the short run, but not in the long run.

a. If the Fed secretly increases the rate at which the money supply is growing, then economic agents will underestimate the actual inflation rate.

b. Job searchers, therefore, are fooled into accepting jobs sooner than they otherwise would have.

c. The shorter duration of unemployment caused by unanticipated inflation causes the unemployment rate to fall; hence higher inflation rates have "bought" a lower unemployment rate in the short run, and the short-run Phillips curve is negatively sloped.

d. In the long run the actual inflation rate will be correctly anticipated, the duration of unemployment will return to its prior level, and the unemployment rate will return to the natural rate of unemployment and the economy will be operating on its LRAS curve.

e. The long-run Phillips curve, therefore, is vertical; in the long run monetary policy affects only the price level; real GDP and employment are unchanged.

6. An unanticipated expansionary monetary policy causes the AD curve to shift rightward and the short-run AS curve to remain constant; hence real national income (output) and employment will rise with the price level.

7. In the long run the AS curve is vertical; hence expansionary monetary policy will increase only the price level.

8. The *rational expectations hypothesis* (REH) contends that economic agents will try to anticipate future stabilization policy and its effects.

a. Economic agents will allocate resources to predict stabilization policy and its effect on the value of future economic variables—especially the future inflation rate.

b. The REH predicts that policymakers cannot cause economic agents to make consistent forecasting errors; workers will not consistently and systematically underestimate the inflation rate; sometimes they will overestimate the inflation rate.

c. Eventually, once economic agents know that policymakers are trying to fool them, not even a *short-run* (systematic) trade-off between inflation and unemployment exists.

i. The REH predicts that an anticipated (announced) stabilization policy will have little impact on the employment rate and on real national income.

ii. Expansionary demand policies in the past may have worked because economic agents had not been fooled by *previous* government stabilization policies.

iii. In recent years stabilization policy has been more difficult to conduct because economic agents have found it rational to allocate resources to economic forecasting.

9. The new classical model incorporates the assumptions of the rational expectations model, and adds the assumptions that (a) all markets are highly competitive and (b) all prices and wages are perfectly competitive.

10. The policy irrelevance proposition, an implication of the new classical model, is that policy actions have no real effects in the short run if the policy actions were anticipated, and not in the long run even if the policy actions were unanticipated.

11. The new classical model seems to imply that fluctuations in real variables are a result of *mistakes*, either on the part of policymakers, or economic agents.

12. Various theories have been developed to explain fluctuations in real variables (business cycles) that are *not* due to mistakes.
    a. Small-menu cost theory hypothesizes that it is costly for firms to change prices in response to demand changes, hence some price rigidity is rational.
    b. The efficiency wage theory maintains that high wages tend to increase labor productivity and worker loyalty, hence wage reductions might interfere with both; employers are therefore reluctant to lower wages in recessions and wage rates are inflexible downward.
    c. Real business cycle theory maintains the assumption of price and wage flexibility, but suggests that the source of business cycles is changes in supply.
        i. Supply shocks such as the oil supply disruption or the sudden increase in the price of oil in the 1970s, or any significant change in the price of a crucial resource shift the SRAS curve (and maybe the LRAS curve) and change real economic variables.
        ii. Technological changes and changes in the composition of the labor force are additional (nonmonetary) supply shocks that have short run and long run effects on real economic variables.

13. New growth theorists believe that encouraging innovations which contribute to economic growth (and contribute to business cycles) is more important than stabilizing the economy in the short run.

KEY TERMS

Phillips curve	Natural rate of unemployment
New Keynesian economics	New classical model
Real business cycle theory	

KEY CONCEPTS

Active policymaking	Small-menu costs theory
Passive policymaking	NAIRU
Policy irrelevance proposition	Rational expectations hypothesis
Efficiency wage theory	

COMPLETION QUESTIONS
Fill in the blank or circle the correct term.

1. The Phillips curve posits a trade-off between the _____ rate and the _____ rate.

2. In recent years in the United States, the Phillips curve relationship (is, is not) supported by empirical evidence.

3. The natural rate of unemployment prevails in the (short, long) run when the economy is in (equilibrium, disequilibrium); when the natural rate of unemployment is reached, the actual inflation rate (is less than, is greater than, equals) the expected inflation rate, and there (is, is not) a tendency for the inflation rate to accelerate.

4. In order to keep the actual unemployment rate below the natural unemployment rate, the actual inflation rate must be (greater than, less than, equal to) the expected inflation rate; thus the inflation rate must always be (constant, accelerating, decelerating).

5. The rational expectations hypothesis contends that policymakers (can, cannot) induce economic agents to make systematic forecasting errors. According to this model, if a government stabilization policy is announced it will have (much, little) effect on output and unemployment; if a stabilization policy is not announced and is unanticipated by economic agents, it (will, will not) have a short-run impact on the economy, and the impact (will, will not) be systematic on output and employment.

6. If inflationary expectations are high and the Fed pursues an unanticipated contractionary policy, the unemployment rate will (fall, rise), because economic agents will (underestimate, overestimate) the future inflation rate. If the Fed announces a contractionary policy and such a policy is believed by economic agents, the rational expectations hypothesis predicts that the unemployment rate (will, will not) rise significantly.

7. The new classical model accepts the assumptions of the rational expectations hypothesis, and adds the assumptions of _____ and _____; that model implies that fluctuations in real variables are a result of mistakes on the part of _____ and _____.

8. The policy irrelevance proposition states that if policy actions are anticipated, such actions will have (no, a great) effect on real variables in the short run; if policy actions are unanticipated then they (will, will not) have an effect on real variables in the short run, but that effect (is, is not) predictable; in the long run unanticipated policy (will, will not) have real effects.

9. Small-menu cost theory maintains that if the cost of frequent changes in prices exceeds the costs of not changing such prices, it is (rational, irrational) to leave prices unchanged in the face of changes in demand; this theory suggests that prices and wages (are, are not) perfectly flexible.

10. The efficiency wage hypothesis maintains that (high wages lead to high productivity, high productivity leads to high wages), and therefore producers may be reluctant to reduce wages in recessions; hence this theory suggests that wage rates are (inflexible, flexible) in the downward direction.

11. Real business cycle theory assumes that prices and wages are (inflexible, flexible) and that changes in real economic variables result from (supply, demand) shocks; this theory suggests that changes in _____, _____, and _____ could affect real economic variables.

12. New growth theorists believe that short-run stabilization policy (is, is not) a worthwhile pursuit.

TRUE-FALSE QUESTIONS
Circle the **T** if the statement is true and the **F** if it is false. Explain to yourself why a statement is false.

T F   1.   The Phillips curve relates inflation rates to growth rates.

T F   2.   If workers underestimate the true inflation rate, the Phillips curve will be negatively sloped.

T F   3.   If workers overestimate the true inflation rate, the unemployment rate could rise as inflation rises.

T F   4.   The Friedman-Phelps model predicts that no trade-off exists between inflation and unemployment in the short run.

T F   5.   In recent years in the United States, there seems to be no systematic, negative relationship between the inflation rate and the unemployment rate.

T F   6.   New growth theorists think that we should be more concerned with growth rates, and less concerned with short-run stabilization.

T F   7.   Monetary policy works by fooling people only in the long run.

T F   8.   The new classical model predicts that if the government announces its stabilization policy, the unemployment rate will be affected greatly.

T F   9.   Both the Friedman-Phelps model and the rational expectations model predict that in the long run the actual unemployment rate equals the natural rate.

T F   10.   In macroeconomic equilibrium, the actual unemployment rate exceeds the natural unemployment rate.

T F   11.   The Friedman-Phelps model contends that high inflation does not keep unemployment down; only not fully anticipated rising inflation does.

T F   12.   If the inflation rate falls unexpectedly, the unemployment rate will fall, according to the Friedman-Phelps model.

T F   13.   The rational expectations hypothesis argues that policymakers cannot systematically change the unemployment rate in the short run.

T F   14.   The rational expectations/new classical model argues that policymakers simply cannot affect the unemployment rate in the short run.

T F   15.   Traditional Keynesians believe that capitalism is stable, and that stabilization policy is too difficult to conduct.

T F   16.   Keynesians and classical economists all believe that the demand for money is sensitive to the interest rate.

MULTIPLE CHOICE QUESTIONS
Circle the letter that corresponds to the best answer.

1. Which of the following is most **UNLIKE** the others
    a. Theories that assume fixed prices in the short run
    b. Efficiency wage theory
    c. Real business cycle theory
    d. Small-menu cost theory

2. The Phillips curve relates
    a. inflation rates and productivity rates.
    b. inflation rates and unemployment rates.
    c. unemployment rates and growth rates.
    d. the natural unemployment rate and the actual unemployment rate.

3. A trade-off between inflation and unemployment
    a. exists only in the long run.
    b. can exist if workers underestimate the true inflation rate.
    c. can exist if workers underestimate the natural inflation rate.
    d. is depicted by the production possibilities curve.

4. If workers underestimate the true inflation rate, then
    a. more inflation can "buy" less unemployment.
    b. the Phillips curve will be vertical in the short run.
    c. the Phillips curve will be positively sloped.
    d. the unemployment rate will rise.

5. If workers anticipate a 10 percent inflation rate, they will
    a. add 10 percent to their wage requests.
    b. subtract 10 percent from their wage requests.
    c. quit work.
    d. work longer hours.

6. New growth theorists maintain that
    a. short-run stabilization policy is overrated.
    b. economic growth is overrated.
    c. innovations are harmful.
    d. None of the above.

7. In the Friedman-Phelps model, if the inflation rate falls unexpectedly, then
    a. workers will overestimate the true inflation rate.
    b. the unemployment rate will rise.
    c. the short-run Phillips curve will be negatively sloped.
    d. All of the above

8. If the actual unemployment rate equals the natural unemployment rate, then
    a. no inflation is possible.
    b. macroeconomic equilibrium exists.
    c. no unemployment exists.
    d. All of the above

9.   Under the Friedman-Phelps model
    a.   the short-run Phillips curve is vertical.
    b.   a short-run Phillips curve exists for each actual inflation rate.
    c.   a short-run Phillips curve exists for each expected inflation rate.
    d.   only one Phillips curve exists, and it is negatively sloped at the natural unemployment rate.

10.   The natural rate of unemployment equals the actual unemployment rate
    a.   in the long run.
    b.   only when the actual inflation rate is zero.
    c.   only when the natural inflation rate is zero.
    d.   only in the short run.

11.   The natural rate of unemployment
    a.   occurs when the inflation rate is correctly anticipated.
    b.   is always above the actual rate of unemployment.
    c.   is always below the actual rate of unemployment.
    d.   occurs usually in the short run.

12.   The only way to keep the actual unemployment rate below the natural unemployment rate is to
    a.   have the actual inflation rate be less than the expected inflation rate.
    b.   have the actual inflation rate be higher than the expected inflation rate.
    c.   constantly reduce the inflation rate.
    d.   provide job security.

13.   The rational expectations hypothesis
    a.   rejects the Friedman-Phelps model.
    b.   maintains that policymakers cannot get economic agents to make systematic forecasting errors.
    c.   maintains that economic agents will use all information, including expected stabilization policies, when they estimate the future inflation rate.
    d.   All of the above

14.   The irrelevancy proposition maintains that
    a.   anticipated government stabilization policies cannot reduce unemployment below the natural rate.
    b.   unanticipated stabilization policies cannot reduce unemployment below the natural rate.
    c.   anticipated stabilization policies cannot reduce the increase in actual unemployment resulting from a decrease in the inflation rate.
    d.   unanticipated stabilization policies are very effective in reducing actual unemployment below natural unemployment.

15.   The new classical model
    a.   rejects the rational expectations approach.
    b.   assumes that price and wages are flexible.
    c.   maintains that monetary policy cannot affect real variables in the short run.
    d.   was developed by Keynes.

16.   When expansionary monetary policy is unanticipated, in the short run
    a.   the unemployment rate will fall.
    b.   actual inflation will exceed anticipated inflation.
    c.   workers are fooled into accepting jobs sooner.
    d.   All of the above

17. Which of the following models predicts that capitalism is not inherently stable?
    a. traditional classical
    b. traditional Keynesian
    c. new classical
    d. new Keynesian

18. Which of the following economic schools of thought is most unlike the others?
    a. traditional classical
    b. new Classical
    c. traditional Keynesian
    d. new Keynesian

19. Real business cycle theory
    a. assumes that prices and wages are flexible.
    b. maintains that real economic variables can change even if mistakes are not made.
    c. suggests that supply creates its own demand.
    d. All of the above

MATCHING
Choose the item in column (2) that best matches an item in column (1).

(1)	(2)
a. Phillips curve	h. vertical LRAS curve
b. new growth theory	i. efficiency wage hypothesis
c. NAIRU	j. noninflationary unemployment
d. price-wage rigidity	k. innovations
e. long-run Phillips curve	l. supply creates its own demand
f. policy irrelevancy proposition	m. rational expectations hypothesis
g. real business cycle theory	n. relationship between inflation and
	unemployment

WORKING WITH GRAPHS

1. Suppose you are given the Phillips curve in the graph below.

a. If the rate of 7 percent unemployment constitutes "full" employment, what rate of inflation should the economy expect at full employment?
b. Suppose the government were to set a goal of lowering inflation to 4 percent. If the Phillips curve above is accurate and stable, what level of unemployment will have to be tolerated if the goal for inflation is to be achieved?
c. Suppose the Phillips curve above describes the inflation-unemployment trade-off with individuals anticipating inflation of 6 percent. If individuals suddenly begin to expect inflation of 8 percent, and this raises the level of unemployment for each level of actual inflation by 1.5 percent, draw in the new Phillips curve.
d. What will be the level of unemployment if the actual rate of inflation is the anticipated rate, 8 percent?
e. If the actual rate of inflation turns out to be 6 percent rather than 8 percent, what will the level of unemployment be?
f. What conclusion can be drawn from answers to parts c through e?

2. Analyze the graphs below, then answer the questions that follow.

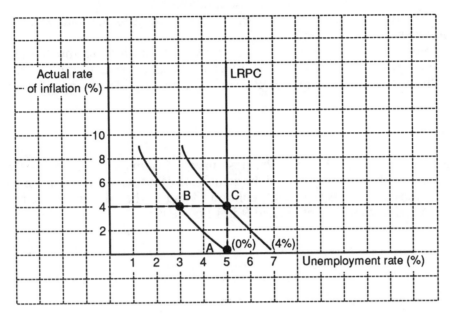

a. What is the natural rate of unemployment for the economy depicted in the graphs above?
b. Starting from point A and assuming that economic agents anticipated 0 percent inflation, what will be the actual unemployment rate if the actual inflation rate is 4 percent? 6 percent?
c. If the anticipated inflation rate is 4 percent, and the actual inflation rate is 4 percent, what will be the actual unemployment rate? The natural unemployment rate?
d. When does the short-run Phillips curve shift?

3. Consider the graphs below and then answer the questions that follow.

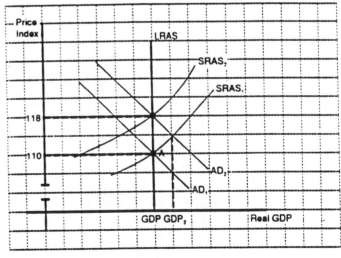

   a. Assume that we begin at point A. Now the Fed increases the money supply in secret. Which curve is affected? What is the new equilibrium?
   b. Continuing (a) above, what has happened, at this point in our analysis, to employment, unemployment, and real GDP?
   c. In the long run economic agents will now fully anticipate the higher price level, consequently which curve will now be affected? What is the new equilibrium point?
   d. What is the new equilibrium real GDP level? The new equilibrium price level?

PROBLEMS

1. In the table below are three short-run Phillips curves. Columns 1 and 2 show the relationship between the unemployment rate (U) and the actual rate of inflation (R) when the anticipated rate of inflation in the economy is 0 percent; columns 3 and 4 when the anticipated R is 6 percent; and columns 5 and 6 when the anticipated R is 12 percent.

Phillips Curve 1		Phillips Curve 2		Phillips Curve 3	
(1) U	(2) $R_{0\%}$	(3) U	(4) $R_{6\%}$	(5) U	(6) $R_{12\%}$
10	0	10	6	10	12
9	1	9	7	9	13
8	3	8	9	8	15
7	6	7	12	7	18
6	10	6	16	6	22
5	15	5	21	5	27
4	21	4	27	4	33

   a. Suppose the anticipated rate of inflation and the actual rate of inflation are 0. The unemployment rate U is _____ percent.

   b. If expansionary monetary or fiscal policies are used to increase aggregate demand and to reduce U to 7 percent, the actual R will (increase/decrease) to _____ percent.

   c. When the economy comes to anticipate this R, U will be _____ percent; and if expansionary stabilization policies are again used to reduce U to 7 percent, the actual R will _____ to _____ percent.

   d. And when the economy comes to anticipate this R, U will be _____ percent; if stabilization policies are once more used to reduce U to 7 percent, the actual R will _____ to _____ percent; and when the economy comes to anticipate this R, U will again _____ to _____ percent.

e. Use your answers to parts (a), (b), (c), and (d) above to show U in the long run at each of the actual R's in the table.

R	U
0	_____
6	_____
12	_____

CASE STUDY

Economist Phillip Cagan analyzed the post-World War I German hyperinflation period, during which that economy experienced high and variable money supply growth and inflation rates. Over the period from 1921 to 1923 the inflation rate ranged from about 0 percent to 500 percent *per month*. Cagan found that during that period relatively small changes occurred in the levels of real national output and total employment.

It became extremely difficult for economic agents to predict the inflation rate—and therefore to determine the "best" nominal interest rate at which to lend or borrow.

1. Does this historical experience lend some support to the rational expectations hypothesis? Why?

2. What would you predict happened to the number of loans made at nominal interest rates, during that period?

3. Would you guess that important redistribution of income effects occurred during that period? Why?

ANSWERS TO CHAPTER 18

COMPLETION QUESTIONS

1. inflation, unemployment
2. is not
3. long; equilibrium; equals; is not
4. greater than; accelerating
5. cannot; little; will; will not
6. rise; overestimate; will not
7. pure competition; price/wage flexibility; policymakers; economic agents
8. no; will; is not; will not
9. rational; are not
10. high wages lead to high productivity; inflexible
11. flexible; supply; oil prices; technology; composition of the labor force
12. is not

TRUE-FALSE QUESTIONS

1. F It relates inflation rates to unemployment rates.
2. T
3. T
4. F It predicts no trade-off in the long run.
5. T
6. T
7. F It fools people only in the short run.
8. F Unemployment will not be affected very much, if policy is announced.
9. T
10. F In equilibrium they are equal.
11. T
12. F It will rise as workers prolong their job search.
13. T
14. F They can change unemployment, but the direction is uncertain.
15. F They believe it is unstable, and that stabilization policy is possible.
16. F Classical economists believed the demand for money was insensitive to the interest rate.

MULTIPLE CHOICE QUESTIONS

1.c;	2.b;	3.b;	4.a;	5.a;	6.a;	7.d;	8.b;	9.c;	10.a;
11.a;	12.b;	13.d;	14.a;	15.b;	16.d;	17.b;	18.c;	19.d	

MATCHING

a and n;   b and k;   c and j;   d and i;   e and h;   f and m;   g and l

WORKING WITH GRAPHS

1. a. 6 percent
   b. 10 percent
   c. see graph below
   d. 7 percent
   e. between 8 and 8.5%
   f. When actual inflation is less than anticipated inflation, unemployment rises.

2. a. 5 percent
    b. 3 percent; 2 percent
    c. 5 percent; 5 percent
    d. Every time the anticipated inflation rate changes.

3. Your new graphs should be labeled as indicated below.

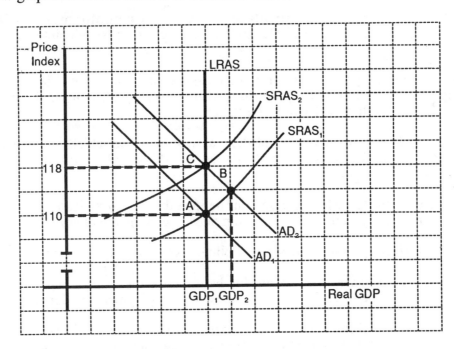

a. The AD curve shifts to AD$_2$, point B; See graph above.
b. employment increases because the duration of unemployment falls, unemployment falls,
    real GDP rises to GDP$_2$.
c. The short run aggregate supply curve shifts upward to SRAS$_2$, the new equilibrium point
    is point C; See graph above.
d. GDP$_1$, 118.

PROBLEMS

1. a. 10
   b. increase, 6
   c. 10, increase, 12
   d. 10, increase, 18; increase, 10
   e. 10 percent, 10 percent, 10 percent

CASE STUDY

1. Yes, some support. Apparently economic agents tried to anticipate money supply changes and, therefore, real variables did not change very much.
2. Decreased, because people would be forced to speculate on the inflation rate if they borrowed or lent at nominal interest rates.
3. Yes; borrowers who owed *nominal* debts gained at the expense of lenders.

GLOSSARY TO CHAPTER 18

Active (discretionary) policymaking Monetary and fiscal policies undertaken in response to, or anticipation of, an actual or potential change in the economy.

Efficiency wage theory The hypothesis that the productivity of workers depends on the level of the real wage rate.

NAIRU, or non accelerating-inflation rate of unemployment That rate of unemployment below which the rate of inflation tends to rise and above which the rate of inflation tends to fall.

Natural rate of unemployment That rate of measured unemployment that is estimated to prevail in long-run macroeconomic equilibrium with no money illusion when employees and employers both correctly anticipate the rate of inflation.

New classical model A modern version of the classical model in which wages and prices are flexible and there is pure competition in all markets. Additionally, the rational expectations hypothesis is assumed to be working.

New Keynesian economics Models based on the idea that demand creates its own supply as a result of various possible government fiscal and monetary coordination failures.

Passive (nondiscretionary) policymaking Policymaking carried out in response to a rule.

Phillips curve A curve showing the relationship between unemployment and changes in wages or prices. The Phillips curve gives the trade-off between unemployment and inflation.

Policy irrelevance proposition The new classical conclusion that policy actions have no real effects in the short run if the policy actions were anticipated, and not in the long run even if the policy actions were unanticipated.

Price inertia A tendency for the level of prices to resist change with the passage of time.

Rational-expectations hypothesis A hypothesis or theory stating that people combine the effects of past policy changes on important economic variables with their own judgment about the future effects of current and future policy changes.

Real business cycle theory   An extension of the new classical economists' theories, in which money is neutral, and only real factors matter.

Small-menu cost theory   A hypothesis that it is costly for firms to change prices in response to demand changes because of the cost of negotiating contracts, printing price lists, etc.

CHAPTER 19

CONSUMER CHOICE

PUTTING THIS CHAPTER INTO PERSPECTIVE

Chapter 19 analyzes consumer choice. The body of this chapter is concerned with the traditional, or classical, theory of consumer behavior, which is referred to as utility analysis. In the appendix to this chapter (which is analyzed separately immediately following this section), the more modern approach to the study of consumer behavior—indifference curve analysis—is presented.

Your understanding of Chapter 19 and its appendix will be aided immeasurably by your learning to distinguish between an ordinal measure and a cardinal measure. (See footnote 1, in the text.) In this chapter we deal with utility as something that can be measured cardinally. The analysis in the appendix, however, requires only that utility be measured ordinally—a less stringent, and therefore more analytically powerful—requirement.

You are also well-advised to study carefully the distinction between total utility and marginal utility—and how they are related. As long as marginal utility is positive, total utility will rise; if marginal utility is rising, total utility will rise at an *increasing* rate; if marginal utility is constant, total utility will rise at a constant rate (the total utility curve would be linear); if marginal utility falls, then total utility will rise at a *decreasing* rate. Memorize, and then learn, how "marginal" and "total" are related now, because we shall return to these concepts often.

Equally important is the relationship between marginal utility and average utility (or "average" and "marginal" anything); marginal pulls and tugs average. Thus, if marginal is above average, then average will rise; if marginal is below average, then average will fall; if marginal equals average, then average will remain constant. The relationship between marginal and average is also a recurring thread in this text; learn it now, once and for all.

Another important (and recurring) topic is the concept "marginal utility per dollar's worth," which in equation form is MU/P, or marginal utility divided by price. Play around with this ratio; convince yourself that given MU, changes in price lead to changes in marginal utility per dollar's worth of a good. Also, learn exactly what the inequality $MU_1/P_1 > MU_2/P_2$ means, and *exactly* what the inequality $MU_1/P_1 < MU_2/P_2$ means, and learn what such an inequality implies about consumer optimization behavior.

Time spent now on the concepts stressed here will pay handsome dividends in the future. If you really master these concepts, then the analysis that lies ahead in later chapters will be much easier.

LEARNING OBJECTIVES

After you have studied this chapter you should be able to

1.   define utility, util, marginal utility, marginal analysis, diminishing marginal utility, consumer optimum, substitution effect, principal of substitution, purchasing power, and real income effect.

2.   distinguish between total utility and marginal utility, and answer questions that require an understanding of how they are related.

3.   distinguish between marginal utility and average utility, and answer questions that require an understanding of how they are related.

4.   apply the concept of diminishing marginal utility to the law of demand.

5.   predict what happens to the marginal utility per dollar's worth of a good when (a) its price changes, other things being constant and (b) more or less is consumed, other things being constant.

6.   predict what a consumer will do if the marginal utility per dollar's worth of good A is greater (less) than the marginal utility per dollar's worth of good B.

7.   predict how a change in price generates a real income effect, and a substitution effect.

8.   answer questions that require an understanding of how economists can explain the diamond-water paradox.

CHAPTER OUTLINE

1.   *Utility analysis* is the study of consumer decision making based on utility maximization.
     a.   A *util* is an artificial unit by which *utility* is measured.
     b.   *Total utility* is the sum of all the utils derived from consumption; *marginal utility* is the change in total utility due to a one-unit change in the quantity of a good consumed.
     c.   Economists maintain that economic decisions are made by comparing the marginal benefit of an activity with its marginal cost.
     d.   When relative price changes, it is the *marginal* buyers who respond, not the average buyers.
     e.   As long as marginal utility is positive, total utility will rise.
     f.   If marginal utility becomes negative—the good becomes a nuisance—total utility will fall.

2.   The principle of *diminishing marginal utility* states that as more of any good or service is consumed, eventually its extra benefit declines.

3.   Consumers are assumed to optimize their consumption choices; the consumer attempts to maximize total utility subject to such constraints as income and relative prices.

4.   When relative price changes, the *consumer optimum* is affected and the consumer reacts consistently and predictably.
     a.   A consumer is optimizing when she allocates all of her money income in such a way that the marginal utility per dollar's worth of goods and services purchased is equated.
     b.   If the relative price of a good falls, consumers will substitute it for the now relatively more expensive substitutes; this is the substitution effect.

    c.   If the price of a good falls, given money income and given the prices of all other goods, a consumer's real income rises and she normally will purchase more of that good whose price has fallen; this is the real income effect.

    d.   The substitution effect and the income effect help to explain the law of demand.

5.   The "law" of diminishing marginal utility can account for the law of demand; because the marginal benefit falls to consumers as they consume more per unit of time, price must fall to induce them to purchase more.

6.   The *diamond-water paradox* is that diamonds are unessential to life and have a high relative price, while water is essential to life yet has a low relative price.

    a.   The total utility of water to humans far exceeds the total utility of diamonds to humans; but the *marginal utility* of water is relatively low and the marginal utility of diamonds is high.

    b.   The price of a good, therefore, reflects its value on the margin—not its total or average value.

KEY TERMS

Utility   Marginal utility
Util

KEY CONCEPTS

Utility analysis   Real income effect
Purchasing power   Consumer optimum
Diminishing marginal utility   Principal of substitution
Substitution effect

COMPLETION QUESTIONS
Fill in the blank or circle the correct term.

1.   The want-satisfying power that a good or service possesses is referred to as _____.

2.   The _____ is an artificial unit by which utility is measured.

3.   The change in total utility due to a one-unit change in quantity consumed is called _____; _____ analysis is the study of what happens when small changes take place relative to the status quo.

4.   When relative price changes, the (average, marginal) buyer responds; economists maintain that (average, marginal) analysis is the key to understanding human behavior.

5.   If marginal utility is positive, total utility must (fall, rise); if marginal utility is negative, total utility must _____; if marginal utility falls (but is positive) then total utility must (fall, rise) at a decreasing rate.

6.   Economists maintain that as more of a good or service is consumed, per unit of time, its marginal benefit (falls, rises); therefore before buyers will purchase more and more of a good, its price must (fall, rise).

7. The consumer optimum exists when consumers _____ their total utility, subject to such constraints as _____ and relative price; in order to optimize, a consumer should allocate his income so that the marginal utility per dollar's worth of each good or service he purchases is _____.

8. Assume a consumer is in consumer optimum and then the price of good A rises, other things being constant. It is now true that the marginal utility per dollar's worth of good A is (less, greater) than the marginal utility per dollar's worth of other goods; the consumer will now feel (richer, poorer) and probably spend (more, less) on good A; furthermore, the consumer will tend to substitute (A for other goods, other goods for A).

9. Although the (marginal, total) utility of water is greater than that of diamonds, the (marginal, total) utility of diamonds is higher; the price of a good reflects its (marginal, average, total) utility.

TRUE-FALSE QUESTIONS
Circle the **T** if the statement is true, the **F** if it is false. Explain to yourself why a statement is false.

T F 1. Economists today maintain that utility can be measured cardinally.

T F 2. Economists maintain that decisions are made on the margin; hence the concept of "margin" is usually more important than that of "average."

T F 3. Positive economics permits economists to say that person 1 gets more utility from ice cream than does person 2.

T F 4. If total utility rises at a decreasing rate, then marginal utility must be falling.

T F 5. If marginal utility is less than average utility, then average utility must rise.

T F 6. Economists typically assume that as a person consumes more of any good, that good's total utility must fall.

T F 7. If the MU of good X/price of good X exceeds the MU of good Y/price of good Y, the consumer can increase her total utility by substituting good X for good Y.

T F 8. The law of diminishing marginal utility implies the law of demand, assuming consumers wish to optimize.

T F 9. When the price of hamburgers falls, other things constant, everyone's real income will rise.

T F 10. When the price of butter falls, other things constant, people will tend to substitute butter for margarine.

T F 11. Because price reflects average utility rather than total utility, diamonds are more expensive than water.

MULTIPLE CHOICE QUESTIONS
Circle the letter that corresponds to the best answer.

1. If marginal utility is positive, but falling, then total utility
    a. falls.
    b. falls at a decreasing rate.
    c. rises.
    d. rises at a decreasing rate.

2. Which of the following words is most unlike the others?
    a. marginal
    b. average
    c. incremental
    d. extra

3. When the relative price of good A rises, the
    a. average buyer is affected.
    b. marginal buyer is affected.
    c. total buyer is affected.
    d. marginal utility of good A falls.

4. As more of good A is consumed per week, over broad ranges
    a. the marginal utility of good A falls.
    b. the total utility of good A rises.
    c. the total utility of good A rises at a decreasing rate.
    d. All of the above

5. If marginal utility is negative, then
    a. total utility falls.
    b. total utility rises at a decreasing rate.
    c. total utility must be negative.
    d. None of the above.

6. Which of the following helps to explain the law of demand?
    a. the law of diminishing marginal utility
    b. the substitution effect
    c. the income effect
    d. All of the above

7. Consumer optimizing requires that the consumer
    a. maximize income.
    b. maximize total utility, subject to an income constraint.
    c. maximize marginal utility, subject to an income constraint.
    d. maximize average utility, subject to an income constraint.

8. If the marginal utility per dollar's worth of good A exceeds that of good B for Mr. Capra, then he
    a. is optimizing.
    b. will substitute good A for good B.
    c. will substitute good B for good A.
    d. is minimizing, not maximizing.

9.   If the price of good A rises, other things being constant, then
     a.   the marginal utility of good A falls.
     b.   the marginal utility of good A rises.
     c.   the marginal utility per dollar's worth of good A falls.
     d.   the relative price of good A falls.

10. If the price of steak rises, other things constant,
     a.   everyone's real income will rise.
     b.   everyone's money income will rise.
     c.   the real income of steak buyers will rise.
     d.   the real income of steak buyers will fall.

11. If the price of steak rises, other things constant,
     a.   a real income effect will induce people to purchase less steak.
     b.   people will substitute hamburgers for steak.
     c.   the quantity demanded for steak will fall.
     d.   All of the above

12. Diamonds have a higher price than water because
     a.   people are shallow and shortsighted.
     b.   price reflects total, not marginal, utility.
     c.   price reflects marginal, not total, utility.
     d.   the total utility of diamonds is greater, but the marginal utility of water is greater.

WORKING WITH GRAPHS

1.   Use the information given below to complete the table.

Hamburgers consumed per month	Total utility (in utils)	Marginal utility (in utils)
0	0	_____
1	5	_____
2	14	_____
3	22	_____
4	28	_____
5	33	_____
6	36	_____
7	35	_____
8	32	_____

a) Graph the total and marginal utility curves on the graph provided below. (Plot the marginal utilities at the midpoint between quantities.)

b) At what quantity does diminishing marginal utility set in?

2. Consider the graphs below, then answer the questions that follow.

a. Which panel indicates constant marginal utility?
b. Which panel indicates increasing marginal utility?
c. Which panel indicated decreasing marginal utility?

PROBLEMS

1. Consider the following information.

Quantity Consumed per week	Candy Bars		Apples	
	Total utility	Marginal utility	Total utility	Marginal utility
0	0	_____	0	_____
1	10	_____	15	_____
2	18	_____	24	_____
3	25	_____	30	_____
4	29	_____	32	_____
5	31	_____	31	_____
6	30	_____	29	_____

   a. Complete the columns containing the marginal utilities of each good.
   b. With unlimited income, a consumer described by the above information would consume _____ candy bars and _____ apples.
   c. If candy bars cost 25 cents each and apples are two for a quarter (12.5 cents each) and the consumer has $1.50 to spend on candy and apples, what quantity of candy bars and apples will put the above consumer into an equilibrium situation?
   d. Now suppose the consumer suffers a loss of income and has 20 cents to spend. In addition, the price of candy bars is now 10 cents and the price of apples is 2 cents. What quantities of each will put the consumer in equilibrium?

2. Mr. Smith does not believe that economists are correct when they say that diminishing marginal utility is the rule for most goods. He claims that *increasing* marginal utility is the rule: as he consumes more and more of any good, his marginal utility rises.

   Assume that Mr. Smith spends his income one dollar at a time, and that he can purchase one dollar's worth of any good. Assume further that he wishes to maximize his total utility.

   On what good does Mr. Smith spend his first dollar? The second? The third? What predictions can you make about his behavior? Do most people behave that way? Does anyone?

3. Conduct the same analysis that you did in question (2) above for Mrs. Smith, who claims that for her *constant* marginal utility is the rule.
   a. How do your answers differ from those in question (2)?
   b. Can you think of *anything* for which diminishing marginal utility does not occur eventually, *per unit of time*?

ANSWERS TO CHAPTER 19

COMPLETION QUESTIONS

1. utility
2. util
3. marginal utility; marginal
4. marginal; marginal
5. rise; fall; rise

6. falls; fall
7. maximize, income; equal
8. less; poorer, less; other goods for A
9. total, marginal; marginal

TRUE-FALSE QUESTIONS

1. F They need only to assume that it can be measured ordinally.
2. T
3. F Interpersonal utility comparisons require normative judgments.
4. T
5. F If marginal is less than average, average will fall
6. F They assume that its *marginal utility* falls.
7. T
8. T
9. F Only hamburgers buyers will experience an increase in real income.
10. T
11. F Price reflects marginal utility.

MULTIPLE CHOICE QUESTIONS

1.d;   2.b;   3.b;   4.d;   5.a;   6.d;   7.b;   8.b;   9.c;   10.d;
11.d;   12.c

WORKING WITH GRAPHS

1. a. 0; 5; 9; 8; 6; 5; 3; 1; -3

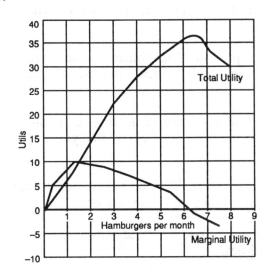

   b. with the third hamburger consumed each month

2. a. 3
    b. 1
    c. 2

PROBLEMS

1. a. marginal utility of candy bars: 0, 10, 8, 7, 4, 2, -1; marginal utility of apples: 0, 15, 9, 6, 2, -1, -2
    b. 5, 4
    c. 4 candy bars and 4 apples
    d. 1 candy bar and 4 apples. Note that the consumer has 2 cents left over, cannot purchase another candy bar, and will not purchase another apple, since the additional apple has a negative marginal utility (total utility declines).

2. Mr. Smith will spend every dollar of his income on the same good—that which gives him the highest marginal utility per dollar's worth of his first dollar spent. Only drug addicts, perhaps, behave that way.

3. a. The answers are the same as in (2) above.
    b. Given the qualifications in the question, its difficult to think of any good for which that is not the case.

GLOSSARY TO CHAPTER 19

Consumer optimum   A choice of a set of goods and services that maximizes the level of satisfaction for each consumer, subject to limited income.

Diminishing marginal utility   The principle stating that as more of any good or service is consumed, its extra benefit declines. Otherwise stated, there are smaller and smaller increases in total utility from the consumption of a good or service as more is consumed during a given time period.

Marginal utility   The change in total utility due to a one-unit change in the quantity of a good consumed.

Principal of substitution   The principal that consumers and producers shift away from goods and resources that become relatively higher priced, in favor of goods and resources that are now relatively lower priced.

Purchasing power   The value of your money income in buying goods and services. If your money income stays the same but the price of one good that you are buying goes up, your effective purchasing power falls.

Real-income effect   The change in people's purchasing power that occurs when, other things being constant, the price of one good they purchase changes.

Substitution effect   The tendency of people to substitute in favor of cheaper commodities and against more expensive commodities.

Util   Representative unit by which utility is measured.

Utility   The want-satisfying power that a good or service possesses.

Utility analysis   The analysis of consumer decision making based on utility maximization.

APPENDIX E

MORE ADVANCED CONSUMER CHOICE THEORY

In Appendix E the more modern, but more difficult, theory of consumer demand is analyzed. Here we assume that utility *cannot* be measured cardinally; instead it can be measured only ordinally. In other words, people can only rank one combination of goods and services as being more preferable to, less preferable to, or equally preferable to another combination of goods. Another way to think of this is to realize that 30 utils is preferable to 15 utils, but 30 utils are not necessarily *twice* as preferable as 15 utils (as would be the case if utility were cardinally measurable).

In this appendix we introduce the indifference curve, explore its properties, and develop an indifference map. Then a budget line is constructed, and its properties are explored. By graphing an indifference map and a budget line, a more sophisticated analysis of the consumer optimum position is possible.

Then we turn to some of the fun topics. We show what happens to consumer optimum when income, and then price, changes; next we derive a price-consumption line; finally we derive a demand curve using the indifference curve-budget line model.

LEARNING OBJECTIVES

After you have studied Appendix E you should be able to

1. define indifference curve, budget constraint, income-consumption curve, and price-consumption curve.

2. draw an indifference curve based on data presented in a table.

3. answer questions that require a proper interpretation of an indifference curve and of an indifference map.

4. recognize properties of indifference curves.

5. interpret the meaning of the slope of an indifference curve and the slope of a budget line.

6. recognize the consumer optimum combination of goods, given an indifference map and a budget line.

7. interpret and sketch an income-consumption curve and a price-consumption curve.

8. predict what happens to a budget line when each price changes and when income changes.

APPENDIX OUTLINE

1.   This appendix presents a more rigorous and more formal analysis of consumer behavior.
   a.   An *indifference curve* is the set of consumption alternatives which yield the same total amount of satisfaction.
   b.   Indifference curves have important properties.
       i.   Indifference curves are negatively sloped.
       ii.   Indifference curves are never linear; they are convex with respect to the origin.

    c.   The slope of an indifference curve is referred to as the *marginal rate of substitution*, which is the change in the quantity of one good that just offsets a one-unit change in the consumption of another good, so that total satisfaction remains constant.

2.   An *indifference map* is a set of indifference curves; higher indifference curves represent higher levels of satisfaction (because they permit more consumption of *both goods*), and lower indifference curves represent less preferred combinations of goods.

3.   A *budget constraint* represents the set of opportunities facing a decision maker.
    a.   The budget line is derived assuming a fixed money income and a given set of relative prices.
    b.   The slope of a budget line is (the negative of) the ratio of the prices of the relevant goods.
    c.   The position of a budget line depends on the level of nominal income; if nominal income changes, a parallel shift in the budget line results.

4.   *Consumer optimum* exists at that point (combination of goods and services) where the slope of the indifference curve equals the slope of the budget line; at that point the consumer is maximizing utility.

5.   If nominal and relative prices are held constant and *income is increased*, an *income-consumption curve* can be derived.

6.   A *price-consumption curve* is the set of consumer optimum combinations of two goods that results when the price of one good changes, holding money income and the price of the other good constant.

7.   A demand curve can be derived from the indifference map-budget line model; as the price of one good changes, other things being constant (the price of the other good and money income), consumer optimum changes so as to indicate an inverse relationship between price and quantity demanded.

KEY TERMS

Income–consumption curve   Price–consumption curve

KEY CONCEPTS

Indifference curve   Budget constraint

COMPLETION QUESTIONS
Fill in the blank or circle the correct term.

1.   A curve that indicates combinations of goods and services that yield an equal level of satisfaction is called a(n) _____ curve; such a curve is (positively, negatively) sloped.

2.   Ignoring its sign, the slope of an indifference curve (falls, rises) as we move down the curve; a set of indifference curves is called an indifference _____.

3. If indifference curve B lies below indifference curve A, it is (less, more) preferred; if indifference curve C lies above indifference curve A, indifference curve C permits a consumer to consume (less, more) of both goods.

4. A budget constraint line is derived holding relative _____ constant and holding nominal _____ constant; the slope of a budget constraint line is determined by _____, and the position of such a line depends on _____.

5. Consumer optimum exists where the budget constraint line is _____ to a(n) _____ curve; at such a point the (lowest, highest) indifference curve is achieved.

6. If income falls, other things being constant, the budget line _____; generally a reduction in income will lead to a(n) (decrease, increase) in its quantity demanded.

7. If the price of one good changes, the slope of an indifference curve (remains constant, changes); if the price of one good changes, the slope of a budget constraint line (remains constant, changes); if nominal income changes, the slope of a budget constraint line (remains constant, changes).

8. Along a price-consumption curve, which relates the combinations of good A and good B that a consumer will purchase, the price of good A falls while the price of good B (rises, falls, remains constant) and nominal income (rises, falls, remains constant).

TRUE-FALSE QUESTIONS
Circle the **T** if the statement is true, the **F** if it is false. Explain to yourself why a statement is false.

T F   1. Along an indifference curve, a consumer has the same level of marginal utility.

T F   2. Indifference curves are negatively sloped.

T F   3. Indifference curves are usually linear.

T F   4. The slope of the budget constraint curve is referred to as the marginal rate of substitution.

T F   5. Points below a budget constraint line are not attainable goods combination for a consumer.

T F   6. If indifference curve 3 lies above indifference curve 2, it is less preferable to the consumer.

T F   7. Indifference curves that lie entirely above a budget constraint line are unattainable for the consumer.

T F   8. If nominal income changes, then the slope of an indifference curve changes.

T F   9. If nominal income changes, then the slope of a budget constraint line changes.

T F 10. If relative prices change, then the slope of a budget constraint line changes, but the slope of an indifference curve is unaltered.

T F 11. Consumer optimum is attained where the budget constraint line is tangent to the highest possible indifference curve.

T F 12. Along an income-consumption curve, prices remain constant.

T F 13. Along a price-consumption curve, relative prices change, but money income is constant.

MULTIPLE CHOICE QUESTIONS
Circle the letter that corresponds to the best answer.

1. Along an indifference curve,
    a. total utility stays the same.
    b. marginal utility stays the same.
    c. average utility stays the same.
    d. All of the above

2. In indifference curve analysis, if combination A is preferred to combination B and combination B is preferred to combination C, then
    a. A is on a higher indifference curve than B or C.
    b. C is on a lower indifference curve than A or B.
    c. A, B, and C are on different indifference curves.
    d. All of the above

3. Indifference curves
    a. are upward sloping.
    b. are linear.
    c. are convex with respect to the origin.
    d. indicate objective, not subjective, valuations of a consumer.

4. As we move down an indifference curve, the marginal rate of substitution
    a. remains constant.
    b. remains constant, but total utility rises.
    c. changes.
    d. changes, but total utility rises.

5. The negative of the slope of a(n) _____ is the marginal rate of substitution.
    a. production possibilities curve
    b. budget constraint line
    c. income-consumption curve
    d. indifference curve

6. Where consumer optimum is reached,
    a. the slope of the budget constraint line equals the slope of an indifference curve.
    b. the ratio of relative prices equals the marginal rate of substitution.
    c. the consumer attains the highest indifference curve, given the budget constraint line.
    d. All of the above

7. The slope of the budget constraint line
    a. reflects the relative prices of the two goods in question.
    b. reflects the consumer's income.
    c. varies as nominal income varies.
    d. always equals the slope of the indifference curve.

8. If income rises, other things being constant, then
   a. an indifference curve shifts outward.
   b. a parallel, rightward shift in the budget constraint line occurs.
   c. the slope of the budget constraint line falls.
   d. the slope of the budget constraint line rises.

9. When a price-consumption curve is derived,
   a. the relative price of both goods changes.
   b. the relative price of only one good changes.
   c. money income changes.
   d. consumer optimum is not attained.

10. When an income-consumption curve is derived,
    a. relative prices remain constant.
    b. income changes.
    c. consumer optimum exists at each point along such a curve.
    d. All of the above

11. When the price of good A rises, other things being constant,
    a. the indifference map does not change.
    b. the slope of the budget constraint line changes.
    c. a new consumer optimum is reached, where less of good A is purchased.
    d. All of the above

WORKING WITH GRAPHS

1. Suppose that a consumer is faced with the choice of only two goods: food and entertainment. After some consideration, the consumer provides the following information about various combinations of food and entertainment per month to which she is indifferent, given some particular level of satisfaction.

Units of entertainment per month	Units of food per month
35	7
20	11
10	15
5	20
3	30
2	45

   a. Use this information and the following grid to plot this consumer's indifference curve for entertainment and food for a given level of satisfaction. Label the curve I.

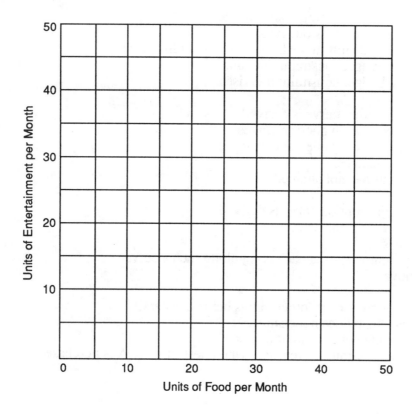

Suppose the consumer is asked to provide the same type of information for some higher level of satisfaction. In this case the consumer supplies the information given below.

Units of entertainment per month	Units of food per month
40	11
30	15
25	18
15	25
10	35
7	45

b. Use this new information and the grid above to plot this additional indifference curve. Label this curve II.

2.   Suppose that the consumer in problem 1 has a monthly income of $400 and that the price of entertainment is $10 per unit and the price of food is $20 per unit.
  a. Plot the consumer's budget line on the above grid and label it BL1.
  b. Given the consumer's indifference map and the above prices and income, what combination of entertainment and food will put the consumer at an optimum point?
  c. Suppose that the price of food drops to $10 per unit but the price of entertainment and the consumer's income remain unchanged. Draw the new budget line in the above grid and label it BL2.
  d. After the change in part (c), which combination of entertainment and food will put the consumer at an optimum point?

3.   Draw a price-consumption curve for each of the following combinations of goods.
  a. Hot dogs and hot dog buns with the price of buns changing.
  b. Coke and Pepsi with the price of Pepsi changing.
  c. Potatoes and guitar strings with the price of guitar strings changing.

ANSWERS TO APPENDIX E

COMPLETION QUESTIONS

1. indifference; negatively
2. falls; map
3. less; more
4. prices; income; relative prices; income
5. tangent; indifference; highest

6. shifts inward (parallel); decrease
7. remains constant; changes; remains constant
8. remains constant; remains constant

TRUE-FALSE QUESTIONS

1. F Total utility stays the same, not marginal
2. T
3. F A linear indifference curve implies a constant marginal rate of substitution.
4. F The slope of the budget line reflects relative prices.
5. F They are attainable, but not optimal.
6. F It is more preferable if it lies above 2.
7. T
8. F Indifference curves are independent of income.
9. F Slope stays the same, but the budget line shifts.
10. T
11. T
12. T
13. T

MULTIPLE CHOICE QUESTIONS

1.a; 2.d; 3.c; 4.c; 5.d; 6.d; 7.a; 8.b; 9.a; 10.d; 11.d

WORKING WITH GRAPHS

1. a. see graph below; b. see graph below

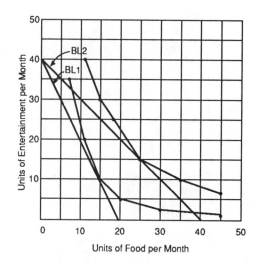

2. a. see graph above; b. 10 units of entertainment per month and 15 units of food per month; c. see graph above; d. 15 units of entertainment per month and 25 units of food per month.

3.

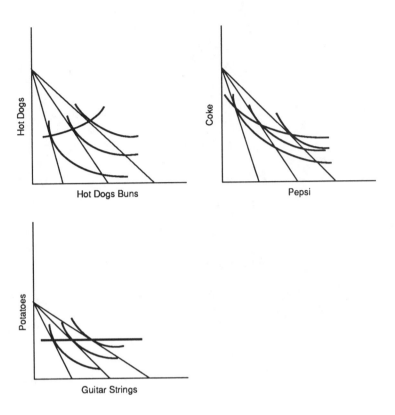

GLOSSARY TO APPENDIX E

Budget constraint The resource constraint imposed on households and firms at any point in time; it represents the set of opportunities facing each decision maker.

Income-consumption curve The set of optimum consumption points that would occur if income were increased, nominal and relative prices remaining constant.

Indifference curve A curve composed of the set of consumption alternatives, each yielding the same total amount of satisfaction.

Price-consumption curve The set of consumer optimum combinations of two goods that the consumer would choose as the relative price of the goods changes, while money income remains constant.

DEMAND AND SUPPLY ELASTICITY

PUTTING THIS CHAPTER INTO PERSPECTIVE

Chapter 20 is the second chapter in Part Six, in which the micro-economics portion of this text continues. You have already analyzed supply and demand in Chapter 3; this chapter is concerned with demand and supply elasticity.

The law of demand posits an inverse relationship between price and quantity demanded, other things being constant. Knowing that quantity demanded will rise if price falls and that quantity demanded will fall if price rises, other things being constant, is useful information—to be sure. But the concept of price elasticity of demand goes one step further; it is concerned with how responsive quantity demanded is to changes in price. If price rises, will quantity demanded fall by a little or a lot? If price falls, will quantity demanded rise by just a little bit, or by a great amount?

Price elasticity of demand is defined as the percentage change in quantity demanded divided by the percentage change in price. Because of the law of demand, the price elasticity of demand coefficient (number) will always be negative. By convention, therefore, economists ignore the sign; and if the coefficient is greater than one, less than one, or equal to one, we refer to a good (in the relevant price range) as being elastic, inelastic, or unit elastic, respectively.

Price elasticity of demand is a very useful concept. If you are in business and you know the price elasticity of demand coefficient for your good, you can raise your total revenues (and perhaps profits) by raising or lowering your sales price, depending on whether the elasticity coefficient is less than or greater than one. If you are in charge of raising revenues for a government, you would be well-advised to tax only those goods for which at current prices the price elasticity of demand coefficient is quite low. Many other issues, in this chapter and throughout the remainder of this text, will revolve around the value of the price elasticity of demand coefficient.

In Chapter 20 we analyze how price elasticity of demand coefficients can be measured; we also analyze cross elasticities of demand, income elasticities of demand, and the price elasticity of supply.

There are several pitfalls that you should be careful to avoid. Many students think in terms of whether a *good* is price elastic or inelastic; instead you should realize that for each good (given a linear demand curve) there are ranges of price elasticity and price inelasticity. For that reason you should always be careful to specify the *price range* when analyzing elasticity of demand. Finally, many students believe that a business can increase its profits by raising selling price; but as the text indicates, if a firm raises price when the demand is highly price elastic at the current price, its total revenues will fall dramatically; so too, probably, will its profits.

LEARNING OBJECTIVES

After you have studied this chapter you should be able to

1. define price elasticity of demand, elastic demand, unit elastic demand, inelastic demand, perfectly inelastic demand, perfectly elastic demand, cross elasticity of demand, income elasticity of demand, price elasticity of supply, perfectly elastic supply, and perfectly inelastic supply.

2. calculate price elasticity of demand in two ways, given the relevant information.

3. predict what will happen to a firm's total revenues if the firm changes price, given price elasticity of demand.

4. classify an elasticity coefficient as indicating whether demand is elastic, unit elastic, or inelastic, in the relevant price range.

5. recognize from a graph whether the demand for a good is perfectly elastic or perfectly inelastic in the specified price range.

6. identify the determinants of price elasticity of demand.

7. calculate the cross elasticity of demand coefficient, and determine from the sign of that coefficient whether or not the goods in question are substitutes or complements.

8. calculate income elasticity of demand from relevant information and distinguish price elasticity of demand from income elasticity of demand.

9. calculate price elasticity of supply, identify the determinants of price elasticity of supply, and recognize a graph of a perfectly elastic supply curve and a perfectly inelastic supply curve.

CHAPTER OUTLINE

1. Elasticity measures quantity responsiveness to price changes.
    a. *Price elasticity of demand* is defined as the percentage change in quantity demanded divided by the percentage change in price.
        i. Because of the law of demand, the price elasticity of demand is always negative; by convention the sign is ignored.
        ii. Price elasticity of demand relates percentage changes, not absolute changes.
    b. There are two ways to calculate the price elasticity of demand.
        i. Price elasticity of demand may be calculated by dividing the change in quantity demanded over the original quantity demanded by the change in price over the original price; this method yields a different elasticity over the same range of the demand curve, depending on whether price rises or falls.
        ii. In order to get consistent results over the same range of a demand curve, it is possible to calculate price elasticity by using average values for base price and base quantity.

2. If the calculated price elasticity of demand for a good is greater than one, the demand is called *elastic*; if it is equal to one, the demand is called *unit elastic*; if it is less than one, the demand is called *inelastic*.

3. Elasticity is related to a firm's *total revenues*.
    a. In the range of elastic demand, if a firm lowers price its total revenues will rise; if it raises price its total revenues will fall.
    b. In the range of unit elastic demand, small changes in price leave the firm's total revenues unaltered.
    c. In the range of inelastic demand, if a firm lowers price its total revenues will fall; if it raises price its total revenues will rise.
    d. Along a linear demand curve (which has a constant slope, by definition), a good has a elastic, a unit elastic, and an inelastic range.
    e. There are two extreme price elasticities of demand.
        i. *Perfectly inelastic demand* indicates no change in quantity demanded as price changes; such a demand curve is vertical at the given quantity.
        ii. *Perfectly elastic demand* indicates that even a slight increase in price will lead to a zero quantity demanded; such a demand curve is horizontal at the given price.

4. There are three major determinants of the price elasticity of demand.
    a. The closer the substitutes for a particular good, and the more available they are, the greater will be its price elasticity of demand.
    b. The higher the proportion of total expenditures that people allocate to a good, the higher will be that good's price elasticity of demand.
    c. The longer any price change persists, the greater the price elasticity of demand; the distinction between the short-run and long-run consumer adjustment period varies with the good in question.

5. *Cross elasticity of demand* is defined as the percentage change in the quantity demanded of one good (holding its price constant) divided by the percentage change in the price of a related good.
    a. If the sign of the cross elasticity of demand is positive, the two goods are *substitutes*.
    b. If the sign of the cross elasticity of demand is negative, the two goods are *complements*.

6. *Income elasticity of demand* is defined as the percentage change in the quantity demanded for a good (holding its price constant) divided by the percentage change in money income.

7. *Price elasticity of supply* is defined as the percentage change in quantity supplied divided by the percentage change in price.
    a. One extreme is *perfectly elastic supply*, where a slight decrease in price leads to a zero quantity supplied; such a supply curve is horizontal at the given price.
    b. Another extreme is *perfectly inelastic supply*, where quantity supplied is constant, regardless of what happens to price; such a supply curve is vertical at the given quantity.
    c. The longer the time for adjustment, the more price elastic is the supply curve.
    d. Empirical evidence indicates that short-run elasticities for goods are considerably smaller than long-run elasticities.

8. Governments tax products that are considered demand inelastic; however, the long-run demand elasticities are higher because buyers can find alternative sources for such goods.

KEY TERMS

Elastic demand   Inelastic demand
Unit elasticity of demand

KEY CONCEPTS

Price elasticity of demand
Perfectly inelastic demand
Perfectly elastic demand
Perfectly elastic supply

Cross elasticity of demand
Price elasticity of supply
Income elasticity of demand
Perfectly inelastic supply

COMPLETION QUESTIONS
Fill in the blank or circle the correct term.

1.   Price elasticity of demand is a measure of buyer _____ to price changes.

2.   Price elasticity of demand is defined as the percentage change in _____ divided by the percentage change in _____; the problem with this measure is that we get (the same, a different) numerical value when we move up, as opposed to down, the same range of the demand curve.

3.   In order to correct for the problem in question 2 above, the _____ value method of calculating the price elasticity of demand can be used.

4.   Assume a 1 percent change in price. If quantity demanded changes by less than 1 percent then we say that in that range the demand for the good is _____; if quantity demanded changes by 1 percent then in that range demand is _____; if quantity demanded changes by more than 1 percent then in that range demand is _____.

5.   If price falls and total revenues rise, then in that range demand was price _____; if price falls and total revenues remain constant, then in that range demand was price _____; if price falls and total revenues fall, then in that range demand was price _____.

6.   If price rises and total revenues fall, then demand was price _____; if total revenues rise, then demand was price _____; if total revenues remain constant, then demand was _____.

7.   A demand curve that exhibits zero responsiveness to price changes is _____; such a demand curve is (horizontal, vertical) at the given quantity; a demand curve in which even the slightest increase in price will lead to a zero quantity demanded is _____; such a demand curve is (horizontal, vertical) at the given price.

8.   The determinants of price elasticity of demand are _____, _____, and _____.

9.   Cross elasticity of demand is defined as the percentage change in the _____ for one good, holding its _____ constant, divided by the percentage change in the _____ of another good.

10.   If the cross elasticity of demand is positive, then the two goods are _____; if it is negative, the two goods are _____.

11.   The income elasticity of demand is defined as the percentage change in _____ for a good, holding its _____ constant, divided by the percentage change in _____.

12. The price elasticity of supply measures the responsiveness of the _____ of a good to a change in its price; a supply curve in which a slight decrease in price leads to a zero quantity supplied is _____; if quantity supplied remains constant no matter what happens to price, the supply curve is _____.

TRUE-FALSE QUESTIONS

Circle the **T** if the statement is true, the **F** if it is false. Explain to yourself why a statement is false.

T F   1. Price elasticity of demand measures the responsiveness of price to changes in quantity demanded.

T F   2. Because of the law of demand, price elasticity of demand will always (implicitly) be a negative number.

T F   3. Price elasticity of demand deals with absolute, not relative values.

T F   4. When price elasticity of demand is used by the average-value approach, price elasticity is the same whether price rises or falls over a given demand curve range.

T F   5. If the price elasticity of demand is 3, then over the relevant price range, demand is inelastic.

T F   6. If price falls and total revenues rise, then over that price range demand is inelastic.

T F   7. If a firm discovers that at current prices the price elasticity of demand is 1/2, the firm may want to raise prices to increase profits.

T F   8. The price elasticity of demand for McDonald's hamburgers is less than the price elasticity of demand for hamburgers.

T F   9. If the demand for good A is perfectly elastic, its demand curve is vertical at that price.

T F   10. If the demand for good A is perfectly inelastic over *all* prices, good A violates the law of demand.

T F   11. The less time people have to respond to a price change, the higher is the price elasticity.

T F   12. If the cross elasticity of demand for goods A and B is negative, A and B are complements.

T F   13. Income elasticity of demand is calculated for a horizontal shift in the demand curve, given price.

T F   14. If supply is perfectly inelastic, the curve will be horizontal at the given quantity.

MULTIPLE CHOICE QUESTIONS
Circle the letter that corresponds to the best answer.

1. Price elasticity of demand measures responsiveness of
    a. quantity demanded to changes in price.
    b. quantity demanded to changes in income.
    c. price to changes in quantity demanded.
    d. price to changes in demand.

2. If the price elasticity of demand is 1/3, then
    a. demand is inelastic.
    b. demand is inelastic over that price range.
    c. demand is elastic.
    d. demand is elastic over that price range.

3. Which of the following is **NOT** true concerning the price elasticity of demand?
    a. Its sign is always negative, due to the law of demand.
    b. It is a unitless, dimensionless number.
    c. It equals the percentage change in price divided by the percentage change in quantity demanded.
    d. It measures the responsiveness of quantity demanded to changes in price.

4. If price elasticity of demand is calculated using the original price and quantity, then over a given range in the demand curve price elasticity of demand
    a. differs depending on whether price rises or falls.
    b. is the same, regardless of whether price rises or falls.
    c. is equal to 1.
    d. rises as price falls.

5. If price falls by 1 percent and quantity demanded rises by 2 percent, then the price elasticity of demand
    a. is inelastic over that range.
    b. is 1/2.
    c. is elastic over that range.
    d. cannot be calculated from this information.

6. If price rises and total revenue rises, then the price elasticity of demand over that range is
    a. elastic.
    b. inelastic.
    c. unitary elastic.
    d. equal to 1.

7. If price falls and over that price range demand is inelastic, total revenues will
    a. remain constant.
    b. fall.
    c. rise.
    d. fall, then rise.

8. If the demand for good A is perfectly inelastic at all prices,
    a. quantity demanded does not change as price changes.
    b. the law of demand is violated.
    c. the demand curve is vertical at the given quantity.
    d. All of the above

9. If the demand for good A is perfectly elastic,
   a. quantity demanded does not vary with price.
   b. the demand curve is horizontal.
   c. the demand curve is vertical.
   d. the demand curve is positively sloped.

10. Which of the following is **NOT** a determinant of the price elasticity of demand?
    a. existence and closeness of substitutes
    b. proportion of the good to the consumer's budget
    c. price elasticity of supply
    d. length of time allowed for adjustment to a price change

11. If the cross elasticity of demand between good A and good B is positive, the goods are
    a. substitutes.
    b. complements.
    c. unrelated.
    d. necessities.

12. If the cross elasticity between good A and good B is -10, then A and B are
    a. close substitutes.
    b. near substitutes.
    c. strongly complementary.
    d. mildly complementary.

13. Baseballs and baseball bats are
    a. substitutes.
    b. complements.
    c. not related goods.
    d. necessities.

14. When the income elasticity of demand for good A is calculated,
    a. the price of good A varies.
    b. income changes, which lead to horizontal shifts in the demand curve for good A, are measured.
    c. a movement along the demand curve for good A is measured.
    d. All of the above

15. *Analogy*: A movement along a demand curve is to price elasticity of demand as a shift in the demand curve is to
    a. an increase in demand.
    b. changes in taxes or subsidies.
    c. income elasticity of demand.
    d. substitutes and complements.

16. At current prices for salt, salt is highly price
    a. elastic.
    b. inelastic.
    c. cross elastic.
    d. unitary elastic.

17. Which of the following goods is probably the most highly income elastic?
    a. salt
    b. food
    c. alcoholic beverages
    d. private education

18. A perfectly inelastic supply curve
    a. shows great quantity supplied responsiveness to price changes.
    b. is horizontal at the given price.
    c. indicates zero quantity supplied responsiveness to price changes.
    d. is a normal situation.

19. If the supply of good B is perfectly elastic and price falls, quantity supplied will
    a. remain unchanged.
    b. rise.
    c. fall.
    d. fall to zero.

20. If price rises, the quantity supplied will be greater the
    a. longer the time that elapses.
    b. more income elastic is the good.
    c. higher the price elasticity of demand for the good.
    d. All of the above

MATCHING
Choose the item in column (2) that best matches an item in column (1).

(1)	(2)

a. perfectly inelastic demand   h. elasticity coefficient less than 1
b. perfectly elastic demand   i. horizontal supply curve
c. perfectly inelastic supply   j. complementary or substitute goods
d. perfectly elastic supply   k. quality of substitutes
e. determinant of price elasticity   l. horizontal demand curve
f. cross-price elasticity of demand m. vertical demand curve
g. inelastic   n. vertical supply curve

PROBLEMS

1. Suppose you are given the following data on the market demand and supply for CD's in a small record store. (Use the average elasticity measure.)

Price	Quantity demanded (per week)	Quantity supplied (per week)
$4.00	50	10
4.50	45	15
5.00	40	25
5.50	35	35
6.00	30	45

   a. What is the equilibrium price for CD's?
   b. What is the price elasticity of demand over the price range $4.50 to $5? Over the range $5.50 to $6?
   c. What is the price elasticity of supply over the same two ranges of price?
   d. Now suppose that most students in the area are working for the minimum wage and that the minimum wage has gone up. As a result, at each price, two more CD's per week are demanded. Calculate the price elasticity of demand over the same ranges as in part (b).
   e. After comparing your answers from parts (b) and (d), what can you conclude about the price elasticity of demand as the demand curve shifts to the right?

2. Suppose we have the following information for a low-income family:

	Income per month	Quantity of hamburger demanded per month	Quantity of steak demanded per month
Period 1	$750	8 lbs.	2 lbs.
Period 2	950	5 lbs.	4 lbs.

   a. What is the income elasticity of demand for hamburger?
   b. What is the income elasticity of demand for steak?
   c. From our study of demand in an earlier chapter, we know _____ is a normal good, whereas _____ is an inferior good.

3. Suppose the price of color print film has recently risen by 10 percent due to an increase in the cost of the silver that is used to make film. As a result, less film is being sold in the camera store where you work. You do some checking and find that camera sales are down by 4 percent. What is the cross-price elasticity of cameras and film? Are these two goods complements or substitutes?

CASE STUDY

High prestige private American universities (and state universities as well) charge different prices to different students, even though they provide the same service to students. By charging tuition (giving scholarships) based solely on "need" (essentially, the income and wealth of the students' parents), such universities are pricing according to the price elasticity of demand.

1. Is the demand for an education at a high prestige university likely to be less elastic for high-income parents, or for low-income parents? Why?
2. How would a revenue-maximizing university charge tuition to students?

ANSWERS TO CHAPTER 20

COMPLETION QUESTIONS

1. responsiveness
2. quantity demanded; price; a different
3. average
4. inelastic; unit elastic; elastic
5. elastic; unit elastic; inelastic
6. elastic; inelastic; unit elastic
7. perfectly inelastic; vertical; perfectly elastic; horizontal
8. closeness of available substitutes; proportion of the good in consumer budgets; length of time to respond
9. quantity demanded; price; price
10. substitutes; complements
11. quantity demanded; price; money income
12. quantity supplied; perfectly elastic; perfectly inelastic

TRUE-FALSE QUESTIONS

1. F It measures quantity demanded responsiveness to price changes.
2. T
3. F It deals with relative values.
4. T
5. F It is price elastic because the coefficient exceeds 1.
6. F It must have been elastic.
7. T
8. F It is greater, because there are more substitutes for *McDonald's* hamburgers than for hamburgers.
9. F It is horizontal at that price.
10. T
11. F Elasticity increases over time because substitutes become more readily available over time.
12. T
13. T
14. F It will be vertical, at the given quantity.

MULTIPLE CHOICE QUESTIONS

1.a; 2.b; 3.c; 4.a; 5.c; 6.b; 7.b; 8.d; 9.b; 10.c;
11.a; 12.c; 13.b; 14.b; 15.c; 16.b; 17.d; 18.c; 19.d; 20.a.

MATCHING

a and m; b and l; c and n; d and i; e and k; f and j; g and h

PROBLEMS

1. a. $5.50
   b. 1.12; 1.77
   c. 4.75; 2.88
   d. 1.07; 1.67
   e. As the demand curve shifts to the right, for any price range, demand becomes less elastic— or, alternatively stated, more inelastic.

2. a. -1.96
   b. 2.83
   c. steak; hamburger

3. -0.43; complements

CASE STUDY

1. Demand is less elastic for high-income parents, who will view other universities as inferior substitutes for high-prestige universities.
2. The same way that the prestigious universities do; it would, however, give fewer 100% tuition scholarships, unless long-run profit considerations required that minority or low income students who are very likely to be successful in the future be advertisements for *that* school.

GLOSSARY TO CHAPTER 20

Cross elasticity of demand   The percentage change in the demand of one good (holding its price constant) divided by the percentage change in the price of a related good.

Elastic demand   A demand relationship in which a given percentage change in price will result in a larger percentage change in quantity demanded. Total expenditures and price are inversely related in the elastic portion of the demand curve.

Income elasticity of demand   The percentage change in demand for any good, holding its price constant, divided by the percentage change in money income; the responsiveness of the demand to changes in income, holding its relative price constant.

Inelastic demand   A characteristic of a demand curve in which a given percentage change in price will result in a less-than-proportionate percentage change in the quantity demanded. Total expenditures and price are directly related in the inelastic region of the demand curve.

Perfectly elastic demand   A demand curve that has the characteristic that even the slightest increase in price will lead to a zero quantity demanded.

Perfectly elastic supply   A supply curve characterized by a reduction in quantity supplied to zero when there is the slightest decrease in price.

Perfectly inelastic demand   A demand curve that exhibits zero responsiveness to price changes; that is, no matter what the price is the quantity demanded remains the same.

Perfectly inelastic supply   The characteristic of a supply curve for which quantity supplied remains constant, no matter what happens to price.

Price elasticity of demand   The responsiveness of the quantity demanded of a commodity to changes in its price. The price elasticity of demand is defined as the percentage change in quantity demanded divided by the percentage change in price.

Price elasticity of supply   The responsiveness of the quantity supplied of a commodity to a change in its price. Price elasticity of supply is defined as the percentage change in quantity supplied divided by the percentage change in price.

Unit elasticity of demand   A demand relationship in which the quantity demanded changes exactly in proportion to the change in price. Total expenditures are invariant to price changes in the unit elastic portion of the demand curve.

CHAPTER 21

THE FINANCIAL ENVIRONMENT OF BUSINESS

PUTTING THIS CHAPTER INTO PERSPECTIVE

Chapter 21 is the third chapter in Part Six, and it introduces you to the various forms of business organization and provides some background information that will be helpful in Part Seven.

Problems arise because a separation of ownership and control exists in large corporations, enabling managers to place their own interests above those of the shareholders. Economists refer to this as the principal-agent problem; also the problems of asymmetric information, adverse selection, and moral hazard are related to financial transactions.

LEARNING OBJECTIVES

After you have studied this chapter you should be able to

1. define financial capital, proprietorship, partnership, corporation, unlimited liability, limited liability, dividends, share of stock, bond, primary market, secondary market, reinvestment, asymmetric information, adverse selection, moral hazard, principal-agent problem, separation of ownership and control, collateral, incentive-compatible contract, random walk theory, and inside information.

2. state the distinctions among proprietorships, partnerships, and corporations.

3. state the advantages and disadvantages of proprietorships, partnerships, and corporations.

4. recognize how owners can reduce the principal-agent problem that arises from the separation of ownership and control.

5. recognize how asymmetric information can contribute to a moral hazard problem and an adverse selection problem.

6. enumerate the three principal methods of corporate financing.

7. distinguish between primary and secondary markets.

8. predict the consequences of the efficient market theory.

CHAPTER OUTLINE

There are three basic forms into which U.S. businesses have chosen to organize: proprietorship, partnership, and corporation.

1. A proprietorship is owned by a single individual who makes the business decisions, receives all the profits, and is legally responsible for all the debts of the firm.
    a. Advantages: a proprietorship is easy to form and dissolve; all decision-making powers reside with the sole proprietor; a proprietorship is taxed only once.
    b. Disadvantages: the proprietorship faces unlimited liability for debts of the firm and has limited ability to raise funds; the business normally ceases to exist with the death of the proprietor.

2. A partnership is owned by two or more who share profits or losses.
    a. Advantages: partnerships are easy to form, experience relatively low costs of monitoring job performance, permit more specialization than sole proprietorships, and are only taxed once.
    b. Disadvantages: partnerships face unlimited liability and more difficulty in decision-making (relative to proprietorship); dissolution of the partnership is usually necessary when a partner dies or leaves the partnership.

3. A corporation is a legal entity that may conduct business in its own name, just as an individual does. The owners of the corporation are its shareholders.
    a. Advantages: shareholders enjoy limited liability; a corporation continues to exist even if some owners cease to remain owners; a corporation has the ability to raise large sums of money for investments.
    b. Disadvantages: owners are subject to double taxation because corporations pay taxes on profits and shareholders pay taxes on dividends received; ownership and control are separated in a corporation.
        i. Professional managers, who may have little or no ownership in the firm, may pursue their own, not shareholder-owner, interests.
        ii. Shareholders may experience high costs to monitor the behavior of professional managers.

4. Stocks, bonds, and reinvestment of retained earnings are the most important sources of corporate financing.
    a. From the investor's point of view, stocks offer the highest risk (and, therefore, the highest potential rate of return), and the greatest control over the firm's decisions.
    b. Bonds are relatively safer (and yield a correspondingly lower rate of return) and provide little control over decision-making.

5. Both businesses and investors engage in financial transactions in primary and secondary markets.
    a. In primary markets, purchases and sales of newly issued securities are made.
    b. In secondary markets, purchases and sales of previously issued securities are made.

6. Some people believe that the stock market is an efficient market, in the sense that it follows a random walk.
    a. The random walk theory predicts that the best forecast of tomorrow's stock price is today's price, because today's price incorporates all the information important to stock price determination.
    b. Only inside information will permit people to beat the stock market.

7. Technological advances in computers, telecommunications, and travel, along with an increased decentralization and opening of economies, have helped to make the world a global economy; as is always the case in economics, a trade-off exists.

8. Leading the way toward a globalized economy is worldwide financial integration.
    a. Legal and technological changes have blurred the distinctions among financial institutions and between financial and non-financial institutions.
    b. Multinational corporations with a wide array of financial services operate worldwide.
    c. Markets for U.S. government securities, interbank lending and borrowing, foreign exchange trading, and common stock are now operating continuously, in vast quantities, around the clock and around the world; along with technological and legal changes, the U.S. trade deficit has helped to spur such markets.

9. When financial transactions take place, asymmetric information may exist.
    a. If asymmetric information exists *before* a transaction takes place, adverse selection exists; borrowers who are the worse credit risks know better than lenders that they are poor risks, and such borrowers can outbid other borrowers for funds.
    b. If asymmetric information exists *after* a transaction, moral hazard may exist; after borrowing funds, the borrowers may be able to use the money to make investments riskier than was otherwise expected by the lender.
    c. A moral hazard problem arises *within* a firm; because modern business is characterized by a separation of ownership (stockholders) and control (management) a principal-agent problem exists; management has an incentive to pursue its own, and not stockholder, interest.
    d. In order to reduce the problems that arise from asymmetric information, various countermoves have evolved.
        i.   Lenders can reduce the problem of *adverse selection* in general ways.
             (a) Lenders can purchase information from independent businesses who rate the credit worthiness of borrowers.
             (b) Lenders can require borrowers to put up collateral.
        ii. Lenders can reduce the problem of *moral hazard* by requiring an incentive-compatible contract, which assures that borrowers also place a good deal of their own assets at risk; such a scheme makes the interests of borrowers and lenders more closely aligned.

KEY TERMS

Proprietorship	Dividends	Financial capital
Partnership	Share of stock	Collateral
Corporation	Bond	

KEY CONCEPTS

Unlimited liability	Adverse selection	Incentive-compatible contract
Limited liability	Reinvestment	Asymmetric information
Separation of ownership	Primary market	Random walk theory
and control	Secondary market	Inside information
Moral hazard	Principal-agent problem	

COMPLETION QUESTIONS
Fill in the blank or circle the correct term.

1.   The three major forms of U.S. business organizations are _____, _____, and _____.

2.   While the highest percentage of U.S. firms are (proprietorships, partnerships, corporations), the highest percentage of total business revenue is attributed to _____.

3.   A _____ is a legal entity that may conduct business in its own name, just as an individual does; its owners are called (shareholders, bondholders), and such owners enjoy (unlimited, limited, partially limited) liability.

4.   The income that corporations earn is taxed (once, twice).

5.   When transactions take place, _____ information may exist; if such a situation exists before the transaction occurs, the _____ problem exists; if it exists after the transaction exists then the _____ problem exists.

6.   Because modern corporations are characterized by a separation of ownership and _____, a _____ hazard problem exists.

7.   Lenders can reduce the problem of adverse selection by purchasing information regarding a borrower's _____; lenders can also require borrowers to put up _____.

8.   Lenders can reduce the moral hazard problem by requiring a(n) _____ contract, which requires borrowers to assume part of the _____.

9.   A separation of ownership and control could lead to the _____ problem.

10. The three main sources of corporate finance are _____, _____, and _____; of these a _____ denotes ownership in the corporation and a _____ is a legal claim against the firm, entitling the owner to receive a fixed annual coupon, plus a lump sum at _____.

11. Because professional managers usually own a very small percentage of the firms they manage, a separation of ownership and _____ exists; this separation can lead to a situation in which managers can maximize (their own; shareholders') interests.

12. Previously issued stocks and bonds are sold in _____ markets; new issues are sold in _____ markets.

13. According to the efficient markets theory, the stock market is a _____ walk; the best prediction of tomorrow's price is _____.

TRUE-FALSE QUESTIONS
Circle the **T** if the statement is true, the **F** if it is false. Explain to yourself why a statement is false.

T   F   1.   Corporations are the most common form of business organization in the United States.

T F   2.   Proprietorships account for the highest percentage of total business revenues in the United States.

T F   3.   Proprietorships and partnerships face unlimited liability for the debts of their firms.

T F   4.   The main advantage of corporations is that they offer limited liability to shareholders.

T F   5.   Corporate shareholders are taxed twice on the corporation's earnings.

T F   6.   A separation of ownership and control often exists in large corporations.

T F   7.   In large corporations, managers can possibly pursue their own, not shareholders', interests.

T F   8.   The adverse selection problem results due to asymmetric information after a transaction.

T F   9.   Borrowers who do not intend to repay loans might be able to outbid honest borrowers for the funds.

T F 10.   Stocks offer a higher risk and return, relative to bonds, but bonds offer investors greater control over the firm's decisions.

T F 11.   Reinvestment of retained earnings is the most important source of corporate finance.

T F 12.   In a secondary market, previously issued securities are bought and sold.

T F 13.   The principal-agent problem implies that management will pursue the public's interest, not stockholder interests.

T F 14.   When lenders insist that borrowers put up collateral they are trying to avoid the principal-agent problem.

T F 15.   According to the efficient market theory, the best prediction of tomorrow's stock price is today's price.

T F 16.   According to the efficient market theory, the only way to earn abnormal profits (in the long run) is to have inside information.

MULTIPLE CHOICE QUESTIONS
Circle the letter that corresponds to the best answer.

1.   Which of the following is **NOT** true, concerning a proprietorship?
   a.   Most U.S. firms are proprietorships.
   b.   They are easy to form and to dissolve.
   c.   They offer limited liability.
   d.   The owner is taxed only once on business income.

2.   Which of the following is a disadvantage of a proprietorship?
   a.   Unlimited liability for the firm's debts.
   b.   Limited ability to raise funds.
   c.   The firm ends with the death of the proprietor.
   d.   All of the above

3. Which of the following is **NOT** true, concerning partnerships?
    a. There are fewer partnerships than proprietorships in the United States.
    b. They permit more effective specialization than proprietorships.
    c. Business income is taxed only once.
    d. Partners have limited liability for the firm's debts.

4. Which of the following is an advantage of partnerships?
    a. Partners have unlimited liability.
    b. They enjoy reduced cost in monitoring job performance.
    c. They must be dissolved if one partner dies.
    d. All of the above

5. A corporation
    a. is a legal entity that conducts business in its own name.
    b. permits unlimited liability to shareholders.
    c. must be dissolved if a majority stockholder dies.
    d. has severely limited abilities to attract financial resources.

6. According to the efficient market theory, in an efficient market
    a. only lucky people can earn abnormal profits in the long run.
    b. tomorrow's price is easily determined.
    c. only inside information permits abnormal profits.
    d. a pattern of price changes will emerge.

7. Regarding asymmetric information:
    a. if it exists before a transaction, adverse selection may occur.
    b. it exists only after the transaction.
    c. it presents a problem that cannot be reduced.
    d. if it exists after a transaction, adverse selection may occur.

8. Which of the following helps to reduce the problem of asymmetric information?
    a. Require borrowers to put up collateral.
    b. Purchase information regarding the credit rating of borrowers.
    c. Require an incentive-compatible contract.
    d. All of the above

9. Which of the following is **NOT** an example of a problem resulting from asymmetric information?
    a. moral hazard problem
    b. efficient markets
    c. adverse selection problem
    d. principal-agent problem

10. Which of the following has **NOT** evolved to solve a problem resulting from asymmetric information?
    a. collateral
    b. incentive-compatible contracts
    c. globalized stock markets
    d. credit rating agencies

11. Shareholders
    a. are the owners of corporations.
    b. are less at risk than are bondholders.
    c. are subject to unlimited risk.
    d. have less control over firm decisions than do bondholders.

12. In a large corporation
    a. ownership is usually concentrated in a few hands.
    b. separation of ownership and control is unlikely.
    c. managers may try to maximize their own (not shareholders') wealth.
    d. shareholders are guaranteed a fixed dividend.

MATCHING
Choose the item in column (2) that best matches an item in column (1).

(1)	(2)
a. secondary market	h. corporate debt
b. share of stock	i. purchase and sale of previously issued securities
c. bond	j. limited liability
d. separation of ownership and control	k. total revenues minus total costs
e. total profits	l. corporate ownership
f. corporation	m. principal-agent problem
g. asymmetric information	n. adverse selection

CASE STUDY

Niels Bohr, a Nobel Laureate physicist, divided the stock market into three groups: smart investors who study a corporation's finances to determine if its price is overvalued or undervalued, people who play randomly (throwing darts to pick stocks), and people with inside information. He reasoned that, as a group, the third group must be winners and the second group will break even.

1. Who must be the losers?

2. Given this theory, what should the losing group do after it discovers that its analysis indicates that Stock A is overpriced? (HINT: Remember inside information could exist).

ANSWERS TO CHAPTER 21

COMPLETION QUESTIONS

1. proprietorships; partnerships; corporations
2. proprietorships; corporations
3. corporation; shareholders; limited
4. twice
5. asymmetric; adverse selection; moral hazard
6. control; moral
7. credit rating; collateral
8. incentive-compatible; risk
9. principal-agent
10. stocks; bonds; reinvestment; stock; bond; maturity
11. control; their own
12. secondary; primary
13. random; today's price

TRUE-FALSE QUESTIONS

1. F Proprietorships account for about 70 percent of total business organizations.
2. F Corporations do.
3. T
4. T
5. T
6. T
7. T
8. F Before a transaction.
9. T
10. F Stocks also give investors greater control than bonds.
11. T
12. T
13. F It implies that managers pursue their own interests.
14. F They are trying to prevent the adverse selection problem.
15. T
16. T

MULTIPLE CHOICE

1.c; 2.d; 3.d; 4.b; 5.a; 6.c; 7.a; 8.d; 9.b; 10.c; 11.a; 12.c.

MATCHING

a and i; b and l; c and h; d and m; e and k; f and j; g and n

CASE STUDY

1. Group one, the "smart" investors, assuming a zero-sum game (some must lose if some win).
2. If smart investors think a stock is overpriced they should *buy* it, because people with inside information are purchasing it.

GLOSSARY TO CHAPTER 21

Adverse selection The problem that arises in financial markets when borrowers that are the worst credit risks are most likely to receive loans.

Asymmetric information Information that is possessed by one side of a transaction only. If, for example, sellers have relatively more information than buyers, they will be at an advantage.

Bond A legal claim against a firm entitling the owner of the bond to receive a fixed annual coupon payment, plus a lump sum payment at the bond's maturity date; bonds are issued in return for funds lent to the firm.

Collateral   An asset pledged as security for the payment of a loan.

Corporation A legal entity that may conduct business in its own name just as an individual does; the owners of a corporation, called shareholders, own shares of the firm's profits and enjoy the protection of limited liability.

Dividends Portion of a corporation's profits paid to the firm's owners.

Financial capital The money available to purchase capital goods such as plant and equipment.

Incentive-compatible contract A loan contract under which a significant amount of the borrower's assets are at risk.

Inside information Information about what is happening in a corporation that only "insiders" know and is not available to the general public.

Limited liability   A legal term meaning that the responsibility, or liability of the owners of a corporation is limited to the value of their ownership shares in the firm.

Moral hazard A problem that occurs because of asymmetric information after a transaction occurs. In financial markets, a person to whom money has been lent may indulge in more risky behavior, thereby increasing the probability of default on the debt.

Partnership A business owned by two or more co-owners, or partners, who share the responsibilities and profits of the firm, and who are individually liable for all of the debts of the partnership.

Primary market A financial market in which purchases and sales of newly issued securities such as new bonds are made.

Principal-agent problem The conflict of interest that occurs when agents—managers of firms—pursue their own objectives to the detriment of the principals'—owners of the firm—goals.

Proprietorship   A business owned by one individual who makes the business decisions, receives all of the profits, and is legally responsible for all of the debts of the firm.

Random walk theory A theory that there are no predictable trends in prices, so today's prices cannot be used to predict future prices.

Reinvestment Profits or depreciation reserves used to purchase new capital equipment.

Secondary market A financial market in which purchases and sales of previously issued securities are made.

Separation of ownership and control A situation that exists in corporations in which the owners—shareholders—are different from those who control the operation of the corporation—the managers. The goals of these two groups often are different.

Share of stock A legal claim to a share of a corporation's future profits; if it is common stock, it incorporates certain voting rights regarding major policy decisions of the corporation; if it is preferred stock, its owners are accorded preferential treatment in the payment of dividends.

Unlimited liability A legal term meaning that the personal assets of the owner(s) of a firm may be seized to pay off the debts of the firm.

THE FIRM: COST AND OUTPUT DETERMINATION

PUTTING THIS CHAPTER INTO PERSPECTIVE

Chapter 22 is the first chapter in Part Six. It is an important chapter because the material it contains is essential to the remaining five chapters in Part Six.

Chapter 19 analyzed consumer behavior in detail, and it provided the ingredients for a proper understanding of demand. Chapter 22 lays the foundation for supply because it analyzes business costs of production. Many economists refer to microeconomics—the second major topic of this text—as "price theory." The modern theory of price is that market price is determined by supply and demand; because supply is intimately related to a firm's cost of production, this chapter is obviously important.

In this chapter we analyze again the relationship between "average" and "marginal" concepts; more specifically, Chapter 22 analyzes the relationship between marginal cost and average cost. As expected, marginal cost pulls and tugs average cost: if marginal cost is above average cost, then average cost will rise; if marginal cost is below average cost, then average cost will fall; if marginal cost equals average cost, then average cost remains constant. If you truly understand this, then you can easily see why the marginal cost curve intersects the average variable cost curve and the average total cost curve at their minimum points.

In this chapter we also introduce the law of diminishing returns. It is important to understand that this law is a purely technological statement; it indicates what happens to output when inputs are changed in a specific way. By itself the law has nothing to do with costs or profits—each of which, after all, is denominated in money. The law, however, does have *implications* for firm production costs (and therefore for profits), and you should concentrate on how the law accounts for the upward sloping portion of the marginal cost, the average variable cost, and the average total cost curves. Pay particular attention to the marginal cost curve; it is the most important because, as we stress again and again, economic decisions are made on the margin. The profit maximizing firm will compare the marginal cost of producing another unit of output with the marginal benefit of doing so.

Chapter 22 also makes the important distinction between accounting profits and economic profits; it also distinguishes between long-run and short-run cost curves. Note well that it is the law of diminishing returns that determines the shape of the short-run average cost curve, and that it is the existence (or lack thereof) of economies or diseconomies of scale that determines the shape of the long-run average cost curves.

LEARNING OBJECTIVES

After you have studied this chapter, you should be able to

1. define firm, explicit costs, implicit costs, accounting profit, normal rate of return, opportunity cost of capital, economic profits, short run, long run, production, production function, law of diminishing (marginal) returns, average physical product, marginal physical product, total costs, fixed costs, variable costs, average fixed costs, average variable cost, average total costs, marginal costs, planning horizon, long-run average cost curve, planning curve, economies of scale, constant returns to scale, diseconomies of scale, minimum efficient scale.

2. distinguish between accounting profits and economic profits.

3. distinguish between explicit costs and implicit costs.

4. distinguish between the firm's short run and its long run.

5. apply the law of diminishing (marginal) returns to account for the shape of the firm's short-run marginal cost curve, average total cost curve, and average variable cost curve.

6. classify firm costs as fixed or variable costs.

7. calculate average total cost, average fixed cost, and marginal cost, given sufficient information.

8. apply the concepts of economies of scale, diseconomies of scale, and constant returns to scale to predict the shape of a firm's long-run average cost curve.

9. list reasons for economies of scale and for diseconomies of scale.

10. understand the concept of minimum efficient scale (MES).

CHAPTER OUTLINE

1. A *firm* is an organization that brings together different factors of production, such as labor, land, capital, and entrepreneurial skill, to produce a product or service which it is hoped can be sold for a profit.
    a. *Accounting profits* equal total revenues minus explicit costs.
    b. The opportunity cost of capital, or the normal rate of return to invested capital, is the rate of return that must be paid to an investor to induce him or her to invest in a business.
    c. There is also an opportunity cost to labor; single-owner proprietors, after all, could earn wages elsewhere.
        i.   There is an opportunity cost to all inputs.
        ii. Economic profits equal total revenues minus the opportunity cost of all inputs; stated differently, total profits equal total revenues minus the sum of explicit and implicit costs.

2. It is widely assumed by economists that the goal of the firm is to maximize total profits.

3. The short run is defined as that time period in which a firm cannot alter its current size of plant; the long run is that time period in which all factors of production can be varied.

4. *Total costs* are identical to total *fixed costs* plus total *variable costs.*
    a. Total fixed costs do not vary with output.
    b. Total variable costs are the sum of all those costs that vary with output.
    c. There are several short-run average cost curves.
        i.   Average total costs equal total costs divided by output.
        ii. Average variable costs equal total variable costs divided by output.
        iii. Average fixed costs equal total fixed costs divided by output.
    d. *Marginal cost* equals the change in total costs divided by the change in output.
    e. When marginal cost is above average cost, average cost rises; when marginal cost is below average cost, average cost falls; when marginal cost equals average cost, average cost remains constant.
    f. The marginal cost curve intersects the average total cost curve and the average variable cost curve at their respective *minimum points.*

5. The *production function* is a relationship between inputs and outputs; it is a technological, not an economic, relationship.
    a. The law of *diminishing (marginal) returns* comes into play when the firm increases output in the short run.
    b. The marginal physical product is the change in total product that occurs when a variable input is increased and all other inputs are held constant.
    c. The law of diminishing (marginal) returns implies that the marginal physical product of labor eventually falls.

6. Diminishing marginal product causes the marginal cost curve, the average total cost curve, and the average variable cost curve to rise.

7. In the *long run,* all inputs are variable, and long-run cost curves must take this into account.
    a. The *long-run average cost curve* is the locus of points representing the minimum unit cost of producing any given rate of output, given current technology and resource prices.
    b. Another name for the long-run average cost curve is the *planning horizon.*

8. The long-run average cost curve is also U-shaped.
    a. Initially a firm experiences *economies of scale* due to specialization, a dimensional factor, or improved productive equipment.
    b. Eventually a firm might experience *diseconomies of scale* because a disproportionate increase in management and staff may be needed, and because the costs of information and communication also grow more than proportionally with output.

9. The minimum efficient scale is the lowest rate of output per unit time period at which average costs reach a minimum for a particular firm.

10. At the output rate when economies of scale end and constant economies of scales start, the minimum efficient scale for the firm occurs. It is the lowest rate of output at which long-run average costs are minimized.

KEY TERMS

Average physical product
Marginal physical product
Total costs
Fixed costs
Variable costs
Average fixed costs
Average variable costs

Average total costs
Marginal costs
Long-run average cost curve
Planning curve
Economies of scale
Constant returns to scale
Production

KEY CONCEPTS

Explicit costs
Implicit costs
Accounting profit
Normal rate of return
Economic profits
Long run
Diseconomies of scale

Short run
Production function
Law of diminishing returns
Planning horizon
Minimum efficient scale
Firm
Opportunity cost of capital

COMPLETION QUESTIONS
Fill in the blank or circle the correct term.

1. (Explicit, Implicit) costs are usually considered by accountants, but _____ costs typically are not.

2. Economists consider implicit costs because such costs (do, do not) include the opportunity costs of the resources used.

3. Accounting profits equal _____ minus _____; economic profits equal _____ minus _____; economic profits are less than accounting profits because economic profits subtract _____ costs from total revenues.

4. Economists usually assume that the firm's goal is _____.

5. Our definition of the short run is the time during which _____ is fixed, but _____ is variable; in the long run (no, all) factors are variable.

6. Fixed costs (do, do not) vary with output; variable costs (do, do not) vary with output; _____ and _____ are examples of fixed costs; _____ and _____ are examples of variable costs.

7. Short-run average cost curves eventually are upward sloping due to _____; at the minimum of the average total cost curve, marginal cost is (less than, greater than, equal to) average total cost; if marginal cost exceeds average total cost, then average total cost will (fall, rise, remain constant).

8. Because of diminishing (marginal) returns, in the (short, long) run the marginal product of labor will eventually (fall, rise, remain constant).

9. The long-run cost curve may also be U-shaped, because initially as a firm expands its scale of operations, it realizes _____ of scale; then it may realize _____ returns to scale; eventually it realizes _____ of scale.

10. Reasons for economies of scale include _____, _____, and _____; a firm might experience diseconomies of scale due to _____ and _____.

TRUE-FALSE QUESTIONS
Circle the **T** if the statement is true, the **F** if it is false. Explain to yourself why a statement is false.

T F   1.   Accountants typically do not consider implicit costs.

T F   2.   Explicit costs include the opportunity cost of a resource.

T F   3.   Accounting profits equal total revenues minus explicit costs.

T F   4.   Accounting profits always exceed economic profits.

T F   5.   Economists usually assume that the firm's goal is to maximize profits.

T F   6.   Short-run cost curves that include variable costs eventually reflect the influence of the law of diminishing marginal returns.

T F   7.   Fixed costs vary with output.

T F   8.   Eventually, as output expands, the short-run marginal cost curve must rise.

T F   9.   When average costs exceed marginal cost, marginal cost must be rising.

T F 10.   At the minimum average total cost output level, marginal cost equals average total cost.

T F 11.   In the short run, the supply of labor to the firm is usually fixed.

T F 12.   Because of the law of diminishing marginal returns, the marginal product of labor will rise.

T F 13.   Long-run cost curves are U-shaped due to the law of diminishing returns.

MULTIPLE CHOICE QUESTIONS
Circle the letter that corresponds to the best answer.

1.   Explicit costs
   a.   are considered by accountants.
   b.   are greater than implicit costs.
   c.   are considered irrelevant by economists.
   d.   are considered by accountants, but not by economists.

2.   Implicit costs
   a.   are considered important to accountants, but not to economists.
   b.   are usually less than explicit costs.
   c.   include the opportunity costs of resources.
   d.   are considered irrelevant by businesses.

3.   Accounting profits
   a.   equal total revenues minus explicit costs.
   b.   exceed economic profits.
   c.   do not take implicit costs into account.
   d.   All of the above

4. The opportunity cost of capital is
    a. an explicit cost of doing business.
    b. not an important cost of doing business.
    c. the normal rate of return on capital invested in a business.
    d. purely a technological concept.

5. Which of the following is unlike the others because it is not explicit?
    a. wages
    b. opportunity cost of capital
    c. taxes
    d. rent

6. *Analogy*: Rent is to explicit costs as _____ are to implicit costs.
    a. labor services of a proprietor
    b. taxes
    c. wages
    d. accounting profits

7. Which of the following goals of the firm is most widely assumed by economists?
    a. staff maximization
    b. sales maximization
    c. growth maximization
    d. profit maximization

8. In the short run, for our purposes,
    a. all factors are variable.
    b. labor is variable.
    c. capital is variable
    d. both capital and labor are variable.

9. The long run
    a. permits the variation of all factors of production.
    b. is different for different firms.
    c. permits a firm to avoid the consequences of the law of diminishing returns.
    d. All of the above

10. Fixed costs
    a. vary with output.
    b. do not vary with output.
    c. reflect the effect of diminishing returns.
    d. include labor and raw material costs.

11. Which cost is most unlike the others because it is not fixed?
    a. rent
    b. wages
    c. opportunity cost of capital
    d. interest payments on borrowed money

12. If marginal cost is above average total cost, then average total cost
    a. will rise.
    b. will fall.
    c. will remain constant.
    d. cannot be calculated.

13. At that output where average total cost is at a minimum,
    a. marginal cost equals average total cost.
    b. marginal cost equals average variable cost.
    c. average total cost is rising.
    d. total cost is constant.

14. Which short-run curve is **NOT** U-shaped?
    a. average total cost
    b. marginal cost
    c. average variable cost
    d. average fixed cost

15. The production function
    a. is a technological relationship.
    b. is not an economic relationship.
    c. relates output to inputs.
    d. All of the above

16. Because of the law of diminishing marginal returns,
    a. long-run average cost eventually rises.
    b. marginal cost falls.
    c. the marginal product of labor eventually falls.
    d. the average total cost curve falls.

17. Which is **NOT** due to the law of diminishing marginal returns?
    a. rising short-run marginal cost
    b. rising long-run average total cost
    c. rising short-run average variable cost
    d. rising short-run average total cost

18. *Analogy*: Diminishing returns is to rising short-run average total costs as _____ is to rising long-run average total costs.
    a. economies of scale
    b. diseconomies of scale
    c. law of diminishing returns
    d. constant returns to scale

19. Which of the following helps to account for a U-shaped short-run average total cost curve?
    a. economies of scale
    b. diseconomies of scale
    c. law of diminishing (marginal) returns
    d. constant returns to scale

20. A firm might experience diseconomies of scale due to
    a. disproportionate rises in specialization.
    b. dimensional factors.
    c. information and communication costs that rise disproportionately.
    d. the ability to use larger-volume machinery that is efficient only at large outputs.

21. If the minimum efficient scale is relatively low, then
    a. there will likely be a relatively large number of firms in the industry.
    b. there will likely be a relatively small number of firms in the industry.
    c. economies of scale are very great.
    d. long-run average costs decline over broad ranges of output.

MATCHING
Choose the item in column (2) that best matches an item in column (1).

(1)	(2)
a. long run	i. falling long-run average cost
b. short run	j. rising long-run average cost
c. fixed cost	k. fixed plant size
d. variable cost	l. diminishing marginal product
e. opportunity cost of capital	m. overhead
f. economies of scale	n. wages of laborers
g. diseconomies of scale	o. implicit cost
h. law of diminishing returns	p. all factors variable

WORKING WITH GRAPHS

1. Assume that the High Rise Bakery produces a single product: loaves of bread. Further assume that the bread is produced using a fixed plant size, with ten ovens and varying quantities of labor. John Doe notices that as he hires additional workers, the total output of bread goes up for a while. Then he finds that after hiring several additional workers, the workers begin to get in one another's way and extra output begins to decline. John knows the principles of economics and something about diminishing marginal physical product. Given the information below, calculate the marginal physical product of John's bakers. Graph total and marginal products on the next page and tell John how many bakers he can employ before diminishing marginal returns set in. (Plot the marginal product at the midpoint between the number of bakers employed.)

Bakers	Output (loaves per day)	Marginal product
0	0	___
1	8	___
2	19	___
3	32	___
4	45	___
5	60	___
6	71	___
7	75	___
8	77	___
9	77	___
10	75	___
11	65	___

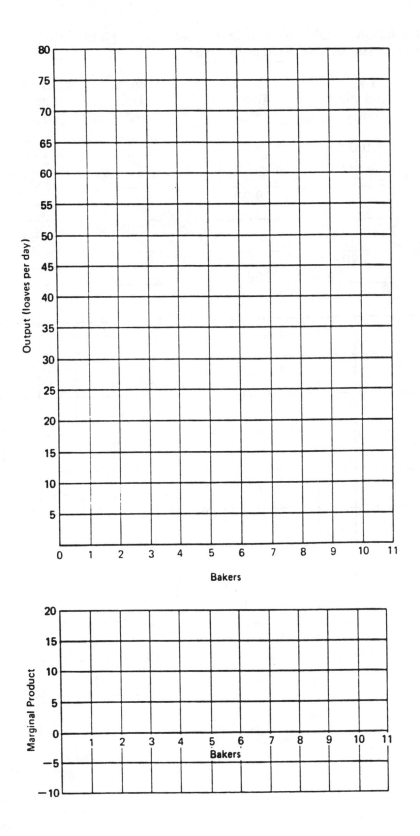

2. Complete the following table of cost figures and then graph the information on the graphs provided below. Assume total fixed costs are $3.

Output	Total variable costs	Total costs	Average variable cost	Average total cost	Marginal cost
0	0.00	3.00	___	___	___
1	3.00	___	___	___	___
2	___	___	___	4.00	___
3	___	9.20	___	___	___
4	___	___	___	___	2.30
5	___	___	2.38	___	___
6	___	___	___	___	5.00
7	23.90	___	___	___	___
8	___	36.90	___	___	___

3. Use the graphs below to answer the questions that follow.

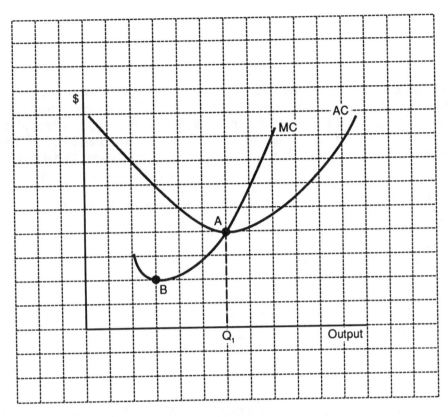

    a. At what point do diminishing marginal returns begin?
    b. At any output less than Q_1, why is AC falling?
    c. At any output greater than Q_1, why is AC rising?
    d. What is AC doing at the exact output Q_1?

4. Use the graphs below to answer the questions that follow. Assume that A and B are minimum points.

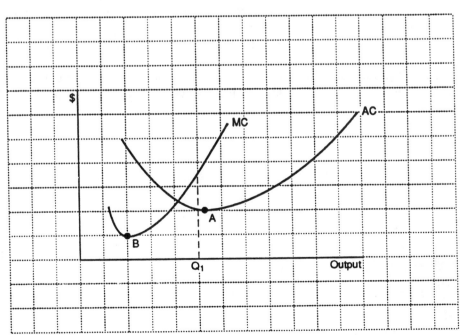

*a. Something is wrong with the graphs above. What is it?
b. According to the graphs above, what is happening at output Q_1, with respect to MC and AC? Is this possible?

PROBLEMS

1. Mr. DeMato owns his own car repair business. His annual total revenues are $200,000, and his total costs are $160,000. Upon further investigation it is discovered that Mr. DeMato did not include an estimate of the worth of his own wages in calculating his annual total profits of $40,000. Nor, it seems, did he estimate the annual rate of return that he could have earned on the $100,000 of his own savings that he used to enter his business. What advice would you give him?

2. Fill in the information in each blank below so that the equation is correct. (Note: Q is quantity of output.)

   a. TC = TFC + _____
   b. AFC = _____ - AVC
   c. ATC = (TVC/Q) + _____
   d. TFC = Q x _____
   e. AVC = (TC/Q) - _____ /Q
   f. TVC = (Q x ATC) - Q x _____

CASE STUDY

Economists think that the distinction between marginal cost and fixed costs is crucial to decision making. They define fixed costs as costs that do not change with the decision at hand. For example, assume that you own a restaurant that is open only at night, and you now want to decide whether you should open for lunch. The $1,000 per month rent and the $500 per month payment on a loan used to start your restaurant are fixed costs. *Moreover, such fixed costs should be ignored in making your decision.* Instead, you should compare the change in your total revenues (marginal revenues) to the change in your total costs (marginal costs) after you tried serving lunch for a reasonable period of time.

1. Suppose that your monthly revenues (due to your lunch trade) rise by $2,000 per month and your marginal costs (additional costs for labor, food and beverages, and so on) rise by $1,000 per month. Should you continue to open the restaurant for lunch? Why or why not?

2. Suppose your accountant tells you to allocate half your rent payment and half your loan payment as a "cost" of your lunch trade. Should you heed his advice? Why or why not?

ANSWERS TO CHAPTER 22

COMPLETION QUESTIONS

1. Explicit; implicit
2. do
3. total revenues; explicit costs; total revenues; implicit plus explicit costs; implicit
4. profit maximization
5. capital; labor; all
6. do not; do; rent; interest payments on mortgages; wages; raw material costs
7. diminishing (marginal) returns; equal to; rise
8. short; fall
9. economies; constant; diseconomies
10. specialization; dimensional factors; improved productive equipment; disproportionate requirements for managers and staff; disproportionate costs of information and communication

TRUE-FALSE QUESTIONS

1. T
2. F   Implicit costs do.
3. T
4. T
5. T
6. T
7. F   By definition they do not.
8. T
9. F   Not necessarily.
10. T
11. F   Capital is fixed in the short run.
12. F   It falls due to the law of diminishing returns.
13. F   Diminishing marginal returns occurs in the short run.

MULTIPLE CHOICE QUESTIONS

1.a;   2.c;   3.d;   4.c;   5.b;   6.a;   7.d;   8.b;   9.d;   10.b;
11.b;   12.a;   13.a;   14.d;   15.d;   16.c;   17.b;   18.b;   19.c;   20.c;
21.a

MATCHING

a and p;   b and k;   c and m;   d and n;   e and o;   f and i;   g and j;   h and l

WORKING WITH GRAPHS

1. Marginal product: 8; 11; 13; 13; 15; 11; 4; 2; 0; -2; -10
    Diminishing returns set in when John hires the sixth baker.

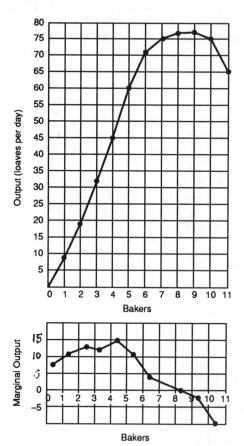

2.

Output	Total variable costs	Total costs	Average variable cost	Average total cost	Marginal cost
0	0.00	3.00	--	--	--
1	3.00	6.00	3.00	6.00	3.00
2	5.00	8.00	2.50	4.00	2.00
3	6.20	9.20	2.07	3.07	1.20
4	8.50	11.50	2.13	2.88	2.30
5	11.90	14.90	2.38	2.98	3.40
6	16.90	19.90	2.82	3.32	5.00
7	23.90	26.90	3.41	3.84	7.00
8	33.90	36.90	4.24	4.61	10.00

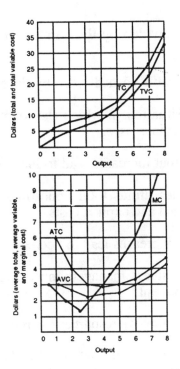

3. a. B
    b. MC is below AC, due to specialization
    c. MC is above AC
    d. AC is constant, because MC = AC.

4. a. MC cuts the AC curve to the left of AC's minimum point.
    b. MC > AC, yet AC is falling. No.

PROBLEMS

1. Determine the opportunity cost of his labor, and the interest he can earn on $100,000. If the sum is greater than $40,000, he is not covering all explicit and implicit costs, and he might consider working for someone else and earning interest on his money, unless he really enjoys being his own boss, that is.

2. a.TVC b.ATC c.AFC d.AFC e.TFC f.AFC

CASE STUDIES

a. Yes, because MR > MC and your profits will now rise by $1000 per month, or your losses will now fall by $1000 per month.
b. No; those costs are fixed costs—they remain whether you are open for lunch or not—so they are irrelevant to this decision.

GLOSSARY TO CHAPTER 22

Accounting profit Total revenues minus total explicit costs. Losses are negative profits.

Average fixed costs Total fixed costs divided by the number of units produced.

Average physical product Total product divided by the variable input.

Average total costs Total costs divided by the number of units produced; sometimes called average per unit total costs.

Average variable costs Total variable costs divided by the number of units produced.

Constant returns to scale A situation in which the long-run average cost curve of a firm remains flat, or horizontal, as output increases.

Diseconomies of scale When output increases lead to increases in long- run average costs.

Economic profits Total revenues minus total opportunity cost of all inputs used, or total revenues minus the total of all implicit and explicit costs.

Economies of scale When output increases lead to decreases in long-run average costs.

Explicit costs Those costs that business managers must take account of because they must be paid; for example, wages, taxes, and rent.

Firm A business organization that employs resources to produce goods or services for a profit.

Fixed costs Those costs that do not vary with output. Fixed costs include such things as rent on a building. These costs are fixed for a certain period of time; in the long run they are variable.

Implicit costs Expenses that managers do not have to pay out of pocket. Those costs that business managers do not normally calculate, such as the opportunity cost of factors of production that are owned; for example, owner-provided capital and owner-provided labor.

Law of diminishing (marginal) returns After some point, successive increases in a variable factor of production, such as labor, added to fixed factors of production, will result in smaller increases in output.

Long run That time period in which all factors of production can be varied.

Long-run average cost curve (LAC) The locus of points representing the minimum unit cost of producing any given rate of output, given current technology and resource prices.

Marginal costs The change in total costs due to a one-unit change of production rate.

Marginal physical product The physical output that is due to the addition of one more unit of a variable factor of production; the change in total product occurring when a variable input is increased and all other inputs are held constant.

Minimum efficient scale The lowest rate of output per unit time period at which average costs reach a minimum for a particular firm.

Normal rate of return The normal rate of return to investment; otherwise known as the opportunity cost of capital.

Opportunity cost of capital The normal rate of return or the amount that must be paid to an investor to induce her or him to invest in a business. Economists consider this a cost of production and it is included in our cost examples.

Planning curve Another name for the long-run average cost curve.

Planning horizon Another name for the long-run. All inputs are variable during the planning horizon.

Plant size Physical size of factories that a firm owns.

Production Any process by which resources are transformed into goods or services.

Production function The relationship between inputs and output. A production function is a technological, not an economic relationship.

Short run That time period in which a firm cannot alter its current size of plant.

Total costs The sum of total fixed costs and total variable costs.

Variable costs Those costs that vary with the rate of production. They include wages paid to workers and the costs of materials.

CHAPTER 23

PERFECT COMPETITION

PUTTING THIS CHAPTER INTO PERSPECTIVE

Chapter 23 is the first of three chapters (the others are Chapters 24 and 25) that are concerned with how firms determine price and output under different market structures. The market structures studied are perfect competition (the subject of this chapter), monopoly (Chapter 24), monopolistic competition (Chapter 25), and oligopoly (also in Chapter 25).

Your understanding of the economic analysis of firms operating in various market structures will be facilitated if you see the "big picture." In effect, the same pattern of methodology can be found under each market structure analysis. First note well the specific characteristics of each particular market structure; memorize those characteristics and then try to see how each one helps to make the specific market structure unique.

Secondly, try to determine the firm's short-run (and then long-run) equilibrium output and price. You might find it helpful to know that regardless of the model we analyze, the firm's equilibrium output will occur where marginal benefit (MB) equals marginal cost (MC). Under different circumstances, the MB to an economic agent (firm, consumer, employer, laborer, etc.) will be called different things; so too will the specific economic agent's MC be called different things in different models and situations. Nevertheless, our assumption of the goal of maximization usually allows us to predict the optimal decision point. For example, in this chapter the competitive firm's MB is its selling price, or its marginal revenue; the marginal cost of a particular output is found on its marginal cost curve. The competitive firm maximizes at the point where MB = MC; that is, it produces up to the point where price = MC or where marginal revenue (MR) equals MC. Thus the profit maximizing output for the competitive firm is at that level for which MR = MC. (Note: you should always be able to show why the economic agent is not maximizing if MB > MC or if MB < MC.)

The final component of our "pattern" is to determine the extent to which the specific market structure is socially efficient or socially inefficient. That is, does price equal marginal cost? Is output at a level at which average total cost is minimized? Do economic profits persist in the long run?

If you try to see the pattern of analysis you may save yourself a lot of study time, and you can more easily *compare* the various market structures (a task which your instructor may well ask you to perform).

LEARNING OBJECTIVES

After you have studied this chapter, you should be able to

1. define price taker, total revenues, marginal revenue, short-run shutdown price, short-run break-even price, industry supply curve, long-run industry supply curve, constant-cost industry, increasing-cost industry, decreasing-cost industry, and marginal-cost pricing.

2. list four characteristics of the perfect competition market structure.

3. recognize the shape of a competitive firm's demand curve and recognize reasons for its shape.

4. determine a perfect competitor's optimal output rate, given sufficient information.

5. calculate the value of a perfect competitor's short-run profits, given sufficient information.

6. recognize and determine the perfectly competitive firm's short-run shutdown price and its short-run break-even price.

7. recognize a perfectly competitive firm's short-run supply curve and recognize how an *industry* short-run supply curve is derived.

8. distinguish among constant-cost, increasing-cost, and decreasing-cost industries.

9. recognize the long-run equilibrium position for a firm in a perfectly competitive industry.

10. indicate why a perfectly competitive market structure is socially efficient.

11. recognize how the asymmetry of information problem affects the perfect competition model.

CHAPTER OUTLINE

1. There are four major characteristics of the perfect competition market structure: a large number of buyers and sellers, homogeneous product, unimpeded industry exit and entry, and equally good information for both buyers and sellers.

2. Because in the perfect competition model many firms produce a homogeneous product, a single firm's demand curve is perfectly elastic at the "going" market price.

3. In order to predict how much the perfect competitor will produce, we assume that it wants to maximize total profits.
   a. Total revenues equal quantity sold times price per unit.
   b. In the short run, total costs are the sum of total fixed costs and total variable costs.
   c. Total revenues minus total costs equal total profits.
   d. Marginal revenue equals the change in total revenue divided by the change in output.
   e. Total profits are maximized at that rate of output where marginal revenue equals marginal cost.

4. Because a normal rate of return to investment is included in the average total cost curve, the "profits" we calculate are *economic profits*.

5. The firm's *short-run shutdown price* occurs at its minimum average variable cost value; at a higher price the firm should produce and contribute to payment of fixed costs; it should not produce at a lower price.

6. The firm's *short-run break-even price* is found at the minimum point on its average total cost curve; at a higher price the firm will earn abnormal profits; at a lower price it suffers economic losses; at the minimum point, economic profits equal zero.

7. The firm's *short-run supply curve* is its marginal cost curve above the short-run shutdown point.

8. The *short-run industry supply curve* is derived by summing horizontally all the firm supply curves; the industry supply curve shifts when nonprice determinants of supply change.

9. In a competitive market, the "going" price is set where the market demand curve intersects the industry supply curve.

10. In the long run, because abnormal industry profits induce entry and because negative industry profits induce exit, firms in a competitive industry will earn *zero economic profits*.
    a. Long-run supply curves relate price and quantity supplied after firms have time to enter or exit from an industry.
    b. A *constant-cost industry* is one whose long-run supply curve is horizontal, because input prices are unaffected by output.
    c. An *increasing-cost industry* is one whose long-run supply curve is positively sloped, because the price of specialized (or essential) inputs rises as industry output increases.
    d. A *decreasing-cost industry* is one whose long-run supply curve is negatively sloped, because specialized input prices fall as industry output expands.

11. In a perfectly competitive industry, a firm operates where price equals marginal revenue equals marginal cost equals short-run minimum average cost equals long-run minimum average cost—in the long run.
    a. Perfectly competitive industries are efficient from society's point of view because for such industries price equals marginal cost in long-run equilibrium.
    b. They are also efficient because in long-run equilibrium the output rate is produced at minimum average cost.
    c. The perfectly competitive model is not a realistic description of any real-world industry; nevertheless it helps economists explain and predict economic events.

12. If asymmetry of information exists—producers know the true quality of their good but buyers don't—the perfect competition condition is not met; this can create the lemons problem.

KEY TERMS

Total revenues
Marginal revenue
Short-run shutdown price
Short-run breakeven price
Market failure

Long-run industry supply curve
Perfectly competitive firm
Total costs
Industry supply curve
Lemons problem

KEY CONCEPTS

Profit maximizing rate of production   Marginal cost pricing
Perfect competition   Increasing cost industry
Price taker   Decreasing cost industry
Signals   Constant cost industry

COMPLETION QUESTIONS
Fill in the blank or circle the correct term.

1. The four major characteristics of a perfect competition market structure are
    _____, _____, _____, and _____.

2. The demand curve facing a perfect competitor is _____ elastic.

3. We assume that the goal of the firm is to _____; if so, the perfect
    competitor should produce up to the point where MR equals _____; total profits are
    defined as _____ minus _____.

4. Marginal revenue equals _____ divided by _____.

5. Because we include the opportunity cost of capital as a cost of production, the profits we
    define are (accounting, economic) profits.

6. If the firm's selling price cannot cover its short-run variable costs, then it should
    _____; if selling price equals minimum average total cost, the
    firm is just _____, and its economic profits are (negative, positive,
    zero).

7. If the firm is earning zero economic profits, it (would, would not) continue to operate.

8. The competitive firm's short-run supply curve is the portion of its _____ curve
    lying above minimum AVC; the industry short-run supply curve is derived by
    _____ all the firm supply curves.

9. In the long run, a firm in a perfectly competitive industry will earn exactly zero economic
    profits. This is true because if economic profits are positive, some firms will
    _____ the industry and price will fall; if economic profits are negative, some
    firms will _____ the industry and price will rise.

10. If an industry expands and input prices do not change, such an industry is a(n)
    _____-cost industry and the long-run supply curve is horizontal; if input
    prices rise, the industry is a(n) _____-cost industry and the long-run
    industry supply curve is _____ sloping; if input prices fall, the
    industry is a(n) _____-cost industry and the industry's long-run
    supply curve is _____ sloping.

11. In the long run a perfectly competitive firm will earn (negative, positive, zero) economic
    profits. Its price will be (greater than, less than, equal to) marginal cost, and output (will,
    will not) be produced at minimum average total cost. From society's point of view, all of
    this is (efficient, inefficient).

12. Prior to the sale of goods producers know better than buyers do concerning the quality of the good, hence this asymmetric information causes the (adverse selection, moral hazard) problem; producers therefore have an incentive to maintain price but reduce quality, causing the _____ problem.

TRUE-FALSE QUESTIONS

Circle the **T** if the statement is true, the **F** if it is false. Explain to yourself why a statement is false.

T   F   1.   A firm in a perfectly competitive industry is a price taker.

T   F   2.   Because firms in a perfectly competitive industry are all price takers, price cannot change in that industry.

T   F   3.   The demand curve facing a perfect competitor is perfectly elastic.

T   F   4.   The perfectly competitive firm attempts to maximize marginal profits.

T   F   5.   The total profit maximization output occurs at the point where the firm's marginal cost equals its marginal revenue.

T   F   6.   Average revenue minus average cost equals total profits.

T   F   7.   If price is below minimum average variable costs in the short run, the firm will shut down, assuming output is where MR = MC.

T   F   8.   If price is below minimum average total cost, economic profits will be negative, assuming that output is where MR = MC.

T   F   9.   The firm's short-run supply curve is its average variable cost curve.

T   F   10.   The industry supply curve is derived by summing horizontally all the firm supply curves.

T   F   11.   Because of the law of diminishing returns, the firm's short-run supply curve will be upward sloping.

T   F   12.   Because of free exit and entry, long-run accounting profits for a perfect competitor must be zero.

T   F   13.   A constant-cost industry has an upward sloping long-run industry supply curve.

T   F   14.   If demand falls in a decreasing-cost industry, in the long run both output and price will fall.

T   F   15.   In the long-run equilibrium situation, the perfectly competitive firm will earn zero economic profits and produce at minimum average cost.

T   F   16.   Because of excessive competition, the perfectly competitive industry is believed to be inefficient from society's point of view.

T   F   17.   The lemons problem is an example of symmetry of information.

MULTIPLE CHOICE QUESTIONS
Circle the letter that corresponds to the best answer.

1. Which of the following is **NOT** a characteristic of the perfect competition market structure?
    a. equally good information for both buyers and sellers
    b. homogeneous product
    c. large number of buyers and sellers
    d. restricted entry and exit

2. The demand curve facing the perfect competitor is
    a. perfectly elastic.
    b. vertical at the going price.
    c. perfectly inelastic.
    d. negatively sloped.

3. In the perfect competition model
    a. each seller is a price taker.
    b. all firms together can affect price.
    c. all firms produce a homogeneous product.
    d. All of the above

4. We assume the firm wants to maximize _____ profits.
    a. marginal
    b. average
    c. total
    d. fixed

5. The firm maximizes total profits at that output at which
    a. MC = MR.
    b. MC > MR.
    c. P = AC.
    d. AR = AC.

6. In which of these cases are economic profits negative?
    a. Total revenues exceed total costs.
    b. Average revenues exceed average costs.
    c. Price is below minimum average total cost.
    d. Average revenue is equal to price.

7. The perfect competitor
    a. can sell all it wants to sell at the going price.
    b. can sell nothing at a price higher than the going price.
    c. faces a perfectly elastic demand curve.
    d. All of the above

8. The competitive firm's short-run total profits equal
    a. average revenue minus average cost times quantity sold.
    b. average revenue minus average cost.
    c. price minus marginal cost.
    d. price minus average variable cost.

9. If selling price equals the firm's minimum average variable cost, then
   a. that is the firm's shutdown point.
   b. economic profits are negative.
   c. the firm is indifferent between producing and shutting down.
   d. All of the above

10. At the short-run break-even price,
    a. accounting profits equal economic profits.
    b. economic profits are negative.
    c. economic profits are zero.
    d. economic profits are positive.

11. The firm's short-run supply curve is its
    a. marginal cost curve above the shutdown point.
    b. average cost curve, above its minimum point.
    c. average variable cost curve, above the shutdown point.
    d. marginal revenue curve.

12. The industry supply curve is derived by summing horizontally all the firms'
    a. marginal cost curves above their shutdown points.
    b. average revenue curves.
    c. total revenue curves.
    d. marginal revenue curves.

13. Which of the following will **NOT** shift the industry supply curve?
    a. change in price
    b. change in the cost of raw materials
    c. change in number of firms in the industry
    d. change in wage rates

14. If economic profits are negative in an industry, then
    a. firms will enter that industry.
    b. some firms will exit from that industry.
    c. price is above minimum average total costs.
    d. accounting profits must also be negative.

15. In long-run equilibrium, a competitive firm
    a. earns zero economic profits.
    b. produces at minimum average cost.
    c. produces where price equals marginal cost.
    d. All of the above

16. If demand falls in an increasing-cost industry, then in the long run
    a. price will fall.
    b. price will return to its previous level.
    c. output will rise.
    d. output will return to its previous level.

17. In a decreasing cost industry, the long-run industry supply curve is
    a. downward sloping.
    b. upward sloping.
    c. horizontal.
    d. perpendicular.

18. The marginal cost of producing good A
     a.   includes fixed costs.
     b.   represents the opportunity cost to society of producing one more unit of good A.
     c.   is found by reading the average variable cost curve.
     d.   includes only labor costs.

19. The lemons problem
     a.   results from asymmetric information.
     b.   is an example of adverse selection.
     c.   violates one of the perfect competition assumptions.
     d.   All of the above

MATCHING
Choose the item in column (2) that best matches an item in column (1).

(1)	(2)

a. lemons problem
b. constant returns to scale
c. price taker
d. decreasing cost-industry
e. short-run shutdown price
f. short-run supply curve
g. profit maximizing output

h. horizontal long-run industry supply
      curve (given input prices)
i. perfectly competitive firm
j. asymmetry of information
k. marginal cost curve above shut-down point
l. falling long-run industry supply curve
m. P = minimum AVC
n. MR = MC

WORKING WITH GRAPHS

1. Use the graphs below to answer the following questions. Assume that the firm is a profit maximizer operating in a competitive market.

    a. How many units of output will the firm produce and sell?
    b. What is TR at this level of output?
    c. What is the ATC at this level of output?
    d. What is the TFC at this level of output?
    e. What is the AVC at this level of output?
    f. What is TC at this level of output?
    g. What is the total profit or loss at this level of output?
    h. What is wrong with the ATC curve as it is drawn?

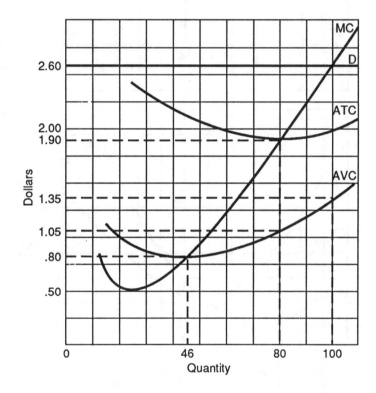

2.   Use the graphs below to answer the questions that follow.

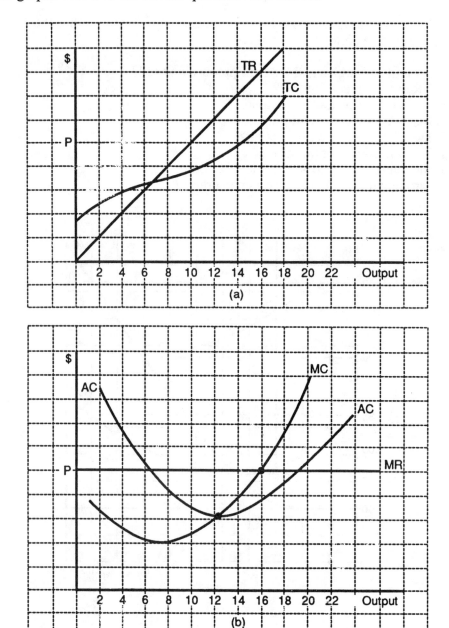

a. The total revenue curve is linear; therefore its slope is a _____; its slope equals what economic concept?

b. The slope of a tangent to a point on the TC curve is defined as what?

c. The firm tries to (minimize, maximize)_____ the positive difference between TR and TC. At what output level does that occur?

d. In panel (b), what is the firm's profit-maximizing output? Why?

e. How are your answers to parts c and d related?

PROBLEMS

1. Suppose you are hired as an economic consultant for Profmax Consulting Company. Your job is to advise the company's clients on the appropriate action to take in the short run in order to maximize the profits (or minimize the losses) of each firm. The firms you are to analyze produce different products, and each operates independently in a different perfectly competitive market. You may assume that each is currently operating at an output level where marginal cost is increasing. Fill in the missing information, and make your suggestions about the appropriate action for each firm by placing one of the following symbols in the last row of the table of information that follows.

    C = currently operating at the correct level of output
    I = increase the level of output
    D = decrease the level of output
    SD = shut down the plant

Firm	A	B	C	D	E	F	G
Price	$0.50	___	$3.50	___	$3.00	$5.00	___
Output	___	300	750	700	___	___	1000
TR	$500	$300	___	$2800	$1800	$4000	$5000
TC	___	$525	$2625	$2975	___	___	___
TFC	___	___	___	___	$180	$1200	___
TVC	$300	___	___	$2450	___	___	$3000
ATC	$0.40	___	Minimum	___	___	$5.50	$5.50
AVC	___	$1.20	$3.00	___	$2.00	Minimum	___
MC	$0.40	$1.00	___	$4.00	$3.50	___	$5.75
Suggestion	___	___	___	___	___	___	___

ANSWERS TO CHAPTER 23

COMPLETION QUESTIONS

1. large number of buyers and sellers; homogeneous product; equally good information for both buyers and sellers; unimpeded entry or exit
2. perfectly
3. maximize total profits; MC; total revenues; total costs
4. change in total revenue; change in output
5. economic
6. shut down; breaking even; zero
7. would
8. MC; summing horizontally
9. enter; exit
10. constant; increasing; upward; decreasing; downward
11. zero; equal to; will; efficient
12. adverse selection; lemons

TRUE-FALSE

1. T
2. F Price is a constant to an *individual* firm, but not to the group of firms.
3. T
4. F Firms attempt to maximize *total* profits.
5. T
6. F It equals average profits.
7. T
8. T
9. F The firm's marginal cost curve above minimum AVC is its short-run supply curve.
10. T
11. T
12. F Long-run *economic* profits must be zero.
13. F It is horizontal
14. F Price will rise.
15. T
16. F It is efficient because P = MC and economic profits = 0 in the long run.
17. F Asymmetry of information causes the lemons problem.

MULTIPLE CHOICE QUESTIONS

1.d;   2.a;   3.d;   4.c;   5.a;   6.c;   7.d;   8.a;   9.d;   10.c;
11.a;   12.a;   13.a;   14.b;   15.d;   16.a;   17.a;   18.b;   19.d

MATCHING

a and j;   b and h;   c and i;   d and l;   e and m;   f and k;   g and n

WORKING WITH GRAPHS

1. a. 100
   b. $260
   c. $2
   d. $65
   e. $1.35
   f. $200
   g. $60 profit

h. ATC times quantity *should* be the same value at every point along the ATC curve. ($200)

2. a. constant; MR (or P)
   b. MC
   c. maximize; 16 units of output
   d. 16 units of output; because MC = MR at that output level
   e. MC = MR at 16 units of output

PROBLEMS

Firm	A	B	C	D	E	F	G
Price	$0.50	$1.00	$3.50	$4.00	$3.00	$5.00	$5.00
Output	1000	300	750	700	600	800	1000
TR	$500	$300	$2625	$2800	$1800	$4000	$5000
TC	$400	$525	$2625	$2975	$1380	$4400	$5500
TFC	$100	$165	$375	$525	$180	$1200	$2500
TVC	$300	$360	$2250	$2450	$1200	$3200	$3000
ATC	$0.40	$1.75	Minimum	$4.25	$2.30	$5.50	$5.50
AVC	$0.30	$1.20	$3.00	$3.50	$2.00	Minimum	$3.00
MC	$0.40	$1.00	$3.50	$4.00	$3.50	$4.00	$5.75
Suggestion	I	SD	C	C	D	I	D

GLOSSARY TO CHAPTER 23

Constant-cost industry An industry whose total output can be increased without an increase in long-run per unit costs; an industry whose long-run supply curve is horizontal.

Decreasing-cost industry An industry in which an increase in industry output leads to a reduction in long-run per unit costs, such that the long-run industry supply curve is downward sloping.

Increasing-cost industry An industry in which an increase in industry output is accompanied by an increase in long-run per unit cost, such that the long-run industry supply curve is upward sloping.

Industry supply curve The locus of points showing the minimum prices at which given quantities will be forthcoming; also called the market supply curve.

Lemons problem The situation in which consumers, because they don't know about the quality of a product, are only willing to pay the price of a low-quality product, even if a higher-quality product at a higher price exists.

Long-run industry supply curve A market supply curve showing the relationship between price and quantities forthcoming after firms have been allowed the time to enter into or exit from an industry, depending on whether there have been positive or negative economic profits.

Marginal cost pricing A system of pricing in which the price charged is equal to the opportunity cost to society of producing one more unit of the good or service in question. The opportunity cost is the marginal cost to society.

Marginal revenue The change in total revenues resulting from a change in output (and sale) of one unit of the product in question.

Market failure A situation in which an unrestrained market operation leads to either too few or too many resources going to a specific economic activity.

Perfect competition A market structure in which the decisions of individual buyers and sellers have no effect on market price.

Perfectly competitive firm A firm that is such a small part of the total industry that it cannot affect the price of the product it sells.

Price taker Another definition of a competitive firm. A price taker is a firm that must take the price of its product as given. The firm cannot influence its price.

Profit-maximizing rate of production That rate of production which maximizes total profits, or the difference between total revenues and total costs; also that rate of production at which marginal revenue equals marginal cost.

Short-run break-even price The price where a firm's total revenues equal its total costs. In economics the break-even price is where the firm is just making a normal rate of return on its capital investment. (It is covering its explicit and implicit cost.)

Short-run shutdown price The price that just covers average variable costs. This occurs just below the intersection of the marginal cost curve and the average variable cost curve.

Signals Compact ways of indicating to economic decision makers information needed to make decisions. A "true signal" not only conveys information but also provides the incentive to "act appropriately" to the signal given. Economic profits and economic losses are such signals.

Total costs The sum of total fixed costs and total variable costs.

Total revenues The price per unit times the total quantity sold.

CHAPTER 24

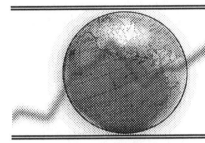

MONOPOLY

PUTTING THIS CHAPTER INTO PERSPECTIVE

Chapter 24 is the second chapter devoted to market structure analysis; the first was Chapter 23, which analyzed the perfect competition model. Chapter 24 introduces the monopoly market structure, and you should be able to compare the perfect competition model to the monopoly model. Here we follow the "pattern" of analysis suggested in Chapter 23 of this student learning guide.

First we consider the characteristics of the monopoly market structure. In the monopoly model one firm produces a homogeneous product and entry into the industry is impeded for one reason or another. Contrast this market structure with perfect competition, in which *many* firms produce a homogeneous product and entry into the industry is easy.

Because there is only one firm in the monopoly market structure, the firm's demand curve is the market demand curve; like all market demand curves, the monopolist's demand curve is negatively sloped. This, of course, is to be contrasted with the perfectly elastic demand curve facing the perfect competitor. Stated differently, there are many close substitutes for the output of the perfect competitor (who is a price taker), but there are no close substitutes for the output of the monopolist (who is a price searcher).

The second part of the pattern of analysis leads us to determine the equilibrium output-price combination. Because we assume that the monopolist desires to maximize profit, we (as usual) predict that the firm will produce output up to the point where the marginal benefit (MB) equals the marginal cost (MC) of doing so. In this chapter we assume that the cost of the monopolist is not unlike that of the perfect competitor; therefore its rising marginal cost is found by reading the marginal cost curve. The marginal benefit to the monopolist of producing one more unit of output is a bit more troublesome. As was true for the perfect competitor, for the monopolist the marginal benefit equals the marginal revenue. Unlike the situation under perfect competition, however, under monopoly marginal revenue falls, because the monopolist's demand curve is downward sloping. Marginal revenue is a constant to the perfect competitor because the demand curve is horizontal (and therefore average revenue is constant). Once the profit maximizing output is determined, the monopolist's price is already determined; the quantity produced can be sold only at one price, read from the monopolist's demand curve. Note that because average revenue equals price and because marginal revenue is less than average revenue, in equilibrium the monopolist must be producing where price exceeds marginal revenue (more about this later). Note that all of this assumes that the monopolist sells all of its output at the same price. If we relax that assumption, as we do near the end of Chapter 24, then we can analyze price discrimination.

Because entry into the monopoly industry is impeded, it is possible (but not necessary) for the monopolist to earn economic profits even in the long run—unlike the perfect competitor, who operates in an industry in which entry is easy.

Finally, we consider whether the monopoly market structure is efficient or inefficient from society's point of view. In equilibrium, price exceeds marginal cost (hence society wants *more* of this good) and long-run economic profits may be positive (also implying that too few resources are allocated to a monopoly industry)therefore, it is inefficient. In short, price is too high and output is too low in the monopoly market structure.

LEARNING OBJECTIVES

After you have studied this chapter, you should be able to

1. define monopolist, natural monopoly, price discrimination, price differentiation, price searcher, tariffs, and cartel.

2. list the characteristics of a monopoly and distinguish them from the characteristics of the perfectly competitive firm.

3. distinguish between the monopolist's demand curve and the perfect competitor's demand curve.

4. determine the profit maximizing output for the monopolist, given sufficient information; and determine the price that a monopolist would charge, given the profit-maximizing output.

5. list possible barriers to entry into an industry.

6. calculate a monopolist's total profits, given sufficient information.

7. recognize some misconceptions concerning monopoly.

8. distinguish between price discrimination and price differentiation, and list the conditions necessary for price discrimination.

9. list and recognize two costs to society of monopolies.

CHAPTER OUTLINE

1. A *monopolist* is a single supplier that constitutes an entire industry; the monopolist produces a good for which there are no close substitutes.

2. *Barriers to entry* are impediments that prevent new firms from entering an industry; there are numerous potential barriers to entry.
   a. Some monopolists gain power through the exclusive ownership of a raw material that is essential to produce a good.
   b. If an enormous capital investment is required to enter an industry, such a sum could be a barrier to entry.
   c. Licenses, franchises, and certificates of convenience also constitute potential barriers to entry.
   d. Patents issued to inventors constitute, for a time, effective barriers to entry.
   e. If economies of scale are great relative to market demand, new entrants into an industry will be discouraged; persistent economies of scale could lead to a natural monopoly.
   f. Governmental safety and quality regulation may raise fixed costs to firms in an industry significantly enough so as to deter new entrants.
   g. If tariffs on imports are sufficiently high, then producers can gain some measure of monopoly power.

3. The monopolist faces the industry demand curve because the monopolist is the entire industry; examples of monopolies include local electric power companies and the post office.

4. It is instructive to compare the monopolist with the perfect competitor.
    a. The perfect competitor's demand curve is perfectly elastic at the "going" price; price is the same as average revenue, and average revenue equals marginal revenue in this model.
    b. The monopolist's demand curve is negatively sloped; price (or average revenue) falls, and therefore marginal revenue is less than price because the monopolist must lower its price on all the units it sells, and not just on the marginal unit.

5. Where marginal revenue equals zero, total revenue is maximized; at the point on the demand curve corresponding to zero marginal revenue, the price elasticity of demand equals 1; at higher prices (lower outputs) demand is elastic, and at lower prices (higher outputs) demand is inelastic.

6. By assuming that the monopolist wants to maximize total profits and that the short-run cost curves are similar in shape to those of the perfect competitor, we can determine the monopolist's optimal output-price combination.
    a. The monopolist's total revenue curve is nonlinear (unlike the perfect competitor's); optimal output exists where the positive difference between total costs and total revenues is maximized.
    b. Stated differently, optimal output exists where MR = MC.
    c. If MR > MC, the firm can increase total profits by increasing output; if MC > MR, then the firm can increase total profits by reducing output.
    d. Once the profit-maximizing output is determined, the monopolist's price is already determined; it is read on the demand curve at that quantity.

7. Graphically, total profits are calculated by subtracting average costs from average revenues and multiplying that value by the quantity produced.

8. If the monopolist's average cost curve lies entirely above its demand curve, it will experience economic losses.

9. If the monopolist can prevent the resale of its homogeneous output and if it can separate its customers into different markets with different price elasticities, then it can price discriminate—and earn higher profits.

10. Monopolies are inefficient because they charge a price that is too high (P > MC) and because they produce an output that is too low.

KEY TERMS

Monopolist   Tariffs
Price discrimination   Cartel
Price differentiation

KEY CONCEPTS

Price searcher   Natural monopoly

COMPLETION QUESTIONS
Fill in the blank or circle the correct term.

1. A monopolist is a _____ supplier that constitutes the entire industry; its demand curve is _____ sloped.

2. Before a monopolist can earn long-run monopoly profits, there must be _____ to entry.

3. Examples of barriers to entry include _____, _____, _____, _____, _____, and _____.

4. Because the perfect competitor's demand curve is perfectly elastic, its selling price is constant; therefore its average revenue (falls, rises, remains constant) and its marginal revenue (falls, rises, remains constant).

5. Because the monopolist's demand curve is negatively sloped, its selling price falls with output; therefore its average revenue (falls, rises, remains constant) and its marginal revenue (falls, rises, remains constant).

6. If a monopolist must charge the same price to everyone, when it produces more, its marginal revenue will be (less than, greater than, equal to) its price.

7. When marginal revenue equals zero, total revenue is (minimized, maximized); at that point on the demand curve, the price elasticity of demand equals the number _____; at a higher price total revenues would fall, and therefore demand is (elastic, inelastic); at a lower price total revenues would fall, and therefore demand is _____.

8. One misconception about monopoly is that the monopolist can sell any quantity that it chooses to at any _____; instead the monopolist can sell any specific quantity at only one price. Another misconception is that a monopolist must earn economic profits; it won't, however, if the _____ curve is above the monopolist's demand curve.

9. The monopolist maximizes total profits at that output for which _____ equals _____; given its profit-maximizing output, the monopolist (need not, must) charge a price consistent with that quantity.

10. If a monopolist need not charge the same price to everyone, then it can _____, and its profits will rise; a monopolist can charge different prices to different groups if it can prevent the _____ of its product.

11. A monopolist charges a price that is too _____, and it produces an output that is too _____; therefore monopoly is (less, more) socially efficient than perfect competition.

TRUE-FALSE QUESTIONS
Circle the T if the statement is true, the F if it is false. Explain to yourself why a statement is false.

T F   1.   The more broadly we define an industry, the less likely it is to be a monopoly.

T F   2.   Because of barriers to entry, a monopolist must earn long-run profits.

T F   3.   The monopolist's marginal revenue curve lies below its demand, or average revenue, curve.

T F   4.   A monopolist must charge the same price to all buyers.

T F   5.   The monopolist's total revenue curve is linear.

T F   6.   At that output for which total revenue is maximized, price elasticity of demand equals 1.

T F   7.   The profit maximizing monopolist will never produce on the inelastic portion of its demand curve.

T F   8.   Total profits are maximized where total revenue equals total costs.

T F   9.   If MR > MC, the firm can increase profits if it produces less.

T F   10.   A monopolist can select only one profit-maximizing price, given the output it chooses to produce, assuming no price discrimination.

T F   11.   If possible, a monopolist will charge a higher price to a price inelastic group than to a price elastic group.

T F   12.   A monopolist tends to produce too little and to sell at a price that is too high.

T F   13.   A monopolist is a price taker.

T F   14.   Because there are no close substitutes for a monopolist's output, its demand curve is inelastic throughout.

MULTIPLE CHOICE QUESTIONS
Circle the letter that corresponds to the best answer.

1.   Which of the following is *not* a characteristic of the monopoly market structure?
     a.   one seller
     b.   homogeneous product
     c.   restricted entry
     d.   price taker

2.   Which of the following is a potential barrier to entry?
     a.   government license requirement
     b.   sole ownership of a key resource
     c.   great economies of scale, relative to demand
     d.   All of the above

3.   Which is **NOT** true about monopolies?
     a.   linear total revenue curve
     b.   may earn long-run economic profits
     c.   negatively sloped demand curve
     d.   marginal revenue below price

4.   The firm maximizes total profits at that output where
     a.   total revenue equals total cost.
     b.   marginal revenue equals marginal cost.
     c.   the elasticity of demand equals 1.
     d.   All of the above

5.   Once a monopolist produces a profit-maximizing output,
     a.   the price is determined for it, given its demand curve.
     b.   it can select any price it wants.
     c.   its competitors select price.
     d.   price cannot be determined.

6.   If MR < MC, then the firm
     a.   is maximizing total profits.
     b.   can increase total profits by producing more.
     c.   can increase total profits by producing less.
     d.   is maximizing total revenues.

7.   Monopoly profit
     a.   equals (average revenue - average cost) times quantity sold.
     b.   equals price times quantity sold.
     c.   exists only in the short run.
     d.   exists because no entry barriers exist.

8.   A monopolist will price discriminate if
     a.   price differentiation exists.
     b.   it can separate markets by different price elasticities of demand and prevent resales.
     c.   it chooses to maximize average revenues.
     d.   all buyers have the same price elasticity of demand.

9.   Which of the following is price differentiation?
     a.   Students pay a higher rental price for apartments than do nonstudents because they cause more damage.
     b.   Women pay higher prices for haircuts because it takes longer to cut their hair.
     c.   People in ghetto areas pay higher prices for individual items because costs are greater in such areas.
     d.   All of the above

10. Assume that at a given output a monopolist's marginal revenue is $10 per unit and its marginal cost is $5. If the monopolist increases output, then
     a.   price, marginal cost, and total profit will fall.
     b.   price will fall, marginal cost will rise, and total profit will rise.
     c.   price will rise, marginal cost will fall, and total profit will rise.
     d.   price, marginal cost, and total profit will rise.

MATCHING
Choose the item in column (2) that best matches an item in column (1).

(1)	(2)
a. perfect competitor	g. nonlinear total revenue curve
b. monopolist	h. firm with a downward sloping demand curve
c. price differentiation	i. great economies of scale
d. price discrimination	j. price taker
e. barrier to entry	k. students pay higher rents for apartments than do non-students
f. price searcher	l. students pay different tuition costs depending on need

WORKING WITH GRAPHS

1. Suppose you are given the demand schedule for a monopolist and the total cost figures below. Plot the monopolist's demand curve, marginal revenue curve, and marginal cost curve on the graph provided. Determine the optimal level of output for the monopolist. What do total profits equal? (Plot MC and MR on the mid-points.)

Output per unit of time	Price	Total Cost
0	$ 32	$ 12
1	28	20
2	24	25
3	20	31
4	16	41
5	12	56
6	8	79
7	4	117

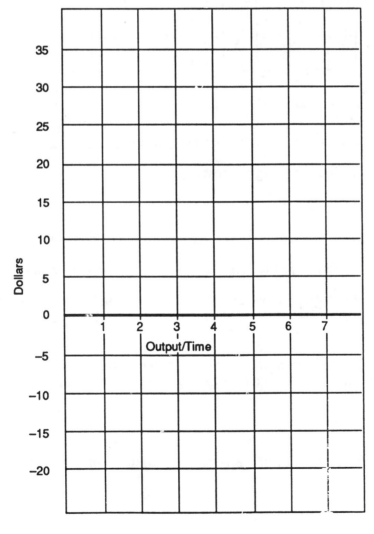

2. Suppose you are given the graphical summary of a monopolist below. Answer the following questions using this information.

a. The optimal short-term output level for the monopolist is _____.

b. At the optimal level of output, marginal cost is _____.

c. At the optimal level of output, total cost is _____.

d. At the optimal level of output, price is _____ and total revenue is _____.

e. The monopolist is earning a (profit, loss) of _____ in the given situation.

f. Suppose that the above graph represented a competitive industry and the demand curve given was the market demand curve for the entire industry. The competitive level of output would be _____, sold at a price of _____.

g. The average total cost per unit of output in the competitive case would fall by _____, as compared with the average total cost under a monopoly.

PROBLEMS

1. Indicate whether the following may characterize the perfect competitor (PC), the monopolist (M), or both (B).

_____ a. perfectly elastic demand curve

_____ b. increasing marginal cost curve

_____ c. downward sloping demand curve

_____ d. linear total revenue curve

_____ e. total profit maximizer

_____ f. possibility of earning long-run economic profits

_____ g. P>MR

_____ h. homogeneous output

_____ i. price discriminator

_____ j. barriers to entry

_____ k. free exit and entry

_____ l. price searcher

_____ m. price taker

_____ n. produces where MR = MC

_____ o. P = MC in equilibrium

_____ p. long-run equilibrium at minimum AC

_____ q. P = MR

_____ r. P = AR

CASE STUDY

In 1937 New York City issued 11,787 medallions (non-expiring, resaleable, licenses to operate a taxicab) for $10 each; that same number of medallions exists today. As the demand for taxicab services has increased over time, clearly the market price for a medallion has risen. At the end of the 1990s the price was around $240,000 per medallion. In effect, this licensing arrangement is a barrier to entry, and it bestows monopolistic advantages to medallion owners.

1. What does the price of a medallion reflect?

2. Who benefits from such a licensing arrangement—new medallion buyers or original medallion recipients?

3. If New York City were to eliminate this system and permit anyone who has a driver's license to drive a cab, who would benefit, and who would be harmed?

ANSWERS TO CHAPTER 24

COMPLETION QUESTIONS

1. single; negatively
2. barriers
3. ownership of resources without close substitutes; large capital requirements to enter industry; legally required licenses; franchises; or certificates of convenience; patents, economies of scale; safety and quality regulation; high tariffs

4. remains constant; remains constant
5. falls; falls
6. less than
7. maximized; 1; elastic; inelastic
8. price; average total cost
9. MR; MC; must
10. price discriminate; resale
11. high; low; less

TRUE-FALSE QUESTIONS

1. T
2. F   An inefficient monopolist need not earn economic profits.
3. T
4. F   A monopolist can price discriminate under certain conditions.
5. F   It is not linear because price falls as the monopolist produces more.
6. T
7. T
8. F   Profit maximization occurs where MR = MC; if TR = TC, then economic profits are zero.
9. F   If MR > MC, profits will rise if the firm produces more.
10. T
11. T
12. T
13. F   A monopolist is a price searcher.
14. F   A monopolist's demand curve has various ranges of elasticity.

MULTIPLE CHOICE QUESTIONS

1.d;   2.d;   3.a;   4.b;   5.a;   6.c;   7.a;   8.b;   9.d;   10.b.

MATCHING

a and j;   b and g;   c and k;   d and l;   e and i;   f and h

WORKING WITH GRAPHS

1.

The profit-maximizing level of output is 3 units sold at a price of $20 each. This can be seen graphically. Total profits equal $29 at that output.

2.   a. 300;   b. $2;   c. $1890;   d. $5, $1500;   e. loss, $390;   f. 400, $4;   g. $0.30

PROBLEMS

1.   a. PC   b. B   c. M   d. PC   e. B   f. M   g. M   h. B   i. M
      j. M   k. PC   l. M   m. PC   n. B   o. PC   p. PC   q. PC   r. B

CASE STUDY

1. Demand conditions, because supply is fixed.
2. Original recipients, because the price to new buyers will reflect the monopolistic advantage.
3. New drivers would benefit, as well as customers; old owners, who paid a price for medallions that reflected the barrier to entry, would be harmed.

GLOSSARY TO CHAPTER 24

Cartel Any arrangement or agreement made by a number of independent entities to coordinate either buying or selling decisions, so that all of them will earn either monopsony or monopoly profits.

Monopolist The single supplier that comprises the entire industry for a good or service for which there is no close substitute.

Natural monopoly A monopoly that arises when there are large economies of scale relative to industry demand.

Price differentiation   Price differences for similar products which reflect only differences in marginal cost in providing those commodities to different groups of buyers.

Price discrimination   Selling a given product at more than one price with the price difference being unrelated to cost difference.

Price searcher   A firm that, because it faces a downward sloping demand curve, must determine the price-output combination that maximizes profit.

Tariffs   A taxes on imported goods.

CHAPTER 25

MONOPOLISTIC COMPETITION, OLIGOPOLY, AND STRATEGIC BEHAVIOR

PUTTING THIS CHAPTER INTO PERSPECTIVE

Chapter 25 is the third chapter that deals with market structures; Chapter 23 analyzed the perfect competition model and Chapter 24 analyzed the monopoly model. Chapter 25 examines two more market structures—monopolistic competition and oligopoly. Because this is a long chapter we suggest that you break it into several parts; let the first part cover the monopolistic competition model and the second part cover the oligopoly model (and the issues and applications).

In the monopolistic competition model the assumptions are (1) a significant number of sellers in a highly competitive (but not perfectly competitive) market, (2) differentiated products, (3) existence of advertising, and (4) easy entry into the industry.

Because of assumptions 1 through 3, the monopolistic competitor has some control over its selling price. This means that its demand curve is negatively sloped, which in turn means that its marginal revenue curve must be below its demand curve and that in equilibrium, price must exceed marginal cost. In short, assumptions 1 through 3 imply that monopolistic competition is less efficient than perfect competition because such assumptions necessitate that in equilibrium P > MC.

Because of assumption 4 we know that in the long run each monopolistic competitor must earn exactly zero economic profits. This means that the demand (average revenue) curve must be tangent to the monopolistic competitor's AC curve. Furthermore, because the demand curve is negatively sloped, the demand curve must be tangent to the AC curve somewhere to the left of AC's minimum point. (By definition, at AC's minimum point the slope must equal zero; therefore, as long as the demand curve is not horizontal, the demand curve cannot be tangent to AC at AC's minimum point.) This gives us another reason to believe that the monopolistic competition model leads to a less efficient solution than the perfect competition model: in equilibrium output will not be produced at minimum average cost.

Because there is independence among oligopolistic competitors, it is difficult to predict the price/output outcome resulting from their behavior. As a consequence economists have developed an approach, called game theory, that gives some insights into the oligopoly model. Your text introduces you to this fascinating topic.

If we assume that an oligopolist's rivals will find it in their own interest to match a price decrease but to ignore a price increase, then a kinked demand curve for each oligopolist is the result. The demand curve is negatively sloped, the marginal revenue curve is below it—and discontinuous. Ultimately this means social inefficiency because it implies that P > MC.

In order to help you sort out the different market structures, the text summarizes their main features in Table 25-3. After you have completed your study of this chapter, you should analyze that exhibit.

LEARNING OBJECTIVES

After you have studied this chapter you should be able to

1. define monopolistic competition, product differentiation, oligopoly, strategic dependence, concentration ratio, horizontal and vertical mergers, reaction function, game theory, cooperative and noncooperative games, zero sum, positive sum, and negative sum games, strategy, dominant strategy, prisoner's dilemma, payoff matrix, opportunistic behavior, tit-for-tat strategic behavior, price leadership, limit-pricing model, price war, and entry-deterrence strategy.

2. list the characteristics of the monopolistic competition market structure and of the oligopoly market structure.

3. distinguish between the monopolistic competitor's demand curve and the perfect competitor's demand curve

4. recognize reasons why the monopolistic competition market structure and the oligopoly market structure are socially inefficient.

5. compare the main features of perfect competition, monopoly, monopolistic competition, and oligopoly.

6. list three reasons for the existence of oligopolies.

7. calculate concentration ratios and recognize their limitations.

8. distinguish between a cooperative and a noncooperative game.

9. answer questions concerning the essence of the kinked demand curve and enumerate criticisms of the kinked demand curve model.

10. distinguish among zero sum, positive sum, and negative sum games.

11. recognize three ways that existing oligopolists deter entry into the industry.

CHAPTER OUTLINE

1. The theory of *monopolistic competition* was developed simultaneously by Edward Chamberlin and Joan Robinson in 1933; we analyze Chamberlin's model.
   a. There are four characteristics of monopolistic competition: a significant number of sellers in a highly competitive market, differentiated products, advertising, and easy entry.
   b. Although there are many sellers, there are not as many as there are in the perfect competition model; each monopolistic competitor has a little control over its price, but collusion is difficult and each firm acts independently of the others.
   c. Perhaps the most important feature of this model is *product differentiation*.
      i. Differentiation refers to differences in physical characteristics.
      ii. Each separate differentiated product has close substitutes.

      d.   Because the monopolistic competitor has at least some monopoly power, it may be profitable for it to advertise.
          i.   Advertising may provide useful information to buyers.
      e.   In the long run, entry into such a market structure is easy.

2.   It is possible to predict the optimal price-output combination of the monopolistic competitor.
      a.   The monopolistic competitor's demand curve is downward sloping; therefore its marginal revenue curve lies below its demand curve.
      b.   Short-run equilibrium exists where MR = MC; economic profits or losses are possible in the short run.
      c.   In the long run, because of free entry, the monopolistic competitor must earn exactly zero economic profits.

3.   For the monopolistic competitor, social inefficiency exists because P > MC and because in the long run its rate of output lies to the left of the minimum point on the ATC curve.

4.   *Oligopoly* is a market situation in which there are a very few sellers, each of which expects a reaction from its rivals to changes in its price and quantity; there are two major characteristics of oligopolies: a small number of firms and interdependence.

5.   There are at least three reasons for the emergence of oligopolistic industries: economies of scale, barriers to entry, and merger (horizontal or vertical).
      a.   Four- or eight-firm *concentration ratios* are often calculated to determine the extent to which an industry is "monopolized."
      b.   Over time some industries experience drastic changes (up or down) in their concentration ratios; others show little change.

6.   Before an oligopoly situation can be analyzed with respect to price and output, specific assumptions about rival *reactions* must be made; a different model arises with each assumption regarding the oligopolist's reaction function.

7.   Because there is interdependence among oligopolistic competitors economists have developed an approach, called game theory, to describe how such firms interact rationally.
      a.   If firms collude and form a cartel, the game is referred to as cooperative game.
      b.   If cartels are too expensive to form or enforce, then a noncooperative game is played among oligopolists.
      c.   Games are classified as being zero sum, positive sum, or negative sum.

8.   Oligopolistic decision makers derive a strategy, or rule used to make a choice; a dominant strategy is one that always yields the highest benefit, regardless of what the other oligopolists do.

9.   The most famous example of game theory is called the prisoner's dilemma in which it can be shown that (under specified conditions) in situations in which there is more than one party to a crime, the dominant strategy for each prisoner is to confess.

10. A payoff matrix indicates the consequences of the strategies chosen by the players in the game.

11. Another oligopoly model results from assuming that rivals will match a price reduction, but ignore a price increase.
      a.   In such a situation, for the oligopolist the price elasticity of demand above the current price will be very high, and the price elasticity of demand below the current price will be

very low; the result is a kinked demand curve and a discontinuous marginal revenue curve.

   b.   One implication of the kinked demand curve model is price rigidity; any change in marginal costs in the discontinuous gap of the marginal revenue curve will leave price unaltered.

   c.   One criticism of this analysis is that it offers no explanation of how the current price was established; empirical evidence indicates that oligopolies tend to change price more frequently than do monopolies.

12. Sometimes even if no formal cartel arises among oligopolists, tacit collusion in the form of price leadership can occur; the largest firm announces its price and smaller competitors then follow this lead.

13. On occasion smaller rivals may set price too far below the price leader and a price war results.

14. Strategic decision making could lead to pricing or investing policies that deter entry by potential competitors; entry-deterrence strategies include threats of a price war, investment in excess capacity by existing firms, inducing governments to restrict entry, and raising switching costs to customers.

15. The limit-pricing model suggests that existing oligopolists collude to set the highest price they can without encouraging entry into the industry.

KEY TERMS

Monopolistic competition	Reaction function	Cooperative game
Oligopoly	Price war	Noncooperative game
Concentration ratio	Payoff matrix	Game theory
Horizontal merger	Vertical merger	

KEY CONCEPTS

Zero sum game	Entry-deterrence strategy	Dominant strategies
Positive sum game	Price leadership	Prisoner's dilemma
Negative sum game	Limit pricing model	Opportunistic behavior
Tit-for-tat strategy behavior		

COMPLETION QUESTIONS
Fill in the blank or circle the correct term.

1. The four characteristics of monopolistic competition are _____, _____, _____, and _____.

2. Under monopolistic competition, collusion is (easy, difficult); each firm (must, need not) take into account the reactions of rivals, and each firm has (a little, much, no) control over its selling price.

3. The goal of advertising is to _____. The perfect competitor (does, does not) advertise; the monopolistic competitor (does, does not) advertise because it has a _____ product.

4. Advertising is useful to the extent that it provides _____ to buyers.

5. The demand curve for the monopolistic competitor is _____ sloped; therefore its marginal revenue curve is (below, above) its demand, or AR curve; therefore in equilibrium price must be (less than, greater than, equal to) marginal cost; therefore social (inefficiency, efficiency) exists in the monopolistic competition market structure.

6. In the long run, ease of entry causes the monopolistic competitor to earn _____ economic profits; therefore its negatively sloped demand curve must be (above, below, tangent to) its ATC curve. As a consequence, in long-run equilibrium, output must be produced at a cost (below, above, at) minimum average total cost.

7. Two key characteristics of oligopoly are _____, and _____; oligopolies may emerge because of _____, _____, and _____.

8. Concentration ratios (fall, rise) as the definition of "industry" is narrowed, and they _____ as the definition is broadened.

9. Economists have developed an approach to analyze the interdependence among oligopolists called _____ theory; if oligopolists collude and form a cartel this is a _____ game; if cartels are too expensive to form or enforce then oligopolists will play a _____ game.

10. Games are referred to as _____ sum if one player's benefit is exactly equal to the expense of the other, _____ sum if the sum of the players' benefit is positive, and _____ sum if the sum of the players' benefit is negative.

11. The most famous example of game theory is _____ in which the dominant strategy of prisoners (usually) is to (confess, not confess).

12. Assume that firm B is an oligopolist. If its rivals match its price reductions but ignore its price increases, firm B will have a _____ demand curve; its marginal revenue curve will be _____; firm B probably (will, will not) change its price very often. Because its demand curve is negatively sloped, in equilibrium firm B's (P = MC, P > MC, P < MC) and from society's point of view it will produce (too little, too much, just enough) and its price will be (too low, too high, just right).

13. Even if no formal cartel arises in an oligopolistic industry, tacit collusion in the form of _____ leadership may result; occasionally such a system breaks down and a price _____ results.

14. Existing oligopolists can use the following strategies to deter entry: _____, _____, and _____; the _____ model suggests that existing firms set the highest price they can without encouraging entry.

TRUE-FALSE QUESTIONS
Circle the **T** if the statement is true, the **F** if it is false. Explain to yourself why a statement is false.

T F   1. The monopolistic competitor has a negatively sloped demand curve.

T F   2. The monopolistic competitor must take into account the reactions of its competitors.

T F   3.   The most important feature of the monopolistic competitive market is product differentiation.

T F   4.   Product differentiation exists in the wheat industry.

T F   5.   One important goal of advertising is convey quality information.

T F   6.   The monopolistic competition model leads to social efficiency because in the long run P = MC.

T F   7.   The main characteristic of the oligopoly market structure is that an oligopolist must consider the reaction of its rivals.

T F   8.   Perhaps the strongest reason for the existence of oligopolies is economies of scale relative to market demand.

T F   9.   Concentration ratios provide an accurate measure of the degree of monopoly power in an industry.

T F   10.   If an oligopolist's rivals match all of its price changes, its demand curve will be kinked.

T F   11.   Cartels are usually expensive to set up and enforce.

T F   12.   A dominant strategy is one that is always preferred by a player, regardless of what other players do.

T F   13.   Price wars result because all players are in a positive sum game.

T F   14.   The limit-pricing model suggests that oligopolists set price at the highest price they can.

T F   15.   Collusion may be found in both formal and tacit arrangements.

MULTIPLE CHOICE QUESTIONS
Circle the letter that corresponds to the best answer.

1.   Which is *not* a characteristic of monopolistic competition?
     a.   significant number of sellers
     b.   differentiated products
     c.   advertising
     d.   must take into account rival's reaction to price changes

2.   Under monopolistic competition, collusion is
     a.   easy.
     b.   difficult.
     c.   impossible.
     d.   nonexistent.

3.   Which firm has the **LEAST** control over price?
     a.   perfect competitor
     b.   monopolistic competitor
     c.   oligopolist
     d.   monopolist

4. Product differentiation is the *central* feature of the _____ model.
    a. monopoly
    b. oligopoly
    c. monopolistic competition
    d. perfect competition

5. Which market structure is most **UNLIKE** the others, regarding its demand curve?
    a. perfect competition
    b. oligopoly
    c. monopolistic competition
    d. monopoly

6. *Analogy*: Product differentiation is to monopolistic competition as _____ is to oligopoly.
    a. competition
    b. interdependence
    c. advertising
    d. economies of scale

7. Advertising
    a. attempts to increase demand for one's product.
    b. helps to differentiate one's product.
    c. can lead to more information for buyers.
    d. All of the above

8. Which firm's demand curve is **NOT** negatively sloped?
    a. oligopolist
    b. perfect competition
    c. monopolist
    d. monopolistic competition

9. Only when a firm's demand curve is negatively sloped will
    a. its MR curve lie below its demand curve.
    b. in equilibrium, MR = MC.
    c. economic profits equal zero in the long run.
    d. All of the above

10. For the monopolistic competitor, in the long run
    a. the demand curve must be tangent to the ATC curve.
    b. output is too high, from society's point of view.
    c. output is produced to the right of the minimum ATC point.
    d. economic profits can be positive.

11. In which of the following will the players' sum of benefits be positive?
    a. negative sum game
    b. zero sum game
    c. positive sum game
    d. prisoner's dilemma

12. If oligopoly B's rivals ignore its price increases but match its price decreases, then B's demand curve will be
    a. discontinuous.
    b. kinked at the going price.
    c. below its marginal revenue curve.
    d. proportionate to the industry demand curve.

13. In long-run equilibrium for the oligopolist,
    a. MR = MC.
    b. P > MR.
    c. economic profits are zero.
    d. All of the above

14. Which firms must have zero economic profits in the long run?
    a. monopolist, perfect competitor
    b. oligopolist, monopolistic competitor
    c. perfect competitor, monopolistic competitor
    d. perfect competitor, oligopolist

15. The *best* explanation for the existence of oligopolies is
    a. no economies of scale exist.
    b. large economies of scale relative to market demand.
    c. advertising.
    d. one firm has exclusive ownership of an important raw material.

16. In an oligopolistic industry, entry will result if
    a. normal profits exist.
    b. the industry LAC curve is below the market demand curve.
    c. the industry LAC curve is above the market demand curve.
    d. advertising is permitted.

17. The kinked demand curve theory
    a. is supported by empirical evidence.
    b. requires that an oligopolist's rivals exactly match its price changes.
    c. predicts price rigidity.
    d. requires collusion.

18. Which of the following is a strategy to deter entry by potential competitors?
    a. raising switching costs to customers
    b. investment in excess capacity by existing firms
    c. limit-pricing strategy
    d. All of the above

MATCHING

(1)	(2)
a. monopolistic competition	g. horizontal demand curve
b. positive sum game	h. all players benefit
c. oligopoly	i. one seller
d. concentration ratio	j. product differentiation
e. price taker	k. kinked demand curve
f. monopoly	l. measure of concentration

WORKING WITH GRAPHS

1. Use the graphs of a monopolistic competitor below to answer each of the following questions.

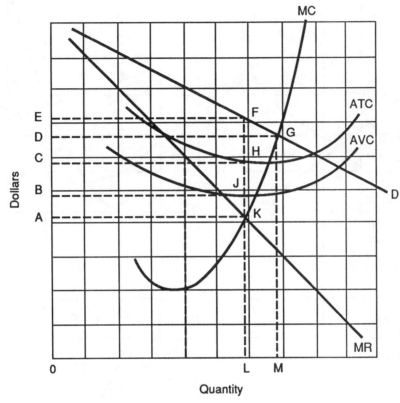

a. At what level of output will this firm operate? _____
b. What is marginal revenue at this level of output? _____
c. What price will this firm charge for its product? _____
d. The area of what rectangle is equal to total revenue? _____
e. What is the firm's average cost in equilibrium? _____
f. The area of what rectangle is equal to the firm's total cost? _____
g. Is the firm making profits or incurring losses? _____
h. The area of what rectangle is equal to profits or losses? _____

2. Use the graphs below to answer the questions that follow.

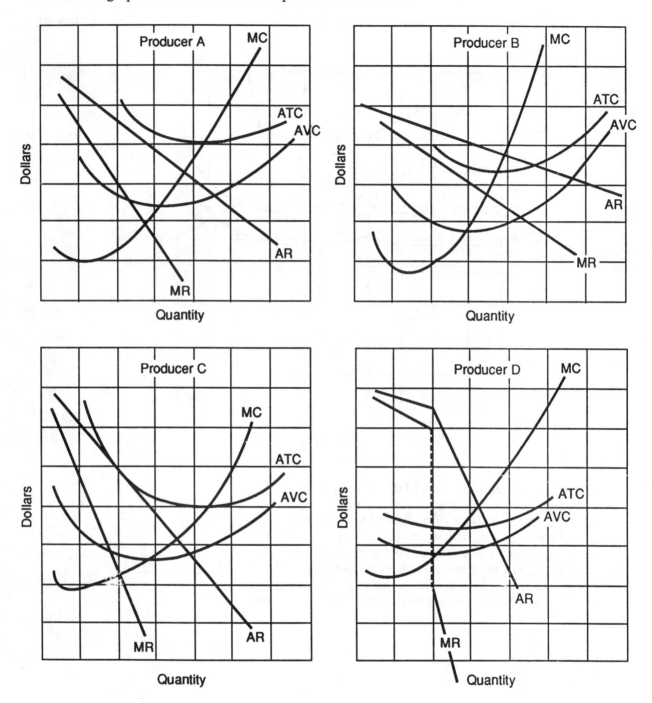

a. Which of the producers is a monopolistic competitor making positive economic profits? _____

b. Which of the producers appears to be in an industry that may have reached a long-run equilibrium? _____

c. Which of the producers is most likely to leave the industry in which it is currently operating? _____

d. If costs increase by a small amount, which producer is most likely to maintain its present price-quantity combination? _____

e. Which of the producers is in an industry that is most likely to attract additional firms? _____

f. Which of the producers is most probably in the industry with the fewest competitors? _____

g. If all the firms in Producer C's industry are currently in a similar situation, what will most probably happen if there is a decrease in demand for the products of that industry? _____

h. Which producer(s) is/are incurring short-run losses? _____

i. Which producer is in the industry that is most probably characterized by some type of barrier to entry? _____

3. Use the graphs of the oligopolist below to answer each of the questions that follow.

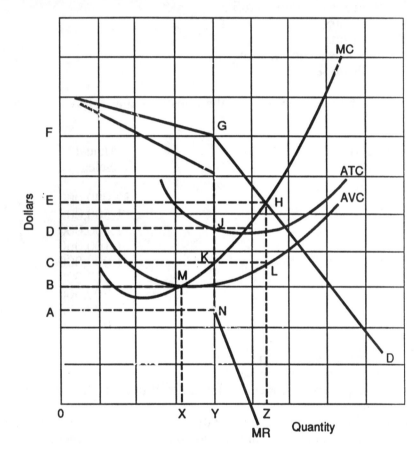

a. At what level of output will this firm operate? _____
b. What is the marginal cost at this level of output? _____
c. What price will the firm charge for its product? _____
d. The area of what rectangle equals total revenue? _____
e. What is the firm's average cost? _____
f. The area of what rectangle is equal to the firm's total cost? _____
g. The area of what rectangle is equal to the firm's profit? _____
h. Suppose the firm is operating at an output level of Y units. How low would marginal costs at Y units of output have to drop before the firm would lower its price? _____

PROBLEMS

1. Let PC = perfect competition, M = monopoly, MC = monopolistic competition, and O = oligopoly. Indicate by writing down the appropriate initials which of the following may be consistent with one, several, or all of those markets.

   _____ a. profit maximizer
   _____ b. advertising
   _____ c. long-run economic profits
   _____ d. social inefficiency
   _____ e. P > MC in equilibrium
   _____ f. product differentiation
   _____ g. large economies of scale relative to market demand
   _____ h. long-run equilibrium at minimum ATC
   _____ i. short-run economic profits
   _____ j. easy entry
   _____ k. few firms
   _____ l. interdependence of firms
   _____ m. ability to set price

2. Consider the table below, then answer the questions that follow. All information is for domestic firms.

Domestic Firms in Industry A	Annual Sales
1	$2,000,000
2	1,500,000
3	1,400,000
4	1,100,000
5	1,000,000
6	700,000
7	200,000
8	100,000
9-20 (remaining firms)	1,000,000

   a. What is the 4-firm concentration ratio?
   b. What is the 8-firm concentration ratio?
   c. What would happen to the concentration ratios if industry B's product is a substitute for Industry A's product?
   d. What would happen to the concentration ratios if the sales of imported goods in Industries A and B that are sold in domestic markets were included?

CASE STUDY

Many noneconomists believe that they can cite exceptions to the law of demand. They point to instances in which some company changed the "image" of its good through advertising, raised the price of the good, and sold more. Their interpretation is that an increase in price led to an increase in quantity demanded; hence the law of demand is wrong.

Actually, if advertising convinces people that Good A is of higher quality, or if people can now receive more "prestige" by purchasing Good A, this is an increase in the demand for Good A; that is, the demand curve for Good A shifts rightward.

1. If the demand for Good A shifts rightward (due to advertising) given the supply of Good A, what happens to the equilibrium price? The equilibrium quantity?

2. What mistake have noneconomists made in interpreting the law of demand?

3. Does the law of demand hold along *each* demand curve—the old and the new?

ANSWERS TO CHAPTER 25

COMPLETION QUESTIONS

1. significant number of sellers; differentiated product; advertising; easy entry.
2. difficult; need not; a little
3. increase demand; does not; does; differentiated
4. information
5. negatively; below; greater than; inefficiency
6. zero; tangent to; above
7. small number of firms; interdependence; economies of scale; barriers to entry; product differentiation and advertising; merger

8. rise; fall
9. game; cooperative; noncooperative
10. zero; positive; negative
11. the prisoner's dilemma; confess
12. kinked; below its demand curve and discontinuous; will not; P > MC; too little; too high
13. price; war
14. threats of price wars; investment in excess capacity; get government to restrict entry; limit-pricing; raising switching costs to customers.

TRUE-FALSE

1. T
2. F There are so many rivals, they can be ignored.
3. T
4. F Wheat is largely homogeneous.
5. T
6. F Social inefficiency exists because the monopolistic competitor's demand curve is negatively sloped; therefore, P > MC in equilibrium.
7. T
8. T
9. F They are very inaccurate, if only because inter-industry competition exists; foreign competition exists too.
10. F Its demand curve will be proportionate to the industry demand curve.
11. T
12. T
13. F They result when price leadership strategies break down.
14. F They set price at the highest level that *will still discourage entry*.
15. T

MULTIPLE CHOICE QUESTIONS

1.d;   2.b;   3.a;   4.c;   5.a;   6.b;   7.d;   8.b;   9.a;   10.a;
11.c;   12.b;   13.d;   14.c;   15.b;   16.b;   17.c;   18.d

MATCHING

a and j;   b and h;   c and k;   d and l;   e and g;   f and i

WORKING WITH GRAPHS

1. a. 0L; b. 0A; c. 0E; d. 0EFL; e. 0C; f. 0CHL; g. profits; h. CEFH
2. a. B; b. C; c. A; d. D; e. B; f. D; g. some firms will exit the industry; h. A; i. D;
3. a. 0Y; b. 0C; c. 0F; d. 0FGY; e. 0D; f. 0DJY; g. DFGJ; h. below 0A

PROBLEMS

1. a. PC, M, MC, O;   b. M, MC, O;   c. M, O;   d. M, MC, O;   e. M, MC, O;
    f. MC, O;   g. M, O;   h. PC;   i. PC, M, MC, O;   j. PC, MC;   k. O;   l. O;
    m. M, MC, O
2. a. 6/9 (or .67)   b. 8/9 (or .89)   c. They would fall.   d. They would fall.

CASE STUDY

1. The equilibrium price and equilibrium quantity both rise.
2. The law of demand is derived holding other things constant; in the example, price would increase *and* perceived quality and/or taste changed along with price.
3. Yes.

GLOSSARY TO CHAPTER 25

Concentration ratio The percentage of all sales contributed by the leading four or leading eight firms in an industry; sometimes called the industry concentration ratio.

Cooperative game A game in which the players explicitly collude to make themselves better off. As applied to firms, it involves companies colluding in order to make higher than competitive rates of return.

Dominant strategies Strategies that always yield the highest benefit, i.e., regardless of what other players do, a dominant strategy will yield the most benefit for the player using it.

Entry-deterrence strategy Any strategy undertaken by firms in an industry, either individually or together, with the design or effect of raising the cost of entry into the industry by a new firm.

Game theory   Away of describing possible outcomes involving two or more interacting individuals.

Horizontal merger The joining of firms that are producing or selling a similar product.

Limit-pricing model A model that hypothesizes a group of colluding sellers will together set the highest common price that they believe they can charge without new firms seeking to enter that industry in search of relatively high profits.

Monopolistic competition A market situation where a large number of firms produce similar but not identical products. There is relatively easy entry into the industry.

Negative-sum game A game in which the sum of the players' gains is negative at the end of the game.

Non-cooperative game A game in which the players neither negotiate nor collude in any way. As applied to firms in an industry, the common situation in which there are relatively few firms, and when each firm has some ability to change price.

Oligopoly A market situation in which there are very few sellers. Each seller knows that the other sellers will react to its changes in prices and quantities.

Opportunistic behavior   Actions that ignore possible long-run benefits of cooperation and focus solely on short-run gains.

Payoff matrix A matrix of outcomes, or consequences, of the strategies chosen by players in a game.

Positive-sum game A game in which the sum of the players' gains is positive at the end of the game.

Price leadership A purported pricing practice in many oligopolistic industries in which the largest firm publishes its price list ahead of its competitors, who then follow those prices already announced. Also called parallel pricing.

Price war A pricing campaign designed to drive competing firms out of a market by repeatedly cutting prices.

Prisoner's dilemma The most famous of strategic games in which two prisoners have a choice between confessing and not confessing to a crime. If neither confesses, they serve a minimum sentence. If both confess, they serve a maximum sentence. If one confesses and the other doesn't, the one who confesses goes free. The dominant strategy is always to confess.

Product differentiation The distinguishing of products by brand name, color, minor attributes, and the like. Product differentiation occurs in other than perfectly competitive markets where products are, in theory, homogeneous, such as wheat or corn.

Reaction function The manner in which one oligopolist reacts to a change in price (or output or quality) of another oligopolist.

Strategic dependence A situation in which one firm's actions with respect to, for example, price changes, may be strategically countered by one or more other firms in the industry. Such dependence can only exist when there are a few major firms in an industry.

Strategy Any rule that is used to make a choice, e.g., always pick "heads". An alternative definition of strategy is any potential choice that can be made by players in a game.

Tit-for-tat strategic behavior In the theory of games, behavior that involves cooperation, usually by signaling other players of our good intentions, that continues so long as other members continue to cooperate.

Vertical merger The joining of a firm with another to which it sells an output or from which it buys an input.

Zero-sum game A game in which one player's losses are exactly offset by the other player's gains.

CHAPTER 26

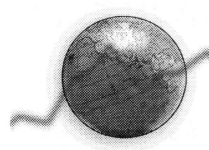

REGULATION AND ANTITRUST POLICY

PUTTING THIS CHAPTER INTO PERSPECTIVE

Chapter 26 is the last chapter in Part Seven, which deals with market structure, and it returns to analyze again the monopoly model. You should not have much trouble with this chapter because it presents relatively little new theory; much of what you have learned in previous chapters of Part Seven is discussed again in Chapter 26.

Natural monopoly describes a situation in which enormous economies of scale (relative to industry demand) lead to persisting declines in average cost and marginal cost. Therefore the firm that gets larger and larger, before other firms, will reap tremendous cost advantages and will price its output so as to drive out all competitors. Presumably, after it has attained monopoly status, it will maximize profits by charging a higher price and producing a lower output than social efficiency requires. (Interestingly enough, because of the advantages of economies of scale, it is possible that it would produce more, at a lower price, than would the perfect competition market structure.)

There are two basic approaches for coming to grips with a natural monopoly: antitrust policy and regulation. Antitrust, in essence, attempts to prevent the monopoly from arising in the first place; it makes "monopolizing" actions illegal. The regulation approach is to permit the monopoly to emerge (indeed, to *help* it to do so) and then to force it to behave in socially desirable ways.

One form of regulation forces the monopolist to price at the firm's marginal cost of output. Unfortunately (as your text points out), in such a situation marginal cost is below average cost; hence the monopolist would suffer economic losses. In order to deal with that problem, natural monopolists are regulated via rate regulation, which takes two forms. First, there is "cost of service" regulation, which requires the natural monopolist to charge according to the *average* cost of production (rather than the marginal cost, and therefore is socially inefficient). Second is the "rate of return" regulation which permits the natural monopolist to earn only a "normal" or competitive rate of return on the investment in the business.

This chapter also analyzes the behavior of regulators. The model maintains that regulators are just like the rest of us: they usually, but not always, do things that are in their own self-interest—and not society's. Two hypotheses are presented: the capture hypothesis and the share the gains/share the pains theory.

Then Chapter 26 explores the phenomenon of deregulation.

LEARNING OBJECTIVES

After you have studied this chapter you should be able to

1. define cost-of-service regulation, rate-of-return regulation, capture hypothesis, share the gains/share the pains theory, deregulation, theory of contestable markets, monopolization, market share test, and creative response.

2. indicate the problem with requiring a natural monopolist to engage in marginal cost pricing and list two ways to counter this problem.

3. distinguish between cost-of-service regulation and rate-of-return regulation, and answer questions that indicate an understanding of the difficulties involved with such regulation.

4. apply the regulator behavior model to predict the behavior of regulators.

5. recognize the essentials of the Supreme Court definition of monopolization.

6. enumerate the essential features of the major antitrust laws.

7. recognize the difficulties in applying the market share test.

8. list four exemptions to the antitrust laws.

CHAPTER OUTLINE

1. A natural monopoly arises when there are large economies of scale relative to industry demand and one firm can produce at a lower cost than can be achieved by multiple firms.

2. When long-run average costs are falling, the long-run marginal cost curve is below the long-run average cost curve; the first firm to take advantage of decreasing costs can drive out all competitors by underpricing them.
    a. If regulators force the natural monopolist to engage in marginal cost pricing, the firm will suffer economic losses and will shut down.
    b. In such a situation, regulators might subsidize the natural monopolist to engage in marginal cost pricing.

3. There are three types of government regulation: regulation of natural monopolies, regulation of inherently competitive industries, and social regulation.
    a. Economic regulation typically concerns controlling prices that regulated enterprises are allowed to charge.
        i.   Cost-of-service regulation allows regulated companies to charge in accordance with actual average costs.
        ii. Rate-of-return regulation allows regulated firms to earn a normal rate of return on their investment in the business.
    b. Regulators can control prices, but because quality is difficult to measure and control, regulated firms can change their price per constant-quality unit when forced to underprice services.
    c. Regulated firms engage in creative response, which is a response to a regulation that conforms to the letter of the law while undermining its spirit.

4. The regulator behavior model suggests that regulation benefits firms already in a regulated industry—not potential entrants or consumers.

    a.   The capture hypothesis predicts that regulators will eventually be controlled by the special interests of the industry that is being regulated.

    b.   The share the gains/share the pains theory maintains that regulators must take into account the demands of three groups: legislators, firms in the industry, and consumers of the regulated industry.

5.   By some estimates, regulation costs our nation over $600 billion per year, or about 8 percent of yearly national income.

6.   Deregulation can create costs and benefits.

    a.   In the short run firms and workers can be hurt by deregulation, but the long-run effects are largely beneficial.

    b.   The contestable market theory suggests that regulation should be concerned with ease of entry into an industry—and not with the current structure of an industry.

7.   Antitrust policy attempts to prevent the emergence of monopoly and monopolistic behavior.

    a.   In 1890 the Sherman Act was passed; it made illegal every contract and combination, in the form of a trust, that restrained trade.

    b.   In 1914 the Clayton Act was passed; it made price discrimination and interlocking directorates illegal.

    c.   The Federal Trade Commission Act of 1914 established that commission to prevent "unfair competition"; the 1938 Wheeler-Lea Act amended the 1914 act to allow the FTC to battle against false or misleading advertising.

    d.   The Robinson-Patman Act of 1936 was aimed at preventing large producers from driving out small competitors by means of selective discriminatory price cuts.

    e.   Numerous antitrust acts serve to exempt certain business (and union) practices from antitrust action.

8.   The Sherman Act does not define monopoly, but the Supreme Court has defined the term monopolization as involving

    a.   the possession of monopoly power in the relevant market, and

    b.   the willful acquisition or maintenance of the power as distinguished from growth, or development as a consequence of a superior product, business acumen, or historic accident.

9.   In practice it is difficult to measure (and define) market power.

10.   The relevant market consists of two elements: a relevant product market and a relevant geographic market.

KEY TERMS

Cost-of-service regulation   Deregulation
Rate-of-return regulation

KEY CONCEPTS

Monopolization   Market share test
Capture hypothesis   Theory of contestable markets
Share the gains/share the pains theory   Creative response

COMPLETION QUESTIONS
Fill in the blank or circle the correct term.

1. A natural monopoly arises when there are large _____ of scale relative to _____; in such a case the firm's average total costs persistently _____ and its marginal cost curve lies (below, above) its average cost curve; the first firm to expand will be able to offer a price that is _____ than those of its rivals and drive them out of business.

2. If a natural monopolist were forced to engage in marginal cost pricing for social efficiency, that firm would experience _____ economic profits; in order to counter that, regulators might _____ the natural monopolist.

3. There are three types of government regulation: regulation of _____, _____, and _____.

4. Cost of service regulation requires firms to charge customers based on actual (marginal, average) costs; rate-of-return regulation permits regulated firms to earn _____ profits. Because price is easier to measure and regulate than quality, regulated firms can (lower, raise) the price per constant-quality unit even if price is constant.

5. Regulated firms often try to avoid the effects of regulation, so they react to regulation by making a _____ response; that is they follow the letter, but not the spirit, of a regulation.

6. The regulator behavior model suggests that much regulation is for the benefit of (consumers, firms already in the industry); two such theories are _____ and _____.

7. Monopolization is the possession of monopoly power in the _____ market, and the _____ acquisition or maintenance of the power, as distinguished from growth as a consequence of a _____, _____, or _____.

8. One predictable short-run result of deregulation is _____; long-run results include _____ and _____.

9. The Sherman Act makes illegal those contracts or trusts that act to _____ trade; the provisions of this act are (vague, clear); the Clayton Act makes price _____ illegal if it substantially lessens competition.

10. The Federal Trade Commission (FTC) Act attempts to prevent_____ competition; the Wheeler-Lea Act amended the FTC Act and permits the FTC to battle against false or misleading _____. The FTC Act was formed to protect _____, while the Wheeler-Lea Act attempts to protect _____.

11. The _____ Act is aimed at preventing producers from driving out competitors by means of selected discriminatory price cuts; it is commonly referred to as the _____ act.

12. Four exemptions to antitrust laws are _____, _____, _____ and _____.

13.   The primary measure of monopoly is the _____ test, which is determined by the _____ of a market that a firm controls.

14.   The contestable markets theory suggests that regulation should be more concerned with the _____ into an industry and not the current _____ of the industry.

TRUE-FALSE QUESTIONS
Circle the **T** if the statement is true, the **F** if it is false. Explain to yourself why a statement is false.

T F   1.   Natural monopolies arise mainly due to large economies of scale.

T F   2.   If a natural monopolist is required to engage in marginal cost pricing, it will earn abnormal profits.

T F   3.   Everyone benefits from deregulation.

T F   4.   Traditionally in the United States inherently competitive industries have not been regulated.

T F   5.   Regulated firms often follow the letter of a rule, but violate its spirit.

T F   6.   Regulators can easily regulate the price per constant-quality unit of regulated firms.

T F   7.   According to the regulator behavior theory, regulators are mostly concerned with the well-being of consumers.

T F   8.   Monopolization, according to the Supreme Court, requires a willful act.

T F   9.   One predictable result of deregulation is bankruptcy for the less efficient firms.

T F   10.   The Wheeler-Lea Act attempts to protect small competitors, while the FTC Act attempts to protect consumers.

T F   11.   The Robinson-Patman Act was aimed at preventing producers from driving out smaller competitors by means of selected discriminatory price cuts.

T F   12.   Labor unions are exempted from antitrust laws, even if their actions restrain trade.

T F   13.   Monopolization requires a willful acquisition of monopoly power in the relevant market.

MULTIPLE CHOICE QUESTIONS
Circle the letter that corresponds to the best answer.

1.   A natural monopoly results because
      a.   of large economies of scale.
      b.   of persisting declining average and marginal costs.
      c.   the largest firm can underprice its competitors.
      d.   All of the above

2. If the natural monopolist were forced to price at marginal cost, it would earn
   a. abnormal profits.
   b. economic profits.
   c. economic losses.
   d. zero economic profit.

3. If an industry is deregulated,
   a. short-run costs to some existing producers can be significant.
   b. all producers would be hurt.
   c. all consumers would be helped.
   d. All of the above

4. Which of the following is **NOT** a recognized type of government regulation?
   a. regulation of natural monopolies
   b. regulation for the benefit of Congress
   c. regulation of inherently competitive industries
   d. regulation for public welfare across all industries

5. Which of the following is probably the most difficult to regulate?
   a. price
   b. output
   c. quality
   d. profit

6. Which of the following is **NOT** consistent with the regulator behavior model?
   a. Regulators are concerned with benefiting themselves.
   b. Regulators are concerned with benefiting vocal customers.
   c. Regulators are concerned with benefiting firms already in the industry.
   d. Regulators are concerned with benefiting potential entrants into an industry.

7. Which of the following is a predictable consequence of deregulation?
   a. increased bankruptcies in the short run
   b. long-run abnormal profits
   c. Long-run price is even greater than MC.
   d. short-run misallocation of resources

8. Which action is considered monopolization?
   a. willful acquisition of monopoly power
   b. producing a superior product
   c. business acumen
   d. historic accident

9. Which of the following are **NOT** exempt from antitrust laws?
   a. labor unions
   b. professional sports
   c. suppliers of military equipment
   d. all unincorporated businesses

10. The contestable market theory maintains that regulators should be primarily concerned with
    a. the degree to which entry into an industry is possible.
    b. concentration ratios.
    c. profits today.
    d. past profits.

MATCHING
Choose the item in column (2) that best matches an item in column (1).

(1)	(2)

a. contestable markets   f. willful acquisition of monopoly power
b. monopolization   g. persistent fall in long run AC
c. natural monopoly   h. behavior of regulated firms
d. creative response   i. behavior of regulators
e. capture hypothesis   j. ease of entry into industry

WORKING WITH GRAPHS

1. Suppose you are an analyst for a regulatory board that is in charge of the regulation of local monopolies. Given the information in the graph that follows, answer the list of questions submitted by your supervisor.

a. If this monopolist is not regulated, what will be the level of
output? _____
price? _____
total revenue? _____
total costs? _____
profit or loss? _____

b. If this monopolist is regulated by marginal cost pricing, what will be the level of
   output? _____
   price? _____
   total revenue? _____
   total costs? _____
   profits or loss? _____
   Will the monopoly need a subsidy? _____
   If so, how much? _____

c. If cost-of-service regulation is imposed on this monopolist, what will be the level of
   output? _____
   price? _____
   total revenue? _____
   total costs? _____
   profit or loss? _____

CASE STUDY

Brian Goff, an economist at Western Kentucky University, recently published a book (*Regulation and Macroeconomic Performance*, Kluwer Academic Press, 1996) in which he attempted to estimate the costs of regulation to the U.S. economy. He constructed what he termed an Effective Regulation Index (ERI) which is a composite of number of pages in the Federal Register (which indicates specific regulations), the number of people employed by the Environmental Protection Agency (EPA), the ratio of workers in the U.S. Agricultural Department to the number of people employed on farms, the ratio of federal civil trials to total trials, and so on. He then tracked his composite variable over time (1950 to 1990) and using statistical techniques concluded that over that period regulation reduced GDP growth by almost 1 percent per year, increased unemployment by one-half percent per year, decreased employment by 0.3 percent per year, and reduced productivity growth by over one-half percent per year. In dollar figures these effects are much higher than those indicated in the studies cited in your text.

1. If you believe that small changes in growth rates lead to enormous changes in living standards, what does this suggest about Goff's findings?

2. Many of the presidential election campaigns have focused on government spending as well as changes in our federal tax structure. Might time be spent wisely regarding how regulation affects our living standards too?

ANSWERS TO CHAPTER 26

COMPLETION QUESTIONS

1. economies; industry demand; fall; below; lower
2. negative; subsidize
3. natural monopoly; inherently competitive industries; social regulation
4. average; normal; raise
5. creative
6. firms already in the industry; capture theory; share the gains/share the pains theory
7. relevant; willful; a superior product; business acumen; historic accident
8. increased bankruptcies; prices closer to marginal cost; smaller abnormal profits
9. restrain; vague; discrimination
10. unfair; advertising; small competitors; consumers
11. Robinson-Patman; chain store
12. labor unions; public utilities; professional sports; cooperative acts among American exporters; hospitals; public transit and water systems; suppliers of military equipment; joint publishing arrangements by two or more newspapers in a single city
13. market-share; percentage
14. degree to which entry is permitted; market structure

TRUE-FALSE QUESTIONS

1. T
2. F   It will realize losses.
3. F   Some firms and workers are hurt in the short run.
4. F   Inherently competitive industries such as trucking and airlines have been regulated.
5. T
6. F   It is difficult to regulate quality.
7. F   They, like the rest of us, are assumed to be concerned with their own well-being.
8. T
9. T
10. F   Just the opposite.
11. T
12. T
13. T

MULTIPLE CHOICE QUESTIONS

1.d;   2.c;   3.a;   4.b;   5.c;   6.d;   7.a;   8.a;   9.d;   10.a.

MATCHING

a and j;   b and f;   c and g;   d and h;   e and i

WORKING WITH GRAPHS

1. a. 1700 units, $3.50, $5950, $5440 (or 1700 x $3.20), profit of $510 (**note**: dollar figures are approximations.)
   b. 3000 units, $1.50, $4500, $7500, loss of $3000, yes, $3000
   c. 2000, $3, $6000, $6000, $0

CASE STUDY

1. They would doubtless favor reductions in regulations.
2. If regulations reduce our living standards by so much, a complete cost-benefit analysis is in order.

GLOSSARY TO CHAPTER 26

Capture hypothesis   A theory of regulatory behavior that predicts that the regulators will eventually be captured by the special interests of the industry that is being regulated.

Cost-of-service regulation   A type of regulation based on allowing prices that reflect only the actual cost of production and do not include monopoly profits.

Creative response   A firm's behavioral modification that allows it to comply with the letter of the law without complying with the spirit of the law so that the law's effects are lessened significantly.

Deregulation   The elimination or phasing out of past regulations of economic activity.

Market share test   The primary measure of monopoly power. A firm's market share is the percentage of a market that a firm controls.

Monopolization   The possession of market power in the relevant market and the willful acquisition or maintenance of the power, as distinguished from growth or development as a consequence of a superior product, business acumen, or historic accident.

Rate-of-return regulation   Regulation that seeks to keep the rate of return in the industry at a competitive level by not allowing excessive prices to be charged.

Share the gains/share the pains theory   A theory of regulatory behavior in which the regulators must take account of the demands of three groups: legislators, who established and who oversee the regulatory agency; those in the regulated industry; and consumers of the regulated industry.

Theory of contestable markets   The hypothesis concerning the pricing behavior of firms in which even though there are only a few in the industry, they are forced to price their products more or less competitively because of the ease of entry by outsiders. The key aspect of a contestable market is relatively costless entry into and exit from the industry.

CHAPTER 27

LABOR DEMAND AND LABOR SUPPLY

PUTTING THIS CHAPTER INTO PERSPECTIVE

Fortunately, much of what you learned in Part Seven can be applied to Part Eight. Most fundamentally, you can apply the maximization or rational behavior model that you learned earlier. Recall that a rational person—supplier, buyer, owner, or manager of a firm—will do any activity up to the point where the marginal benefit (MB) of doing so equals the marginal cost (MC) of doing so. For this model to work, eventually marginal cost must rise relative to marginal benefit. If MB > MC, then maximizing behavior requires that the person (or firm) do more; if MC > MB, then maximizing behavior requires that less be done. If MB = MC (and MC is rising relative to MB), then the person or firm is maximizing.

The trick is to identify the MB and the MC of any activity. If you keep this in mind, and if you remember the rules in the previous paragraph, then Part Eight (and Part Seven) will be much easier for you to understand as you analyze the various market structures.

The first input market structure analyzed in Chapter 27 is perfect competition in both the product market and the labor market. The activity in question is hiring labor; as usual we assume that the firm wants to maximize profits. The firm's marginal benefit from hiring labor is the marginal physical product of labor multiplied by the price of the good sold (MRP); thus MB = MRP. The MRP falls because the marginal physical product of labor falls (due to the law of diminishing marginal returns) and price, P, is constant because the firm is a price taker. The marginal cost of hiring labor is the wage rate, which is constant because the firm is a price taker in the labor market, too. Predictably, the firm hires labor up to the point where MB = MC, as in this model where the MRP of labor equals the wage rate, respectively.

The second major model analyzed in Chapter 27 assumes perfect competition in the labor market, but imperfect competition (monopoly, actually, but the conclusions are the same for monopolistic competition and oligopoly) in the product market. Because an imperfect competitor must reduce price in order to sell more, in this model marginal benefit is more complicated. The MB for hiring labor is marginal revenue (MR) multiplied by the marginal physical product, or MRP, of labor. Recall that if demand is negatively sloped, then price, P, must exceed MR. Because we assume perfect competition in the labor market, the firm is there a price taker; hence the MC of hiring labor is again the wage rate, W. Thus the profit maximizing quantity of labor to hire occurs where MB equals MC, or in this model MRP of labor = W. Note that in this model, MR, or MRP, falls for two reasons: the marginal physical product of labor falls due to diminishing returns, and price falls because the firm is a monopolist in the product market and faces a downward-sloping demand curve.

In Chapter 27 the industry demand for labor curve is also derived; so too is an industry supply of labor curve. Wage rates are determined, of course, at the intersection of the industry demand for labor curve and the industry supply of labor curve. Theories such as the efficiency wage and insider-outsider models imply that under certain circumstances workers can earn wages somewhat above their MRP.

LEARNING OBJECTIVES

After you have studied this chapter you should be able to

1. define marginal factor cost, marginal physical product of labor, derived demand, marginal revenue product, labor market, signaling, efficiency wages, and insider-outsider theory.

2. determine the profit-maximizing quantity of labor to hire for a firm that is a perfect competitor in both the product and the labor market.

3. determine the profit-maximizing quantity of labor to hire for a firm that is a perfect competitor in the labor market and a monopolist in the product market.

4. distinguish between the MRP of labor curve for a perfect competitor and the MRP of labor curve for a monopolist.

5. determine the equilibrium wage rate, given the supply of labor and the demand for labor.

6. list four determinants of the price elasticity of demand for an input.

7. recognize how workers can actually earn wages above the equilibrium wage rate.

8. list three factors that cause the total demand curve for labor to shift.

9. list two factors that cause the total supply of labor curve to shift.

10. recognize the minimum total cost condition for producing a given rate of output.

CHAPTER OUTLINE

1. What is the profit-maximizing quantity of labor to hire for a firm that is a perfect competitor in both the labor market and the product market?
   a. The marginal physical product of labor is the change in total output accounted for by hiring one worker, holding all other factors of production constant.
   b. Because of the law of diminishing returns, the marginal physical product of labor eventually declines.
   c. Because this firm is in a competitive labor market, it is a price taker; it can hire as much labor as it wants to hire at the going wage rate.
   d. The marginal benefit from hiring one more unit of labor is that laborer's marginal physical product multiplied by the firm's constant product selling price, or the marginal revenue product (MRP).
   e. The profit maximizing rule for hiring is to hire laborers up to the point where the wage rate equals the MRP of labor.

2. The demand for labor is a derived demand; laborers (or other inputs) are desired only because they can be used to produce products that are expected to be sold at a profit.

3. The market demand for labor curve is negatively sloped.

4. There are four principal determinants of the price elasticity of demand for an input. The price elasticity of demand for a variable input will be greater
    a. the greater the price elasticity of demand for the final product.
    b. the easier it is to substitute for that variable input.
    c. the larger the proportion of total costs accounted for by a particular variable input.
    d. the longer the time period being considered.

5. The industry supply of labor curve is upward sloping from left to right.
    a. As wage rates rise in an industry, more laborers are willing to accept jobs there.
    b. Nevertheless, the individual firm faces a horizontal supply curve at the going wage rate.

6. The equilibrium market wage rate is determined where the industry demand for labor curve intersects the industry supply of labor curve.

7. There are two alternative theories of wage determination.
    a. Some workers may earn efficiency wages (above equilibrium) due to
        i.   firms trying to reduce turnover costs.
        ii. firms attempting to attract higher quality workers.
        iii. firms encouraging existing workers to work harder in order to keep relatively high-paying jobs.
    b. The insider-outsider theory predicts that wages may remain above equilibrium for insiders even though outsiders may be willing to work for lower wages because the firm would have to incur costs by replacing insiders with outsiders.

8. When nonwage determinants of the supply of and the demand for labor change, those curves shift.
    a. The labor demand curve shifts if there is a change in (1) the demand for the final product, (2) labor productivity, or (3) the price of related factors of production.
    b. The labor supply curve shifts if there is a change in the (1) alternative wage rate offered in other industries, or (2) nonmonetary aspects of the occupation under study.

9. What is the profit-maximizing quantity of labor to hire for a firm that is a perfect competitor in the labor market but a monopolist in the product market?
    a. Such a firm's demand for labor (or any other input) is negatively sloped because (1) the marginal physical product falls and (2) the price (and, therefore, MR) falls as output increases.
    b. Such a firm's MB curve, or demand curve, is its MRP curve, which equals labor's marginal physical product multiplied by the firm's MR; thus MRP = MR x MPP.
    c. Given the going market wage rate, this firm hires up to the point where MRP equals the wage rate.
    d. The monopolist hires fewer workers than a perfectly competitive producer would, other things being constant.

10. How much of *each* variable factor should the firm use when combining those factors to produce a given output?
    a. The firm will hire all variable inputs up to the point where each input's MRP equals its price.
    b. In order to minimize the total cost of producing a given output, the firm should equate the ratios of each factor's marginal physical product to its respective price; this condition is referred to as the *least-cost combination of resources*.

KEY TERMS

Marginal physical product (MPP) of Labor   Marginal revenue product (MRP)
Marginal factor cost (MFC)

KEY CONCEPTS

Derived demand   Insider-outsider theory
Efficiency wages   Labor market signaling

COMPLETION QUESTIONS
Fill in the blank or circle the correct term.

1. To a firm that is a perfect competitor in both the labor and the product market, the marginal benefit from hiring labor equals labor's _____ times _____, or MRP.

2. A competitive firm's MRP curve is negatively sloped because labor's _____ falls, due to the law of _____.

3. To such a competitive firm, the marginal cost of hiring labor is the _____, which (falls, rises, remains constant) as the firm hires more laborers; in the labor market, such a firm is a price (taker, maker).

4. The competitive firm hires labor up to the point where _____ equals _____; at that point it is maximizing _____.

5. The demand for labor is a _____ demand; therefore if the product's selling price increases, the competitive firm's demand for labor curve will shift to the _____; the market demand curve for labor will be _____ sloped.

6. Determinants of the price elasticity of demand for an input include _____, _____, _____, and _____.

7. The supply of labor to a competitive firm is _____ elastic, therefore its labor supply curve is (vertical, horizontal); the supply of labor curve for the industry, however, is _____ sloped.

8. Workers may earn wages above equilibrium, or _____ wages, because firms _____, _____, or _____.

9. The industry demand for labor curve shifts if there is a change in the _____, _____, or _____; the industry supply curve shifts if there is a change in _____ or _____.

10. Assume a firm is a perfect competitor in the labor market but a monopolist in the product market. Its marginal benefit from hiring labor equals _____ times _____, or MRP of labor. This firm's MRP curve is negatively sloped because _____ falls due to the law of _____ and because _____ falls due to the fact that this firm must reduce its _____ as it produces more. This firm will hire labor up to the point where _____ equals _____.

11. If a competitive firm hires more than one variable input, its equilibrium condition is that _____; stated alternatively, it can minimize the total cost of producing a given output by equating _____.

12. The insider-outsider theory maintains that insiders will earn (less, more) than equilibrium wages because firms incur costs such as _____, and _____ if they replace insiders with outsiders.

TRUE-FALSE QUESTIONS
Circle the **T** if the statement is true, the **F** if it is false. Explain to yourself why a statement is false.

T F 1. A firm that is a competitor in all markets will discover that its demand for labor curve is horizontal at the going wage rate.

T F 2. A competitive firm will hire labor up to the point where MRP equals the going wage rate.

T F 3. The marginal physical product of labor declines due to diseconomies of scale.

T F 4. Because the demand for labor is a derived demand, it shifts when wage rates change.

T F 5. The price elasticity of demand for labor will be higher the lower is the price elasticity of demand for the final good.

T F 6. A competitive firm's supply of labor curve is perfectly elastic, but the entire industry supply of labor curve is upward sloping.

T F 7. Existing workers can earn efficiency wages because employers are generous.

T F 8. If labor productivity rises, the demand for labor increases.

T F 9. A firm that is a competitor in the labor market but a monopolist in the product market hires labor up to the point where the MRP of labor equals the going wage rate.

T F 10. If a firm suddenly monopolizes a perfectly competitive industry, more workers will be hired.

T F 11. If a competitive firm hires two factors of production it will hire up to the point where the MRP of one factor divided by that factor's price equals the MRP of the other factor divided by that factor's price.

T F 12. Outsiders cause wage rates to be lower than equilibrium for insiders.

MULTIPLE CHOICE QUESTIONS
Circle the letter that corresponds to the best answer.

1. Which of the following is **NOT** true about a firm that is a perfect competitor in all markets?
   a. Its supply of labor curve is perfectly elastic.
   b. Its demand for labor curve is downward sloping.
   c. Its price falls as it produces more output.
   d. Its marginal physical product of labor falls as it hires more labor.

2.   For a firm that is a perfect competitor in all markets, the profit-maximizing quantity of labor to hire occurs where
     a.   a falling MRP equals a rising wage rate.
     b.   a rising MRP equals a rising wage rate.
     c.   a falling MRP equals a falling wage rate.
     d.   a falling MRP equals a constant wage rate.

3.   A firm that is a perfect competitor in all markets finds that its MRP for labor falls because as it hires more labor
     a.   the marginal physical product of labor falls.
     b.   the price of output falls as output increases.
     c.   Both of the above
     d.   None of the above

4.   The marginal factor cost of labor
     a.   equals the going wage rate to a competitive firm.
     b.   equals the change in wage rates divided by the change in labor.
     c.   rises for the competitive firm.
     d.   equals the change in total cost divided by the change in wage rates.

5.   The demand for labor
     a.   is a derived demand.
     b.   shifts as selling price of the good produced changes.
     c.   shifts to the right if labor productivity increases.
     d.   All of the above

6.   Which of the following will **NOT** lead to a relatively high price elasticity of demand for labor?
     a.   high price elasticity of demand for the final product
     b.   no good substitutes for the labor skill in question
     c.   high ratio of labor to total costs
     d.   a very long period of time after the wage change

7.   The supply of labor
     a.   to a perfect competitor is positively sloped.
     b.   for the entire industry is perfectly elastic.
     c.   is positively sloped for the industry.
     d.   depends on labor's marginal physical product.

8.   Efficiency wages
     a.   are greater than MRP.
     b.   are profitable for employers.
     c.   reduce turnover costs, attract higher quality workers, and encourage workers to be more productive.
     d.   all of the above

9.   The insider-outsider theory maintains that
     a.   outsider competition reduces insider wages.
     b.   insiders set up entry barriers to outsiders.
     c.   insiders earn wage rates below equilibrium.
     d.   employers are altruistic.

10. Which of the following will **NOT** lead to an increase in the demand for labor?
    a. price of labor falls
    b. increase in the productivity of labor
    c. increase in the price of a labor substitute input
    d. increase in the demand for the final product

11. If firm B is a competitor in the labor market and a monopolist in the product market, then
    a. its demand for labor is negatively sloped.
    b. its supply of labor is positively sloped.
    c. its selling price is a constant.
    d. its wage rates rise as it hires more labor.

12. If firm B is a competitor in the labor market and a monopolist in the product market, then
    a. its supply of labor curve is perfectly elastic at the going wage rate.
    b. it hires labor up to the point where MRP of labor equals the going wage rate.
    c. its MRP curve falls because the marginal product of labor falls and its selling price falls.
    d. All of the above

13. The monopolist in the product market finds that its MRP for labor falls as it hires labor because
    a. the MPP of labor falls and output price is constant.
    b. the MPP of labor falls and output price falls.
    c. the MPP of labor is constant and output price falls.
    d. the MPP of labor rises but output price falls faster.

14. If a perfectly competitive market is suddenly monopolized, the amount of labor hired will
    a. remain constant.
    b. fall.
    c. rise.
    d. fall in the short run, rise in the long run.

15. If a firm hires two variable inputs, A and B, it is minimizing costs when
    a. MPP of A/price of A = MPP of B/price of B.
    b. MPP of A/price of B = MPP of B/price of A.
    c. MRP of A/MPP of B = MRP of B/MPP of A.
    d. MRP of A/price of B = MRP of B/price of A.

MATCHING
Choose the item in column (2) that best matches an item in column (1).

(1)	(2)
a. MPP	g. insider-outsider theory
b. MPP x MR	h. MRP of competitive firm
c. MPP x price	i. MRP of monopolistic firm
d. least cost combination	j. labor demand curve
e. derived demand	k. change in output for a unit input change
f. wage rate above MRP	l. equate MPP/price of all factor inputs

WORKING WITH GRAPHS

1. Analyze the graphs below, then answer the questions that follow. Assume that the minimum wage rate is $4.50 per hour.

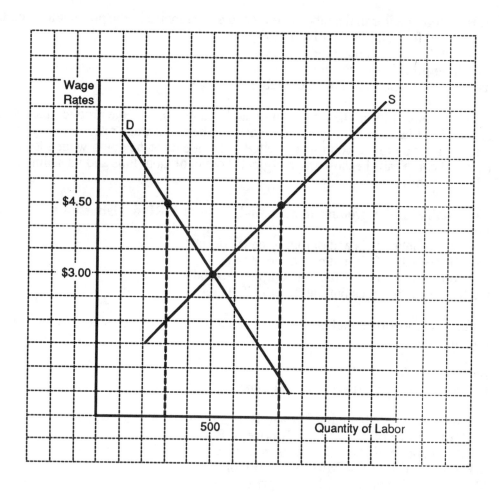

a. What is the equilibrium wage rate in this market?

b. What is the quantity supplied of labor at the minimum wage rate?

c. What is the quantity demanded for labor at the minimum wage rate?

d. What market situation exists at the minimum wage rate?

e. How many workers were laid-off, due to the minimum wage rate?

f. How many workers entered the labor force, seeking a job, due to the minimum wage rate?

g. Are workers in this industry better off or worse off as a result of this minimum wage?

h. Which workers are more likely to be laid off?

PROBLEMS

1. In the following table you are given information about a firm operating in a competitive market. Consider all factors of production fixed at the moment, with the exception of labor services. The other factors of production cost the firm $50 per day, which may be thought of as a fixed cost. Assume the firm is a profit maximizer.

Labor input (workers per day)	Total physical product (units per day)	Marginal physical product (units per day)	Marginal revenue product ($ per worker)
0	0		
1	22	_____	_____
2	40	_____	_____
3	56	_____	_____
4	70	_____	_____
5	82	_____	_____
6	92	_____	_____
7	100	_____	_____
8	106	_____	_____

a. Assume that the firm sells its output at $3 per unit. Complete the last two columns in the table above.

b. If the going market wage is $36 per day, the firm will hire _____ workers per day and produce _____ units of output.

c. Given your answer to part b, the firm will have total revenues of _____ per day and total costs of _____ per day.

d. The above will result in a (profit, loss) of _____ per day.

2. Suppose you work for a firm that sells its output in a monopoly market. Answer the following questions.

a. If you hire an additional worker, output goes up by 50 units to 125 units per day. If you wish to sell the additional 50 units, you must lower your price from $3 per unit to $2 per unit. What is the maximum wage you would be willing to pay the additional worker?

b. Assume you hired the worker from part a and output now stands at 125 units per day. If another worker is hired, output rises to 165 units per day. Given the demand curve for your product, you know that in order to sell the additional output, price will have to be dropped from $2 per unit to $1 per unit. What is the maximum wage you would be willing to pay this additional worker?

CASE STUDY

Many news stories indicate that since the 1970s real (inflation-adjusted) wages in the United States have either remained constant, or have even fallen somewhat. Economist Richard McKenzie, however, says that stagnating or declining wages for U.S. workers is a myth. McKenzie has pointed out that the relevant measure of a person's living standard is *real total compensation*—which includes the real value of fringe benefits plus real wages. Additionally, says McKenzie, the consumer price index (CPI) weighting system was changed in 1983, so that the CPI series before that date is not consistent with the series after that date.

Thus, McKenzie points out that if we use a consistent CPI series to measure real total compensation since 1970 we show a significant rise.

1. Why has the ratio of fringe benefits to total compensation increased over time? (HINT: consider taxes)

2. What are the implications of McKenzie's results?

ANSWERS TO CHAPTER 27

COMPLETION QUESTIONS

1. marginal physical product; price
2. marginal physical product; diminishing returns
3. wage rate; remains constant; taker
4. MRP of labor; wage rate; total profits
5. derived; right; negatively
6. price elasticity of demand for final good; ease with which other inputs can substitute for this input; price elasticity of supply of other inputs; proportion of total costs accounted for by the input in question; length of time period being considered
7. perfectly; horizontal; positively
8. efficiency; try to reduce turnover costs; attempt to attract higher quality labor; and encourage existing workers to work harder in order to keep their jobs.

9. demand for final good; labor productivity; price of related factors; wage rate in other industries; nonmoney job aspects
10. marginal physical product of labor; MR; marginal physical product; diminishing returns; MR; price; MRP; the wage rate
11. the ratio of MRP to price of factor is equated for all factors; the ratio of marginal physical product to factor price for all factors.
12. more; termination wages; litigation expenses.

TRUE-FALSE QUESTIONS

1. F It's demand for labor curve is negatively sloped.
2. T
3. F It declines due to the law of diminishing returns.
4. F If wage rates change, we move along a given labor demand curve.
5. F It will be lower.
6. T
7. F Employers may find it profitable to offer efficiency wages because they could reduce turnover costs, among other things.
8. T
9. T
10. F Fewer workers will be hired, because output falls.
11. T
12. F Insiders can reduce outsider competition by increasing entry barriers.

MULTIPLE CHOICE QUESTIONS

1.c;   2.d;   3.a;   4.a;   5.d;   6.b;   7.c;   8.d;   9.b;   10.a;
11.a;   12.d;   13.b;   14.b;   15.a.

MATCHING

a and k;   b and i;   c and h;   d and l;   e and j;   f and g.

WORKING WITH GRAPHS

1. a. $3.00
   b. 800
   c. 300

    d. surplus, or excess quantity supplied of labor
    e. 200
    f. 300
    g. Those who kept their jobs are better off; those who became unemployed are worse off. Group income fell from $1500 to $1350 because demand was (here) price elastic.
    h. younger, lower income—lower productivity workers.

PROBLEMS

1.   a. MPP: 22, 18, 16, 14, 12, 10, 8, 6
      MRP: 66, 54, 48, 42, 36, 30, 24, 18
    b. 5, 82
    c. $246, (5 x $36) + $50 = $230
    d. profit, $16

2.   a. $25 per day since MRP = $25
    b. A negative wage, because the price decrease necessary to sell the additional output causes total revenues to decline (MR < 0), MRP for this worker is negative, and the firm must be paid to hire another unit of labor.

CASE STUDY

1. Most fringe benefits are not taxable income, therefore they are popular with workers.
2. Things are much better for U.S. workers than many believe; also, one should be careful when interpreting data.

GLOSSARY TO CHAPTER 27

Derived demand Input factor demand derived from demand for the final product being produced.

Efficiency wages Wages that are above competitive wages that increase labor productivity and profits by enhancing the efficiency of the firm because of (1) lower turnover rates, (2) ease of attracting higher quality workers, and (3) better work efforts by existing workers.

Insider-outsider theory A theory of labor markets in which workers who are already employed have an influence on wage bargaining in such a way that outsiders who are willing to work for lower real wages cannot get a job.

Labor market signaling The process by which potential worker's acquisition of credentials, such as B.A. or an M.S., is utilized by the employer to predicate future productivity.

Marginal factor cost (MFC) The cost of using an additional unit of an input. For example, if a firm can hire all the workers it wants at the going wage rate, the marginal factor cost of labor is the wage rate.

Marginal physical product (MPP) of labor The change in output resulting from the addition of one more worker. The MPP of the worker equals the change in total output accounted for by hiring the worker, holding all other factors of production constant.

Marginal Revenue Product (MRP) The marginal physical product (MPP) times marginal revenue. The MRP gives the additional revenue obtained from a one-unit change in labor input.

UNIONS AND LABOR MARKET MONOPOLY POWER

PUTTING THIS CHAPTER INTO PERSPECTIVE

Chapter 28 is the second chapter devoted to an analysis of the labor market; the next chapter is devoted to the other factors of production. It is important for you to keep a proper perspective about the labor market. Even though this chapter considers noncompetitive labor markets—monopoly supply and monopoly demand—the U.S. labor market is inherently very competitive. There are millions of employers and almost a hundred and forty million people in the labor force. It is not likely that monopoly demand or monopoly supply could arise under such conditions. To be sure, in our past there have been "company towns," but by and large they are the exceptions; and it is true that some major employers have dominated at the local level. Still, our laborers traditionally have had both the freedom and the willingness to relocate; labor mobility, then, has certainly limited the economic power that any particular employer could exert on workers.

What does a competitive market imply? Because employers compete for workers, wage rates will be driven up to labor's true MRP. Similarly, because workers compete for jobs, wage rates will be driven down toward labor's true MRP. In short, competitive supply and demand set wage rates at market-clearing values and workers get paid (approximately) their MRP.

One major source of monopolistic power in the labor market is the government. Because employers know that their competition for labor will drive wage rates up toward labor's MRP, they have exerted time and effort to obtain special privilege from the government—usually in the form of exemption from antitrust action. Examples can be taken from professional sports. Also, witness the intercollegiate athletics monopsony considered in this chapter.

Monopoly power on the seller side of the labor market also is derived from government sources. As mentioned in Chapter 27, unions are exempted from antitrust action even though they act in restraint of trade. Similarly, the American Medical Association and scores of other professional associations attempt to restrict the supply of labor into specific occupations through licensing; note how government sanction is necessary for such monopsonistic power to arise. Laborers know only too well that if they compete, their wage rates will be driven down to competitive levels.

Consider first a firm that is a perfect competitor in the product market, but a monopsonist in the labor market. Such a firm faces a downward sloping demand for labor curve; its MB for hiring labor is labor's MRP, which falls due to a declining marginal physical product of labor. That firm faces an upward sloping supply of labor curve, however, because it is the only buyer of labor. In order to obtain another worker it must pay a higher wage rate—to the new worker and to all the previously employed workers. Hence that firm's MC of hiring labor is the marginal factor cost (MFC) of labor, which exceeds the wage rate and rises as the firm hires more labor. The profit-maximizing quantity of labor to hire occurs where the decreasing MRP of labor curve intersects the rising marginal factor cost curve. That firm then sets the wage rate at a level consistent with obtaining that quantity of labor—as given by the industry supply of labor curve.

In the second model, consider a labor-hiring firm that is a monopolist in the product market and a monopsonist in the labor market. Its MB curve is labor's MRP curve, which falls due to decreasing marginal product of labor *and* a falling output price. Its MC curve is its MFC curve, which rises because it must pay higher wages (to new and old workers) as it hires more labor. The profit maximizing quantity of labor to hire occurs where the rising MFC of labor equals the declining MRP of labor; that is, at the point where the MC = MB of hiring labor, the firm maximizes total profits. You will do well to study Figure 28-7.

Also theoretically noteworthy in this chapter is the treatment of unions as a monopolistic seller of labor. The issue becomes: what do unions maximize? It is not clear what unions maximize; once this is decided, then it becomes easier to predict their behavior. You should be aware that unions can set wage rates, or they can choose the quantity of labor employed; they cannot do both. In general, unions redistribute income to high-seniority workers (who keep their jobs when unions set wage rates above equilibrium) from low-seniority workers (who lose their jobs when unions so behave). Because low seniority job losers find work elsewhere—thereby increasing the supply of labor in other areas—unions don't raise *overall* wage rates. Union action causes wage rates to rise in some areas and to fall in other areas.

LEARNING OBJECTIVES

After you have studied this chapter you should be able to

1. define labor unions, craft unions, collective bargaining, industrial unions, right-to-work laws, closed shop, union shop, jurisdictional dispute, sympathy strike, secondary boycott, featherbedding, monopsonist, monopsonistic exploitation, strikebreakers, and bilateral monopoly.

2. identify the key provisions of major legislation dealing with unions.

3. distinguish between craft unions and industrial unions.

4. list three possible union goals and predict the quantity of labor that will be employed under each union strategy.

5. show how unions can redistribute income from low seniority to high seniority workers.

6. predict the quantity of labor hired and the wage rate that will result, given a market structure in which a firm is a perfect competitor in the product market and a monopsonist in the labor market.

7. predict the quantity of labor hired and the wage rate that will result, given a firm that is a monopolist in the product market and a monopsonist in the labor market.

8. list reasons why the NCAA qualifies as a cartel with monopsony power.

CHAPTER OUTLINE

1. Unions are workers' organizations that usually seek to secure economic improvements for their members.
   a. The American labor movement started with *craft unions*, which are composed of workers who engage in a particular skill or trade.

b. The American Federation of Labor (AFL), a craft union, was formed by Samuel Gompers in 1886; its membership growth flourished until World War I, when government withdrew its support.

c. The Great Depression brought the National Recovery Act in 1933, which attempted to raise wages to predepression levels; its key provision was to guarantee the right of labor to bargain collectively.

d. The Wagner Act, labor's "Magna Carta," also guaranteed *collective bargaining*; it guaranteed workers the right to form unions.

e. In 1938 John L. Lewis formed the Congress of Industrial Organizations (CIO), which was composed of *industrial unions*, that is, unions with membership from an entire industry.

f. The Taft-Hartley Act was enacted to stem union power; it allows individual states to pass *right-to-work* laws, which make illegal the requirement of union membership for continued employment. It also bans the closed shop everywhere and the union shop in states with right-to-work laws, and makes illegal jurisdictional disputes, sympathy strikes, and secondary boycotts.

g. The percentage of the labor force that is unionized has fallen because of the following: higher percentages of women are in the labor force, persistent illegal immigration, and the number of white collar workers in the service sector has increased relative to the number of blue collar manufacturing workers.

2. Unions can be analyzed as setters of minimum wages; the strike is the ultimate bargaining tool for unions.

3. It is not clear what unions wish to maximize. Unions can either set wage rates or select the quantity of its membership that will be employed; they can't do both.

a. To the extent that unions set wage rates above equilibrium, they create a surplus of labor, or a shortage of jobs that they ration.

b. If unions wish to employ all members, they must accept a relatively low wage rate.

c. If unions wish to maximize total wages, they set wage rates where the price elasticity of demand equals 1; some members will be unemployed.

d. If unions maximize wage rates for a given number of workers—presumably high-seniority workers—low-seniority workers will become unemployed because wage rates probably will be set above equilibrium.

e. One union strategy is to limit total union membership to the original quantity; over time, if demand increases, wage rates will rise.

f. Unions can raise wage rates for members by (a) limiting membership, and (b) increasing the demand for union labor by increasing labor productivity and increasing the demand for union labor relative to nonunion labor.

4. It is not apparent that unions have raised *overall* wage rates; on average, unions redistribute income within unions from low- to high-seniority workers.

5. Recent studies indicate that unions can both (a) act as monopolies that redistribute income from low-seniority to high-seniority members and (b) increase labor productivity.

6. Consider a firm that is a perfect competitor in the product market and a *monopsonist* in the labor market.

a. That firm faces an upward sloping supply of labor curve; before it can hire more labor it must raise wage rates for *all* of its employees.

b. As a consequence, the marginal factor cost of hiring labor to that firm exceeds the wage rate; the MFC curve is that firm's MC to hiring labor, and it rises as the firm hires more labor.

c. The marginal benefit to hiring labor to such a firm is its MRP curve, which falls (due to declining marginal product of labor) as it hires more labor.

d. The profit-maximizing employment level occurs where the decreasing MRP curve intersects the rising MFC curve; the wage rate is set on the supply curve, consistent with that quantity of labor.

e. In such a situation monopsonistic exploitation of labor results, because the wage rate is below the MRP of labor.

7. A summary of monopoly, monopsony, and perfectly competitive situations is presented in Figure 28-7.

8. The NCAA qualifies as a cartel and therefore behaves in an economically predictable way; it sets "wage rates" to college athletes below the value of their marginal product.

9. In spite of declining union membership, there have occasionally been highly publicized union victories. One of those was the strike by the Teamsters against UPS in 1997. Ultimately, though, the Teamsters won very little from that strike.

KEY TERMS

Craft unions   Jurisdictional dispute   Strikebreakers
Collective bargaining   Monopsonist   Industrial unions
Right-to-work laws   Labor unions

KEY CONCEPTS

Featherbedding   Union shop   Bilateral monopoly
Closed shop   Sympathy strike   Secondary boycott
Monopsonistic exploitation   Marginal factor cost (MFC)

COMPLETION QUESTIONS
Fill in the blank or circle the correct term.

1. The American labor movement started with local _____ unions, which are comprised of workers in a particular _____; the other major type of union is the _____union, which consists of workers from a particular _____.

2. The Great Depression generated legislation that (helped, hurt) the union movement.

3. The Taft-Hartley Act of 1947 (is, is not) considered pro-labor union; it allows states to pass _____ laws. The act makes illegal the following union practices: _____, _____, a _____ strike, and a _____ boycott.

4. The original craft unions were the _____.

5. The ultimate bargaining tool for the union is the _____.

6. If a union sets wage rates above market-clearing levels, it creates a _____ of labor; viewed alternatively, it creates a _____ of jobs, which it must then ration to workers.

7. If a union chooses to employ all of its members, it (must, need not) accept a relatively lower wage rate; if the union wants to maximize the value of total wages, it sets wage rates where the price elasticity of demand for labor equals the number _____; if the union wants to set relatively high wages for its high-seniority members, its _____ members will be laid off.

8. Assume that a firm is a perfect competitor in the product market and a monopsonist in the labor market. The marginal benefit to hiring labor for such a firm is its _____ curve, which is (horizontal, negatively sloped, positively sloped), due to the law of _____; the marginal cost to hiring labor for such a firm is its _____ curve, which is (horizontal, positively sloped, negatively sloped). The firm's MFC curve rises because as it hires more labor, wage rates (fall, rise, remain constant) because the industry supply of labor curve is _____ sloping; the firm's MFC is (equal to, greater than, less than) the wage rate.

9. Assume a firm is a monopolist in the product market and a monopsonist in the labor market. The marginal benefit to hiring labor for that firm is its _____ curve, which falls due to _____ and _____ as output increases. The marginal cost to hiring labor is that firm's _____ curve, which rises because in order to hire more labor, that firm must _____ wage rates of _____ employees; this is because the firm's supply of labor curve is _____ sloping.

10. A firm maximizes total profits by hiring labor up to the point where the (MB > MC, MB < MC, MB = MC) of doing so. Suppose Firm A is a perfect competitor in the product market and a monopsonist in the labor market. Firm A will hire labor up to the point where a downward sloping _____ curve intersects an upward sloping _____ curve; given that quantity of labor, the wage rate will be set at that level consistent with the (supply, demand) curve of labor.

11. Firm B is a monopolist in the product market and a monopsonist in the labor market. If it wants to maximize total profits, it will hire labor up to the point where a downward sloping _____ curve intersects an upward sloping _____ curve.

12. The NCAA qualifies as a cartel because it_____, _____, _____, and _____.

13. When a resource is paid less than its _____, monopsonistic exploitation exists.

TRUE-FALSE QUESTIONS
Circle the T if the statement is true, the F if it is false. Explain to yourself why a statement is false.

T F   1. The growth rate of unions and the extent to which unions are effective has depended on government support.

T F   2. The Wagner Act increases union power, but the Taft-Hartley Act reduces it.

T F   3. Union power was decreased during the Great Depression.

T F   4. In recent years, public employee union membership has increased significantly.

T F   5. Unions tend to create a shortage of labor and a surplus of jobs.

T   F   6.   In the United States, unions can set wage rates or determine the quantity of labor hired, but they can't do both.

T   F   7.   If a union wants to maximize the value of total wages, it sets wage rates as high as it possibly can.

T   F   8.   If a union can restrict the total quantity of laborers to a fixed number, its members must earn higher wages in the future.

T   F   9.   Recent studies indicate that unions do not increase labor's productivity.

T   F   10.   A profit-maximizing firm that is a perfect competitor in the product market but a monopsonist in the labor market will hire labor up to the point where MRP of labor equals the going wage rate.

T   F   11.   A firm that is a monopolist in the product market and a monopsonist in the labor market maximizes total profit by hiring labor up to the point where the MRP of labor equals the MFC of labor.

T   F   12.   The NCAA qualifies as a cartel with monopsony power.

T   F   13.   Monopsonistic exploitation exists when workers receive a wage below their MRP.

MULTIPLE CHOICE QUESTIONS
Circle the letter that corresponds to the best answer.

1.   Which of the following is **NOT** associated with a craft union?
   a.   United Auto Workers
   b.   AFL
   c.   Knights of Labor
   d.   Pipefitters Union

2.   Which of the following acts is **NOT** pro labor union?
   a.   National Industrial Recovery Act
   b.   Wagner Act
   c.   Taft-Hartley Act
   d.   National Labor Relations Act

3.   Which of the following is legal in **NON** right-to-work states?
   a.   closed shop
   b.   union shop
   c.   sympathy strike
   d.   secondary boycott

4.   Which of the following is true about the union movement?
   a.   The growth and effectiveness of unions depends in part on the extent of government help.
   b.   Since 1968 private-employee union membership has risen.
   c.   Since 1968 public-employee union membership has fallen dramatically.
   d.   All of the above

5. Unions tend to
    a. set minimum wages for members above the market clearing level.
    b. create unemployment for low-seniority members.
    c. create surpluses of labor and shortages of union jobs.
    d. All of the above

6. If a union sets wage rates above market clearing levels, then
    a. jobs must be rationed among union members.
    b. a surplus of jobs is created.
    c. a shortage of labor is created.
    d. high-seniority members will complain.

7. Which of the following is inconsistent with the others?
    a. surplus of labor
    b. shortage of jobs
    c. wage rate above market-clearing level
    d. wage rate below market-clearing level

8. If unions want to maximize the value of total wages, they set wage rates
    a. as high as they can.
    b. as low as they can.
    c. where the price elasticity of demand for labor equals 1.
    d. in the inelastic range of the product demand curve.

9. If unions maximize the wage rate of high-seniority workers, then
    a. low-seniority workers will become laid off.
    b. all union members will remain employed.
    c. they violate the Wagner Act.
    d. they violate the Taft-Hartley Act.

10. Which of the following statements probably best describes the impact of unions on wage rates?
    a. Unions have increased all wage rates in the economy.
    b. Unions have increased all union worker wage rates.
    c. Unions increase the wage rates of some workers at the expense of other workers.
    d. Unions cannot raise wage rates for their members.

11. Unions
    a. can set wage rates, but not employment levels.
    b. can set wage rates and employment levels.
    c. can set neither wage rates nor employment levels.
    d. can set either wage rates or employment levels, but not both.

12. Unions, according to the Freeman-Medoff analysis,
    a. on net, probably raise social efficiency.
    b. reduce wage inequality.
    c. create workplace practices valuable to workers and costless to management.
    d. All of the above

13. If Firm B is a monopsonist in the labor market and a perfect competitor in the product market, then
    a. it faces a horizontal supply of labor curve.
    b. it faces a horizontal demand for labor curve.
    c. its wage rate equals its MFC.
    d. its MB to hiring labor equals the MRP of labor.

14. Firm B, in the previous question (No. 13), can maximize total profits by hiring labor up to the point where
    a. a decreasing MRP of labor curve intersects a decreasing MFC of labor curve.
    b. a decreasing MRP of labor curve intersects a rising MFC of labor curve.
    c. a decreasing MRP of labor curve intersects a horizontal supply of labor curve, at the going wage rate.
    d. a horizontal MRP of labor curve is intersected by a rising MFC of labor curve.

15. Firm B, in questions 13 and 14, faces a(n)
    a. rising MFC of labor.
    b. declining labor MRP
    c. upward sloping supply of labor curve.
    d. All of the above

16. If Firm A is a monopolist in the product market and a monopsonist in the labor market, then
    a. it faces a horizontal labor supply and a horizontal labor demand curve.
    b. it faces a downward sloping supply of labor curve.
    c. its MB of hiring labor falls and its marginal cost to hiring labor rises.
    d. its MB to hiring labor is constant and its marginal cost to hiring labor rises.

17. Firm A, in the previous question (No. 16), can maximize total profits by hiring labor up to the point where
    a. a downward sloping MRP of labor curve intersects an upward sloping MFC of labor curve.
    b. an upward sloping MRP of labor equals a constant wage rate.
    c. a constant MRP of labor curve equals a falling MFC of labor.
    d. a horizontal MRP of labor curve is intersected by a rising supply of labor curve.

18. Firm A in question 16
    a. observes a MFC that exceeds the wage rate.
    b. observes a selling price that exceeds the marginal revenue of an extra unit of output.
    c. maximizes profits by hiring where MRP of labor = MFC of labor.
    d. All of the above

19. The NCAA
    a. cannot regulate the number of athletes a university can "hire."
    b. cannot enforce its regulations and rules.
    c. sets the prices, wages, and conditions under which universities can "hire" student athletes.
    d. sets the "wage rates" for student athletes at levels above their market value.

20. Which of the following is probably an example of monopsony exploitation, as defined in this text?
    a. A low-skilled laborer is paid $1 per hour in a competitive labor market.
    b. A professional athlete gets paid $1 million per year but his MRP is $1.5 million per year.
    c. Mr. Smith can earn $35,000 per year as a plumber but chooses to work as a high school teacher for $20,000 per year.
    d. Mrs. Calvo has a Ph.D. in English, but only earns $10,000 per semester teaching university English because there are so many qualified teachers in that area.

21. Monopsonistic exploitation equals
    a. marginal physical product of labor minus the wage rate.
    b. marginal revenue product of labor minus the wage rate.
    c. marginal physical product of labor minus marginal revenue product of labor.
    d. marginal factor cost of labor minus marginal physical product.

WORKING WITH GRAPHS

1. Suppose you are given the following graphical representation for a monopsonist selling its output in a competitive market. Answer the following questions.

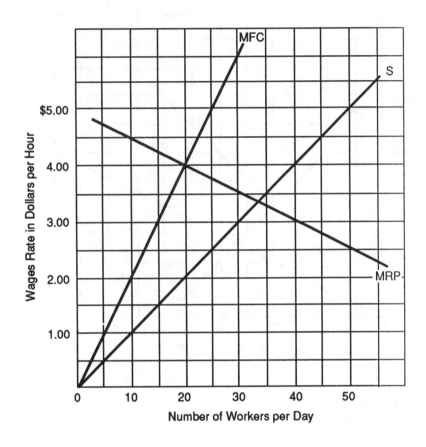

a. Given the market conditions that exist in the above graph, the monopsonist will hire _____ workers per day at a wage of _____ per hour.

b. Suppose that the government (or a labor union) initiates a minimum wage of $2.50 per hour in this particular market. As a result, the monopsonist will (increase, decrease) its employment rate to _____ workers per day at a wage of _____ per hour.

2.   Use the graph below to answer the following questions. Note: define monopolistic exploitation as being equal to the difference between VMP (or price times the marginal product of labor) and MRP—as defined in the text. (Note: VMP is not defined in your text, therefore this is a difficult question. It is purely optional.)

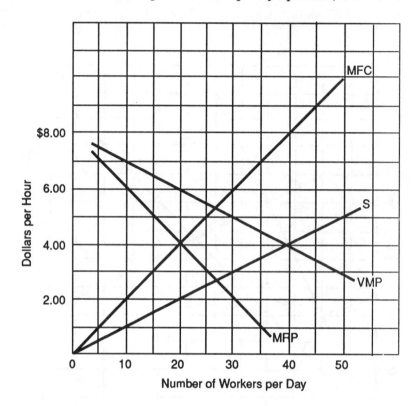

a. This monopolist-monopsonist will hire _____ workers per day and pay a wage of _____ per hour.

b. At this rate of employment, the value of marginal product of labor (VMP) is _____ per hour.

c. With no outside intervention in this market, we will observe (monopsonistic, monopolistic, both monopsonistic and monopolistic) exploitation.

d. The level of monopsonistic exploitation is _____ per hour, and the level of monopolistic exploitation is _____ per hour.

e. The total level of exploitation is _____ per hour, represented by the difference between the _____ and _____.

CASE STUDY

When unions set wage rates above the equilibrium wage rate, they create a surplus of labor at that wage rate. That is, at the union-set wage rate the quantity supplied of labor exceeds the quantity demanded for labor. Another way to view this situation is that at such an above-equilibrium wage rate, a *shortage of jobs exists*. In other words, such (relatively high paying) jobs are now scarcer and, like any scarce resource, they have to be rationed.

Economist Walter Williams has pointed out that historically unions have rationed African Americans out of such jobs; union leaders in union crafts have allocated these artificially scarce jobs to the families of members already in the union. Williams cites as evidence that after the Civil War much higher percentages of African Americans held jobs in the skilled crafts than was the case after World War II. The labor union movement flourished between those two periods.

1. How would African Americans have been able to avoid being rationed out of craft jobs had there been no unions?

2. Can there be a shortage of some jobs, but a surplus of others? Can there be a shortage of all jobs?

ANSWERS TO CHAPTER 28

COMPLETION QUESTIONS

1. craft; skill or trade; industrial; industry
2. helped
3. is not; right-to-work; closed shop (union shop in right-to-work states); jurisdictional disputes; sympathy; secondary
4. European merchant guilds
5. strike
6. surplus; shortage
7. must; l; low-seniority
8. MRP of labor; negatively sloped; diminishing returns; MFC of labor; positively sloped; rise; upward; greater than

9. MRP of labor; diminishing marginal physical product of labor; decreasing product price; MFC of labor; raise; all; upward
10. MB = MC; MRP of labor; MFC of labor; supply
11. MRP of labor; MFC of labor
12. regulates number of student athletes per school; fixes the price of university games; sets prices; wages; and conditions for university hiring of athletes; enforces its rules with sanctions and penalties
13. marginal revenue product

TRUE-FALSE QUESTIONS

1. T
2. T
3. F   It was increased by President Roosevelt.
4. T
5. F   They create a surplus of labor and a shortage of jobs.
6. T
7. F   It sets wage rates where the price elasticity of demand equals l.
8. F   Not necessarily; demand may fall dramatically.
9. F   They may increase productivity by creating a safer and securer environment.
10. F   It hires up to where MRP = MFC of labor
11. T
12. T
13. T

MULTIPLE CHOICE QUESTIONS

1.a;   2.c;   3.b;   4.a;   5.d;   6.a;   7.d;   8.c;   9.a;   10.c;
11.d;   12.d;   13.d;   14.b;   15.d;   16.c;   17.a;   18.d;   19.c;   20.b;
21.b

WORKING WITH GRAPHS

1. a. 20, $2;   b. increase, 25, $2.50
2. a. 20, $2;   b. $6;   c. both monopsonistic and monopolistic;   d. $2,$2;
   e. $4, VMP of $6 per hour, wage of $2 per hour

CASE STUDY

1. They could have offered to work for lower wages (in effect, they could have bid "higher" for jobs).

2. Yes, a shortage of jobs arises when wage rates are set above equilibrium, and a surplus when wage rates are set below equilibrium; when the equilibrium wage rate exists, there is neither a shortage nor a surplus of jobs. A shortage of all jobs cannot exist—unless wage rates are set above equilibrium in all labor markets.

GLOSSARY FOR CHAPTER 28

Bilateral monopoly A market structure consisting of a monopolist and a monopsonist.

Closed shop A business enterprise in which an employee must belong to the union before he or she can be employed. The employee must remain in the union after he or she becomes employed.

Collective bargaining Bargaining between management of a company or of a group of companies and management of a union or a group of unions for the purpose of setting a mutually agreeable contract on wages, fringe benefits, and working conditions for all employees in the union(s). Different from individual bargaining, where each employee strikes a bargain with his or her employer individually.

Craft unions Labor unions composed of workers who engage in a particular trade or skill, such as baking, carpentry, or plumbing.

Featherbedding Any practice that forces employers to use more labor than they would otherwise or to use existing labor in an inefficient manner.

Industrial unions Labor unions that consist of workers from a particular industry, such as automobile manufacturing or steel manufacturing.

Jurisdictional dispute A dispute by two or more unions over which should have control of a particular jurisdiction, such as over a particular craft or skill or over a particular firm or industry.

Labor unions Workers' organizations that usually seek to secure economic improvements for their members.

Monopsonist A single buyer.

Monopsonistic exploitation Paying a worker a wage below that worker's marginal revenue product.

Right-to-work laws Laws that make it illegal to require union membership as a condition of continuing employment in a particular firm.

Secondary boycott A boycott of companies or products sold by companies that are dealing with a company that has already been struck.

Strikebreakers Temporary or permanent workers hired by a company to replace union members who are striking.

Sympathy strike A strike by a union in response to, or in sympathy with, another union's already existing strike.

Union shop A business enterprise that allows nonunion members to become employed, conditional upon their joining the union by some specified date after employment begins.

RENT, INTEREST, AND PROFITS

PUTTING THIS CHAPTER INTO PERSPECTIVE

Chapters 27 and 28 dealt with labor and its payment: wage rates. Chapter 29 analyzes land, capital, and entrepreneurship, and the (roughly) corresponding payments to those factors: rent, interest, and profits.

Probably the most important thing you can learn from this chapter is that rent, interest, and profits (and wage rates too) are *prices*. As such they perform an allocative function; in a market economy, land, capital, and labor flow to the highest (business) bidder. (Profits are a little more difficult to analyze; we deal with them later in this section.) In general, the highest bidders will be those firms that are the most profitable or have the best profit record in the past. Consequently, through the price system, resources flow from less profitable firms to more profitable firms; this means that resources (factors of production) flow from lower-valued to higher-valued uses, and economic efficiency prevails. To the extent that governmental price controls such as usury laws, minimum wage laws and comparable worth laws, and excess profits taxes exist, then economic efficiency suffers. Inefficiency results also when governments subsidize firms that are going bankrupt. Note, however, that just because government economic policies are inefficient does not mean that we *should not* permit such interferences; remember that questions of "should" are normative in nature. Economists can only present the results of their positive economic analysis to society; society can then determine whether or not other matters outweigh efficiency considerations.

Rent is typically regarded as a payment for land. Economists have extended the term *rent* to include the payment to any resource that is fixed in supply. More specifically, we define economic rent as the payment to any resource over and above what is necessary to keep the resource in supply at its current level. This extended concept of rent permits us to analyze economic rents involved with professional athletes and entertainers. Note again the point about price as an allocating, or rationing, device. Suppose the Spice Girls would be *willing* to perform for $500 a night. At such a price they would be in great demand and a shortage of their services would exist. If a law were passed that limited their income to $500 a performance, their economic rents would disappear, but how would we ration their performances? That is, where would they entertain? In a market system, their shows might be bid up to $100,000 a night. The Spice Girls sell their services to the highest bidder and earn economic rents, and economic efficiency obtains. Society maximizes the value of their services, because the highest bidders value their services most highly.

Interest is the cost of obtaining credit; it arises because most people prefer to consume in the present rather than in the future—due to the uncertainty of life. In order to induce people to save now, they are offered interest, which permits them to consume more in the future. Borrowers can reward lenders in the future if they use the funds (saving) so obtained to produce capital goods that increase output in the future. Hence we have a supply of credit by savers and a demand for credit by businesses, and the interest rate is thereby established. The interest rate is a price, and it allocates credit to the highest bidder; ultimately physical capital is being allocated because business-borrowers purchase capital goods with the money they borrow. Capital is allocated to its most profitable use and economic efficiency results.

Profits are less easy to analyze. The economic function of profit is to help society decide which industries, and which firms within an industry, are to expand and which are to contract. In the process, resources move from lower-valued to higher-valued uses.

LEARNING OBJECTIVES

After you have studied this chapter you should be able to

1. define economic rent, interest, nominal rate of interest, real rate of interest, present value, rate of discount, and discounting.

2. understand the allocative function of economic rents.

3. distinguish between the nominal interest rate and the real interest rate.

4. calculate the (approximate) nominal interest rate, given the real interest rate and the anticipated rate of inflation.

5. list three things that account for variations in interest rates.

6. answer questions that require an understanding of the rationing function of rent, interest, and profits.

7. calculate the present value of an amount of money to be received at a future date.

CHAPTER OUTLINE

1. *Economic rent* is a payment for the use of any resource that is in fixed supply.
    a. Land is often believed to be in fixed supply.
    b. Even if land is absolutely in fixed supply, rent payments help society to decide how land is to be used.
    c. Economic rents also accrue to factors of production other than land.
    d. Rents help society decide how to allocate a factor fixed in supply.

2. The term *interest* is used to mean two things: (1) the price paid by debtors to creditors for the use of loanable funds, and (2) the market return earned by capital as a factor of production.
    a. Interest is the payment for obtaining credit.
    b. Interest rates vary with the length of loan, risk, and handling charges.
    c. The equilibrium rate of interest is found at the intersection of the downward sloping demand for loanable funds curve and the upward sloping supply of loanable funds curve.
    d. The *nominal interest* rate is (approximately) equal to the sum of the real interest rate and the expected rate of inflation.
    e. The interest rate, ultimately, allocates physical capital to various firms for investment projects.

3. Interest rates link the present with the future.
    a. A money value in the future can be expressed in today's value by a process referred to as *discounting* to present worth.

    b. Discounting is the method by which the present value of a future sum, or a stream of future sums, is obtained.

    c. The *rate of discount* is the interest rate used in the discounting to present worth equation.

4. Profit is the reward to the entrepreneurial factor of production.

    a. Accounting profits are the difference between total revenues and total explicit costs; economic profits equal the difference between total revenues and the opportunity cost of all factors of production.

    b. Various explanations for profit exist.

        i. Economic profits can be the result of barriers to entry.

        ii. Some economists, notably Joseph Schumpeter, maintain that economic profits result from innovation.

        iii. Frank Knight believed that profit is the reward for assuming uninsurable risk.

    c. The function of economic profit is to (a) spur innovation and investment and (b) allocate resources from lower-valued to higher-valued uses.

KEY TERMS

Interest
Nominal rate of interest
Real rate of interest

Economic profit
Accounting profit
Rate of discount

KEY CONCEPTS

Economic rent
Discounting

Present value

COMPLETION QUESTIONS
Fill in the blank or circle the correct term.

1. A payment for the use of any resource that is _____ in supply is an economic rent.

2. Frank Knight believed that profit was the reward for assuming _____ risk.

3. Interest is the cost of obtaining _____. Interest is used to mean two different things: (1) _____, and (2) _____.

4. Interest rates vary due to _____, _____, and _____.

5. Interest rates are determined at the intersection of the demand for _____ curve and the supply of _____ curve. The supply curve is positively sloped because as people save more, the marginal utility of *present* consumption (falls, rises, remains constant); therefore before people will save more, the interest rate must _____.

6. The three major sources of demand for loanable funds are _____, _____, and _____.

7. The consumer demand for loanable funds exists because people, typically, prefer to consume (earlier than later, later than earlier); businesses demand loanable funds for investments that increase _____.

8. The nominal interest rate equals the real interest rate plus the _____; ultimately the interest rate allocates _____ to various firms for investment projects.

9. If a factor is fixed in supply, society must decide who gets to use it; _____ plays this allocative role.

10. The process of finding the value today of a sum of money in the future is called _____; the interest rate used in that process is called the _____ rate.

TRUE-FALSE QUESTIONS
Circle the T if the statement is true, the F if it is false. Explain to yourself why a statement is false.

T F   1. Economic rent accrues only to the factor land.

T F   2. Economic rent is the price paid to a factor that is perfectly elastic in supply.

T F   3. If economic rent was totally taxed away, society would have to decide who gets to use the resource in question.

T F   4. For a factor fixed in supply, economic rent has no economic function.

T F   5. Economic rent occurs because specific resources have perfect substitutes.

T F   6. If a rock star prices tickets at a price way below equilibrium, that is an efficient way to help poor people.

T F   7. Other things being constant, the greater the risk of nonrepayment, the higher the interest rate.

T F   8. At higher interest rates, businesses will find fewer investments in capital goods profitable, other things being constant.

T F   9. The nominal interest rate (approximately) equals the real rate of interest plus the expected interest rate.

T F   10. Ultimately, the interest rate allocates physical capital to *specific firms* and households.

T F   11. Discounting is the process of converting future money values to present worth.

T F   12. Profits serve no economic function.

T F   13. Accounting profits are less than economic profits.

T F   14. State lotteries understate the true value of their awards.

T F   15. If an inefficient firm goes bankrupt, that is socially efficient.

MULTIPLE CHOICE QUESTIONS
Circle the letter that corresponds to the best answer.

1. For a factor that earns economic rent,
    a. its quantity varies only in the long run.
    b. its supply is perfectly elastic.
    c. its supply curve is perfectly inelastic.
    d. no taxation is possible because no surplus exists.

2. In David Ricardo's economic model,
    a. land was fixed in supply.
    b. wages and salaries were set by government.
    c. land rent falls as industrialization occurs.
    d. All of the above

3. Economic rents
    a. have no allocative function.
    b. have no economic function.
    c. do not bring forth a greater quantity of the resource.
    d. exist only for land.

4. Mr. Pulsinelli earns $800,000 per year as a tennis pro; he could earn, at best, $100,000 per year as an economist. Which statement is the most accurate?
    a. He should be a tennis pro.
    b. He would earn economic rents as a tennis pro.
    c. He would earn economic rents as an economist.
    d. His comparative advantage is as an economist.

5. Credit card interest rates are high because
    a. such loans are unsecured.
    b. of adverse selection.
    c. risks are high to the issuers of credit cards.
    d. All of the above

6. Economic rents
    a. accrue only to land.
    b. accrue only to labor.
    c. accrue only to entrepreneurs.
    d. can accrue to any factor, in principle.

7. Other things being constant, the interest rate varies with the
    a. length of a loan.
    b. risk of nonrepayment.
    c. handling charges.
    d. All of the above

8. Which of the following statements is **NOT** true?
    a. As people save more, their marginal utility for present consumption falls.
    b. In order to induce households to save more, the interest rate must rise.
    c. The supply of loanable funds curve is positively sloped.
    d. At higher interest rates people substitute future consumption for present consumption.

9. Which of the following statements is **NOT** true?
    a. Households demand loanable funds to purchase durable goods.
    b. Governments demand loanable funds to finance surpluses.
    c. Businesses demand loanable funds to purchase investment capital.
    d. Households demand loanable funds to maintain consumption when income falls temporarily.

10. The nominal interest rate approximately equals the real interest rate
    a. minus the expected interest rate.
    b. plus the expected interest rate.
    c. plus the expected rate of inflation.
    d. minus the expected inflation rate.

11. Interest rates
    a. have no economic function.
    b. allocate money capital to less efficient firms.
    c. allocate physical capital to firms in a random manner.
    d. allocate physical capital to specific firms for investment projects.

12. Discounting
    a. converts future dollar values into present values.
    b. connects the future with the present.
    c. uses the interest rate.
    d. All of the above

13. If the interest rate is 5 per cent, the present value of $100 that is to be received one year from now is about
    a. $90
    b. $950
    c. $95
    d. $105

14. Profits
    a. perform no economic function.
    b. move resources from lower-valued to higher-valued uses.
    c. provide useful information, but losses do not.
    d. lead to a misallocation of resources because producers produce for profit, not for consumer needs.

15. When Miller won the $1,000,000 lottery in Florida, he found out that the money would be paid to him at the rate of $50,000 per year for the next twenty years. Which of the following is probably true?
    a. Miller will refuse the money, after he finds out what the lottery is really worth.
    b. The lottery winnings are worth considerably less than $1 million.
    c. Miller would *prefer* to receive his lottery winnings over twenty years, instead of all at once.
    d. Miller would have preferred to receive $25,000 per year for 40 years.

MATCHING
Choose the item in column (2) that best matches an item in column (1).

<table>
<tr><td align="center">(1)</td><td align="center">(2)</td></tr>
<tr><td>a. profit</td><td>e. inflationary expectation</td></tr>
<tr><td>b. real rate of interest</td><td>f. discount rate</td></tr>
<tr><td>c. economic rent</td><td>g. bearing uninsurable risk</td></tr>
<tr><td>d. present value calculation</td><td>h. payment to resource fixed in supply</td></tr>
</table>

WORKING WITH GRAPHS

1. Use the information given below to answer the questions that follow. The figures other than the rate of interest are given in thousands of dollars per month.

Rate of interest	Quantity demanded of: Consumption loans	Investment loans	Total loans	Supply of loanable funds
16	10	30	_____	300
14	20	40	_____	250
12	30	60	_____	200
10	40	100	_____	140
8	50	140	_____	90
6	60	180	_____	50
4	70	210	_____	30

a. On the grid provided above, plot the demand curve for consumption loans and label it D (consumption), and plot the demand curve for investment loans and label it D (investment).

b. Complete the column for the total loans demanded in the above table.

c. On the above grid, plot the total demand curve for loanable funds and the supply curve for loanable funds.

d. The equilibrium rate of interest is _____, and the equilibrium quantity of loanable funds is _____ per month.

e. _____ per month will be lent for the purpose of consumption loans at equilibrium, and _____ will be lent for investment.

2. Use the following graphs to answer the questions that follow.

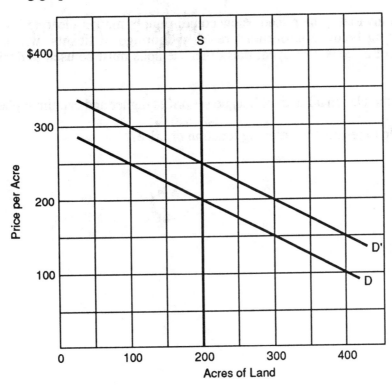

a. If the demand for land is represented by D, what is the total rent received by the owner of the 200 acres of land?

b. If the demand for land increases to D', what is the rent received by the landowner?

PROBLEMS

1. Suppose you win a lottery that offers the following payoff. At the end of each year for the next 3 years you are to receive $1000. At the end of each of the following 3 years you will receive $500, for a total of $4500 over the six-year period. If the current going rate of interest is 8%, what is the present value of your winnings? If someone offered you $3700 today for your lottery ticket, should you take it?

2. Gladstone Gander just learned that a long-lost aunt has set up a trust for him, whereby he will receive $1 million exactly ten years from now. Assume that the relevant interest rate is 10 percent.

    a. Can Gladstone sell his inheritance, right now, for $1 million? Why or why not?

    b. What is the present value of Gladstone's inheritance?

3. Suppose that you had used a discount rate of 20 percent in question (2) above. How would you answer (a) and (b) now?

    c. How are present value and the interest rate related?

CASE STUDY

Super Bowl tickets invariably are priced below equilibrium or market-clearing levels, which is nice for scalpers. Pricing below equilibrium creates a shortage of tickets, which means that the rationing function of price is destroyed; thus other methods must be used to decide who gets the tickets.

1. Why wouldn't the National Football League set prices higher and capture higher revenues?

2. Do scalpers help to restore the rationing function of price?

ANSWERS TO CHAPTER 29

COMPLETION QUESTIONS

1. fixed
2. uninsurable
3. credit; price paid by creditors to debtors, return to capital
4. length of loan, risk of nonrepayment, handling charges
5. loanable funds, loanable funds; rises; rise
6. households, businesses, governments
7. earlier than later; profits or productivity
8. expected inflation rate; physical capital
9. economic rent
10. discounting; discount

TRUE-FALSE QUESTIONS

1. F It accrues to any factor fixed in supply.
2. F It is the price paid to a perfectly *in*elastic resource supply.
3. T
4. F It allocates the fixed factor to its highest-valued use.
5. F Rent is earned by resources that cannot be replicated exactly.
6. F Giving them money income directly would be more efficient.
7. T
8. T
9. F Plus the expected *inflation (not expected interest)* rate.
10. T
11. T
12. F They help to allocate capital, and they help to decide which firms should grow and which should contract.
13. F They normally exceed economic profits because the latter takes into account the opportunity costs of factors of production; accounting profits do not.
14. F They overstate, because they don't tell the discounted value.
15. T

MULTIPLE CHOICE QUESTIONS

1.c;   2.a;   3.c;   4.b;   5.d;   6.d;   7.d;   8.a;   9.b;
10.c;   11.d;   12.d;   13.c;   14.b;   15.b

MATCHING

a and g;   b and e;   c and h;   d and f

WORKING WITH GRAPHS

1. a. See the graph below.

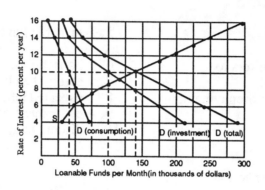

b. 40, 60, 90, 140, 190, 240, 280;
c. See the graph above;
d. 10 percent, $140,000;
e. $40,000, $100,000

2. a. $40,000;   b. $50,000

PROBLEMS

1. From Table 29-2 on page 659 of your text we can see:

Year	Present Value	(Found by)
1	$ 926.00	(.926 x 1000)
2	857.00	(.857 x 1000)
3	794.00	(.794 x 1000)
4	367.50	(.735 x 500)
5	340.50	(.681 x 500)
6	315.00	(.630 x 500)
Total	$3600.00	

Yes, you would be $100 better off, as is seen by the present value calculation.

2. a. No, no one would give him $1 million right now because such a sum could be invested and earn interest for ten years, and at the end of that period it would be worth $1 million plus the accumulated interest.

   b. $\dfrac{\$1,000,000}{(1.1)^{10}} = \dfrac{\$1,000,000}{2.5937425} = \$385,543$ • Or from Table 29-2, use the discount factor of .385.

3. a. See (2) above
   b. $161,506.
   c. They are inversely related.

CASE STUDY

1. We're not sure we know the exact answer, but perhaps TV revenues swamp seat revenues and NFL big shots can impress their friends by giving them very scarce tickets; also high scalping prices might be a good advertising gimmick for the NFL.
2. Yes.

GLOSSARY TO CHAPTER 29

Accounting profit   The difference between total revenues and total explicit costs.

Discounting   The method by which the present value of a future sum or a future stream of sums is obtained.

Economic profit   The difference between total revenues and the opportunity cost of all factors of production.

Economic rent   A payment for the use of any resource that is in fixed supply.

Interest   The payment for current rather than future command over resources; the cost of obtaining credit. Also the return paid to owners of capital.

Nominal rate of interest   The market rate of interest that's expressed in terms of current dollars.

Present value   The value of a future amount expressed in today's dollars; the most that someone would pay today to receive a certain sum at some point in the future.

Rate of discount   That rate of interest used to discount future sums back to present value.

Real rate of interest   The rate of interest obtained by subtracting the anticipated rate of inflation from the nominal rate of interest.

INCOME, POVERTY, AND HEALTH CARE

PUTTING THIS CHAPTER INTO PERSPECTIVE

To this point we have analyzed factor markets and learned how factors of production are evaluated and priced in competitive and noncompetitive markets. Ultimately, payments to factors of production represent income to the people who own those factors. Chapter 30 explores how those incomes are distributed across the population.

It might be helpful for you to think of a "natural" distribution of income that would result from a perfectly competitive economic system. Each person would be paid (approximately, subject to imperfect information limitations) his or her marginal revenue product—for labor and nonlabor resources. Such a distribution of income would doubtless be very uneven because we each have different talents and skills, and we each start out with different degrees of family connections, inherited property, and other variables that potentially affect income. Depending on the tastes of society, a good deal of inequality of income results from the amount of luck (or ill fortune) in the matchup between inherent physical and mental traits and consumer tastes. Then, of course, there are traits that we can acquire by training and/or hard work.

Although such an unequal distribution might be "natural" in some sense, it hardly follows that such a distribution is *desirable*. A "natural" distribution of income can theoretically be consistent with a very small number having extremely high incomes and a large number living at near-subsistence.

This brings us to a potential problem. A "natural" distribution does have some benefits: it is consistent with economic freedom and provides economic incentives for people to improve their marginal productivity through training, education, risk-taking, and old-fashioned hard work. In contrast, a natural distribution of income also reflects mere luck. One's income may be relatively low due to a failure to inherit traits and characteristics that the marketplace (which reflects society's tastes for goods and services) values, or to a failure to inherit wealth from one's ancestors.

Unfortunately, when we tax some to give to others we affect economic incentives and economic freedom. In short, there is a trade-off between income equality and economic efficiency. There is, therefore, an optimal amount of inequality, but such an optimum depends on one's particular value system. The optimal distribution of income cannot be derived through positive economics; once again economic analysis can provide only limited aid in solving a crucial societal problem. Nevertheless, economic analysis can serve to remind us that there are costs, as well as benefits, to redistributing income through government tax and transfer programs. Combating poverty has proven to be a difficult problem.

This chapter is also concerned with the health care problem that seems to have arisen in the United States in recent years. A combination of (a) a population that is getting older, (b) new, expensive, technological advances in medical equipment (and drugs), (c) a third-party payment system, much of which is government subsidized, which creates a moral hazard situation for health care users and (d) a lack of incentives for physicians and hospitals to contain costs, have led to a dramatic increase in the demand for medical care. As a consequence the costs of such care has skyrocketed and so too (predictably) has the cost of health insurance.

LEARNING OBJECTIVES

After you have studied this chapter you should be able to

1. define distribution of income, Lorenz curve, income in\ kind, comparable-worth doctrine, age-earnings cycle, third parties, and medical savings accounts (MSAs).

2. list criticisms of using the Lorenz curve as an indicator of the degree of income inequality in a country.

3. distinguish between income and wealth.

4. recognize facts concerning income distribution and poverty in the United States.

5. list three determinants of income differences.

6. list two normative standards of income distribution and distinguish between them.

7. describe the situation of poverty in the U.S.

8. list ways poverty is reduced in the U.S.

9. relate third party payment systems to the moral hazard problem.

10. enumerate costs associated with forcing more income equality in a nation.

11. enumerate three reasons that explain why medical costs have risen rapidly in the U.S.

12. list benefits and costs to using medical savings accounts to counter the moral hazard problem in the health care industry.

CHAPTER OUTLINE

1. This chapter attempts to define distribution of income and present theories of why income is unevenly distributed across the population.

2. The Lorenz curve is a geometric representation of the distribution of income.
    a. There are some criticisms of using the Lorenz curve to measure the degree of income inequality in a nation.
        i.   The curve does not take into account income in kind.
        ii. It does not account for differences in family size and effort.
        iii. It does not account for age differences.
        iv. It measures pretax money income.
        v.   It does not measure underground economy earnings.

b. Since World War II the distribution of money income in the United States has not changed very much.

c. The distribution of total income, which includes in-kind transfers, has become more equal in the U.S. since 1962.

3. Wealth and income are not synonymous.
   a. Wealth is a stock concept, and income is a flow concept.
   b. A stock is evaluated at a given moment in time; a flow is evaluated during a period of time.
   c. Each of us inherits a different endowment, including human attributes and nonhuman wealth, which strongly affects our ability to earn income in the marketplace.

4. There are numerous determinants of income differences.
   a. The *wage-earnings cycle* typically shows that at a young age income is low; it builds gradually to a peak at around age 50, and then gradually curves down until it approaches zero at retirement age.
   b. In competitive markets, workers can expect to earn, approximately, their marginal revenue product (MRP).
   c. Determinants of an individual's marginal productivity include innate abilities and attributes, education, experience, and training.

5. Inheritance is also a determinant of income differences.

6. Discrimination also contributes somewhat to income differences.
   a. White males, on average, hold jobs in the highest-paying occupations; the lowest-paying jobs are held by nonwhite males, and by white and nonwhite females.
   b. Minorities are often denied equal access to higher education.

7. The comparable-worth doctrine contends that females (or minorities) should receive the same wages as males if the levels of skills and responsibility in their different jobs are equal. Skill and responsibility levels, in practice, are difficult to define and arbitrariness inevitably results in setting such wage rates.

8. Investment in human capital, on average, earns a rate of return on a par with the rate of return to investment in other areas.

9. There are normative standards of income distribution: equality and productivity.

10. Western nations have sustained enough economic growth over the last several hundred years so that mass poverty has disappeared.

11. If poverty is measured in absolute terms, it will be eliminated by economic growth. If poverty is defined in relative terms, it will be mathematically impossible to eliminate it, unless everyone has the same income—an improbable event.
    a. If we correct poverty rates for in-kind transfers, they fall dramatically in the United States.

12. There are a variety of income-maintenance programs designed to help the poor; they include social insurance, Supplemental Security Income, Temporary Assistance to Needy Families, food stamps, and the earned-income tax credit program.

13. In spite of the numerous programs designed to reduce poverty, officially defined poverty rates have shown no long run tendency to drop since their relatively dramatic decline through 1973.

14. More income equality reduces economic incentives to both the people who are taxed and the people who receive transfers, and economic freedoms are reduced if more income equality is enforced; hence a trade-off exists between efficiency and equality of income.

15. In recent years the price of health care services and health care insurance have increased dramatically in the U.S.; American citizens have been spending higher and higher percentages of their income on health care.

16. There are several explanations as to why health care costs have risen rapidly in the United States.
    a. Our population is, on average, getting older and the elderly are the main users of health care.
    b. Technological advances in medicine have spawned expensive machinery that everyone wants to use (both suppliers and demanders).
    c. The state and federal governments account for about 40 percent of total spending on health care; private insurance accounts for about 30 percent of the spending.
       i. Because health care is subsidized by government, people want more than they would otherwise; thus, a moral hazard exists.
       ii. Both government and private-provided health care insurance create a situation in which third parties (insurers) pay most of the costs of medical services; hence people want more health care than if they were paying for it themselves.
    d. The third-party payment system has created a situation in which physicians and hospitals have no incentive to keep health care costs down.

17. Some have suggested a national health care plan to replace the private insurance system that the U.S. has; an essential ingredient of such a system is price ceilings on physician's fees and hospital costs.

18. Others have suggested a national health insurance plan which, presumably, would be offered only to lower income groups.

19. A recent suggestion is the medical savings account, in which people save money in tax-exempt accounts on which they can draw down to pay for health care; what is not spent belongs to the individual. Only catastrophic insurance is purchased.

KEY TERMS

Lorenz curve

KEY CONCEPTS

Distribution of income
Age-earnings cycle
Comparable-worth doctrine

Income in kind
Third parties
Medical savings accounts (MSAs)

COMPLETION QUESTIONS
Fill in the blank or circle the correct term.

1. A Lorenz curve shows what portion of total money income is accounted for by different _____ of a nation's households; if it is a 45 degree line, then _____ income inequality exists.

2. The Lorenz curve as a representation of income inequality has been criticized because it does not _____, or account for _____, _____, _____, and _____.

3. Since World War II, the lowest 20 percent of the income distribution in the United States had a combined money income of _____ percent of the total money income of the entire population; however, if income in kind is taken into account, income inequality has (decreased, increased) since then.

4. (Wealth, Income) is a stock concept, while _____ is a flow concept.

5. One determinant of income inequality is age; the age-earnings cycle indicates that teenagers' incomes are relatively (low, high), then incomes rise gradually to a peak at around age _____, and then gradually fall toward zero as people approach _____. People earn different amounts over their lifetime because age is related to a worker's _____.

6. If a worker's MRP exceeds her wage rate, chances are that she will (change jobs, be laid off); if a worker's wage rate is greater than her MRP, then chances are she will be _____. As long as it is costly to obtain information about a specific worker's MRP, there (will, will not) be some difference between a worker's wage and his or her MRP.

7. Four determinants of an individual's marginal productivity are _____, _____, _____, and _____; other than differences in marginal productivity, income differences are also due to _____ and _____.

8. Two theories of normative standards of income distribution are _____ and _____.

9. (Absolute, Relative) poverty will automatically be eliminated by economic growth, but _____ poverty can never be eliminated, in practice.

10. In the United States there are several income-maintenance programs aimed at eliminating poverty. The best known is _____ Security, which in effect is an intergenerational income transfer; another is SSI, which establishes a nationwide _____ income for the aged, the blind, and the disabled; the TANF program is for families who are _____ in need.

11. In the United States since 1973 there (has, has not) been a long-run trend toward reduced officially defined poverty.

12. Many economists believe that the major cost to increased income equality is _____; hence a trade-off exists.

13. In recent years the percent of total income spent on medical care has (decreased, increased) dramatically because our population, on average, is getting (younger, older), technological advances in medical equipment have caused a(n) (decrease, increase) in the demand for medical services, third-party billing has (decreased, increased) due to health insurance, and because physicians and hospitals have (little, strong) incentives to keep costs down.

14. Most national health care plans incorporate a system to put a (floor, ceiling) on medical fees and services; this will create (surpluses, shortages) eventually.

TRUE-FALSE QUESTIONS

Circle the T if the statement is true, the F if it false. Explain to yourself why a statement is false.

T F   1. In the real world, no country has a linear (straight-line) Lorenz curve.

T F   2. Third party paying avoids the moral hazard problem that exists in the health care system.

T F   3. When in-kind transfers are considered, measured income inequality in the U.S. rises and poverty levels fall.

T F   4. Not considering income-in-kind, the bottom 20 percent of United States income earners earn about 5% of total U.S. income.

T F   5. Income and wealth are unrelated.

T F   6. The comparable-worth doctrine accepts the notion that workers should be paid their MRP, as determined by markets.

T F   7. In the United States, over time, income inequality has increased dramatically.

T F   8. An age-earnings cycle exists because age and marginal productivity are related.

T F   9. In a competitive economy, workers tend to get paid their marginal revenue product.

T F 10. In the United States inheritance and discrimination are more important determinants of income differences than are marginal productivity differences.

T F 11. In the United States, there has been discrimination against African Americans and other minorities regarding access to quality education.

T F 12. In the United States the return to investment in human capital is significantly higher than it is for other investments.

T F 13. Mass poverty is still a problem for even the advanced Western economies.

T F 14. Economic growth will eventually eliminate relative poverty.

T F 15. Despite massive sums of money devoted to income redistribution programs in the United States, officially measured poverty has remained roughly unchanged since 1973.

T F 16. All economists agree that more income equality in the United States is desirable.

T F 17. Because health care is usually paid for by third parties, buyers are largely insensitive to price increases.

T F 18. Physicians and hospitals, like other service providers, have an incentive to keep costs down.

T F 19. Medical savings accounts can help to avoid the moral hazard problem.

MULTIPLE CHOICE QUESTIONS
Circle the letter that corresponds to the best answer.

1. The Lorenz curve
    a. gives a numerical measure of a nation's degree of income inequality.
    b. is a straight line in modern, industrial societies.
    c. is a straight line in socialist countries.
    d. overstates the true degree of income inequality, as it is currently measured.

2. Which of the following is **NOT** a correct statement about the Lorenz curve?
    a. It does not adjust for age.
    b. It does not consider income-in-kind transfers.
    c. It considers income earned in the underground economy.
    d. It considers pretax income.

3. In 1996, in the United States, the lowest 20 percent of income earning families had a combined income of about _____ percent of the total money income of the entire population.
    a. 5
    b. 10
    c. 15
    d. 20

4. Which of the following statements is **FALSE**?
    a. The U.S. population, on average, is getting older.
    b. Technological advances in medicine have reduced health care costs.
    c. Much of health care is subsidized by governments.
    d. Most health care is paid by third parties.

5. Analogy: Income is to flow as _____ is to stock.
    a. wealth
    b. poverty
    c. consumption
    d. investment

6. Total economic wealth
    a. is a flow concept.
    b. includes human attributes.
    c. excludes nonhuman wealth.
    d. is zero for most people in the United States.

7. In the United States the long-run trend shows
    a. increased poverty.
    b. increased income inequality.
    c. little change in officially measured poverty.
    d. increased poverty once income-in-kind adjustments are made.

8. In the United States, over the age-earnings cycle,
    a. productivity changes.
    b. income peaks at about age 65.
    c. income rises with age, throughout.
    d. income first falls with age, then rises with age.

9.   In the United States an age-earnings cycle exists because
     a.   age is unrelated to income.
     b.   age and income are related by law.
     c.   productivity and age are related.
     d.   of minimum wage laws.

10. Which of the following is probably the **MOST** important determinant of income differences
     in the United States?
     a.   differences in marginal productivity
     b.   inheritance of nonhuman wealth
     c.   discrimination
     d.   welfare programs

11. Which is **LEAST** like the others, with respect to productivity?
     a.   innate abilities and attributes
     b.   experience
     c.   education and training
     d.   inheritance of nonhuman wealth

12. Regarding medical savings accounts, they
     a.   could be used to finance catastrophic routine office visits.
     b.   reduce the moral hazard problem.
     c.   are likely to increase health care costs.
     d.   decrease consumer price elasticity of demand.

13. Which of the following does **NOT** occur with economic growth?
     a.   elimination of absolute poverty
     b.   elimination of relative poverty
     c.   increasing living standards
     d.   increasing life expectancy

14. In recent years, in the United States,
     a.   health care costs have increased as a percentage of national income.
     b.   the population, on average, is getting younger.
     c.   technological discoveries have reduced the cost of medical care.
     d.   health care costs have risen, but national income has risen more rapidly.

15. The Earned Income Tax Credit program (EITC) creates
     a.   incentives for those taxed to work.
     b.   disincentives to its recipients to work.
     c.   incentives for its recipients to increase MRP.
     d.   neither incentives nor disincentives for anyone to work.

16. We have to worry about greatly increasing Medicare expenditures because
     a.   the U.S. population is getting older
     b.   there is a moral hazard issue with respect to Medicare
     c.   Congress keeps adding to eligible expenses for Medicare repayment
     d.   All of the above

17. The optimal amount of income inequality
     a.   is zero.
     b.   is a positive economics concept.
     c.   is a normative economics concept.
     d.   is agreed to by all economists.

18. In a nation in which complete income equality has been achieved,
    a. economic incentives would be reduced dramatically.
    b. economic freedom would be curtailed dramatically.
    c. national output and national income would fall dramatically.
    d. All of the above

MATCHING
Choose the item in column (2) that best matches an item in column (1).

| (1) | (2) |

a. Lorenz curve
b. moral hazard
c. comparable-worth doctrine
d. determinant of income inequality
e. wealth
f. income

g. equal pay for equal work
h. inherited traits or MRP
i. stock
j. third party payments
k. flow
l. geometric measure of income distribution

WORKING WITH GRAPHS

1. Use the table below and the grid provided to construct a Lorenz curve.

Cumulative percent of population	Cumulative percent of income
20	5
40	10
60	30
80	70
100	100

2. Below are income figures for two countries. Plot the Lorenz curve for both countries on the grid provided.

Percent of population	Percent of Income Country A	Country B
20	5	10
40	20	20
60	40	30
80	60	50
100	100	100

Which of the two countries has the more equal distribution?

PROBLEM

1. In your text you learned that income and wealth are different concepts. But they can be related via the discounting technique that you learned in Chapter 29. How?

CASE STUDY

It is widely believed that one way to cure poverty in general, and help minority groups in general, is to raise the minimum wage rate. Indeed, in 1996 President Clinton made precisely this argument.

In contrast, economists have long argued that increasing the minimum wage rate will lead to higher unemployment rates among low income wage earners and among teenagers. Recently, that conventional notion has been challenged by Princeton University economists David Cord and Alan Krueger who presented 1995 studies that purported to show that higher minimum wage rates either had no effect or actually *raised* employment. (Their studies obviously influenced President Clinton's proposal.)

The Cord-Krueger results have been criticized by David Neumark (Michigan State) and William Wascher (Federal Reserve Board) who found that higher minimum wages lead to movements from (a) in-school employed and in-school not employed to not-in-school employed, and (b) not-in-school employed to not-in-school not employed categories. More specifically, they found that higher minimum wage rates cause blacks and Hispanics who were not in school to lose their jobs to non-blacks, non-Hispanics who quit school to accept the higher paying jobs. Neumark and Wascher also find a significant but slight, overall impact of higher minimum wages on employment (restoring the conventional conclusion).

1. If Neumark-Wascher are correct, will raising the minimum wage do much to help disadvantaged minorities?
2. What economic law is at issue here?

ANSWERS TO CHAPTER 30

COMPLETION QUESTIONS

1. proportions; zero
2. include income in kind; differences in family size and effort; age; taxes; underground economy earnings
3. about 5; decreased
4. Wealth; income
5. low; 50; retirement; productivity
6. change jobs; laid off; will
7. age; innate abilities and attributes; education; experience or training; inheritance; discrimination
8. equality; productivity
9. Absolute; relative
10. Social; minimum; temporarily
11. has not
12. less economic efficiency
13. increased; older; increase; increased; little
14. ceiling; shortages

TRUE-FALSE QUESTIONS

1. T
2. F   Third party paying causes a moral hazard problem.
3. F   Income inequality falls.
4. T
5. F   The present value of income equals "human" wealth; see the problem section.
6. F   It rejects MRP and substitutes an entirely different approach.
7. F   It has remained constant, or fallen somewhat.
8. T
9. T
10. F   Marginal productivity differences are the most important.
11. T
12. F   The rate of return is about the same.
13. F   Economic growth has eliminated it.
14. F   Relative poverty can never be eliminated.
15. T
16. F   Many believe it undesirable; almost all recognize its costs.
17. T
18. F   No, such a lack of incentive is one reason costs have risen.
19. T

MULTIPLE CHOICE QUESTIONS

1.d;   2.c;   3.a;   4.b;   5.a;   6.b;   7.c;   8.a;   9.c;   10.a;
11.d;   12.b;   13.b;   14.a;   15.b;   16.d;   17.c;   18.d

MATCHING

a and l;   b and j;   c and g;   d and h;   e and i;   f and k

WORKING WITH GRAPHS

1. See graphs below.

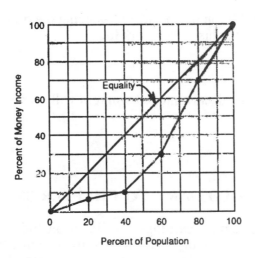

2. See graphs below. Country A has a more equal distribution of income.

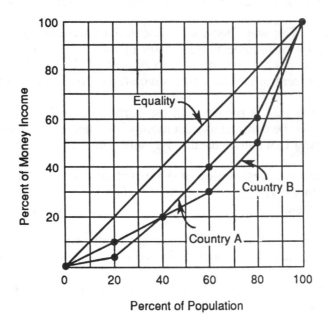

PROBLEMS

1. The value of "human" wealth can be considered as being the present value of the (net) income stream that a person earns over his or her work life.

CASE STUDY

1. Apparently not; low-income disadvantaged workers will be replaced by low-income whites who will quit school.
2. The law of demand.

GLOSSARY TO CHAPTER 30

Age-earnings cycle   The regular earnings profile of an individual throughout his or her lifetime. The age-earnings cycle usually starts with a low income, builds gradually to a peak at around age 45 to 50, and then gradually curves down until it approaches zero.

Comparable-worth doctrine   A doctrine which contends that females should receive the same wages as males if the levels of skill and responsibility in their different jobs are equal.

Distribution of income   The way income is allocated among the population. For example, a perfectly equal distribution of income would result in the lowest 20 percent of income earners receiving 20 percent of national income and the top 20 percent also receiving 20 percent of national income. The middle 60 percent of income earners would receive 60 percent of national income.

Income in kind   Income that is received in the form of actual goods and services, such as housing or medical care. To be contrasted with money income, which is simply income in dollars or general purchasing power that can be used to buy any goods and services.

Lorenz curve   A geometric representation of the distribution of income. A Lorenz curve that is perfectly straight represents perfect income equality. The more bowed a Lorenz curve, the more unequally income is distributed.

Medical savings accounts (MSAs)   A tax-exempt health care account to which individuals would pay into on a regular basis and from which medical care expenses could be paid.

Third parties   The buyer and seller are the first two parties; others who are a party to the transaction are called third parties.

CHAPTER 31

ENVIRONMENTAL ECONOMICS

PUTTING THIS CHAPTER INTO PERSPECTIVE

One of the most important concepts brought out in Chapter 31 is the notion of the socially optimum quantity of a good or service to produce. The optimum quantity, from society's point of view, occurs where the MB to society equals the MC to society; at that quantity the opportunity cost to society of the last unit produced just equals the marginal benefit society derives from it. By now you know that if the MB to society exceeds the MC to society, then society wants more; and if the MB to society is less than the MC to society, then society wants less. In short, from society's point of view, if MB does not equal MC, then a misallocation of resources (or social inefficiency) exists.

In Part Seven you learned that economic agents are rational when they attempt to maximize: businesses maximize total profits and households maximize total utility. In each case the economic agent pursues an activity—either buying or selling in a product or a factor market—up to the point where its private MB equals its private MC. That is, an economic agent pursues its own self-interest and is not concerned (usually) with society's well-being. A major lesson learned in Part Seven is that if firms attempt to maximize total profits in perfectly competitive markets, then social efficiency results. Stated differently, when economic agents pursue their private self-interest, social efficiency results—usually.

As Part Eight indicates, however, if imperfect competition exists in either the product market or the factor market, then if economic agents pursue their own self-interest, social inefficiency results. If a firm is not a perfect competitor, too little will be produced from society's—not the firm's—point of view.

In Chapter 31 you discover yet another instance in which social inefficiency results when individuals pursue their own self-interest: externalities. If society's MC exceeds private MC, then an externality (such as pollution) exists, and social inefficiency results because too much will be produced. Individuals pursue their own self-interest, but in equilibrium the MC to society exceeds the MB to society.

In this chapter you also learn about the common property alternatives to pollution-causing resource use, and recycling.

LEARNING OBJECTIVES

After you have studied this chapter you should be able to

1. define private costs, social costs, externality, optimal quantity of pollution, private property rights, common property, transaction costs, and recycling.

2. distinguish between private costs and social costs.

3. recognize how common property and species extinction are related.

4. list three choices that businesses must make if they are charged to pollute.

5. determine the optimal quantity of pollution, when given sufficient information.

6. distinguish between private property rights and common property, and predict how rational economic agents behave under each.

7. list various ways to reduce pollution toward the optimal quantity.

8. recognize how to test whether or not a resource is becoming scarcer.

9. recognize how voluntary exchange can solve the externality problem.

CHAPTER OUTLINE

1. It is important to distinguish between private costs and social costs.
   a. *Private costs* are those incurred by individuals when they use scarce resources.
   b. *Social costs* include private costs plus the cost of actions borne by people other than those who commit those actions; social costs embody the full opportunity cost of a resource-using action.
   c. When people use resources in production or consumption, pollution may be an unwanted by-product; if so, the social costs of consuming and producing will exceed the private costs of doing so.

2. An *externality* exists when a private cost or benefit diverges from a social cost or benefit; if an externality exists, the costs or benefits of an action are not fully borne by the two parties engaged in an exchange, or by an individual using resources.

3. In theory, it is possible to change the signals in an economy so that individuals can be forced to take into account all the costs of their actions.
   a. If polluters are charged to pollute, they will (i) install pollution-abatement equipment, (ii) reduce pollution-causing activities, or (iii) pay the price to pollute.
   b. In general, charging a uniform price to pollute is inefficient because a given physical quantity of pollution has different social costs in different places.

4. Ultimately, the *optimal quantity of pollution* is a normative, not a positive, economics concept.
   a. The waste-disposing capacity of our ecosystem is a scarce resource that can be analyzed like any other resource; the marginal benefit curve for a cleaner environment declines, and the marginal cost curve for a cleaner environment rises.

b. The optimal quantity of pollution occurs where the declining marginal benefit curve intersects the rising marginal cost curve; in general the optimal quantity of pollution will exceed zero.

5. *Common property* is owned by everyone; hence private property rights, which allow the use, transfer, and exchange of property, do not exist for common property.
    a. If a resource is scarce and it is common property, it will be wasted; certain species will become extinct if people value them but property rights do not exist.
    b. A resource that is scarce, but is not common property, can be used efficiently under certain conditions.
    c. Externalities can be internalized via voluntary contracting even when property rights do not exist:
        i.   if the transaction costs associated with making, reaching, and enforcing agreements are low relative to the expected benefits of reaching an agreement.
        ii. if the number of individuals involved is small.
    d. Private property rights can be assigned (through governments), so that an externality can be internalized.

6. Recycling has the potential to save scarce resources and reduce pollution; unfortunately the existing state of the art is such that recycling processes are costly, and create pollution themselves.

7. The fact that the price of landfills is falling implies that the U.S. is not "running out" of landfills; in fact, the prices of *most* resources have been falling, which means that, in general, the resource base is getting larger!

8. Unfortunately, attempts to protect species often leads to costs imposed on land owners, producers, and consumers; trade-offs exist.

KEY TERMS

Private costs   Transaction costs
Social costs

KEY CONCEPTS

Externality   Optimal quantity of pollution
Recycling   Private property rights
Common property

COMPLETION QUESTIONS
Fill in the blank or circle the correct term.

1. Costs incurred by individuals when they use scarce resources are called _____ costs; _____ costs include private costs and external costs and represent the full cost that society bears when a resource-using action occurs.

2. When we add external costs to internal costs, we get _____ costs; an externality exists if there is a divergence between _____ and _____.

3. In theory, decision makers can be made to take into account all of the costs of their actions if people who impose costs on others are (taxed, subsidized).

4. If polluters are charged to pollute, they have the following three options: _____, _____, and _____.

5. A uniform tax on polluters will not be economically efficient if a given physical quantity of pollution imposes different _____ costs in different places.

6. As more and more pollution is reduced, then the marginal benefit (falls, rises) and the marginal cost _____; the optimal quantity of pollution occurs where _____.

7. If at a zero price the quantity demanded of a resource _____ its quantity supplied, that resource is scarce; if a scarce resource is common property, it probably (will, will not) be wasted.

8. Sheep, cows, and other species are not in danger of extinction because they are valued and _____ rights exist; other species are becoming extinct because they are _____ property.

9. If a businessperson/environmentalist treats pollution voluntarily, he or she will be at a competitive (advantage, disadvantage) in the marketplace.

10. Externalities can be internalized if _____ costs are low and if the number of parties involved is (small, large).

11. Recycling in theory, can save scarce resources; however it is very _____ and itself creates _____.

12. Many people feel that the world is running out of resources; but the evidence is that the inflation-adjusted price of most resources has (fallen, increased) historically.

13. Attempts to protect a specific species usually involve a _____.

TRUE-FALSE QUESTIONS
Circle the **T** if the statement is true, the **F** if it is false. Explain to yourself why a statement is false.

T F 1. Social costs do not include private costs.

T F 2. Private costs do not include external costs.

T F 3. If social costs exceed private costs, too much of the good normally will be produced.

T F 4. Pollution is an example of a social cost.

T F 5. The optimal quantity of pollution is zero.

T F 6. Air pollution is a problem because air is common property.

T F 7. A given quantity of physical pollution causes the same amount of economic damage everywhere.

T   F   8.   If polluters are charged to pollute, we may end up with less pollution.

T   F   9.   If a specific firm pays to reduce its output of pollution, it may be at a competitive disadvantage.

T   F   10.   If private property rights don't exist, the private sector cannot internalize externalities.

T   F   11.   Externalities may be internalized if the government assigns private property rights.

T   F   12.   Private property rights to sheep exist, therefore they are not in danger of extinction.

T   F   13.   Attempts to protect one species may well impose costs on humans.

T   F   14.   Recycling is always a good idea.

T   F   15.   The inflation-adjusted price of most resources has fallen, historically.

MULTIPLE CHOICE QUESTIONS
Circle the letter that corresponds to the best answer.

1.   Social costs
     a.   exclude internal costs.
     b.   exclude external costs.
     c.   exclude both internal and external costs.
     d.   include both internal and external costs.

2.   Air pollution
     a.   is an internal cost to firms.
     b.   is an external cost to firms.
     c.   exists because air is a privately owned resource.
     d.   has the same costs to society everywhere.

3.   A misallocation of resources may result if
     a.   social costs exceed private costs.
     b.   social benefits exceed private benefits.
     c.   a scarce resource is communally owned.
     d.   All of the above

4.   If polluters are charged to pollute, then
     a.   pollution will disappear.
     b.   the environment will be damaged severely.
     c.   less pollution is a probable result.
     d.   less voluntary pollution abatement will result.

5.   Which of the following will **NOT** help to reduce the problem that exists if social costs exceed social benefits?
     a.   subsidize polluters
     b.   subsidize parties damaged by pollution
     c.   charge polluters to pollute
     d.   internalize external costs

6. If polluters are charged to pollute, efficiency requires that
    a. they be charged according to the economic damages they create.
    b. they be charged the same amount.
    c. they be charged according to the physical quantity of pollution they generate.
    d. nonpolluters be charged also.

7. The optimal quantity of pollution exists at that level of pollution at which, for pollution abatement, a
    a. rising marginal benefit equals a falling marginal cost.
    b. rising marginal cost equals a falling marginal benefit.
    c. constant marginal cost equals a falling marginal benefit.
    d. constant marginal benefit equals a rising marginal cost.

8. Externalities can be internalized by the private sector if
    a. transaction costs of doing so are low.
    b. benefits of doing so are high.
    c. the number of people involved is small.
    d. All of the above

9. Which statement is **NOT** true?
    a. Recycling can be costly and can add to pollution.
    b. Attempts to protect one species often harm landowners and consumers.
    c. The evidence is that most natural resources are becoming scarcer.
    d. The inflation-adjusted price of landfills has been falling in the U.S.

10. Recycling
    a. may save resources.
    b. can be very costly.
    c. can create its own pollution problems.
    d. All of the above

WORKING WITH GRAPHS

1. Use the graphs below to answer the questions that follow. Note that S represents the industry supply curve and SS represents the marginal costs to society—which include marginal private costs and external costs. Assume that no positive externalities exist.

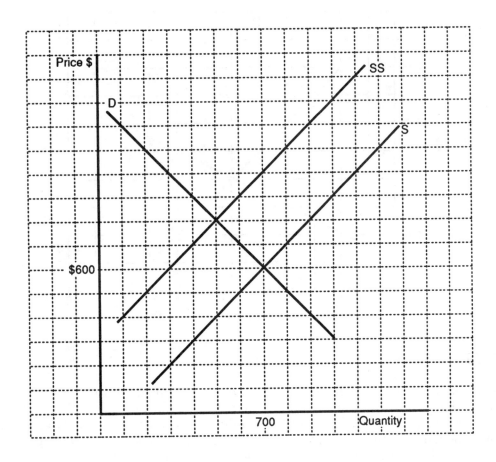

a. Which curve represents the marginal private costs of producing the good in question?

b. Which curve reflects the marginal social costs of producing this good?

c. Which curve represents both the marginal private benefits and the marginal social benefits of this good?

d. How many units of this good will be produced by the private sector? What is the value of the marginal social cost of that quantity? the value of the marginal social benefits?

e. What is the optimal quantity of this good, from society's point of view? Why?

2. Suppose you are given the following graph for the demand and supply of fertilizer per week. As a by-product of fertilizer production, the fertilizer plant dumps harmful chemicals into local streams. A local agency has determined that if fertilizer production were limited to 2 tons per week, the local streams would be able to handle the by-products without harm. The agency has decided to impose a tax on the fertilizer plant. What tax per unit of output is necessary to achieve the agency's goal of no harm to the local streams? Can we conclude that if the agency charges this tax that society is better off? Why or why not?

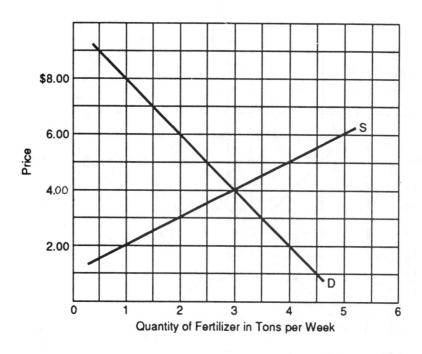

PROBLEMS

1. Suppose you live in a small town with a privately owned solid-waste disposal facility (garbage dump) just west of town that services a larger city about 30 miles away. Because of the prevailing westerly wind, your town suffers from an unpleasant odor generated at the dump. The more garbage that arrives at the dump in a given week, the more unpleasant the odor. A study is undertaken, and the results are partially summarized in the table that follows.

(1) Garbage processed in tons per week	(2) Dump's marginal cost	(3) Consumers' valuation of disposal services	(4) External costs due to odor	(5) Marginal social cost
5	$4.00	$8.00	$0.00	$4.00
10	4.25	7.60	0.20	4.45
15	4.50	6.60	0.50	5.00
20	4.80	5.80	1.00	_____
25	5.20	5.20	1.75	_____
30	5.80	4.80	2.75	_____

Column 1 represents the quantity of garbage disposed of at the dump in tons per week.

Column 2 is the private marginal cost of disposing of various quantities of garbage—the supply of disposal services.

Column 3 represents the demand (willingness to pay) for various quantities of garbage disposal by the consumers of the service in the city to the west.

Column 4 is the external costs that are imposed on residents in your town by the dumping of various quantities of garbage.

Column 5 is the marginal social cost of the dumping services, which includes both private and external costs.

a. Under present conditions, with the disposal plant ignoring external cost, what is the equilibrium price and quantity of disposal services in the market?

b. Complete column 5.

c. Using your answers from a and b, can you tell what is happening in this market at the present?

d. If the disposal plant were forced to internalize all the relevant costs of operation, what would be the equilibrium price and quantity in this market?

CASE STUDY

Title IV of the 1990 amendments to the Clean Air Act of 1970 created tradable pollution permits for sulfur dioxide; these permits are traded on the Chicago Board of Trade.

Dan Dudek, an economist who works for the Environmental Defense Fund, has suggested extending the domestic pollution credits idea to the global economy. As you are probably aware by now, many (but certainly not all) scientists believe that the world will soon experience ill-effects from the "Greenhouse effect"; carbon gases (and other sources) buildup is believed to be causing the world to become warmer.

Fossil fuel burning and land use conversion distribute carbon into the atmosphere, and oceans and plant life absorb carbon; some believe that the first two now outweigh the last two, hence the net effect is carbon buildup.

Some agency can be empowered to issue pollution credits to nations, and credits can be *given* to nations that preserve their forest lands. Thus, tropical rain forest countries in Central and South America can be given credits, which they can then sell. A lively market will develop and the total number of credits issued can change as the Greenhouse effect becomes more or less serious.

1. What will determine the price of such carbon polluting credits?

2. How does this scheme eliminate, at once, both positive and negative externalities?

ANSWERS TO CHAPTER 31

COMPLETION QUESTIONS

1. private; social
2. social; social costs and private costs or social benefits and private benefits.
3. taxed
4. install pollution abatement equipment; reduce pollution-causing activity; pay the price to pollute
5. social
6. falls; rises; MB = MC of pollution reduction
7. exceeds; will
8. private property; common
9. disadvantage
10. transaction; small
11. expensive; pollution
12. fallen
13. tradeoff because property owners; producers; and consumers are harmed

TRUE-FALSE QUESTIONS

1. F They are the sum of private costs and negative externalities (if any).
2. T
3. T
4. T
5. F It is a positive amount, because it costs society resources to have a cleaner environment.
6. T
7. F The next unit of air pollution causes more economic damage in New York City than it does in a small town in Arizona.
8. T
9. T
10. F The private sector, throughout history, has sometimes been able to do so, when transaction costs are low.
11. T
12. T
13. T
14. F Sometimes recycling is too costly, or it creates pollution itself.
15. T

MULTIPLE CHOICE QUESTIONS

1.d; 2.b; 3.d; 4.c; 5.a; 6.a; 7.b; 8.d; 9.c; 10.d

WORKING WITH GRAPHS

1. a. curve S
   b. curve SS
   c. curve D
   d. 700; $1000; $600
   e. 500; that is where the MB to society equals the MC to society

2. $3 per ton of fertilizer; No. We are given no information about how much society values unharmed streams in the area, so we are not justified in concluding that the tax has made society better off.

PROBLEMS

1. a. $5.20, 25 tons per week

b. Marginal social cost: $5.80, $6.95, $8.55
c. With the external costs being ignored, the disposal plants' marginal cost at the equilibrium level is below the true marginal social cost
d. 5.80, 20 tons per week

CASE STUDY

1. Supply and demand conditions; for example, if the greenhouse effect worsens, fewer credits will be issued, such credits will be scarcer, and their price will rise.

2. Positive externalities are eliminated when countries that preserve their rain forests are given salable pollution credits; negative externalities are eliminated when polluting countries are forced to buy credits.

GLOSSARY TO CHAPTER 31

Common property   Property that is owned by everyone and therefore owned by no one. Examples of common property resources which have historically been owned in common are air and water.

Externality   A situation in which a private cost or benefit diverges from a social cost or benefit; a situation in which the costs or benefits of an action are not borne by the two parties engaged in exchange or by an individual engaging in a scarce-resource-using activity.

Optimal quantity of pollution   That level of pollution for which the marginal benefit of one additional unit of clean air just equals the marginal cost of that one additional unit of clean air.

Private costs   Those costs incurred by individuals when they use scarce resources. For example, the private cost of running an automobile is equal to the gas, oil, insurance, maintenance, and depreciation costs. Also called internal costs.

Private property rights   Exclusive rights of ownership which allow the use, transfer, and exchange of property.

Recycling   The reuse of raw materials from used manufactured products.

Social costs   The full cost that society bears when a resource-using action occurs. For example, the social cost of driving a car is equal to all of the private costs plus any additional cost that society bears, including air pollution and traffic congestion.

Transaction costs   All costs associated with making, reaching, and enforcing agreements.

PUBLIC CHOICE: THE ECONOMICS OF INTEREST GROUPS

PUTTING THIS CHAPTER INTO PERSPECTIVE

Chapter 32 deals with the public choice model and then applies it to the United States' farm sector. The text ties these two seemingly disparate topics together by showing how our farm policy can best be understood by viewing it as a specific application of the public choice theory. You should be able to apply the principles of the public choice model to the farm sector after you have studied this chapter.

The public choice model, in effect, applies some of the principles developed in the chapters concerned with the private marketplace. The most important application is the assumption that voters, politicians, and bureaucrats behave just like businesses and consumers: they usually (but not always) pursue their own, not society's, interest. Starting with this premise and drawing on general economic principles, it is possible to gain some very interesting insights into how resources are allocated in the public sector, and into the workings of the U.S. government's farm policy.

One important insight is that voters have only one "all or nothing" vote to cast (unlike consumers, who have dollar votes that enable them to indicate the intensity of wants), and hence cannot indicate the intensity of their wants in the public sector. As a result, logrolling, or vote trading, has evolved. Logrolling permits voters, through their elected representatives, to indicate the intensity of their wants; in that sense logrolling is economically efficient and permits the political process to move more closely to the ideal democracy. In contrast, logrolling permits special interest groups to work efficiently—at the expense of the rest of us. Thus, politicians (and bureaucrats) representing the interest of farmers can, in effect, trade votes with politicians representing other special interest groups; the net effect is that national efficiency suffers.

Another insight yielded by the public choice model is that in many instances it is rational for voters to remain ignorant of political issues because information is costly to obtain and most issues will affect them only slightly. Stated in a more familiar way, the marginal benefit to obtaining political information is often quite low relative to the marginal cost of obtaining such information.

The public choice model also yields insights concerning distributional coalitions. Distributional coalitions form when it is possible for a small group to benefit relatively hugely at the expense of a large group that pays, *individually*, relatively small amounts. How else can we account for our incredibly expensive agricultural policy that helps so few people?

LEARNING OBJECTIVES

After you have studied this chapter, you should be able to

1. define theory of public choice, collective decision making, distributional coalitions, logrolling, bureaucrats, majority rule, proportional rule, incentive structure, rent seeking, deficiency payment, and target price.

2. recognize the fundamental assumptions of the public choice model.

3. predict the conditions under which a voter will choose to remain ignorant about a specific political issue.

4. recognize differences and similarities between market and collective decision-making.

5. predict the conditions under which distributional coalitions will emerge.

6. predict some consequences of a price support system that kept price above the market clearing price.

7. recognize why a private economy would generate a different composition of goods and services than would a representative of government.

8. understand why an agency such as the IRS will probably never be eliminated.

CHAPTER OUTLINE

1. In order to understand how resources are allocated by governments, economists have developed the public choice model, which analyses collective decision making, which involves the actions of voters, politicians, political parties, and special interest groups.

2. There are similarities and dissimilarities in how resources are allocated in the private sector vs. the public (government) sector.
    a. As is true for private economy decision makers, all participants in the political marketplace follow the dictates of rational self-interest.
    b. In the private marketplace firms specialize in the production of private goods, while governments provide political goods at a zero price; in the private sector buyers can reveal the intensity of their wants via a proportional rule (dollar votes), whereas in the political sector an all or nothing majority rule is followed, hence the composition of output would be different under each system.
    c. Logrolling permits elected officials to indicate the intensity of their constituents' wants.

3. The theory of distributional coalitions is that small groups can use the government to redistribute disproportionate benefits to themselves if small amounts can be taken from each of many people.

4. Bureaucrats are nonelected governmental officials who organize special interest groups and defend the rights of such "clients."
    a. Because performance in government is often measured by the number of clients served, bureaucrats have an incentive to expand the size of their clientele.
    b. Bureaucratic rewards do not depend on profits (as would be the case in the private sector); therefore their rewards appear not so much in high salaries but in job perks which provide further incentives for bureaucrats to protect their jobs.

5. For most issues it is not worth the time and effort for citizens to incur the costs of gathering information regarding political issues; hence it is usually rational for citizens in democracies to remain ignorant.

6. In an attempt to stabilize farm incomes, the government attempted to stabilize farm prices; it established *price supports* by setting market price above equilibrium until 1996.
   a. In order to maintain market price above the equilibrium level, the government had to purchase the resulting surplus and store it—or sell it abroad.
   b. Because a price support subsidized farmers per unit of output, those with large farms typically received higher payments; also much of the benefits of a price support system were capitalized in the value of farmland, most of which was owned by such farmers.

7. One scheme that attempted to reduce farm surpluses, while still helping farmers, was the *target price* system.
   a. The government set a target price and paid the farmer the difference between the target price and the market price per unit, multiplied by the quantity sold on the market.
   b. While a target price system reduced the size of the agricultural surplus and permited consumers to pay a lower price for farm goods than a price support system did, taxpayers still had to pay for the farm aid; also, such a program did not reduce the allocation of resources absorbed by the farm sector.

KEY TERMS

Collective decision making
Theory of public choice
Deficiency payment

Bureaucrats
Proportional rule
Majority rule

KEY CONCEPTS

Target price
Distributional coalitions
Government, or political, goods
Incentive structure

Logrolling
Rent seeking
Interest group

COMPLETION QUESTIONS
Fill in the blank or circle the correct term.

1. The public choice model assumes that even though regulators and bureaucrats are (like, unlike) the rest of us, they face a (similar, different) incentive system.

2. The public choice model assumes that politicians, bureaucrats, and regulators pursue (society's, their own) self-interest.

3. Consumer special interest groups to fight (say) milk price supports have never been forthcoming because individual milk buyers endured (low, high) costs as a result of such price supports.

4. Private sector buyers can reveal the intensity of their wants via a _____ through _____ votes; in the political sector the all or nothing _____ rule is followed; we can conclude that the composition of output will (differ, be the same) under those two rules of supplying goods to customer/clients.

5. A _____ will be formed if small groups can use the government to redistribute disproportionate benefits to themselves from small amounts extracted from each of many people.

6. Bureaucrats are (elected, nonelected) governmental officials whose clients are _____ groups; bureaucrats' rewards take the form of _____.

7. Each member of congress has an incentive to (favor, oppose) spending that benefits other Congress members' constituents, but to _____ spending that benefits his or her own constituents; an exception to this rule occurs when politicians find it beneficial to trade votes, in a process called _____.

8. Because information to voters is not _____ and because voters will not be concerned with expenditure programs that affect them only slightly, voters often choose to be _____.

9. Fundamental to the theory of public choice is the idea that voters, bureaucrats, and politicians follow the dictates of rational _____, just as do private decision makers.

10. Distributional coalitions form when a (small, large) number of people can gain relatively large amounts at the expense of a (small, large) number of people, each of whom pays a relatively (small, large) amount.

11. If price is above equilibrium, a _____ exists; normally price will _____ and quantity demanded will _____ while quantity supplied _____; eventually the _____ disappears.

12. Prolonged or long period of surpluses in agricultural goods existed because the government set price (below, above) equilibrium and _____ the surpluses; these actions prevented price from _____ to the equilibrium level.

13. A target price system set a target price for food; if the target price was set above the market price, then farmers produced based on the (target, market) price; farmers received deficiency payments equal to _____ times the quantity they sell; under such a system surpluses tended to be (less, greater) than surpluses existing under a price support system.

14. Price supports were based on an individual farm's output; as a consequence the larger subsidies went to owners of (small, large) farms. The benefits of a price support system were reflected in the price of land; hence owners of (small, large) farms received most of such capitalized benefits.

TRUE-FALSE QUESTIONS
Circle the **T** if the statement is true, the **F** if it is false. Explain to yourself why a statement is false.

T F 1. The public choice model assumes that regulators and bureaucrats are mostly concerned with their own—not the public's—self-interest.

T F 2. The public choice model indicates that households will be provided the same goods by elected representatives as they would by the private sector.

T F 3. The various programs to benefit farmers cost more in dollars than farmers received in dollar payments.

T F   4.   Distributional coalitions benefit everyone in the economy.

T F   5.   It is often rational for voters to remain ignorant of political issues and of candidates.

T F   6.   Bureaucrats can often exert great influence on matters that concern themselves.

T F   7.   In the private marketplace dollar votes indicate majority, not proportional rule.

T F   8.   Logrolling helps politicians to indicate the intensity of wants of their clients.

T F   9.   The U.S. agricultural sector could have always resembled the perfectly competitive market structure, had it not been for government intervention.

T F   10. The combination of price supports and government purchases of surpluses created long periods of food surpluses.

T F   11. Price supports tended to benefit landowners, because the value of supports was reflected in the price of farmland.

T F   12. In an effort to reduce surpluses, the government instituted various schemes to limit farm output.

T F   13. In theory, target prices reduced surpluses.

T F   14. Tax lawyers and accountants are one of the main beneficiaries of our complicated tax system.

MULTIPLE CHOICE QUESTIONS
Circle the letter that corresponds to the best answer.

1. Which of the following characterizes collective, but not market, decision making?
    a.   the legal use of force
    b.   a positive price usually is charged to users
    c.   intensity of wants is easily revealed
    d.   proportional rule

2. People who work in the public sector
    a.   are more competent than other workers.
    b.   are less competent than other workers.
    c.   face a different incentive structure than many workers in the private sector.
    d.   would behave in the same way if they worked for a small private business.

3. If Mr. Ayers loves good A, he can convey the intensity of his wants if good A is
    a.   a private good.
    b.   a public good.
    c.   not subject to the exclusion principle.
    d.   expensive.

4. Which of the following is necessary for prolonged surpluses?
    a.   price supports above equilibrium
    b.   price supports above equilibrium and government purchases of the surplus
    c.   price supports below equilibrium
    d.   target prices

5.   The public-choice theory assumes that voters, bureaucrats, and politicians usually
     a.   attempt to pursue their self-interest.
     b.   are concerned with society's interests.
     c.   exhibit behavior not subject to economic analysis.
     d.   are indifferent to what voters want.

6.   Distributional collectives are more likely to form if
     a.   costs are concentrated in a small number of individuals.
     b.   benefits are dispersed among a large number of individuals.
     c.   the group is small and homogeneous.
     d.   political instability exists.

7.   Distributional collectives are seldom countered because it is not usually worthwhile for
     _____ to fight them.
     a.   those that receive the benefits
     b.   those that pay the costs
     c.   taxpayers
     d.   unions

8.   An individual member of Congress has an incentive to
     a.   vote against expenditures that do not directly benefit his own constituents.
     b.   vote for expenditures that benefit only his constituents.
     c.   vote for expenditures that benefit everyone.
     d.   All of the above.

9.   Voters often find it rational to remain ignorant of issues and candidates because
     a.   ignorance is bliss.
     b.   politicians don't care what voters want anyway.
     c.   information is costly to obtain.
     d.   they don't have to pay for expenditures anyway.

10. Voters tend to be
     a.   very knowledgeable about the issues.
     b.   ignorant of many political issues.
     c.   very knowledgeable about a candidate's political platform.
     d.   willing to spend much time and effort to become knowledgeable.

11. Bureaucrats
     a.   often can exert great influence on matters concerning themselves.
     b.   seldom can exert great influence on matters concerning themselves.
     c.   cannot influence public demand; they only have political influence.
     d.   refrain from exerting political influence because they are concerned with society's
          interests.

12. According to the public choice model, people enter politics mostly to
     a.   maximize their income and wealth.
     b.   do good for society.
     c.   help the poor.
     d.   eliminate economic rents.

13. The U.S. farm industry is characterized by
     a.   production of homogeneous goods
     b.   many buyers and sellers
     c.   fairly easy entry
     d.   All of the above

14. Price supports benefited
    a. farmers at the expense of nonfarmers.
    b. farmland owners.
    c. individual farmers based on their total output.
    d. All of the above.

15. Everyone knows that the Internal Revenue Code is too complicated, yet abolition of the code and thus the IRS will always be fought by those groups that would tend to lose if all deductions and credits were swept away and a single tax rate applied. Some of those groups who would fight against such a change are
    a. current IRS employees.
    b. tax accountants and lawyers.
    c. those who benefit from charitable deductions such as churches and universities.
    d. All of the above.

MATCHING
Choose the item in column (2) that best matches an item in column (1).

(1)	(2)
a. price support	i. union
b. public choice theory	j. deficiency payment
c. distributional coalition	k. trade votes
d. target price	l. proportional rule
e. logrolling	m. zero price
f. government goods	n. information is costly to obtain
g. intensity of wants revealed	o. surpluses
h. rational ignorance	p. self-interested politicians

WORKING WITH GRAPHS

1. Study the following graphs, then answer the questions that follow.

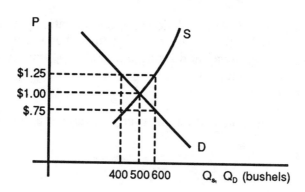

a. The equilibrium price is _____.

b. If the government price support is $1.25 per bushel, quantity supplied by farmers is _____ bushels; quantity demanded by the private sector is _____ bushels; the government must purchase the resulting surplus of _____ bushels, at a total cost of $_____.

c. If instead the government decides to use a target price system and it targets price at $1.25 per bushel, farmers will produce _____ bushels; the market price then will be $_____, and at that price quantity demanded equals _____ bushels; the surplus now equals _____ bushels. The per bushel deficiency payment is $_____, and the target program costs $_____ to taxpayers.

d. The price that food consumers pay is lower under the _____ program.

2. Use the following graphs to answer these questions.

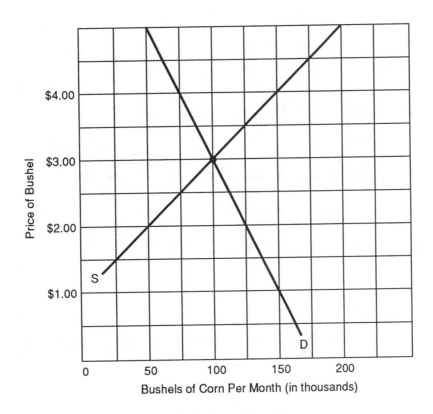

a. In the market for corn, in the absence of any government intervention, the market clearing price per bushel will be _____, with a quantity of _____ bushels per month being sold.

b. The total income of corn farmers in this market will be _____ per month.

c. Suppose that the government has established the need for price supports in the corn market and begins to support the price of corn at $4 per bushel. As a result, farmers will produce _____ bushels per month.

d. Farmers will sell _____ bushels per month to consumers and _____ bushels per month to the government.

e. Total income of farmers will rise to _____ per month, with the government paying out _____ per month of the farmers' incomes.

f. In this case, the government is purchasing the (shortage/surplus) created by the price support for corn.

3. Use the graphs that follow to answer the following questions.

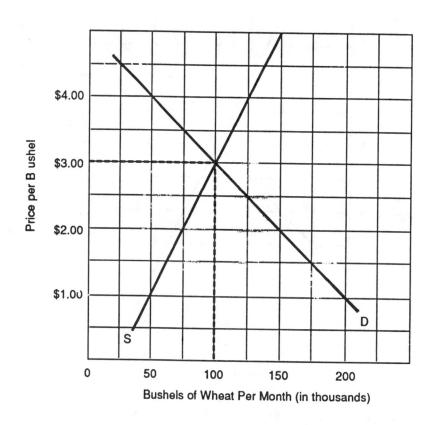

a. In the market for wheat, in the absence of any government intervention, the market clearing price per bushel will be _____, with a quantity of _____ bushels per month being sold.

b. The total income of farmers in this market will be _____ per month.

c. Suppose that the government establishes a target price for wheat of $4 per bushel. As a result, farmers will produce _____ bushels per month.

d. Farmers will now sell _____ bushels per month to consumers at a price of _____ per bushel.

e. The government will pay a subsidy of _____ per bushel to farmers, which will make their total incomes _____ per month.

f. Suppose that the market demand for wheat increases, because of an increase in the foreign demand for U.S. wheat, so that the new market clearing price is $4.50 per bushel. Farmers will now receive a subsidy of _____ per bushel.

CASE STUDY

It is widely assumed that the Food and Drug Administration (FDA) is necessary to regulate drugs, because pharmaceutical companies are concerned only with profits and FDA regulations are concerned with the public's welfare. In contrast, the public choice model maintains that politicians and regulators are just like the rest of us—they usually make decisions that are in their *own* interest, and not in society's.

Assume drug Z has just been invented and it is purported to cure some dreaded disease. Two types of errors can be made. A type I error occurs if the production and sale of drug Z occurs and there are bad side effects. A type II error occurs whenever a drug is not allowed on the market but had it been allowed, people would have been made better off. We often say that a type I error is an error of commission, whereas a type II error is an error of omission. Type I errors can be readily observed. Type II errors are more difficult to observe because people who could have benefited from a drug had it been introduced on the market don't know that fact.

1. If no regulatory agency existed, which error is more likely?

2. If a regulatory agency existed, which error is more likely?

3. Which error is worse?

ANSWERS TO CHAPTER 32

COMPLETION QUESTIONS

1. like; different
2. their own
3. low
4. proportional rule; dollar; majority; differ
5. distributional coalition
6. nonelected; special interest; perks such as large staffs; pensions; etc.
7. oppose; favor; logrolling
8. costless; rationally ignorant
9. self-interest
10. small; large; small
11. surplus; fall; rise; falls; surplus
12. above; purchased; falling
13. target; the target price minus the market price; less
14. large; large

TRUE-FALSE QUESTIONS

1. T
2. F The goods will differ because proportional rule in the private sector can reveal intensity of wants, while majority rule in voting cannot.
3. T
4. F Only relatively small interest groups benefit.
5. T
6. T
7. F Dollar votes indicate a proportional rule system.
8. T
9. T
10. T
11. T
12. T
13. T
14. T

MULTIPLE CHOICE QUESTIONS

1.a;   2.c;   3.a;   4.b;   5.a;   6.c;   7.b;   8.d;   9.c;   10.b;
11.a;   12.a;   13.d;   14.d;   15.d.

MATCHING

a and o;   b and p;   c and i;   d and j;   e and k;   f and m;   g and l;   h and n

WORKING WITH GRAPHS

1. a. \$1.00;   b. 600; 400; 200, \$250 = (200)(\$1.25);   c. 600; \$0.75, 600; 0, \$0.50, \$300;   d. target price.
2. a. \$3, 100,000;   b. \$300,000;   c. 150,000;   d. 75,000, 75,000;   e. \$600,000, \$300,000; f. surplus
3. a. \$3, 100,000;   b. \$300,000;   c. 125,000;   d. 125,000, \$2.50;   e. \$1.50, \$500,000; f. \$0

CASE STUDY

1. A type I error—but only maybe. After all, a "bad" drug reduces sales of all the companies products, eliminates the signaling effect of the companies' previous advertising, and generates law suits.

2. A type II error. A type I error ruins the regulators career, whereas a type II error can almost always be defended; indeed it is likely to go unnoticed! Note also that calls for a pharmaceutical company to do more and more research costs the company money, but the regulators do not bear the research cost.

3. Without specific information it is impossible to tell which is worse—although one's first response is to think that a type I error is worse.

GLOSSARY TO CHAPTER 32

Bureaucrats Non-elected government officials who are responsible for the day-to-day operation of government regulations and laws.

Collective decision making How voters, politicians, and other interested parties act, and how these actions influence nonmarket decisions.

Deficiency payment A direct subsidy paid to farmers equal to the amount of a crop they produce, multiplied by the difference between the target price for that good and its market price.

Distributional coalitions Associations such as cartels, unions, and cooperatives that are formed to gain special government privileges in order to redistribute wealth by taking small amounts from each of many people and giving large amounts to each of only a few.

Government, or political, goods Goods (and services) provided by the public sector; they can be either private or public goods.

Incentive structure The system of rewards and punishments individuals face with respect to their own actions.

Interest group Any organization that seeks to cause government to change spending in a way that will improve the group's members or to undertake any other action that will benefit the group's members. Sometimes called a special interest group.

Logrolling The practice of exchanging political favors by elected representatives. Typically, one elected official agrees to vote for the policy of another official in exchange for the vote of the latter in favor of the former's desired policy.

Majority rule A collective decision-making system in which group decisions are made on the basis of 50.1 percent of the vote. In other words, whatever more than 50 percent of the population votes for, the entire population has to take.

Proportional rule A decision-making system in which actions are based on the proportion of the "votes" cast and are in proportion to those votes cast. In a market system, if 10 percent of the dollar votes are cast for blue cars, 10 percent of the people get to buy blue cars.

Rent seeking The use of resources in an attempt to get government to bestow a benefit on an interest group.

Target price A price set by the government for specific agricultural products. If the market-clearing price is below the target price a **deficiency payment**, equal to the difference between the market price and the target price, is given to farmers for each unit of the good they produce.

Theory of public choice The study of collective decision making.

CHAPTER 33

COMPARATIVE ADVANTAGE AND THE OPEN ECONOMY

PUTTING THIS CHAPTER INTO PERSPECTIVE

Chapter 33 is the first chapter in Part Nine, and the first of two chapters dealing with international trade. International trade and finance have always been important topics in economics, and they have become increasingly important over the past ten years. The percentage of GDP due to exports has increased, our international trade deficit has been an increasing "problem," our nation and many of our trading partners seem to be moving toward "protection from foreign competition," and monetary policy and fiscal policy have become increasingly difficult as recent technological innovations in communications and computers have made the countries of the world more interdependent. For these and other reasons analyzed in Part Nine, it is important for you to understand the principles that underlie international trade and finance.

The most important goal of Chapter 33 is to demonstrate how voluntary trade between nations is based on comparative advantage. Each nation specializes in the production of those goods for which it has a comparative advantage, which means that it produces those goods with the lowest opportunity costs. As a result, world economic growth is fostered and world living standards, with minor short-run exceptions, rise.

Another objective of Chapter 33 is to expose some myths concerning international trade. Many people are induced to favor import restrictions because they believe that imports take jobs away from domestic workers. The truth is that import restrictions merely help save some workers' jobs at the expense of others, and as a by-product consumers must pay higher prices. This chapter analyzes and compares graphically the effects of tariffs and import quotas.

Chapter 33 also analyzes several methods by which nations restrict foreign trade. It is a source of wonderment that the one issue on which virtually all economists agree—that free trade is advantageous—is the same issue on which nearly all non-economists seem to disagree. We don't insist that others agree with us; we merely ask that you try to understand our reasoning. We hope that your text and this *Study Guide* will help you do so.

LEARNING OBJECTIVES

After you have studied this chapter you should be able to

1. define absolute advantage, comparative advantage, quota system, dumping, infant industry argument, General Agreement of Tariffs and Trade (GATT), World Trade Organization (WTO), voluntary import expansion (VIE), and voluntary restraint agreement (VRA).

2.   list the way in which a nation pays for its imports.

3.   distinguish between absolute advantage and comparative advantage and determine each for nations, giving sufficient information.

4.   interpret a graph that shows the effect of an import quota.

5.   interpret a graph that shows the effect of a tariff.

6.   relate comparative advantage to opportunity cost.

7.   list reasons why trade arises between nations.

8.   list potential costs of international trade.

9.   identify the pros and cons of arguments against free trade among nations.

10.   contrast and compare the results of import quotas and tariffs.

CHAPTER OUTLINE

1.   The proportion of GDP accounted for by trade for individual nations varies greatly, but if trade were curtailed, even such nations as the United States (which have relatively low proportions) would be affected significantly.
     a.   A nation ultimately pays for its imports by exports; thus restrictions on imports ultimately reduce exports.
     b.   If trade is voluntary, then both nations participating in an exchange benefit.

2.   A nation has an *absolute advantage* in the production of good A if it can produce more units of good A than other nations can, from a given quantity of inputs; a nation has a *comparative advantage* in producing good A if out of all the goods it can produce, good A has the lowest opportunity cost.

3.   Opportunity costs, and hence comparative advantages, differ among nations.

4.   There are numerous arguments that have been presented as being anti-free trade. Such arguments include the *infant industry argument*, protecting a way of life, stability, protecting domestic jobs, and countering foreign subsidies and dumping. Some of these arguments are simply wrong, and others emphasize costs to the neglect of benefits.

5.   There are numerous methods that nations have used to restrict foreign trade.
     a.   Some nations place *import quotas* on foreign goods.
     b.   Some nations place taxes or *tariffs* on foreign goods.
     c.   Both quotas and tariffs raise prices to domestic consumers and reduce the quantity of goods traded; a tariff, however, generates revenues to the government, while a quota does not.

KEY TERMS

General Agreement on Tariffs and Trade (GATT)   Quota system
Infant industry argument   World Trade Organization (WTO)

KEY CONCEPTS

Comparative advantage
Absolute advantage
Dumping

Voluntary import expansion (VIE)
Voluntary restraint agreement (VRA)

COMPLETION QUESTIONS
Fill in the blank or circle the correct term.

1. A nation ultimately pays for imports by _____.

2. If world trade ceased to exist, all trade-related jobs (would, would not) be lost in the long run; instead nations would simply _____. Nevertheless, worldwide living standards would (fall, rise) significantly.

3. International trade permits each nation to specialize in the production of those goods for which it has a(n) _____ advantage; each nation specializes in the production of goods for which its opportunity costs are the (lowest, highest).

4. Nations have an incentive to specialize and trade because they have different collective tastes and because different nations will always have different _____ costs to producing goods.

5. There are numerous arguments against free trade; they include the _____ industry argument, the argument that trade leads to (increased, decreased) stability as comparative advantage changes with technological changes and changes in taste.

6. Two ways to restrict foreign trade analyzed in the text are _____ on imports and _____ on imported goods.

7. Most restrictions on international trade have one major element in common: they interfere with nations' specializing in the production of goods for which they have a _____ advantage. Therefore they are economically (inefficient, efficient).

8. Because a nation ultimately pays for imports with its _____, restricting imports to save jobs destroys jobs in the _____ sector of the economy; hence, on net, import restrictions (do, do not) save jobs.

TRUE-FALSE QUESTIONS
Circle the **T** if the statement is true, the **F** if it is false. Explain to yourself why a statement is false.

T F 1. If all world trade ceased, import sector jobs and export sector jobs would be permanently destroyed.

T F 2. Because international trade is voluntary in the private sector, both nations benefit from trade that is continued.

T F 3. Imports are paid for by exports.

T F 4. In effect, a tariff makes the supply of the good in question a vertical line at a level below the original equilibrium quantity.

T F   5. A U.S. tariff on Japanese-made goods will lead to an increase in the demand for U.S. goods that are substitutes for those Japanese-made goods.

T F   6. Import quotas harm domestic consumers but help domestic producers of those goods on which quotas are placed.

T F   7. Tariffs harm domestic consumers and harm domestic producers of goods that compete with the goods on which tariffs are placed.

T F   8. A tariff on good X will cause a leftward shift of the supply of good X in the foreign country, and a rightward shift of the demand for good X in the country that imposed the tariff.

T F   9. In a two-country world, it is possible for both countries to have a comparative advantage in the production of a specific good.

T F   10. If the United States has a comparative advantage in producing wheat, it must be true that the opportunity cost for producing wheat in the United States is below that opportunity cost in other nations.

T F   11. Because in the real world nations have different resource endowments and different collective tastes, trade will always be advantageous.

T F   12. It is easy to determine the industries to which the infant industry argument applies.

T F   13. If a nation imposes anti-dumping laws, its consumers will pay lower prices for goods.

T F   14. Free trade may increase a nation's instability in the short run, because over time a nation's comparative advantage can change.

T F   15. When a nation restricts imports to protect jobs it, in effect, preserves less productive employment at the expense of more productive employment.

T F   16. One difference between the economic effects of quotas versus tariffs is that tariffs lead to a higher price to consumers but quotas do not.

T F   17. Tariffs increase government revenues, but import quotas do not.

MULTIPLE CHOICE QUESTIONS
Circle the letter that corresponds to the best answer.

1. A nation pays for its imports by
    a. exporting.
    b. creating money.
    c. extending credit to the exporting nation.
    d. All of the above

2. The U.S. ratio of imports to GDP is about _____ percent.
    a. 7
    b. 9
    c. 12
    d. 15

3. If trade between two nations is voluntary and continued, then
    a. both nations benefit.
    b. one nation could benefit more than the other.
    c. living standards are higher in both nations than if trade were not permitted.
    d. All of the above

4. Country A can produce both wheat and oranges using fewer resources than country B. Which of the following statements is true?
    a. Country A has a comparative advantage in producing both goods.
    b. Country A has an absolute advantage in producing both goods.
    c. Country B has no comparative advantage.
    d. Country B must have an absolute advantage in producing one of the goods.

5. If Country C has a comparative advantage in producing wheat, then its opportunity cost of producing wheat
    a. is maximized.
    b. equals the opportunity cost of producing other goods.
    c. cannot be determined.
    d. is lowest among its trading partners.

6. Nations find it advantageous to trade because they
    a. have different resource endowments.
    b. have different collective tastes.
    c. have different comparative advantages.
    d. All of the above

7. Which of the following is **NOT** an argument used against free trade?
    a. Free trade makes nations more interdependent.
    b. Free trade causes instability in a nation because a nation's comparative advantage changes over time.
    c. Free trade increases average and total worldwide incomes.
    d. Imports may destroy some domestic jobs.

8. Which of the following is most **UNLIKE** the others?
    a. import quota
    b. tariff
    c. free trade
    d. anti-dumping laws

9. Concerning import quotas and tariffs, which of the following statements is true?
    a. Both lead to lower prices for consumers.
    b. Both lead to more imports.
    c. Tariffs lead to higher prices, but quotas do not.
    d. Tariffs generate government revenues, but import quotas do not.

10. Which statement is **NOT** true, concerning the use of import restrictions to save jobs?
    a. The cost to consumers often exceeds the value of the jobs saved.
    b. Some jobs are destroyed in the export sector.
    c. In the long run they do not save jobs in those industries in which a nation has lost its comparative advantage.
    d. They are the most efficient way to help domestic workers threatened by foreign competition.

MATCHING
Choose the item in column (2) that best matches an item in column (1).

(1)   (2)

a. anti-dumping law   e. minimum opportunity cost of production
b. tariff   f. trade restriction
c. comparative advantage   g. tax on foreign-produced goods
d. absolute advantage   h. producing at a lower cost

WORKING WITH GRAPHS

1. Analyze the graphs below, then answer the questions that follow. They deal with an import quota set on foreign-made sugar. Start at point A.

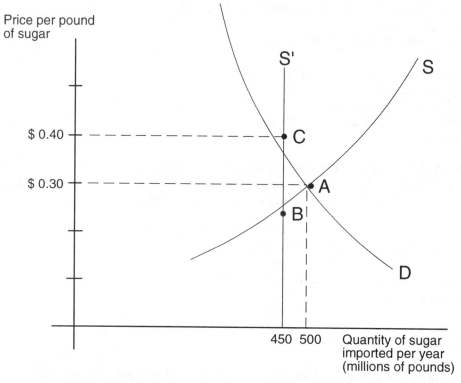

a. What is the price of sugar in this country, without the import quota?
b. What is the maximum amount of imported sugar given the quota?
c. What is the price of sugar, given the import quota?
d. What is the effective import supply curve, given the quota?

2. Analyze the graphs below, which deal with a U.S. tariff placed on Japanese-made autos, then answer the questions that follow. Start with point A.

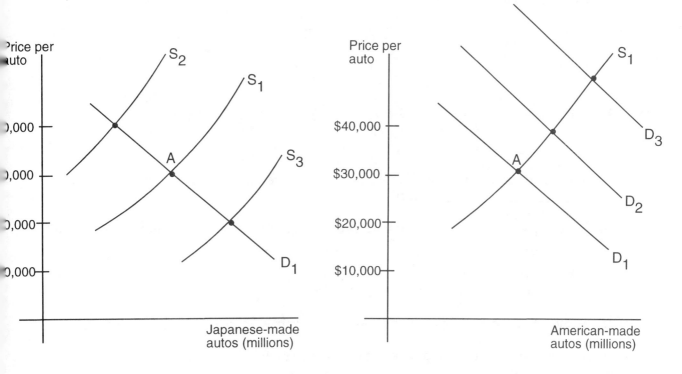

a. What is the price of U.S. and Japanese made autos in the U.S., without the tariff?
b. Which curve represents the supply of Japanese-made autos into the U.S., after the tariff?
c. Which curve shows the demand for American-made autos in the U.S., after the tariff?
d. What is the price of autos in the U.S., after the tariff is imposed?

PROBLEMS

1. Suppose that Germany and the United States are both fully employed and can produce the following amounts of wine and beer per week. Use this information to answer the following questions.

	Wine (gallons)	Beer (gallons)
Germany	600	1200
United States	400	1600

a. Germany has a comparative advantage in the production of _____, whereas the United States has a comparative advantage in the production of _____.

b. What is the cost of wine in terms of beer in Germany? What is the cost of wine in terms of beer in the United States?

2. Let us assume we are again in a two-country world, with the countries being Germany and the United States. Again, to simplify, let us assume that there are only two goods produced, coal and steel. In the table that follows, you will find the production possibilities of both countries. Assume that each country is currently operating at combination B on its production possibilities schedule. Use this information to answer the following questions.

(Hint: Remember that movements along production possibilities curves involve opportunity costs and that comparative advantage and trade depend on opportunity costs.) Entries are in thousands of tons per week.

		A	B	C	D
Germany:	Coal	0	24	48	72
	Steel	18	12	6	0
United States:	Coal	0	36	72	108
	Steel	36	24	12	0

a. Which country has an absolute advantage in the production of coal? _____ steel? _____

b. Which country has a comparative advantage in the production of coal? _____ steel? _____

c. What is the cost of coal in terms of steel in Germany? _____ What is the cost of coal in terms of steel in the United States? _____

(Remember that these are opportunity costs as determined by production possibilities.)

d. What is the current world production of coal and steel? _____

e. If both countries specialize in the production of goods in which they have a comparative advantage, Germany will produce _____ thousand tons of _____, the United States will produce _____ thousand tons of _____, and the world output of coal will increase by _____ thousand tons.

CASE STUDY

During the late 1990's, more and more people are calling for restrictions on free trade. Perhaps they have forgotten the studies conducted in the late 1980's concerning the costs to consumers of protectionism. Robert W. Crandall of the Brookings Institution investigated the cost of "saving" U.S. jobs in the automobile industry. He estimated that import restrictions raised the price of U.S.-produced cars by about $400 per car, and of Japanese-produced cars by about $1000 per car; the total cost to the U.S. consumer was about $4.3 billion. He then estimates that about 26,000 jobs were saved (ignoring the jobs lost in the U.S. export sector). In effect, U.S. consumers could have *given* $80,000 to each unemployed worker to not work and still have been able to save over $2 billion in lower-priced autos.

1. In light of Crandall's findings, why haven't import restrictions been removed?

2. Does it follow from Crandall's findings that import quotas *should* be removed?

ANSWERS TO CHAPTER 33

COMPLETION QUESTIONS

1. exporting
2. would not; produce the goods themselves; fall
3. comparative; lowest
4. opportunity
5. infant; decreased
6. quotas; tariffs
7. comparative; inefficient
8. exports; export; do not

TRUE-FALSE QUESTIONS

1. F Eventually each nation will produce its own goods—but at a higher cost and (perhaps) lower quality.
2. T
3. T
4. F That describes the effect of an import quota.
5. T
6. T
7. F They help domestic producers of such goods.
8. T
9. F Not for a *specific* good.
10. T
11. T
12. F In practice it is difficult to predict which industries will eventually be successful without aid.
13. F Consumers will pay higher prices.
14. T
15. T
16. F Both lead to higher prices for consumers.
17. T

MULTIPLE CHOICE QUESTIONS

1.a;   2.c;   3.d;   4.b;   5.d;   6.d;   7.c;   8.c;   9.d;   10.d

MATCHING

a and f;   b and g;   c and e;   d and h

WORKING WITH GRAPHS

1. a. 30 cents per pound
   b. 450 million pounds
   c. 40 cents per pound
   d. The same as the regular supply curve up to 450 million pounds; vertical from that point on.

2. a. $30,000 per auto.
   b. S2
   c. D2
   d. $40,000 per auto.

PROBLEMS

1.   a.   wine, beer
       b.   1 gallon wine = 2 gallons beer; 1 gallon wine = 4 gallons beer
2.   a.   United States, United States
       b.   Germany, United States
       c.   4000 tons coal = 1000 tons steel; 3000 tons coal = 1000 tons steel
       d.   60,000 tons coal; 36,000 tons steel
       e.   72, coal, 36, steel, 12

CASE STUDY

1.   It is politic to save jobs by imposing import restrictions. Automobile producers and unions have enormous power and they can influence Congress; auto consumers are not united.
2.   Crandall's study merely shows that import quotas are an inefficient method of saving jobs; whether we *should* continue to impose import quotas is a normative issue that cannot be solved through positive reasoning alone.

GLOSSARY TO CHAPTER 33

Absolute advantage   The ability to produce more output from given inputs of resources than others can. For example, America may have an absolute advantage in the production of agricultural goods in the sense that, per unit of labor, we can produce more bushels of wheat than any other country.

Comparative advantage   It is better for individuals and nations to specialize in those activities in which their advantages over other people or nations are greatest (or in which their disadvantages compared to others are the smallest). Comparative advantage always exists as long as the opportunity cost of doing the same job differs for different individuals or different countries.

Dumping   Selling a good or service abroad at a price below its cost of production or below the price charged in the home market.

General Agreement of Tariffs and Trade (GATT)   An international agreement established in 1947 to further world trade by reducing barriers and tariffs.

Infant industry argument   An argument in support of tariffs: Tariffs should be imposed to protect (from import competition) an industry that is trying to get started. Presumably, after the industry becomes technologically efficient, the tariff can be lifted.

Quota system   A government imposed restriction on the quantity of a specific good that another country is allowed to sell in the United States. In other words, quotas are restrictions on imports. These restrictions are usually applied to a specific country or countries.

World Trade Organization (WTO)   The successor organization to GATT.

Voluntary restraint agreement (VRA)   An official agreement with another country that "voluntarily" restricts the quantity of its exports to the U.S.

Voluntary import expansion (VIE)   An official agreement with another country in which it agrees to import more from the U.S.

EXCHANGE RATES AND THE BALANCE OF PAYMENTS

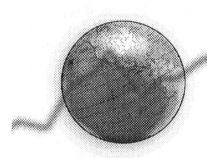

PUTTING THIS CHAPTER INTO PERSPECTIVE

Chapter 34 is the second of two chapters on international economics. Chapter 33 discussed why trade arises between nations, the various arguments against free international trade, and the various restrictions on such trade. Chapter 34 is concerned with how trade between nations is financed. The summary that follows below is somewhat long, but well worth the effort to learn if your teacher emphasizes this chapter. It is, we hope, a rigorous and thorough perspective on this chapter.

For simplicity let's assume a two-country world in which residents of one nation transact with residents of the other nation in three ways. First, they sell (export) to and buy (import) from each other; second, they lend to or borrow from each other; and third, they give gifts to or receive gifts from each other. When a nation exports goods and services to, borrows from, and receives gifts from another country, it (in effect) receives the other country's currency. In contrast, when a nation imports from, lends to, or gives gifts to another country, it (in effect) surrenders its own currency to the other country.

If the value of country A's exports exceeds the value of its imports, then A's balance of trade is a positive number. (Most people would refer to this as a trade surplus.) If the value of its exports is less than the value of its imports, then A's balance of trade is a negative number (also referred to as a trade deficit). In a two-country world, by definition, the other country, B, has a positive balance of trade if A has a negative balance of trade. (B has a trade surplus if A has a trade deficit.)

If the value of the goods and services that A exports plus the value of private and government gifts it receives from B exceed the value of the goods and services that it imports plus the value of private and government gifts it gives to B, then B will have a negative balance on current account and A will have a positive balance on current account.

Countries A and B also transact by direct investments (purchases) of each other's financial assets and by lending to and borrowing from each other. If the value of A's direct investments in B's financial assets plus the value of its loans to B exceed the value of B's investments in A and B's loans to A (A's borrowings from B), then A's balance on capital account will be a negative number and B's balance on capital account, by definition, will be a positive number.

If governments did not enter the picture, then, if A's current account were negative, its capital account would be positive and exactly offsetting. And, by definition, B's current account would be positive and its capital account would be negative and exactly offsetting. In other words, if the residents in A buy more from and give more to B than B buys from and gives to A, then B must "finance" this activity by acquiring A's assets or by lending to A. In the process for each nation the sum of its balance on current account and its balance on capital account is zero.

Once government gets into the act, however, all bets are off. Governments, by mutual agreement, can permit country A to have a negative current account *and* a negative capital account. (A can be a big spender, a big donor, and a big lender!) This is accomplished through *official* (government) transactions that, in effect, finance such activities. By definition, if the sum of A's current account balance plus its capital account balance is nonzero, then the value of official transactions will be that number that makes that sum equal to zero.

Note that all of the above is definitional. That does not mean that negative or positive numbers for the current account plus capital account sum can persist indefinitely; eventually an *equilibrium* in the balance of payments must prevail. If governments do not intervene, forces will be set in motion that see to it that eventually the value of what residents of one nation buy from, give to, and lend to other nations (the other nation in our simple two-country model) will roughly be equal to the value of what those same residents sell to, receive from, and borrow from other nations. Exactly what those forces are depends on what the particular international financial structure is, which is the subject of the second major section of Chapter 34.

Assume, for simplicity, that no government transactions exist. When residents of country A sell (export) goods and services to, receive gifts from, and borrow from residents in country B, then country A receives B's currency, which it supplies on the foreign exchange market because residents of country A ultimately demand their own currency. Thus such activities lead, simultaneously, to a supply of B's currency and a demand for A's currency.

When residents of country A buy (import) goods and services, give gifts to, and lend to residents in country B, then B's residents take A's currency and supply it to foreign exchange markets, because B's residents demand their own currency. Thus, when A's residents import, give gifts, and lend to foreigners (in B), these actions lead, simultaneously, to a demand for B's currency and a supply of A's currency.

In short, when residents of A and B interact economically, a supply of and a demand for each country's currency automatically arises. And foreign exchange markets reflect such supply and demand conditions.

Assume that the sum of A's current account plus its capital account is a negative number and that, therefore, the sum of B's current account plus its capital account is a positive number. This means that there will be an excess demand for (shortage of) B's currency and (by definition) a surplus of A's currency. Under a flexible exchange rate international payments system, B's currency will appreciate and A's currency will depreciate. In other words, it will take more units of A's currency to equal one unit of B's currency. This change in the exchange rate will induce residents in country A to import less from, give less to, and lend less to residents in B; and it will induce residents in country B to import more from, give more to, and lend more to residents in A. Thus, a change in the exchange rate will occur until residents of each nation *voluntarily* behave so as to generate a current account plus capital account sum that is roughly equal to zero. Thus exchange rates will adjust until a payments equilibrium exists.

What if the world is on a gold standard and the sum of A's current account plus its capital account is negative? Then A will pay for its "excess spending" with gold; gold flows from A to B. A's price level (and national income level) falls relative to B's, because gold and currencies are exchangeable under such a system. The results are the same as under the other fixed exchange rate system analyzed in the previous paragraph; under a gold standard gold flows occur (if disequilibrium exists) until relative price levels change sufficiently to create a balance of payments equilibrium.

LEARNING OBJECTIVES

After you have studied this chapter you should be able to

1. define foreign exchange rate, accounting identities, foreign exchange market, flexible exchange rates, appreciation, depreciation, gold standard, balance of trade, balance of payments, special drawing rights (SDR), International Monetary Fund (IMF), dirty float, and par value.

2. distinguish among the balance of trade, the balance on current account, the balance on capital account, and the balance of payments.

3. list three factors that affect a nation's balance of payments.

4. enumerate official reserve account transactions.

5. list transactions that lead to an increase in the supply of a domestic country's currency and an increase in the demand for foreign currency, and distinguish such transactions from transactions that lead to a demand for a domestic country's currency and a supply of a foreign country's currency.

6. recognize the equilibrium exchange rate from graphs, and predict how specific events will change the exchange rate.

7. distinguish between a gold standard international payments system and a flexible exchange rate international payments system.

CHAPTER OUTLINE

1. A *balance of trade* reflects the difference between the value of a nation's merchandise exports and its merchandise imports; the balance of payments reflects all economic transactions between a nation and the rest of the world.
   a. The *current account balance* equals the sum of (1) the balance of trade, (2) the balance of services, and (3) net unilateral transfers (private gifts and government grants). If the current account balance is negative, a current account deficit exists; if it is positive, a current account surplus exists.
   b. *Capital account* transactions consist of direct investment purchases in financial assets among countries and loans to and from foreigners. If the capital account is a negative number, a capital account deficit exists; if it is positive, a capital account surplus exists.
   c. If the sum of a nation's current account and its capital account is negative, that nation has an international *payments disequilibrium (deficit)* that must be financed by official (government) reserve account transactions; of course, another nation must have an international *payments surplus*.
      i. Official reserve account transactions include sales or purchases of foreign currencies, gold, *special drawing rights*, the reserve position in the International Monetary Fund, and financial assets held by official government agencies.
      ii. Official transactions must exactly equal (but be of opposite sign to) the *balance of payments*.

2.   Under a *flexible exchange rate system* of international payments, exchange rates between nations are determined by the forces of supply and demand.
   a.   When U.S. residents import a foreign good or service, this leads to a supply of dollars and a demand for foreign currency on foreign exchange markets.
   b.   When U.S. residents export goods and services to a foreign country, this leads to a supply of foreign currency and a demand for dollars.
   c.   The equilibrium exchange rate is determined in the same way that the equilibrium price for anything is established.
      i.   The U.S. demand curve for (say) French francs is negatively sloped; as the dollar price of the franc falls—it takes fewer dollars to purchase a given quantity of francs—the quantity demanded for francs, by U.S. residents, rises.
      ii.   The U.S. demand for francs is a derived demand; we demand French francs because we demand French goods and services.
      iii. The French supply francs because they want (say) U.S. goods and services; as the dollar price of francs rises—it takes fewer francs to purchase one dollar—the French will increase their quantity supplied of francs in order to purchase more U.S. goods.
      iv.   The equilibrium dollar price per franc is established at the intersection of the U.S. demand for francs curve and the French supply of francs curve; the equilibrium franc price per dollar is automatically determined thereby.
   d.   If U.S. residents experience a change in tastes in favor of French goods, the demand for francs will increase. The dollar price of francs rises and the franc price of dollars falls; the dollar *depreciates* and the franc *appreciates*.
   e.   Other determinants of exchange rates include (relative) changes in real interest rates, changes in productivity, changes in tastes, and perceptions of economic stability.

3.   Between a flexible exchange rate system and a fixed exchange rate is a "dirty float," or a managed exchange rate system, in which governments (through their central banks) intervene in foreign exchange markets in order to affect the price of currencies; such is the current world monetary system.

4.   Under a *gold standard*, each nation fixes its exchange rate in terms of gold; therefore all exchange rates are fixed. Under the pure gold standard, each nation would have to abandon an independent monetary policy; each nation's money supply would automatically change whenever a balance of payments disequilibrium occurred.

5.   In 1944 representatives of the world's capitalist nations met in Bretton Woods to create a new international payments system to replace the gold standard that had collapsed in the 1930s.
   a.   The *International Monetary Fund (IMF)* was established in 1944; the IMF established a system of fixed exchange rates and a means to lend foreign exchange to deficit nations.
   b.   Member governments were obligated to intervene in foreign exchange markets, to maintain the values of their currencies within 1 percent of the declared par value.
   c.   In 1967 the IMF created Special Drawing Rights (SDRs), a new type of international money exchange (only) between monetary authorities.

KEY TERMS

Flexible exchange rates   International Monetary Fund (IMF)
Foreign exchange market   Gold standard
Foreign exchange rate   Balance of trade
Appreciation   Balance of payments
Depreciation   Special drawing rights (SDRs)

KEY CONCEPTS

Dirty float   Par value
Accounting identities

COMPLETION QUESTIONS
Fill in the blank or circle the correct term.

1. When Americans wish to import French-made goods, they supply _____ to the foreign exchange market and demand _____ on that market; when the French wish to import American-made goods, they supply _____ and demand _____ on the foreign exchange market.

2. In a flexible exchange rate system, exchange rates are determined by (governments, supply and demand); if the exchange rate goes from 25 cents per franc to 50 cents per franc, the dollar has (appreciated, depreciated) and the franc has _____.

3. If the franc depreciates, it takes (fewer, more) francs to purchase a dollar; this leads to a(n) (increase, decrease) in the quantity demanded of francs by Americans and a(n) (increase, decrease) in the quantity supplied of francs by the French.

4. If American tastes move in favor of French goods, there will be a(n) _____ in the demand for francs; other things being constant, the franc will (appreciate, depreciate) on the foreign exchange market. This eventually will induce Americans to export (less, more) to the French and import _____ from the French.

5. Under a pure gold standard, exchange rates (float, are fixed).

6. If the value of U.S. imports exceeds the value of its exports, the U.S. balance of trade will be a (negative, positive) number, and another country's balance of trade must be a _____ number; then the United States is said to have a trade (deficit, surplus), while the other nation has a trade _____.

7. If governments do not intervene, by definition the sum of a nation's balance on current account plus its balance on capital account will equal _____; if governments intervene in the balance of payments process, then the sum of a nation's balance on current account plus its balance on capital account must exactly _____, but be of opposite sign to, its official transactions.

8. Official reserve account transactions involve the following assets of individual countries: _____, _____, _____, _____, and _____.

9. A nation's balance of payments is affected by, among other things, relative changes in that nation's _____, and _____.

10. If the value of a nation's exports is less than the value of its imports, it is running a trade_____; its currency will (depreciate, appreciate) under a flexible exchange rate system.

11. When nations intervene in foreign exchange markets in order to affect exchange rates, a freely floating exchange rate system becomes a _____ float.

TRUE-FALSE QUESTIONS
Circle the **T** if the statement is true, the **F** if it is false. Explain to yourself why a statement is false.

T F   1. If you wish to buy German goods, you ultimately offer dollars and demand German currency.

T F   2. If you wish to send money to your relatives in England, you ultimately offer dollars and demand English currency.

T F   3. In a flexible exchange rate system, gold flows lead to international payments equilibrium.

T F   4. If French tastes move in favor of American goods, the supply of dollars on the foreign exchange market rises relative to the demand for dollars.

T F   5. The U.S. demand for French francs rises if the French inflation rate exceeds the U.S. inflation rate.

T F   6. In a flexible exchange rate system, if French tastes move away from American goods (other things being constant), both the dollar and the franc will depreciate.

T F   7. The gold standard is one form of fixed exchange rate system.

T F   8. Under the gold standard, if disequilibrium exists in the world's balance of payments, gold will flow from one nation to another until payments equilibrium is restored.

T F   9. Under a flexible exchange rate system, if disequilibrium exists in the world's balance of payments, exchange rates will change until payments equilibrium is restored.

T F   10. Under a flexible exchange rate system, each nation must give up control over its own monetary policy.

T F   11. In today's world, the sum of a nation's current account balance plus its capital account balance must be zero.

T F   12. If one nation has a current account deficit, another nation must have a current account surplus.

T F   13. A nation can finance a current account deficit with a capital account surplus.

T F   14. A dirty float results because nations do not want to pay the price of adjusting to a balance of payments disequilibrium.

T F   15. Under a flexible exchange rate system, payments equilibrium is brought about by a change in the exchange rate; under a gold standard, national price levels change to restore payments equilibrium.

MULTIPLE CHOICE QUESTIONS
Circle the letter that corresponds to the best answer.

1. If the foreign exchange rate is that $1 is equivalent to 5 francs, then 1 franc is worth
    a. $5.
    b. 50 cents.
    c. 20 cents.
    d. 5 cents.

2. The demand schedule for francs on the foreign exchange market
    a. is derived partially from foreign demand for French goods.
    b. reflects the fact that the French want to import goods and services.
    c. shows the quantity demanded for francs at different income levels.
    d. is unimportant if France is on a fixed exchange rate system.

3. Which of the following does **NOT** lead to an increase in the demand for French francs?
    a. A worldwide change in tastes in favor of French goods occurs.
    b. The French inflation rate exceeds the world inflation rate.
    c. France's interest rate rises relative to world rates.
    d. World real income rises.

4. Which of the following leads to an increase in the demand for the U.S. dollar on the foreign exchange market?
    a. an increase in U.S. exports
    b. an increase in foreign investment in the United States
    c. an increase in gifts from foreigners to U.S. residents
    d. All of the above

5. If a nation has an international payments surplus in a flexible exchange rate system, then
    a. its currency will appreciate.
    b. its price level will rise.
    c. gold will flow from it to nations with a payments surplus.
    d. All of the above

6. Which of the following statements is *not* true?
    a. Under flexible exchange rates, international payments equilibrium is restored through changes in exchange rates.
    b. Under a gold standard, international payments equilibrium is restored through changes in national price levels.
    c. Under a flexible exchange rate system, a nation cannot pursue a monetary policy that is independent of its trading partners.
    d. Under the gold standard, international payments disequilibrium leads to gold flows, which restore equilibrium.

7. If France has a payments deficit, payments equilibrium can be restored if France's
    a. price level rises relative to the world's.
    b. interest rate rises relative to the world's.
    c. real national income rises relative to the world's.
    d. money supply rises relative to the world's.

8. A nation can finance a deficit on its current account with
    a. a surplus on its capital account.
    b. a deficit on its capital account.
    c. official purchases of foreign currencies with its own currency.
    d. purchases of gold from foreign countries with its own currency.

9. If a nation has a deficit on both its current account and its capital account, then
   a. it is in a balance of payments equilibrium.
   b. the world must be on a flexible exchange rate system.
   c. it must have official transactions that are identical to (but opposite in sign to) the sum of those two deficits.
   d. it will experience gold inflows.

10. A nation's balance of payments is affected by its relative
    a. interest rate.
    b. political stability.
    c. inflation rate.
    d. All of the above

11. The dirty float
    a. has emerged in recent years because nations want less flexible exchange rates.
    b. makes fixed exchange rates more flexible.
    c. is common under a gold standard.
    d. is favored over a pure float by people who want their nation to have a monetary policy independent of its trading partners.

MATCHING
Choose the item in column (2) that best matches an item in column (1).

(1)	(2)
a. appreciation	f. rise in one currency's value relative to another's
b. depreciation	g. fall in one currency's value relative to another's
c. fixed exchange rate system	h. balance of payments settlements
d. special drawing right	i. gold standard
e. trade deficit	j. value of exports exceeds value of imports

WORKING WITH GRAPHS

1. Consider a situation in which exchange rates are flexible. Consumers in the United States wish to import a good from Germany.
   a. Calculate the U.S. price of this good, given the German price of the good and the different exchange rates that might prevail as listed in the table below, and place these calculations in the appropriate column. Calculate the quantity of German marks demanded by U.S. consumers in order to purchase the import good at different exchange rates. Enter these numbers in the last column.

Exchange rate ($/DM)	German price of the good	U.S. price of the good	Quantity demanded	Total U.S. DM expenditures
2.20/1	1 DM	_____	90	_____
2.40/1	1 DM	_____	80	_____
2.60/1	1 DM	_____	70	_____
2.80/1	1 DM	_____	60	_____
3.00/1	1 DM	_____	50	_____

By looking at the table above, one can conclude that as it takes more dollars to purchase one German mark (DM), the dollar price of the import good will _____.

b. In the table above, you are given the quantity of the import good at different prices. Graph the demand for German marks on the grid provided below.

c. Let us now assume that people in Germany wish to import from the United States some good that costs $1 per unit. Calculate the German price of the good given the U.S. price and the different exchange rates that might prevail, as listed in the table below, and place these numbers in the appropriate column.

Exchange rate ($/DM)	U.S. price of the good	German price of the good	Quantity demanded	Total German $ expenditures
2.20/1	$ 1	_____	66.7	_____
2.40/1	$ 1	_____	119.0	_____
2.60/1	$ 1	_____	184.2	_____
2.80/1	$ 1	_____	250.0	_____
3.00/1	$ 1	_____	333.0	_____

By looking at the above table, one can conclude that as it takes more dollars to purchase 1 German mark, the mark price of the good will _____.

Quantity of Marks per Unit Time

d. In the last table, you are given the quantity of the import good that German consumers wish to purchase at different German prices. Use this information to calculate the quantity of German marks that German consumers will be willing to supply at different exchange rates in order to import the U.S. good. (Note: Round off to the nearest whole number.) Enter these numbers in the last column. Graph the supply of German marks on the same grid as your graph of part b.

e. Assume for simplicity that the only trade between the United States and Germany involves the two goods discussed above. Under this assumption, the equilibrium exchange rate will be approximately _____ dollars per German mark or _____ German marks per dollar.

f. Suppose that now U.S. consumers undergo a change in tastes and preferences for the German import good. As a result, the U.S. demand for the import good increases as shown in the table below.

Exchange rate ($/DM)	German price of the good	U.S. price of the good	Quantity demanded	Total U.S. DM expenditures
2.20/1	1 DM	_____	120	_____
2.40/1	1 DM	_____	110	_____
2.60/1	1 DM	_____	100	_____
2.80/1	1 DM	_____	90	_____
3.00/1	1 DM	_____	80	_____

Enter in the last column the quantity of German marks now demanded by U.S. consumers for use in purchasing the German import good. Graph the new demand for German marks on the same grid provided for part b.

The new equilibrium exchange rate will be approximately _____ dollars per German mark, or _____ German marks per dollar. As a result of the increase in the U.S. demand for German imports, with all else constant, the dollar will _____ and the mark will _____.

g. Now consider the above problem assuming that the exchange rate was fixed at $2.60/mark. When the U.S. demand for German goods increased, the United States would have purchased _____ units and paid a total of $_____ for German imports. The Germans would have bought _____ units from the United States and paid a total of $_____ for U.S. exports. As a result, the United States would have lost $_____, or approximately _____ marks, in foreign exchange.

2. The figure below shows the supply of, and the demand for, British pounds, as a function of the exchange rate—expressed in U.S. dollars per pound. Assume that Britain and the United States are the only two countries in the world.
    a. How might the shift from D to D' be accounted for?

    b. Given the shift from D to D', what exists at $2.60 = #1?

    c. Will the pound now appreciate or depreciate?

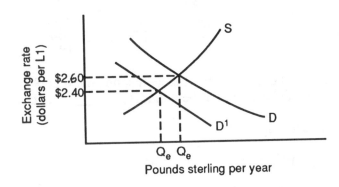

PROBLEMS

1. Below are balance-of-payments figures for Pleasureland during 1997. (All figures are in billions of dollars.

Allocations of special drawing rights	$ 710
Balance on the capital account	-3507
Foreign official assets	10475
Errors and omissions	-1879
Balance on the current account	-5795
Pleasureland official assets	-4

    a. The official settlement balance was (+/-) _____ $_____.

    b. The official reserve transactions were

        (1) the sum of $_____, _____, and _____

        (2) totaled (+/-) _____ $_____

2. Suppose both France and the United States had been on a pure gold standard; and the French government had been willing to buy and sell gold at a price of 140 French francs for an ounce of gold, and the American government had been willing to buy and sell gold at a price of $35 an ounce. In the foreign exchange markets the price of a French franc would have been $_____ and the price of a dollar would have been _____ French francs.

3. Below are hypothetical demand and supply schedules for the German deutsche mark during a week. (The quantities of deutsche marks demanded and supplied are measured in millions and the exchange rate for the deutsche mark is measured in dollars.)

Quantity Demanded	Exchanged Rate	Quantity Supplied
100	$0.28	570
200	0.27	520
300	0.26	460
400	0.25	400
500	0.24	330
600	0.23	260
700	0.22	180

a. The equilibrium exchange rate for the deutsche mark is $_____; and at this equilibrium the rate of exchange for the dollar is _____ deutsche marks.

b. At the equilibrium exchange rate:

(1) _____ million deutsche marks are demanded and supplied each week.

(2) _____ million dollars are bought and sold each week.

c. If the German central bank wished to peg the exchange rate for the deutsche mark at:

(1) $0.26 it would have to (buy/sell) (how many) _____ million deutsche marks for dollars each week.

(2) $0.24 it would have to (buy/sell) (how many) _____ million deutsche marks for dollars each week.

4. Which of the following will cause the yen to appreciate?

a. U.S. real incomes increase relative to Japanese real incomes.

b. It is expected that in the future the yen will depreciate relative to the dollar.

c. The U.S. inflation rate rises relative to the Japanese inflation rate.

d. The after-tax, risk-adjusted real interest rate in the United States rises relative to that in Japan.

e. U.S. tastes change in favor of Japanese-made goods.

CASE STUDY

Politicians and businessmen have long criticized Japan for its huge trade surplus with the United States; in the mid to late 1990's China was similarly criticized. Along with such complaints are the charges that those countries restrict imports and by various clever measures set up barriers to American business who wish to sell their wares in those countries.

While there is some truth in these charges, they are in the main overstated. More importantly, is it sensible to be concerned with *bilateral* (2-country) trade imbalances? What if country A has a large trade deficit with country B, but is in overall balance (i.e., it has trade surpluses with other nations). Clearly the *overall* trade balance is more important than a bilateral trade balance. Indeed, even an *overall* trade imbalance is not necessarily bad if the economy is growing and other countries wish to invest in it (a capital account surplus can drive a current account deficit); after all, the U.S. had trade deficits during most of the 19th century.

1. Mr. Smith has a huge trade deficit with his grocer, who buys nothing from him. Should Smith purchase less from his grocer?

2. What would happen if all nations pursued a policy of bilateral trade balances with each of its trading partners?

ANSWERS TO CHAPTER 34

COMPLETION QUESTIONS

1. dollars; francs; francs; dollars
2. supply and demand; depreciated; appreciated
3. more; increase; decrease
4. increase; appreciate; more; less
5. are fixed
6. negative; positive; deficit; surplus
7. zero; equal
8. foreign currencies; gold; SDRs; reserve position in the IMF; any financial asset held by an official government agency
9. inflation rate; political stability
10. deficit; depreciate;
11. dirty

TRUE-FALSE QUESTIONS

1. T
2. T
3. F Changes in exchange rates lead to payments equilibrium.
4. F The demand for dollars rises relative to the supply of dollars, because the French want to buy relatively more U.S. goods.
5. F Americans will demand fewer francs because French goods are now relatively higher priced.
6. F The dollar will depreciate relative to the franc; the franc therefore must appreciate relative to the dollar.
7. T
8. T
9. T
10. F Floating exchange rate systems permit an independent monetary policy.
11. F In today's world, nations intervene in exchange markets; hence international settlements among governments are necessary.
12. T
13. T
14. T
15. T

MULTIPLE CHOICE QUESTIONS

1.c;   2.a;   3.b;   4.d;   5.a;   6.c;   7.b;   8.a;   9.c;   10.d;
11.a

MATCHING

a and f;   b and g;   c and i;   d and h;   e and j

WORKING WITH GRAPHS

1. a. U.S. prices of the good: 2.20, 2.40, 2.60, 2.80, 3.00. Total U.S. DM expenditures: 90, 80, 70, 60, 50; rise
   b. See graph
   c. German prices of the good: 0.45, 0.42, 0.38, 0.36, 0.33; fall
   d. Total German expenditures in DM: 30, 50, 70, 90, 110. See graph below
   e. 2.60, 0.38
   f. Total U.S. DM expenditures: 120, 110, 100, 90, 80. See graph. 2.80, 0.36; depreciate, appreciate
   g. 100, 260; 184.2, 184.2; 75.8 (or $260 - $184.20), 29 (75.8 ÷ $2.60).

2. a. A decrease in the demand for British pounds will occur if world tastes change away from British-made goods, the British price level rises relative to the world's, world income falls relative to British income, and/or British interest rates fall relative to world interest rates, among other reasons.
    b. A surplus of British pounds, a British balance-of-payments deficit.
    c. depreciate

PROBLEMS

1. a. -, 11181;   b. (1) 710, 10475, -4 (any order) (2) +, 11181
2. 0.25, 4
3. a. 0.25, 4;   b. (1) 400 (2) 100;   c. (1) buy, 160 (2) sell, 170
4. a,c,e

CASE STUDY

1. Obviously that would be foolish; as long as Mr. Smith's overall expenditures are in line with his overall income he will be fine.
2. Trade patterns would be destroyed; nations will not be able to specialize in the production of goods for which they have a comparative advantage; overall world incomes will fall.

GLOSSARY TO CHAPTER 34

Accounting identities   Statements that certain numerical measurements are equal by accepted definition.

Appreciation   An increase in the value of a domestic currency in terms of other currencies. In a fixed exchange rate market, appreciation cannot occur spontaneously; it must be done officially. Then it is called revaluation.

Balance of payments A summary record of a country's economic transactions with foreign residents and governments over a year.

Balance of trade The value of goods and services bought and sold in the world market.

Depreciation A decrease in the value of a domestic currency in terms of foreign currencies.

Dirty float A system in between flexible and fixed exchange rates in which central banks occasionally enter foreign exchange markets to alter rates from where they would be with no such intervention.

Flexible exchange rates Exchange rates that are allowed to fluctuate in the open market in response to changes in supply and demand. Sometimes called free exchange rates or floating exchange rates.

Foreign exchange market The market for buying and selling foreign currencies.

Foreign exchange rate The price of foreign currency in terms of domestic currency. For example, the foreign exchange rate for francs is 20 cents. This means that it takes 20 cents to buy one franc. An alternative way of stating the exchange rate is that the value of the dollar is five francs. It takes five francs to buy one dollar.

Gold standard In its purest form (which is only hypothetical), an international monetary system in which gold plays a prominent part. Nations fix their exchange rates in terms of gold. Thus all currencies are fixed in terms of each other. Any balance-of-payments problems could be made up by shipments of gold.

International Monetary Fund (IMF) An institution set up to manage the international monetary system. It came out of the Bretton Woods Conference in 1944, which established more or less fixed exchange rates in the world.

Par value The legally established value of the monetary unit of one country in terms of that of another.

Special drawing rights (SDRs) A reserve asset created by the International Monetary Fund that countries can use to settle international payments.

CYBERNOMICS

PUTTING THIS CHAPTER INTO PERSPECTIVE

Chapter 35 can be considered a capstone chapter for your text. It deals with how the new world of cyberspace affects economics and vise versa. Of course we are talking about the Internet, as well as its major component, the World Wide Web. Along with the explosion in Internet use and worldwide communications is the growing information technology (IT) sector, not only in the United States, but in the world. The American computing and telecommunications industry has been growing at a prodigious rate, now exceeding $100 trillion a year out of an $8 trillion plus GDP. While business use of the Internet has been going on for some time, household use is increasing even more dramatically. Between 100 and 200 global citizens are connected via the Net and that number is certain to expand.

You can think of the Internet and the World Wide Web as reducers of transaction costs. E-commerce is extensive between businesses. Retail electronic commerce is in its infancy, but is growing, too. When more Americans are certain that their credit cards cannot be "stolen from thin air," e-'tailing will increase, too. The use of intelligent shopping agents over the Web are certain to reduce differentials in prices per constant quality unit for any good or service. Because the Net does not allow customers to touch and feel goods, brand names will become even more important. Marketing and advertising on the Net will become more important, also.

Financial and capital markets are expanding on the Web, making our capitalist system more efficient. Smaller firms can seek capital on the Web now without going through expensive venture capital and underwriting procedures.

Pricing of software that can be distributed on the Net poses a problem. The marginal cost for disseminating one more unit of any given software program is effectively close to zero. Therefore, marginal cost pricing would generate no revenues for traditional software developers. The law of diminishing marginal returns as far as this particular example goes, does not quite work. Software producers must develop additional ways to raise revenues if they are worried that their software will be distributed for free.

A major issue because of the Internet has to do with the protection of intellectual property, in particular CDs, the written word, and computer programs. How such issues will be handled in the future remains to be seen.

LEARNING OBJECTIVES

After you have studied this chapter, you should be able to

1. understand how technological change affects the demand for labor.

2. understand the relationship between increased usage of the Internet and increased economic efficiency.

3. explain the different ways that the Internet can be used for reducing transaction costs.

4. understand the increasing importance of brand names because of Internet retailing.

5. explain how the Internet has changed financial and capital markets.

6. discuss the issue of pricing and the law of diminishing marginal returns for the dissemination of software products on the Internet.

CHAPTER OUTLINE

1. One way that extensive use of the Web will lead to greater efficiency is through a reduction in transaction costs.

2. Most e-commerce is between businesses today

3. Retail business will expand as better encryption methods are used for capturing credit-card numbers.

4. Internet retailing requires no inventory costs for those "malls" that simply send orders to other companies for fulfillment.

5. If more Internet retailing occurs, the demand for traditional retail space will decrease over time.

6. Brands can be established on the Web itself, such as Amazon.com, a now major retailer of books only through the Web.

7. The Internet allows for a better way of reaching more finely tuned groups of potential customers. In this way, it is cheaper and may be more effective than traditional direct-mail marketing methods.

8. Because any Internet transaction may "touch" numerous jurisdictions, unless a uniform taxing policy is adopted, confusion may reign for e-commerce.

9. The buying and selling of securities has become much cheaper with the advent of e-trading. Commissions are less than they used to be, and stock traders can access markets that are open directly from their home cheaply and easily via their computers.

10. The capital market for small firms may become more efficient with the new possibility of raising funds on the Internet.

11.   Pricing decisions for software products that can be downloaded off of the Internet are difficult. After all, the marginal cost becomes zero, but a product given away doesn't yield revenues to pay for its development.

12.   Some firms have succeeded by giving away their programs, but charging for upgrades and updated versions.

13.   The Internet is leading to lower costs of entry, especially in retailing.

KEY TERMS

Protocol
E-commerce

Cybernomics
Intelligent shopping agents

KEY CONCEPTS

Copyright
Monopoly
Marginal cost

Intellectual property
Law of demand

COMPLETION QUESTIONS
Circle the correct term or fill in the blank.

1.   Technological change often reduces the demand for _____ labor services, but it usually increases the demand for _____ types of labor services.

2.   The greatest use of the Internet is _____ _____ .

3.   One way to look at the Internet and the World Wide Web is that the new system is simply a _____ of transaction costs.

4.   Electronic retailing can eventually lead to a reduction in the demand for _____ _____ .

5.   Anybody who puts up a Web home page can sell ad space, but faces a _____ _____ problem for use of this space.

6.   On-line securities trading has lead to _____ commissions.

7.   The marginal cost of one more unit of a software program sold on the Net is close to _____ .

TRUE-FALSE QUESTIONS
Circle the **T** if the statement is true, the **F** if it is false. Explain to yourself why a statement is false.

T F   1.   Electronic retailing will lead to an increase in mass merchandising.

T F   2.   A Web home-page owner has no cost in selling advertising.

T F 3. Nonuniform taxes on the Web will reduce Web commerce.

T F 4. On-line trading has lead to less efficiency in the securities industries.

T F 5. Every bootlegged CD or computer program constitutes a one for one reduction in the revenues of firms selling those products.

T F 6. As Internet shopping becomes more extensive, brand names will become more even important.

T F 7. Technology displaces workers, permanently destroying jobs.

T F 8. Surfing the Net is the most extensive use of the Internet.

MULTIPLE CHOICE QUESTIONS
Circle the letter that corresponds to the best answer.

1. The Internet reduces transaction costs by
   a. making shopping more fun.
   b. increasing the cost of information.
   c. reducing the cost of information.
   d. All of the above.

2. Better encryption's will increase e-commerce because
   a. software programmers will have more work.
   b. retailers will be able to spend more to set up electronic commerce sites.
   c. more consumers will understand what encryption means.
   d. more consumers will feel safer about using credit cards on-line.

3. Brand names may become more important because of electronic shopping
   a. because sales people will not be able to explain differences in different manufactures' products.
   b. because the Internet cannot handle a large number of brands.
   c. because it takes longer to download longer brand names.
   d. All of the above

4. There is an opportunity cost to offering space ads on a home page because
   a. each screen has a limited amount of space.
   b. it takes time to load ads and more screens, and consumers value their time when they are on the Web.
   c. there is always an alternative use of the "real estate" on a home page.
   d. All of the above.

5. The sale of an additional unit of a software program on the Net is
   a. equal to the cost of producing the diskettes for the software program.
   b. equal to the cost of producing the software program in the first place.
   c. equal to the cost of developing the next version of that program.
   d. effectively equal to zero for net distribution.

6. Often organizations calculate the cost to record companies of bootlegged compact disks. These cost estimates usually grossly over state lost revenues
    a. no one can accurately estimate how many bootlegged copies exist.
    b. no revenues are ever lost.
    c. some users of bootlegged copies would not of bought a new copy at the full retail price.
    d. None of the above

MATCHING
Choose the item in column (2) that best matches an item in column (1).

(1)	(2)
a. e-commerce	e. lower commissions
b. encryption	f. shopping over the Net
c. on-line trading	g. decreased transaction costs
d. intelligent shopping agents	h. increased security on the Net

CASE STUDY

There are numerous predictions that traditional textbook publishing will disappear in the foreseeable future because of the richness of the interactive learning possibilities on the Internet. Indeed, the increased ability of motion videos, slides, audio, and the like over the World Wide Web do seem to indicate the possibility of creating on-line courses that are more interesting than traditional textbooks. Publishers, including the one who published this text, are attempting to determine ways to enter this new world of cyber teaching, well at the same time not abandoning traditional textbook publishing.

Even traditional reference book publishers are discovering that the demand for their products are falling. The biggest selling encyclopedia in the world is Microsoft's Encarta—it is on a CD-ROM, with Web links automatically built in. The federal government now puts most of its official statistics on the Web, so those who normally have purchased on a regular basis government statistical publications are not renewing their subscriptions (the authors included).

1. No matter what happens in terms of interactive, distance learning, what can we be sure about the demand for traditional textbooks in the future?

2. Even if a traditional encyclopedia is only sold on CD-ROM's or on Web sites, does that change the amount of work going into developing it?

3. If all publishing goes to the Web, how can anybody make any profits?

ANSWERS TO CHAPTER 35

COMPLETION QUESTIONS

1. traditional, new
2. electronic mail
3. reducer
4. retail space

5. opportunity cost
6. lower
7. zero

TRUE-FALSE QUESTIONS

1. F   More commerce on the Net will reduce the use of mass merchandisers.
2. F   There is an opportunity cost for the space used on each screen.
3. T
4. F   Commissions have dropped dramatically since on-line trading started.
5. F   Because of the law of demand, not everyone would buy the same CD or software program if the full price had to be paid.
6. T
7. F   At least in the U.S., technology has simply meant different jobs are demanded—employment has increased steadily over the years.
8. F   The most extensive use is for e-mail

MULTIPLE CHOICE QUESTIONS

1.c;   2.d;   3.a;   4.d;   5.d;   6.c;

MATCHING

[RLM Please put in answers]

CASE STUDIES

1.   The demand for traditional textbooks will certainly decrease over time. That does not mean the textbooks will disappear, however. It simply means that they will be different, probably linked to Web sites and CD-ROM's (as is your current textbooks). Textbooks in the future will probably be less expensive. The publisher, however, may be able to garner additional revenues by charging small amounts for use of its Web site that accompanies the textbook.

2.   Not necessarily. Just because the encyclopedia Britannica can now be purchased as one CD-ROM does not mean that the research, composition, and proofing of the original document will get any easier. Indeed, it will probably become harder, as publishers attempt to put in more interactive moving videos and color slides in their encyclopedias.

3.   They can start charging for access to their Web sites, such as Microsoft's Slate Magazine did in 1998. It used to be free, and then it became $19.95 per year. Additionally, providers of Web sites can offer for-sale items (called "add ons" in a direct marketing business) in order to obtain profits that way.

GLOSSARY TO CHAPTER 35

Cybernomics   The application of economic analysis to human and technological activities related to the use of the Internet in all of its forms.

E-commerce The use of the Internet in any manner that allows buyers to finds sellers and vice-versa. This may involve business selling directly to other businesses, or business selling to retail customers. Both goods and services can, and are, involved in e-commerce.

Intelligent shopping agents A type of computer program that an individual or business user of the Internet can instruct to carry out a specific task, such as looking for the lowest priced car of a particular brand and model. The "agent" then searches the Internet (usually just the World Wide Web) and may even purchase the product when the best price has been found.

Protocol The agreed-upon systematic way in which computers access each other when they communicate.

Notes

Notes

Notes

Notes

Notes

Notes

Notes

Notes